W9-ARS-452

PINCKNEY ST
WISCONSIN
USA TODAY

BusCapade

PLAIN TALK ACROSS THE USA

Allen H. Neuharth

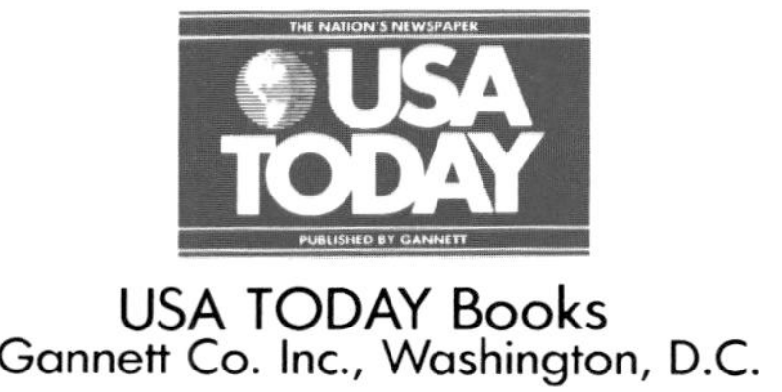

USA TODAY Books
Gannett Co. Inc., Washington, D.C.

 For information, write USA TODAY Books, P.O. Box 450, Washington, D.C. 20044, or call (703) 276-5978.

Printed and bound for USA TODAY Books by Arcata Graphics Co. in Kingsport, Tennessee, the United States of America.

Library of Congress Cataloging-in-Publication Data

Neuharth, Allen H.
BusCapade plain talk across the usa

1. United States — Social life and customs — 1971-
2. United States — Description and travel — 1981-
3. Interviews — United States. I. Title.
E169.04.48 1987 973.927 87-51136
ISBN 0-944347-00-2

Contents

Appreciation

BusCapade was a cooperative venture by USA TODAY, its parent Gannett company, and its sister newspapers and broadcast stations.

Without the contributions of dozens of newsmen and women, support from circulation and promotion and other staffers, such a comprehensive 50-state project would not have been possible in such a short period of time.

I am deeply grateful to all. Those who rode the highways and byways for the entire six months, or for just a few days or weeks. Those who aided in the planning and preparation, editing and publication.

Foremost was my chief of staff and special assistant Ken Paulson. Paulson, 33, bought the bus, outfitted it, recruited the staff and coordinated all news coverage, promotion and logistics.

Other key BusCateers:

■ Lou Brancaccio, 37, managing editor of the Fort Myers, Fla., *News-Press* and a BusCapade editor.

■ Paula Burton, 26, a producer with WXIA-TV in Atlanta and a BusCapade reporter.

■ Lisa Dixon, 32, promotion/market research director with the *The* (Wilmington, Del.) *News-Journal,* who coordinated press relations on BusCapade.

■ Joel Driver, 28, BusCapade bus driver, who logged more than 34,000 miles.

■ Gaynelle Evans, 35, a Gannett News Service and BusCapade reporter.

■ Dan Greaney, 22, editor of the Harvard Lampoon's parody of USA TODAY and a BusCapade reporter.

■ Paul McMasters, 45, deputy editorial director, in charge of editing of the BusCapade interviews for the Inquiry page.

■ Scott Maclay, 37, corporate staff and BusCapade photographer.

■ Mark Pearson, 35, layout editor, and Warren Springer, 37, assistant national editor, prepared BusCapade copy for publication.

■ Juanie Phinney, 23, executive secretary on BusCapade.

■ Phil Pruitt, 36, a corporate staff member who coordinated interviews with the USA's governors and directed the editing and production of this book.

■ Andrea Redding, 33, Suzette Karelis, 38, and Claudia Baldwin, 29, executive secretaries, alternated on BusCapade.

■ Barbara Reynolds, 45, USA TODAY Inquiry page editor, who participated in many BusCapade interviews with governors and celebrities.

■ Bob Roller, 26, corporate staff and BusCapade photographer.

■ David Silk, 22, a USA TODAY circulation manager and BusCapade logistics assistant.

■ Kathleen Smith Barry, 28, *The* (Nashville) *Tennessean* and BusCapade photographer.

Special thanks to Gannett President and Chief Executive Officer John Curley, USA TODAY Editor John Quinn, USA TODAY Executive Editor Ron Martin, USA TODAY Editorial Director John Seigenthaler, USA TODAY Publisher Cathleen Black, USA TODAY President Thomas Curley, Gannett Vice President/News Charles Overby, and Gannett Vice President/Public Affairs and Government Relations Mimi Feller for their support throughout BusCapade.

Also, thanks to the Gannett New Media staff that edited and published this book, especially Nancy Woodhull, Gannett vice president/news services and president of Gannett New Media, and editors Phil Fuhrer, Emilie Davis, Bob Gabordi, Randy Kirk, Lark Borden and Ashley Barnes.

The full roster of BusCateers appears on pages 306-308. Thanks to all for their contributions.

Allen H. Neuharth

Footnotes

Populations: All figures are the latest available. State figures come from U.S. Census Bureau estimates for July 1, 1986; city populations are from census estimates for July 1, 1984; racial and ethnic populations are from the 1980 U.S. Census. Persons of Hispanic heritage can be of any race — so the racial-mix portion of the Snapshots will not add up to 100 percent.

State nicknames and mottos: Some states have more than one nickname or motto. The most commonly used ones are incorporated in this book.

State license plates: All plates pictured are in use. Most states have more than one plate design.

Map points: Largest cities, capitals and some of the other cities and towns visited by BusCapade are included on the state maps.

State trivia: Information for "Uniquely" boxes was provided by USA TODAY research and state commerce, travel and tourism offices.

Cover photo: The scene at Culloden, Ga., 20 miles west of Macon, was photographed from a helicopter by Scott Maclay of Gannett Corporate Publications.

Across the USA

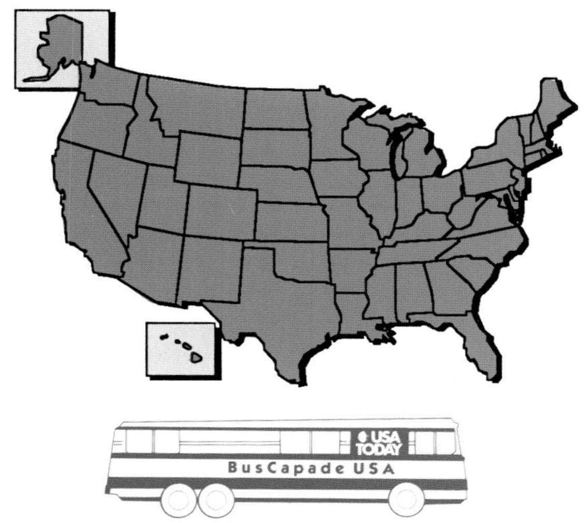

March 16-Sept. 10, 1987

"All 50 states! Are you sure about that?"

Ken Paulson,
Al Neuharth's chief of staff,
to Neuharth in September 1986

Introduction

BusCapade goal: Understanding the USA

The first interviews were with Lynn Merrill and his wife, Rosemary, both 53. On their 45-acre farm near Potosi, Mo. The exact population center of the USA.

The last was with President Ronald Reagan, 76. In the Oval Office of the White House. The action center of the USA.

In between, there were more than 3,000 interviews all across the USA: In cities, large and small. Towns and villages. Farms and factories. With men and women of all races. Young and old. Rich and poor.

All 50 governors. All 50 states. 34,905 miles of highways and byways. Plus JetCapades to Alaska and Hawaii.

BusCapade covered nearly six months. March 16 to Sept. 10, 1987. It was exhausting and exhilarating for me. It was exhausting and exhilarating for the staff that traveled with me.

The BusCateers, as they came to call themselves, often worked past midnight, cramming down room service meals while typing on portable computers. They worked in their rooms and on the bus. And most spent some time typing in bathrooms, airports and airplanes.

■ Why did we do it?

■ What did we hope to learn from it?

BusCapade was conceived because I have long felt that much of the national media has too much of an East Coast perspective.

Agreed, New York City is the financial and commercial center of the world. And, Washington is the news center of the world. But, there is life beyond the Potomac and west of the Hudson.

It seems to me that members of the national media who are desk-bound in New York or Washington — or who only occasionally jet into Atlanta or Chicago or Denver or San Francisco to cover the big story — are missing something. A lot.

They cannot understand the banker in Buffalo. The cowboy in Cheyenne. The doctor in Des Moines. The farmer in Fremont. The homemaker in Hattiesburg. The merchant in Memphis. The preacher in Pocatello. The teacher in Tacoma.

They cannot understand that these people are more alike than they are different. That most of them feel good about their families. Their work. Their communities. Their futures.

Are there concerns? Sure.

Are there problems? Of course.

But the concerns and problems are manageable. The people in this country concentrate on their everyday lives. They're not fretting or biting their nails over foreign problems. Their lives are not going to hell in a handbasket.

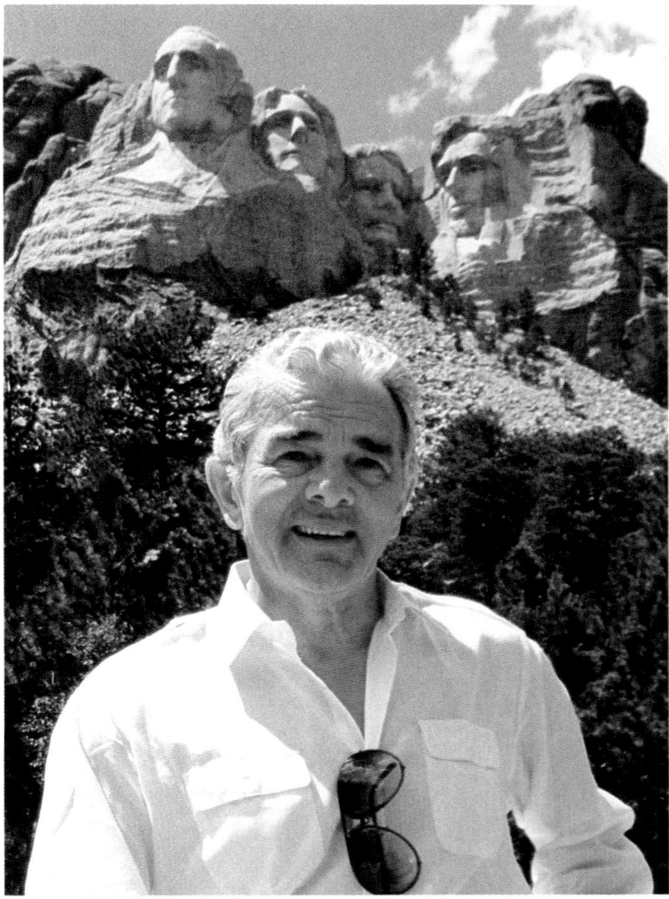

HOMECOMING: Neuharth returned to his home state of South Dakota near the midpoint of the BusCapade tour.

If those in the media do not understand this — and more — they cannot help their readers, viewers or listeners understand.

You won't find a long-winded analysis of the national mood on these pages. You'll find what the readers of USA TODAY found for six months: people talking about their lives. Many of the faces and quotes appeared in USA TODAY; others did not. On the third page of each chapter, you'll find the columns that I wrote twice a week.

Every day USA TODAY carries these words atop its Opinion Page, first expressed by me in Vol. 1, No. 1 on Sept. 15, 1982:

"USA TODAY hopes to serve as a forum for better understanding and unity, to help make the USA truly one nation."

If BusCapade helps contribute to that understanding, it will have been worthwhile.

Allen H. Neuharth
Founder, USA TODAY

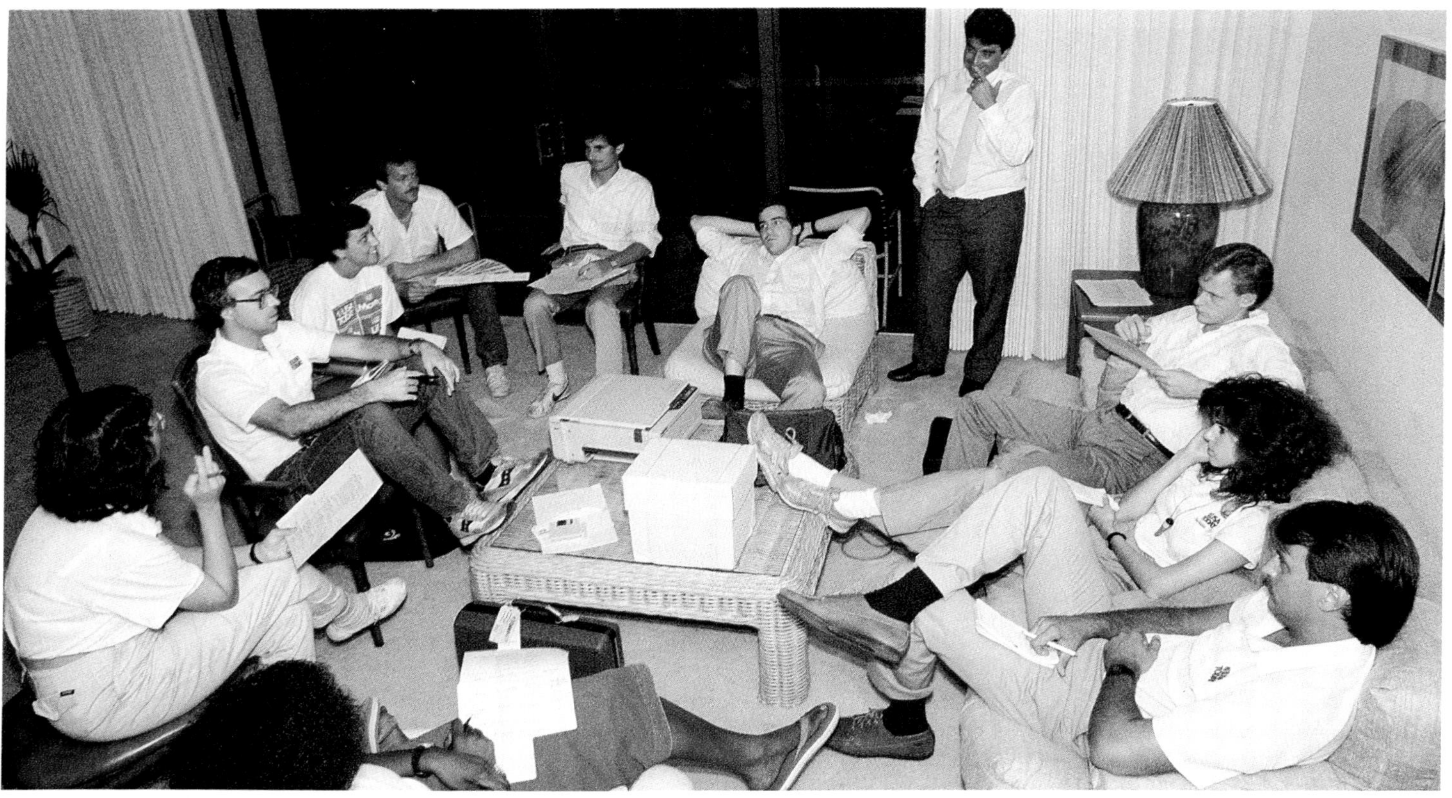

THE PLANNING: As is true in most newsrooms, BusCapade days began or ended with a planning meeting. The difference: BusCapade meetings took place in hotel rooms, on the bus or in airplanes. Ken Paulson, 33, Al Neuharth's chief of staff and the "managing editor" of BusCapade, is seated at far left. Clockwise from Paulson are: Juanie Phinney, 23; Joel Driver, 28; David Silk, 22; Dan Greaney, 22; Lou Brancaccio, 37; Paul Czachowski, 29; Paula Burton, 26; George White, 28; Gaynelle Evans, 35; and Kathleen Smith Barry, 28.

BusCateers at work

THE DETAILS: When Ken Paulson wasn't directing news coverage, he was taking care of logistics. That meant that when the bus made a stop, Paulson headed for the nearest pay phone to handle yet another detail.

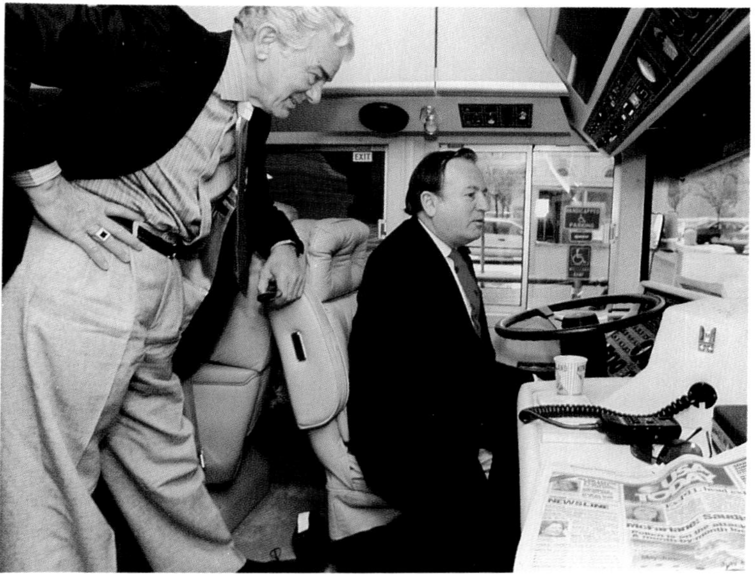

THE GUVS: Rhode Island Gov. Edward DiPrete takes the wheel of the bus as Al Neuharth, 63, looks on. Neuharth met with all 50 governors during the BusCapade tour.

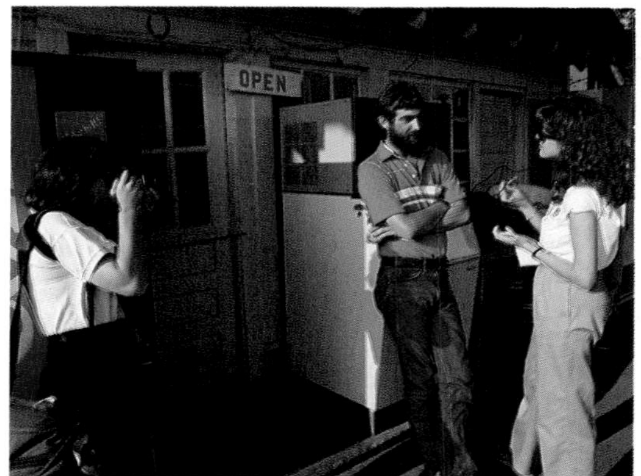

SHOOTING IN GEORGIA: Kathleen Smith Barry, a photographer at Gannett's paper in Nashville, *The Tennessean*, shoots while Paula Burton, a writer/producer at WXIA-TV, Gannett's station in Atlanta, interviews David Clements, 30, in Plains, Ga. Barry and Scott Maclay, in photo at right, shot many of the photos in this book.

SHOOTING IN FLORIDA: Scott Maclay, 37, a photographer for Gannett Corporate Publications, concentrates on next shot while Bo Jim, 41, wrestles an alligator in Ochopee, Fla.

REPORTING IN IDAHO: In Boise, Idaho, Paula Burton talks with Butch Otter, 45, one of the more than 3,000 people interviewed during the six-month journey.

NEUHARTH INTERVIEWED: At many stops, BusCapade made news as well as covered the news. There were 337 local radio and 108 local television stories. Plus 114 newspaper stories and numerous magazine pieces, including in *Newsweek* and *People*. *Good Morning America*, NBC's *Today* Show, *Entertainment Tonight* and *ABC World News Tonight* also did segments.

REPORTING IN IOWA: Dan Greaney, former editor of *The Harvard Lampoon*, interviews Howard Postma, 55, in Sanborn, Iowa.

Alabama

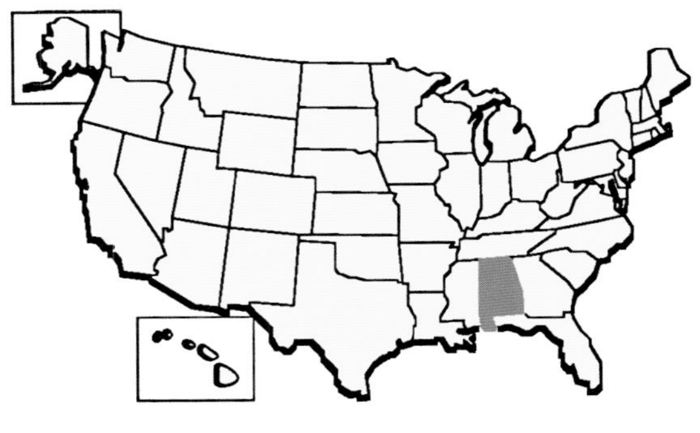

Visited: Aug. 31-Sept. 1, 1987
Featured in USA TODAY: Sept. 4

"I had Dr. Martin Luther King Jr. arrested when he came here in 1955. I was wrong. But race is secondary here now."

Joe Smitherman
Mayor
Selma, Ala.

Alabama

In 'Heart of Dixie,' image is the issue

Dec. 1, 1955. A 42-year-old black seamstress named **Rosa L. Parks** got on a public bus in Montgomery on her way home from work. Took a seat toward the middle. As the bus filled up with white folks, the driver asked Rosa to move to the back.

She refused. No scene, no screams. Just firmly refused. Was arrested and jailed. The civil rights movement had its catalyst. And, Alabama had its image as the racist state.

1987. Image is still an issue in "The Heart of Dixie." Memories remain of the violence-marred march from Selma to Montgomery. Governor **George Wallace** blocking the schoolhouse door to blacks. But issues have changed.

PARKS: Declined back of bus; now has street named for her.

Rosa L. Parks is now the name of an avenue in Montgomery, the state capital (pop. 189,300). She lives in Detroit, which has its own Rosa Parks Boulevard.

Three white and three black councilmen govern Selma (pop. 27,100). Says Mayor **Joe Smitherman**, 59, a white: "I had **Dr. Martin Luther King Jr.** arrested when he came here in 1955. I was wrong. But race is secondary here now."

Adds City Councilman **Lorenzo Harrison**, 55, a black: "We have equal representation on City Council. We have blacks in good jobs. We know more about each other than we did then. The mayor is kind of like George Wallace. He changed with the times."

SMITHERMAN and HARRISON: In Selma, whites and blacks govern together.

Indeed, as times changed, so did Wallace. Guv from 1963-67, '71-'79, '83-'87. A Redneck hero in first term. Parlayed that image into a strong presidential run as an Independent in 1968. Got 9,901,151 votes across the USA. Carried Alabama, Arkansas, Georgia, Louisiana, Mississippi. Enough to deny **Hubert Humphrey** the presidency and elect **Richard Nixon**.

During his last campaign and term as guv, Wallace courted blacks, moved many into his administration. Now 68, retired and suffering very bad health as a result of a bullet in 1972, Wallace is unhappy that his old image lingers. He told the BusCapade at his home this week:

"You reporters still come down and want to talk about my standing in the schoolhouse door a quarter century ago. Let's talk about my honorary degree from Tuskegee Institute (Alabama's leading black institution)."

Today's Alabama leaders look to change the image. Gov. **Guy Hunt**, 54, the first Republican guv since 1872, has proclaimed his priorities: higher teacher salaries, better education, economic development, more and better jobs.

The base to build on is diverse, not as rural as its image.

■ Manufacturing and trade employ over 700,000, about 40 percent of the state's work force. Birmingham (pop. 279,813) has the biggest base.

■ High tech at Huntsville (pop. 151,400) has made that a boom town. NASA's Marshall Space Flight Center and Redstone Arsenal employ 25,000.

■ Farming is shrinking. But cotton, peanuts, soybeans still pour $300 million a year into the state's economy.

Whether on the farms or in the cities, white or black, football unites and divides fans. Very serious stuff. Alabama and Auburn rivalry rivals any in the USA.

Early season fever is especially high at the U of A in Tuscaloosa (pop. 75,600), where new head Coach **Bill Curry**, recruited from Georgia Tech, is in his first season at the Crimson Tide helm.

CURRY: In Bear Bryant's shadow.

Curry knows he's walking in **Bear Bryant**'s shadow. So did **Ray Perkins**, who succeeded the legendary Bear in 1983. Lasted only four seasons. Curry has faced the reality by resurrecting the Bear's famous observation tower of terror near the Tide's practice field. Curry thinks and talks image:

"The most important thing is winning. But a lot of old stupid barriers drop on our football field. The Redneck goes into life better able to accept other people after teaming up with the black. And the black running back figures out the white lineman blocking for him isn't so bad after all. When they play together and win together, they learn to like each other."

That's Plain Talk from Alabama.

Snapshot

Heart of Dixie

ENTERED USA: Dec. 14, 1819, 22nd state

MOTTO: We dare defend our rights
POPULATION: 4,053,000; rank, 22nd
LARGEST CITY: Birmingham, pop. 279,813
CAPITAL: Montgomery, pop. 189,300
LAND: 50,767 square miles; rank, 28th
POPULATION DENSITY: 79.8 per square mile; rank, 25th
RACIAL MIX: 73.8% white; 25.6% black; 0.2% Asian and Pacific islanders. Hispanic heritage: 0.9%.

Uniquely Ala.

MONUMENTAL PEST: The Boll Weevil Monument at Enterprise, unveiled in 1919, is the first statue erected in the USA to an insect pest. Reason: The weevils' destruction of cotton crops forced farmers to diversify.

SOME PARTY: When French General Lafayette visited in 1825, the reception was so lavish that by the time he left, the state treasury was overdrawn by $5,000.

YES, MA'AM: The Women's Army Corps Museum at Fort McClellan at Anniston is the only museum in the world dedicated to women in the military. It opened in 1942.

DEAR DENTIST: The Reynolds Historical Library at Birmingham contains letters written by George Washington to his dentist.

LOG CABIN: The Tower of London has Alabama pine logs in it. In the mid-1880s, W.N. Nichols answered an ad for pine logs placed by Queen Victoria of England.

Voices
of Alabama

Bobby Allison, 49
Professional race car driver
Hueytown

"You can be stopped at a stoplight in Birmingham trying to get directions, and nobody will blow their horn at you. What I enjoy about Alabama is its down-home type of living. People want to accomplish things, but they aren't in such a hurry that they're going to run over the person next to them."

Edd Smartt, 27
Clothing salesman
Huntsville

"A lot of big hi-tech companies are moving here. More young people are going to college. They know that once they have a degree, they will be able to find a job right here at home. They can be successful in Huntsville. There's no reason to go anyplace else."

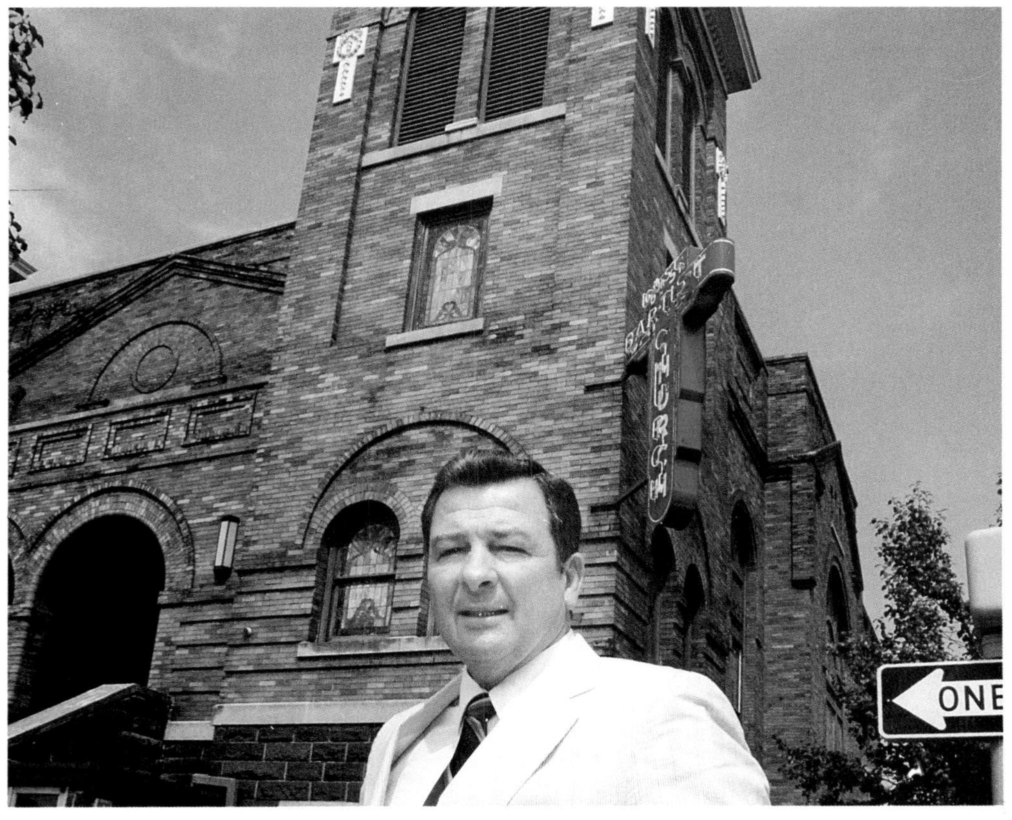

Arthur Deutcsh, 55
Police chief
Birmingham

"Scars of the '60s, they're going to be here. One of the deepest was the bombing of the 16th Avenue Baptist Church, a few blocks from City Hall. That was a turning point. The change has been tremendous. It's a new day in Birmingham."

Linda TeGantvoort, 35
Bookstore cashier
Huntsville

"They say that this is the Bible Belt, and it's true. God is welcome in Huntsville. If rock bands come here and get out of hand, they are not allowed to come back. That's a way the city fathers protect our children. Some cities don't care. We do."

Takayo Ashford, 18
Student
Tuscaloosa

"I don't have to live the Civil Rights movement from day to day. I don't have to worry about being accepted. I think there's not much prejudice on an individual level. But as far as groups are concerned, there still is prejudice. We've made a lot of progress, but I still think we have a long way to go."

David Vaughn, 37
Lawyer
Daphne

"The image of Alabama is still pretty bleak but, these days, undeserved. There's not a dime's worth of difference between us and the rest of the country. We're all pretty much Americans with the same likes and dislikes. We still seem to be taking the rap. It's not all dirt roads and 'Dukes of Hazzard' anymore."

Janie Carlton, 61
Birmingham City Hall
information clerk
Pratt City

"Church is real important to me. Church is where we go to get our souls revived. It's like having a car — you've got to take it to a service station. There's a lot of Christian people in Alabama. The people in the North were maybe living better and working better than the people in the South, so maybe we've had to pray harder to get things to go our way."

Randy Owen, 37, lead singer for the group Alabama, lives in Adamsburg, Ala., where he grew up. Alabama has won several Entertainer of the Year Awards from the Academy of Country Music.

Thank God I'm able to live in Alabama

USA TODAY: What are some of your early memories of Alabama?

OWEN: I remember going with my mother, grandpa and grandma to sell eggs in town. I lived on a farm with my mother, father and two sisters. We had cotton, corn, vegetables and cattle. And I remember the cotton gins in town — they're long gone now, though.

USA TODAY: What are the people like there?

OWEN: They're warm and caring. I think the people have a lot of pride. I love it. I could live anywhere in the world, and I choose to live there.

USA TODAY: What is your home like?

OWEN: It's a nice house, nothing far out. It was very important for me to have my own land and to build a house for my wife and family.

USA TODAY: You went to high school in nearby Fort Payne. Has the town changed?

OWEN: It's still a really neat little place. Sometimes progress can bring about things you don't really want, but I think we've been able to avoid that. People are more aware of Fort Payne, mainly because of the June Jam (an annual music and entertainment fest) and the influx of people — it brings in 60,000 to 70,000 people each year.

USA TODAY: What did you do for fun when you were a teen-ager?

OWEN: We used to drive around and look for girls, to see what's going on, and to be seen. When I was in Fort Payne High School, four or five of my buddies would come out to the farm and we'd play horseshoes. When you live on a farm, there's not a lot of time. You get out of school and mom and daddy are waiting for you to help them.

USA TODAY: When did you start playing music?

OWEN: I started playing guitar when I was 6 years old. I didn't know anything about music. My mother can read music. My daddy didn't know how to play anything. We all knew how to sing, though.

USA TODAY: How do you feel about Alabama?

OWEN: I thank God I've been able to live there. They say once you leave, you can't go home again. I'm glad I have a place to call home.

Topic: ALABAMA

This state has become an economic hot spot

USA TODAY: When you campaigned for governor, one of your themes was the need to change the state's image. What was that image and how has it changed?

HUNT: I think the image of Alabama as a whole was a state of rednecks, a state of people who were behind the times and would not make the adjustments necessary for business to grow and prosper. Now we're really one of the two hot spots of the South in economic development.

USA TODAY: What gives Alabama a competitive edge in trying to attract business?

HUNT: A lot of the companies that have plants in Alabama talk about the high quality of the labor. Also, we've shifted from a farm economy, where you have a lot of people in their 40s and 50s who are trying to get off the farm into something else. Plus we have a training program — said to be one of the best in the country — where we cooperate with the company to train employees.

USA TODAY: Your state tends to show up toward the bottom of lists ranking education spending, income and social services. What's being done to improve your standing?

HUNT: We're pretty high as far as teachers' salaries. Until this past year, we were second to Virginia in the Southeast. One of our goals is to bring teacher salaries up to or above the national level. We have some of the best schools in the country. We're trying to bring about welfare reform and jobs for people on welfare. We also have a tax reform commission.

USA TODAY: Is it true that you want to establish a more down-home atmosphere in the governor's mansion?

HUNT: During the campaign, I told people, "This is your governor's mansion. And when I'm elected, we want you to come for breakfast." So I began that. I had not considered weddings until we had two or three there. There are days when we have hundreds of people through the mansion. We've tried to make people feel it is theirs. Maybe we've succeeded.

Guy Hunt, 54, a Republican, was elected last year. Hunt is a minister and former probate judge.

USA TODAY: How does the presence of the Confederate flag, both in your office and across the street on the old Capitol, fit into the progressive image you're promoting?

HUNT: It has nothing whatsoever to do with it. The Confederate flag has flown here a long time. They began making noises about it after I was elected.

USA TODAY: Do you plan to remove it?

HUNT: I've told my black friends, what we need are more jobs, teen-agers off the streets, more black business people. Let things like that alone, and let's move on the things we can accomplish. If I start removing the rebel flag, a lot of people will never listen to me again. So, we've got to look at meaningful things and not symbols.

USA TODAY: How do you choose between the football teams at the University of Alabama and Auburn University?

HUNT: You don't. Football is a very volatile issue.

USA TODAY: Do you choose sides?

HUNT: They tried to get me involved the other day, and I told them, only if I could get the game transferred to Holly Pond where I live. They didn't ask me about it anymore.

Alaska

Visited by jet: June 24-26, 1987
Featured in USA TODAY: June 29

"This is a completely different lifestyle. Open space for open-minded people."

Tracy Atkins
Cook
Anchorage, Alaska

Alaska

Midnight sun shines on rebels and riches

The sun rose this morning in Fairbanks at 3:07 a.m. It won't set until 12:41 a.m. tomorrow. 21 hours, 34 minutes of daylight.

In December, the sun will rise around noon, set around 3 p.m., 21 hours of darkness.

Such sharp swings in the lifestyles are taken in stride. Nearly all 534,000 Alaskans consider themselves blessed beneficiaries of the bounteous beauty and riches of this biggest state in the USA.

The Call of the Wild has hooked them. When **Jack London** wrote that book, it featured men and dogs. They're still here. But add to that pipelines, oil, women.

The pipeline gave Alaska this generation's boom. An $8 billion, 800-mile tube. Some called it a pipe dream when it was started in 1974. Completed in 1977, it carries up to 1.6 million barrels of oil a day from Prudhoe Bay.

PLANT: Man, dog plus pipeline.

Walt Plant, 41, is a construction worker in Fairbanks (pop. 22,645). Came to work on the pipeline. Stayed. Has a dog. Wanders the wilderness when not working.

"Coming up here was the best move I ever made. I like working outside, even when it's 50 below zero. I like situations where a small mistake can cost you your life."

Sound strange? Not here. Most people are different. Escapists. Gov. **Steve Cowper**, 48, first-term Democrat, is one of them. From North Carolina. Been given the nickname of "The High Plains Drifter."

Says the Guv: "I was one of those rebels. I just woke up one morning and realized I never liked living in the South. So I jumped in my car and drove up here. About 60 percent of the people will give you that kind of answer."

Critics call it a mix of misfits. Too harsh. But people are different. Listen:

Bret Fishell, 26, a bartender in Anchorage, largest city (pop. 226,663). From Vickeryville, Mich. "It takes someone with a pioneer spirit to live here. This brings out the best and the bad in people."

Father **Ron Dunfey**, 65, a Catholic priest in Juneau, state capital (pop. 19,528). From Boston. "Alaska attracts eight balls. But eight balls are important to make the world work."

Tracy Atkins, 31. From Los Angeles. Now a cook in Girdwood section of Anchorage: "This is a completely different lifestyle. Open space for open-minded people."

Lifestyles changed here in the '70s. The pipeline's completion and high oil prices brought a boom. The state income tax was repealed in 1979. Government surplus money was distributed to residents and communities.

The boom busted when oil prices skidded. Times are tougher now. But three basics keep Alaska going.

■ Military. 12 percent of the state's wage earners are recipients of the USA's $1.3 billion annual military spending here.

■ Oil. Even with sharply reduced prices, 175 million barrels brought in $1.27 billion in revenue in 1986. Second only to Texas.

■ Fishing. Alaska salmon is sold around the world. The fish industry rang up $752 million last year. No. 1 in the USA.

The heavy USA military presence seems assured long term. The Soviets are *very* close neighbors. The 154 Alaskans who live on our Little Diomede Island are just 2.5 miles from the Soviets' Big Diomede Island.

Ancestors of many of Alaska's 48,000 Eskimo natives were once under Russian domination. We bought the 377,444,480-acre territory from Russia in 1867 for about 2 cents an acre. $7.2 million. Dubbed "Seward's Icebox" after Secretary of State **William H. Seward**, who pushed the deal through Congress.

MERRY: Santa's North Pole helper.

Many identify Alaska with the North Pole. Actually, its northern tip, Point Barrow, is 1,290 miles south of the North Pole. But there is a North Pole, Alaska (pop. 265).

That's where the postal service delivers all those letters from USA kids addressed to "Santa Claus, North Pole."

About 30,000 a year. Each one is answered by Santa's helpers from the local junior high school.

Merry Christmas Miller, 25, helps her parents run Santa Claus House, a gift shop in North Pole. What's at the top of Merry's Christmas wish list to Santa? She doesn't hesitate: "A trip to Hawaii."

That's Plain Talk from Alaska.

Snapshot

The Last Frontier

INTERNATIONAL DATELINE
POINT BARROW
DIOMEDE ISLAND
FAIRBANKS
NORTH POLE
PALMER
ANCHORAGE
SEMISOPOCHNOI ISLAND
JUNEAU

ALASKA
19 59
The Last Frontier

ENTERED USA: Jan. 3, 1959, 49th state

MOTTO: North to the future
POPULATION: 534,000; rank, 49th
LARGEST CITY: Anchorage, pop. 226,663
CAPITAL: Juneau, pop. 19,528
LAND: 570,833 square miles; rank, 1st
POPULATION DENSITY: 0.9 per square mile; rank, 50th
RACIAL MIX: 77.1% white; 8.5% Eskimo; 5.4% American Indian; 3.4% black; 2% Asian and Pacific islanders. Hispanic heritage: 2.4%.

Uniquely Alaska

ON THE ROCKS: There are more active glaciers and ice fields in Alaska than the rest of the inhabited world — 28,800 square miles.

COMPASS BUSTER: Alaska has the northernmost (Point Barrow), westernmost (Little Diomede Island), and easternmost (Semisopochnoi Island) points in the USA. How possible: It straddles the International Dateline.

LONE TREE: The nation's smallest national forest is in Alaska, far beyond the Arctic Circle. A single black spruce stands inside a white picket fence.

COLD HOUSE: Alaskan igloos are made of driftwood, whalebone and sod — not ice. Canadian Eskimos build ice houses.

THE MAIN EVENT: Traditional events at the annual World Eskimo-Indian Olympics in Fairbanks include seal skinning, fish cutting, greased pole walk, Indian leg wrestling, blanket toss and the knuckle hop.

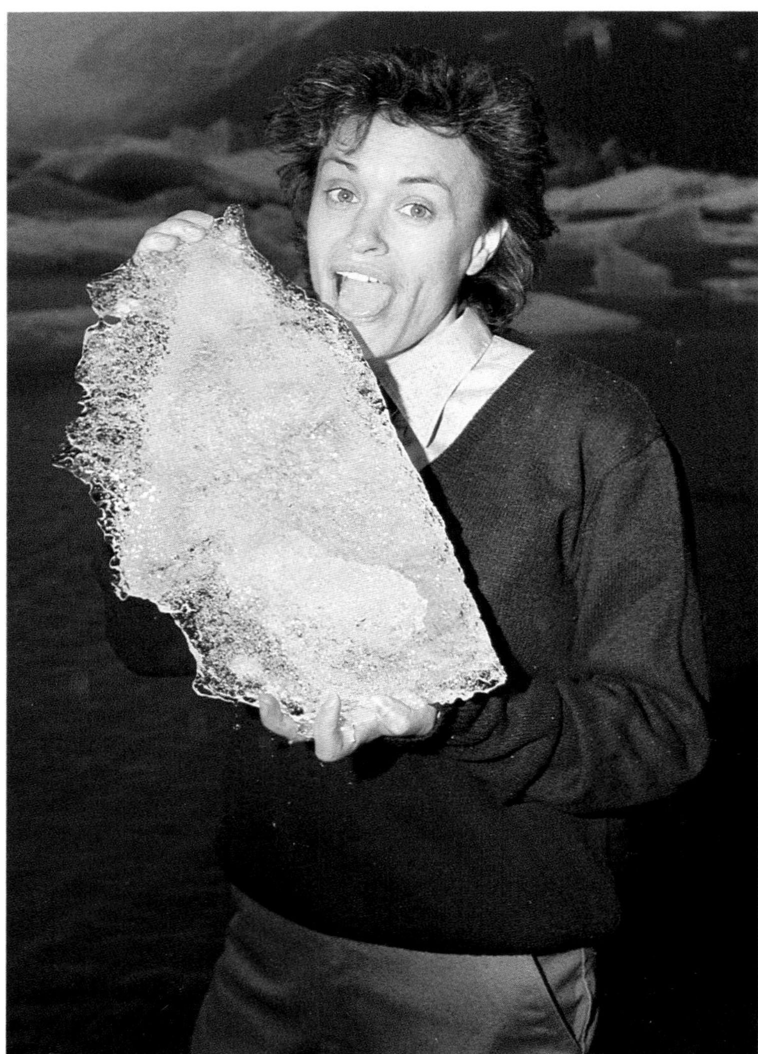

Michaela Smith, 27
Forest guide
Girdwood

"What's interesting about the icebergs is the mood changes every day. When everyone is gone, there's nothing better than to look out and stare. It's like meditating with a giant blue crystal."

Jerry Stinson, 33
Oil worker
Soldotna

"In the Lower 48, you're lucky to catch a minnow. Here, I hooked and landed seven kings (salmon), the biggest at 40 pounds. It is the last frontier. You can't go any further and be outdoors."

Voices
of Alaska

Judy Tankersley, 30
Unemployed
Anchorage

"Salmon fishing and the outdoors. That's what Alaska is all about. I caught a 35-pound king. It gave me a 20-minute fight. I usually bake them or send them to my family in Reno. It's nice to have wildlife on your front porch. The dog was chasing a moose off of it the other day. Everybody thinks this is the ice age here. But the cold doesn't even bother me anymore. I think I developed another layer of skin."

LeRoy Shank, 47
Musher
Fairbanks

"My dogs are a lot more than a piece of machinery. They're part of my family. They're little people. They have personalities. They have senses that we don't even know about. How you name them is how they turn out. Every musher now has a dog named Rambo. Sled dog racing is what Alaska is all about."

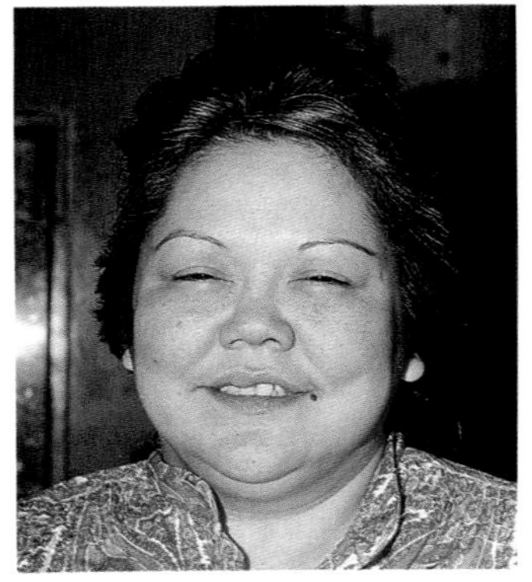

Elaine Hansen, 33
Egg farmer
Palmer

"My grandmother was one of the last pure-bred Eyak Indians. My daughter studies bead making and other native culture in school. She teaches me. I lived in an Eskimo village for four years. We got very close. We did a lot of things together. I enjoy it when the power goes off in town. It's so peaceful."

George King, 40
Teacher
Anchorage

"I own my own plane because you're so restricted to what you see on the highway. I can always jump in my airplane and fly two or three hours and never see a thing made by man. It's feeling more in tune with the world. It's one of the things that's almost spiritual. It's so quiet when man is not around. You get away from all the craziness and the rat race. Dead quiet. It's so quiet it's deafening. Because everywhere else you go, you can feel the rumbling of civilization."

Mary Kelley, 49
Airline clerk
Juneau

"You get very fast at bundling up the kids. If it was warmer than 20 degrees below, they'd go out and play. We're the biggest state and we have the most resources. Being a new state, Alaska has a lot to accomplish in the next few decades. Everything wasn't done a hundred years ago. We're still making the state."

Deedee Hammond, 34
Homemaker
Fairbanks

"The summer is harder than the winter. I never get enough sleep in the summer. I feel like I should use all of that daylight. I'll be out working in the garden, and realize that it's one in the morning. Mount McKinley has its own clouds. It's really choosy about when it shows itself. It doesn't always make an appearance. It plays hard to get. But when the clouds slip away, it's like a celebrity making an entrance."

Susan Butcher, 31, has won the 1,157-mile Iditarod Trail Sled Dog Race twice, in 1986 and 1987. She and her husband live in the Alaskan wilderness in a house without electricity or running water. Butcher has 150 huskies.

You can't be bored in this exciting land

USA TODAY: How popular is sled dog racing? It seems you hear more and more about it.

BUTCHER: It's always been our World Series. It's the state sport. The stars of dog mushing are the state heroes. The nicest thing about that is if you travel by dog team, then you're really welcomed into a village or really welcomed into the bush community. They immediately respect you.

USA TODAY: What were your first impressions when you moved to Alaska?

BUTCHER: When I flew in, it was 40 below, and nobody noticed it. That was a good starter right there. I was just sick and tired of being around people who, as soon as they got a little bit cold, would complain, "Ooooh, it's so cold, it's just terrible."

USA TODAY: Have you changed since you left Colorado for Alaska?

BUTCHER: I don't feel that I've changed except probably in my self-confidence. I think the fact that for 10 years I lived alone in the bush with my dogs and had to completely depend on myself really taught me the confidence that I needed. And, in fact, it's made marriage wonderful because having gone through that, and actually my husband finding all those same answers out on his own, when we got together there was no big deal.

USA TODAY: What kind of place is Alaska?

BUTCHER: It's a place of real freedom. A place where you're counted for what you do. But you have to work maybe twice as hard because of the high cost of living, because of the climate, and because of the fact that there aren't many people up there.

USA TODAY: You went there to be in isolation, and now you're a spokesperson for the state.

BUTCHER: It's ironic. I started dog mushing for absolutely the other reasons. And I never thought I'd make a dollar because of it. I very much believe in the sport of sled dog racing, and it needs to be promoted. And so I have taken it upon myself to help.

USA TODAY: There probably aren't a lot of people who go to your house to do an interview.

BUTCHER: You'd be surprised. We've had quite a menagerie of people. And they all usually get flat tires or stuck in a snowdrift or something of the sort.

Topic: ALASKA

We capitalize on cold and communications

USA TODAY: What do you think people in "the lower 48" think Alaska is all about?

COWPER: Well, too many believe that Alaska is a re-creation of Al Capp's "Lower Slobovia" — snow and ice everywhere, and people's heads poking up at intervals. In fact, the weather in most of the coastal areas, which is where most of the people are, is pretty moderate for northern climes. In Southeast Alaska in some years, the weather doesn't even get below freezing.

USA TODAY: Is Alaska still a frontier state?

COWPER: Yes. I hope it always is.

USA TODAY: Is that what attracts people like you?

COWPER: Yes. There's a kind of a call to the individual that goes on around here which is an interesting myth. But it won't work in the kind of world that we're faced with now. So I want to channel those kinds of energies into a more modern context, without insulting everybody who wants to go out to wrestle a bear.

USA TODAY: People see Alaska as a place to make their fortunes. Does that attract rebels as well as fortune seekers?

COWPER: Over the last 12 years, we have attracted a lot of very talented professional people. An economic opportunity led to their decisions to come up. And then when things kind of went downhill, temporarily, they said, "OK, we're going to tough it out." That's an advantage.

USA TODAY: The oil pipeline construction boom is over. Where is Alaska headed?

COWPER: What I'd like to see happen here is the rapid development of a technologically proficient society. We're spread out all over the place, which, of course, argues for a first-rate communications system, which we do have in place.

USA TODAY: During the boom times, the government distributed surplus money to people. Now, you are faced with reversing that tradition.

Steve Cowper, 48, a Democrat, was elected governor last fall. He formerly was a member of the Alaska House of Representatives.

COWPER: What we're trying to do is really change the whole Alaskan mind-set away from being a place where the government takes care of everything.

USA TODAY: How do you enjoy Alaska's great outdoors?

COWPER: My daughters and I used to go out and run rivers in Western Alaska — we'd be gone for a couple of days and just never see anybody. There's just so much country here that even most Alaskans haven't seen it or even thought about it. You can lose yourself very quickly in this country.

USA TODAY: You have a remarkable range of people in this state. Do they get along?

COWPER: Well, our problem is the value system accepted by Western culture just doesn't apply to indigenous people. I think that urban Alaskans have to bend over backward to try to understand the native people.

USA TODAY: Do Alaskans follow sports down below?

COWPER: Oh, yeah. Like everybody else. We've got a satellite hookup — everybody's become Seattle Seahawk freaks.

USA TODAY: Is Anchorage trying to get the Olympics here in 1994?

COWPER: I think we've got a good chance. We've got a lot to offer here.

Arizona

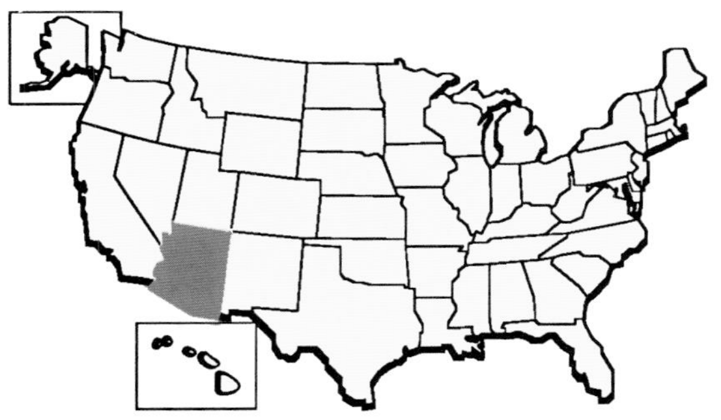

Visited: April 21-23, 1987
Featured in USA TODAY: April 27

"If I'm going to have a second lease on life, this is the place to get it."

Erma Bombeck
Newspaper columnist
Paradise Valley, Ariz.

Arizona

In their 80s or teens, laid-back but not lazy

"They never bury anyone who's moving. So, I keep moving. I'll never retire." **Roy Drachman**, 81. Developer in Tucson (pop. 365,422). That's where many come from across the USA to retire in their 50s and 60s.

"I've lived so long because I didn't touch tobacco, whiskey or women until I was 11." **Sidney Taiz**, 80. Retired and back to school. He's the oldest freshman at the University of Arizona.

Chuck Bryden, 18, one of the younger U of A frosh. "People here do what they want. In Chicago, my father does what he thinks he's expected to do. I wanted to get away from that."

GALLAGHER: Loves back yard.

Mary Gallagher, 25. From Long Island, N.Y., four years ago. Wouldn't think of retiring. A caretaker at Snowbowl on Humphreys Peak, Arizona's highest, near Flagstaff (pop. 34,641). "Nobody back East has a back yard like I have."

All kinds are here. Young and old. Rich and poor. Natives and newcomers. Most look ahead hopefully. Some look back nostalgically. Others look at the present, a little perplexed about growth and traffic gridlock and such.

Arizona attributes:

- People work pretty hard, but don't seem to worry very much.
- Casually comfortable, but also curious. Open collars and open minds.
- 115-plus summer highs in the South. Sub-zero winter lows in the North.

Sun and snow seem to melt or cool people's tensions, without overheating or freezing them.

Politics bubbles as hot as the summer steam bath. Liberal in the South. **Mo Udall** country. Conservative in the middle. **Barry Goldwater** country. Mixed elsewhere.

Right now, first-term Republican Gov. **Evan Mecham,** 62, is a love/hate target.

He rescinded the state holiday for the Rev. **Martin Luther King**'s birthday. Said he considers "pickaninny" for black children "a term of endearment."

Mecham, a car dealer, is a product of the Phoenix area, state capital and largest city (pop. 853,266). An outpost of the John Birch Society and the Eagle Forum. Mecham's friends and foes are outspoken.

"Someone should give the governor a 10-gallon hat and send him back to the 1940s where he belongs." **Mark Crockett**, 28, an IBM employee.

CROCKETT: Guv's outdated.

RICE: Guv's got guts.

"The governor's got guts." **Rade Rice**, 70, retired.

Some of Mecham's musings are too much even for Goldwater, whose 1964 Republican presidential campaign earned him an "extremist" label.

Now 78, retired from the U.S. Senate, Goldwater is still "Mr. Arizona" to many. He is in and out of hospitals for leg surgery, but stays involved.

Recently Goldwater met with Mecham. "He's pretty hard-headed. We haven't had a governor in a long time who did what he wanted and said 'to hell with you.' I'm going to try to get him to come around," Goldwater pledged.

'MR. ARIZONA': Tells Guv to cool it.

Whether they are bothered by problems political or personal, most Arizonans laugh a lot.

Helping them is nationally syndicated newspaper columnist **Erma Bombeck**. Lived here since 1971, after 44 years in Dayton, Ohio. Why did she move here?

"Do you want the funny answer or the real one?" the homespun humorist quipped.

Then, at least semi-serious: "I came in search of the Fountain of Youth. This is like a brand-new place. Still just beginning. I thought, if I'm going to have a second lease on life, this is the place to get it."

That's Plain Talk from Arizona.

Snapshot

Grand Canyon State

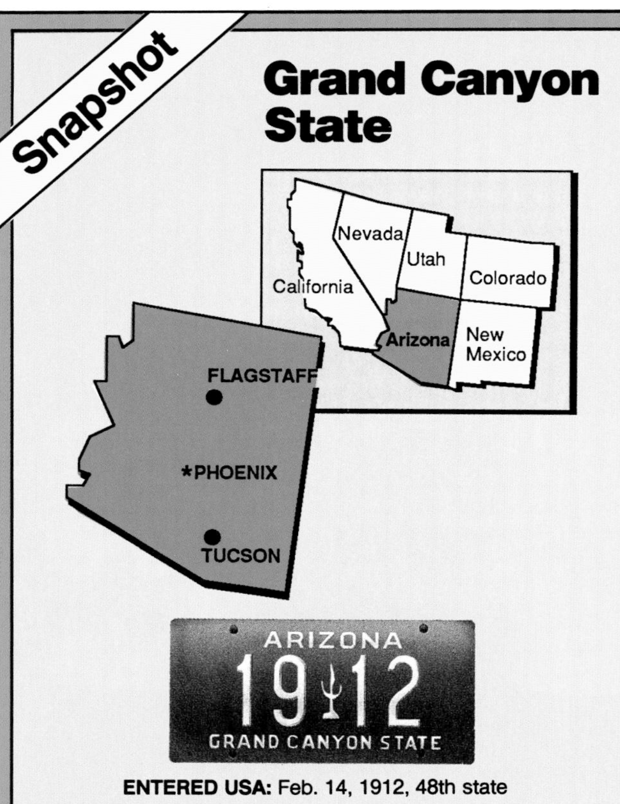

ENTERED USA: Feb. 14, 1912, 48th state

MOTTO: God enriches
POPULATION: 3,317,000; rank, 25th
LARGEST CITY: Phoenix, pop. 853,266
CAPITAL: Phoenix
LAND: 113,508 square miles; rank, 6th
POPULATION DENSITY: 29.2 per square mile; rank, 39th
RACIAL MIX: 82.4% white; 5.6% American Indian; 2.8% black; 0.8% Asian and Pacific islanders. Hispanic heritage: 16.2%.

Uniquely Ariz.

LAND LORDS: Only 15 percent of the land in Arizona is privately owned; most is state or federally owned. Indian reservations cover one quarter of state-owned land.

OLDEST TOWN: The USA's oldest continuously inhabited community is Old Oraibi on the Hopi Indian Reservation — established in 1150.

WHAT'S IN A NAME: Three communities in Arizona are known as the Christmas towns — Santa Claus, Snowflake and Silver Bell. According to local legend, the town of Show Low is so named because it was won in a poker game.

TIE ONE ON: The official state tie is the bola tie, more commonly known as a string tie.

INDIAN TERRITORY: The 25,000-square-mile Navajo reservation in Northeast Arizona is the largest Indian reservation in the USA.

Louise Martinez, 70
Retired
Jerome

"Jerome is the heartbeat of Arizona because it's a living ghost town that keeps Arizona alive. This place is heaven. When I die, I want my ashes thrown across this mountain."

Louise McCall, 62
Artist
Paradise Valley

"There is a sense of something happening that is wonderful and renewing. There is a unique beauty in the landscape that is inspiring to the artist in me. The light here is so fantastic. Light is a tool that we use in our work, like a paint brush."

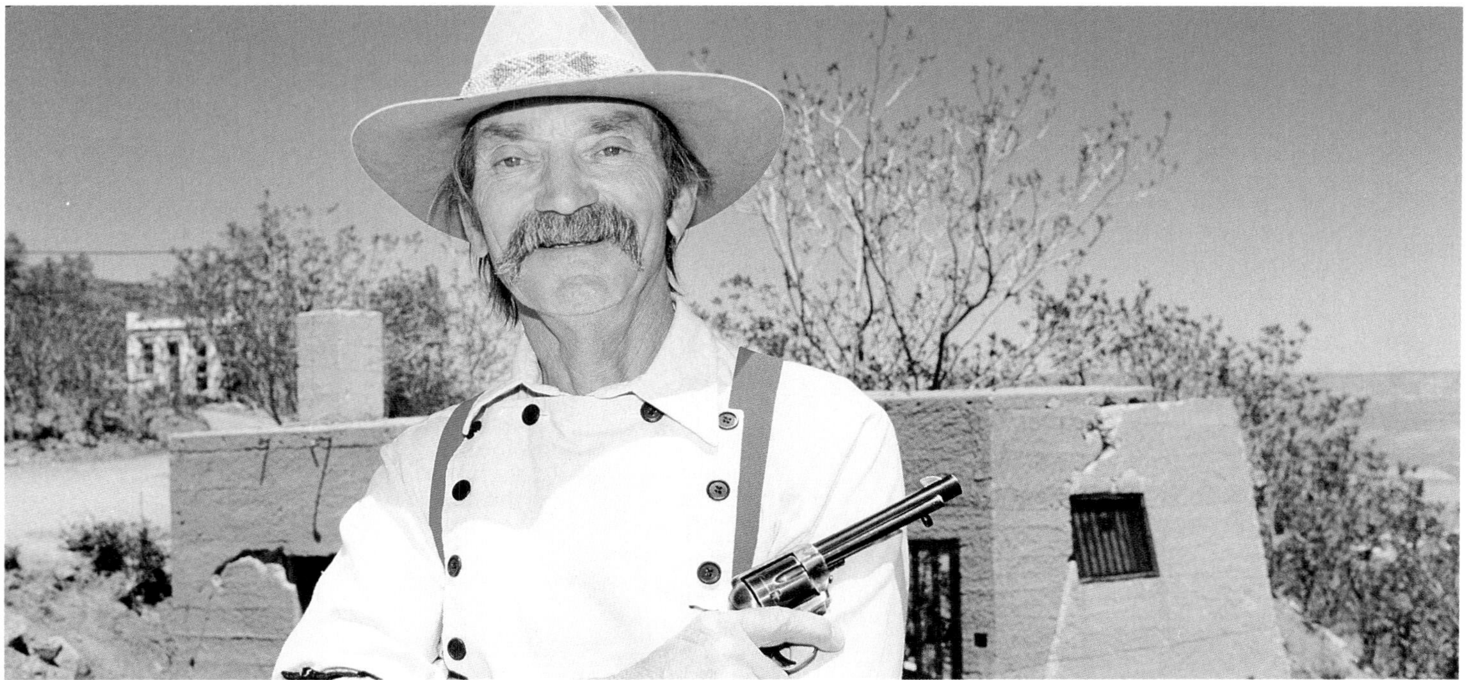

Don McFadden, 64
Rancher/western movie actor
Jerome

"I like to get old maps and retrace the riding trails, like the General Crook Trail that runs from Camp Verde to Prescott. We leave markers and maps for others to follow the path."

Voices
of Arizona

Fred Acosta, 55
Director,
Tucson Job Core Center
Tucson

"*Tucson is a living community. It has a conscience, it has a soul. When I go to Phoenix and other cities, I think that progress has desouled them. Tucson is a place where you want to raise your kids. It's a town that I'd like my grandkids to grow up in.*"

Janet Whalen
Flight nurse
Phoenix

"The state of Arizona offers a wide variety of outdoor experiences. One day you can be snow skiing in the mountains and the next day hiking in the desert. Being an outdoors person, I enjoy the diversity of the Arizona terrain."

Ben Swank, 55
Programmer analyst
Glendale

"Here, I can see the mountains meet the sky. The heat's no problem. You go from your air-conditioned house to your air-conditioned car and drive to your air-conditioned job. On the weekend, you go to the air-conditioned mall."

Alicia Swiszcz, 48
Housekeeper,
University of Arizona
Tucson

"I was born in Arizona. I've lived here all my life. It's beautiful with the desert, cactus and mountains. And the people. I love working around the kids at the university. The lifestyle is slow-paced, and there's great Mexican food!"

Notable

Erma Bombeck, 60, *began writing a weekly humor column in 1963. She now has 31 million readers and has written several books. Bombeck moved to Paradise Valley, Ariz., in 1971.*

Despite road gridlock, home is still paradise

USA TODAY: You moved to Paradise Valley in Arizona from Dayton, Ohio. Why?

BOMBECK: This is almost the truth — not quite. But I gave a speech here in 1970 and they loved it. And I said, "That's the place you should move to. What an audience!" We moved out in '71. The people were just so friendly and so receptive, and it just seemed like a nice, neat place to live.

USA TODAY: Do some regions like humor better than others?

BOMBECK: Everyone has kids who don't clean their room, everyone in the world has husbands who clip things out of the newspaper, and you're reading a lace curtain.

USA TODAY: You're no longer with *Good Morning America.* Did you leave because you were writing a book and a Broadway play?

BOMBECK: No. It was a little more than that. I always have a horror of staying too long at the fair. I'm 60 years old, and I think, my God, I'm going to be standing up there dropping drawers, or doing something and humiliating my entire family.

USA TODAY: Tell me about Paradise.

BOMBECK: Is that adorable or what? Thank you for not laughing when you said that.

USA TODAY: Is it trouble-free?

BOMBECK: Actually, we're in the middle of one of the largest gridlocks in the history of traffic. We're lucky to get out of the house! It better be Paradise, because we can't move!

USA TODAY: So it's not really a Shangri-La.

BOMBECK: I have a little bit of a mountain up here that I can stare out at, it's adjacent to an airport and I did so much traveling for so long. You're still in the middle of things, and yet you're sort of isolated.

USA TODAY: You like the mountains.

BOMBECK: Oh, yeah. You can just sort of stand still, look up, be very quiet and see that those little cactus have a flower on the end and that the mountains will change every few minutes, from the purples to the browns, to the light colors, the yellows — it's just an incredibly beautiful thing.

Topic: ARIZONA

This great melting pot welcomes jobs, visitors

USA TODAY: You've been in office for a few months. How's the job going?

MECHAM: Quite well. We've made a U-turn in many ways. Arizona was headed in the wrong direction. We were escalating spending, increasing taxes. Our educational institutions needed attention. Drugs are so rampant that we're the second worst crime state. Unemployment is creeping up on us.

USA TODAY: After the murder of journalist Don Bolles in 1976, the state's image became linked with organized crime. Is it still a problem here?

MECHAM: Yes. Not as serious as it was. But it's here. I don't think we will get a handle on all of it until we solve the drug problem. When we solve that, that will cut our crime in half.

USA TODAY: How are you fighting the drug problem?

MECHAM: We're engaging everybody in the state. Every school will have an excellent education program on drugs from at least fourth grade right up through our universities. We're going to establish 10 new courts that will deal only with drugs. We're going to hire at least 70 more investigators and 40 prosecutors.

USA TODAY: A new immigration law will take effect in May. Will that help resolve the state's border problems?

MECHAM: It's going to help. We have had an out-of-control situation. Now, we have a law that says, "Let's settle this." I don't think people realize how generous this is on the part of the United States to say, "We don't know how many million people are in our country illegally, but in order not to send people back and split up families, we're going to let you all be citizens."

USA TODAY: How is Arizona coping with its share of the Sunbelt's rapid growth?

MECHAM: We're locked into growth. So many people have come in here to live, we have to make sure that we have industrial development to create the jobs. We're pushing to double tourism in the next four years. That creates a lot of jobs. We expect to do real well with hi-tech.

The Guv

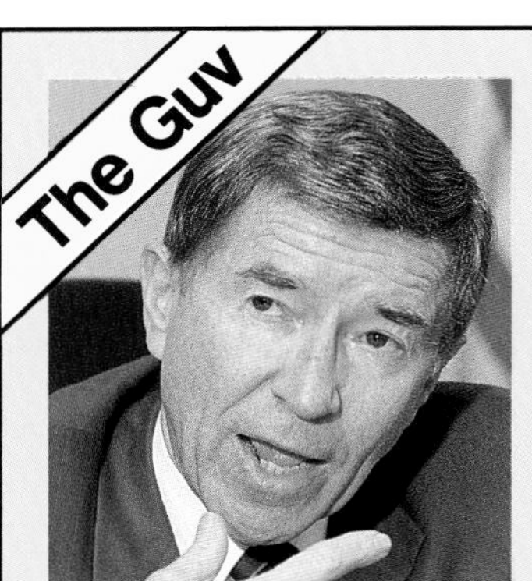

Evan Mecham, 62, *a Republican, won Arizona's governorship last year in a race against two Democrats on his fifth try for the office.*

USA TODAY: Has population growth brought you big-city environmental problems, like the smog in Phoenix and Tucson?

MECHAM: I think our environment statewide is reasonably good. We're very concerned about it; we want to protect our air and water.

USA TODAY: Several groups are boycotting the state because of your stand against the Dr. Martin Luther King Jr. holiday. Is it hurting the state?

MECHAM: Not in the least. There isn't one person in 10,000 who cares what our politics are who wants to come to Arizona.

USA TODAY: What are you proudest of so far?

MECHAM: We've got good people in office who are really working to do their job.

USA TODAY: What do people overlook about this state?

MECHAM: People don't know quite what to think of us. Are we still the swashbuckling Wild West? Are we the sophisticated hi-tech industry? Are we a sand dune where you could die for lack of water at high noon? We're none of those; we're a combination. We're a melting pot.

Arkansas

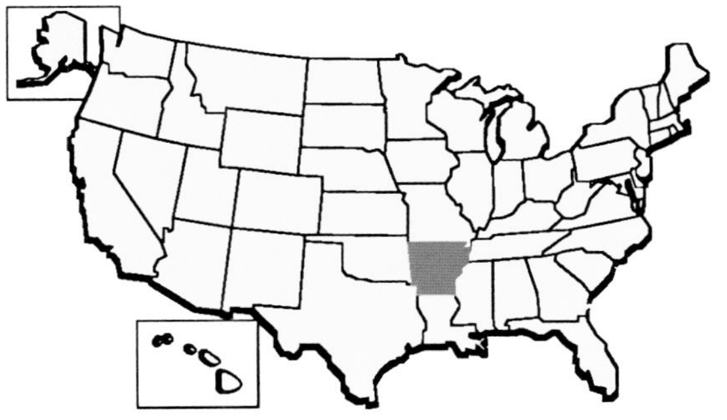

Visited: July 29-31, 1987
Featured in USA TODAY: Aug. 3

"I'm proud to be a Hog. When the fans call the Hogs, it fires me up. I grew up in Arkansas, and I've wanted to play here ever since I started getting serious about football."

Freddie Childress
Student/football player
Fayetteville, Ark.

Arkansas

Rags and riches: Hot springs, warm hearts

Thirty years ago next month, then-Gov. **Orval Faubus** ordered the National Guard to turn away nine black students at Central High School in Little Rock, state capital and largest city (pop. 170,140). Two years of racial turmoil followed.

Now, Central High is one of the most peacefully integrated — and upgraded — public schools in the South. Perhaps in the USA.

Then, Arkansas had a backwoods image. Poverty. Ignorance. Lil' Abner's Dogpatch.

WALTON: Bentonville billionaire.

Now, it is home to the USA's richest person. **Sam Walton**, 69. Worth an estimated $4.5 billion. And he made it all from his Wal-Mart headquarters in his Ozark mountain hometown of Bentonville (pop. 9,900).

Arkansas. Enough beauty in its mountains, rivers, lakes to justify the slogan "The Natural State." But still so rural in character that the hillbilly hallmark hangs on.

What should the real Arkansas image be? Gov. **William Jefferson (Bill) Clinton**, 40, says "I think our biggest problem is that we don't have any image."

Clinton, a charismatic, chic Ivy League graduate and Rhodes Scholar, is working on that. Chaired the National Governors' Conference in Traverse City, Mich., last week. Got high marks for Arkansas' progress in education.

Clinton is serious, but has fun. Entertained the other guvs by hopping on the bandstand and playing the saxophone.

BEA COCKRELL: Pampers tired tourists like Carolyn Senn.

The Arkansas that most across the USA know about is Hot Springs (pop. 28,100). People have been pampered there since Spanish explorer **Hernando DeSoto** found the valley's 47 natural hot springs in 1541.

Bea Cockrell, 69, has been an attendant at the Buckstaff Bathhouse for 37 years. Last week, among those she gave the treatment was **Carolyn Senn**, 26, from Washington, D.C.

"People come with arthritis or broken bones. I bathe them — wash their arms, legs, backs. Have them drink hot water. Use hot towels for aches and pains. They like to be pampered," says Bea.

While visitors from across the USA and around the world unwind in the 143-degree waters at Hot Springs, residents of Arkansas are at work making their living off the land.

■ No. 1 in USA rice crops. 122.5 million bushels last year.

■ No. 1 in broiler chickens. 697 million raised last year. No. 6 in cotton. No. 7 in soybeans.

But paychecks still are paltry for many in Arkansas. Per-person income in 1986 averaged $10,773. That's 47th in the USA. National average was $14,461. Many rural Arkies earn far less than the state average.

Rich or poor, young or old, folks in Arkansas seem at peace with themselves. In the country and in the cities, there's a feeling of warmth toward family, neighbors and visitors. Tolerance and understanding may be the legacies from the racial strife of the 1950s.

After Gov. Faubus barred the blacks on Sept. 2, 1957, **President Eisenhower** sent in the 101st Airborne Division. The military stayed to escort and protect the blacks for the rest of the school year.

When Central opens for the 1987-88 term, it expects about 2,100 students. Last year, 58 percent were nonwhite. Playgrounds this summer are as integrated as the classrooms.

ANN, VINCE: Whites, blacks, others at Central High.

Vince Porter, 17, a junior, is black. "Some teachers talk about the 1957 trouble once in a while. Students don't think much about it. I'm just here to get my grades and get out."

Ann McQueen, 16, also a junior, is white. "I went to an all-white private school and I thought I was too sheltered. You need to meet all different kinds of people. That's how you grow. That's what's so neat about Central. There are whites, blacks, Christians, Jews, atheists. Even people with blue hair."

That's Plain Talk from Arkansas.

Snapshot

Land of Opportunity

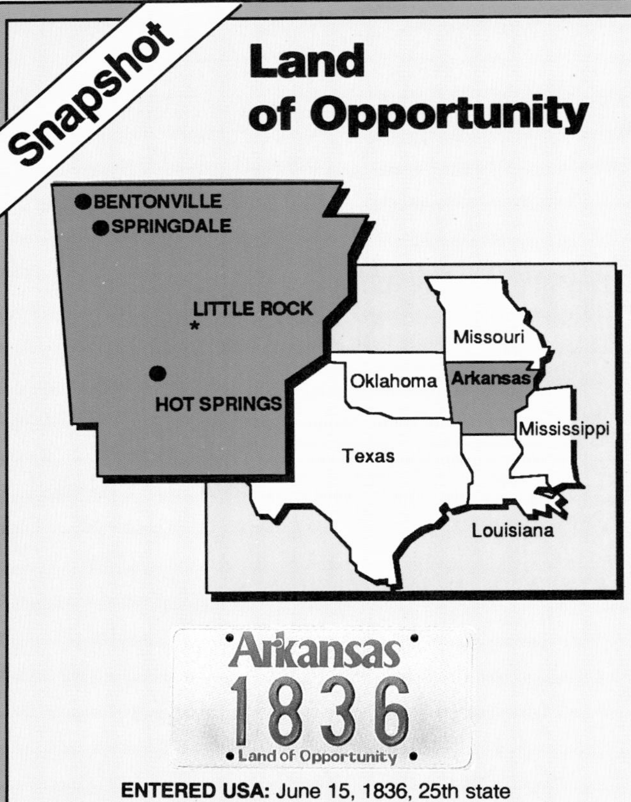

ENTERED USA: June 15, 1836, 25th state

MOTTO: The people rule

POPULATION: 2,372,000; rank, 33rd

LARGEST CITY: Little Rock, pop.170,388

CAPITAL: Little Rock

LAND: 52,078 square miles; rank, 27th

POPULATION DENSITY: 45.5 per square mile; rank, 35th

RACIAL MIX: 82.7% white; 16.3% black; 0.3% Asian and Pacific islanders. Hispanic heritage: 0.8%.

Uniquely Ark.

FINDERS KEEPERS: Arkansas has the USA's only active diamond mine. Visitors to Crater of Diamonds State Park can sift through the diamond-bearing soil and keep any they find. More than 10,000 diamonds have been found since the park opened in 1972.

CLEAN CUT: The official state beverage is milk. Official instrument: fiddle.

FREEDOM FIGHTERS: Davy Crockett and Sam Houston planned the liberation of Texas in the Old Tavern at Washington.

POSTMARK: Texarkana, in Southwest Arkansas and Northeast Texas, has the only USA post office standing equally in two states.

PASSION PLAY: The Great Passion Play, presented on Mount Oberammergau at Eureka Springs, has the largest cast and amphitheater for a religious outdoor drama in the USA. More than 300 actors tell the story of the last week of Christ's life.

Sue McDonald, 32
Pickle packer
Pottsville

"My husband says I smell like pickles at the end of the day. You get used to the smell. Most people relate Atkins, Ark., with pickles because of the labels on the jars in the stores. My mom is proud of my job. She'll be shopping and point to a jar of pickles and say, 'Sue made those.' "

David O'Dell, 46
Bookstore manager
Fayetteville

"The University of Arkansas Hogs are unique. There are lots of bulldogs and tigers and wolves, but there's only one Razorback. You can make a Hog that looks silly or happy. You can't do that with a Crimson Tide or a Golden Hurricane."

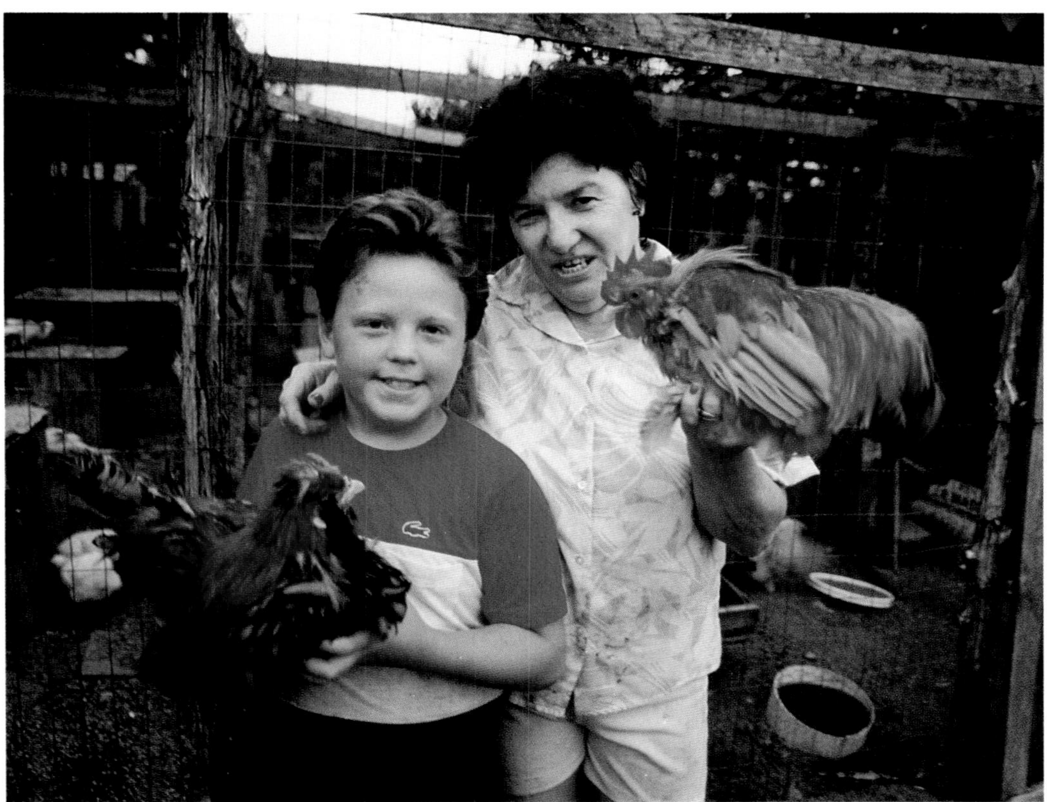

Voices
of Arkansas

Jeremy Murphy, 10
(with Betty Magness, 59)
Student
Lonoke

"The chickens are just like an alarm clock. They always crow at 6. When I hear that, I know it's time to get up and go to school. I take chickens to the county fair. Last year I won $57. I paid my grandparents for feed and I gave $5 to each of my sisters and I spent the rest on toys."

Juliana Moore, 17
Student
Wabaseka

"I've been hunting since I was six. My daddy dragged me along so he could kill my limit and his limit too. I had to sit still and be quiet and not say anything. I like to hunt ducks, but it's usually cold and wet and my waders always leak. My mother was named Miss Duck Gumbo 1986."

Freddie Childress, 20
Student/football player
Fayetteville

"I'm proud to be a Hog. When the fans call the Hogs, it fires me up. I grew up in Arkansas, and I've wanted to play here ever since I started getting serious about football. I figured there was no sense in going out of state and helping somebody else's team when I could stay at home and help my own team."

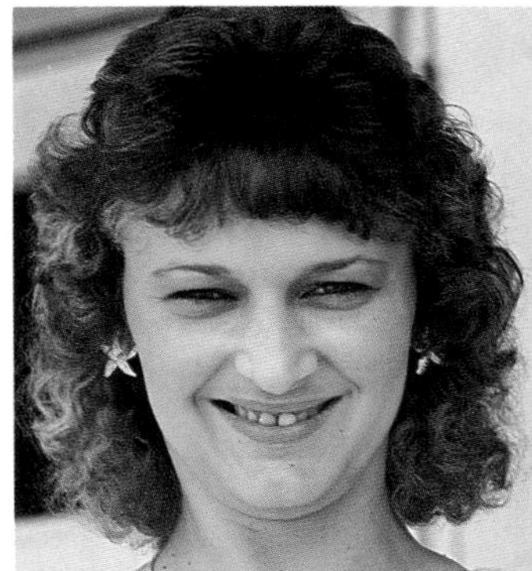

Caron Martin, 30
Traffic clerk
Fort Smith

"I grew up in a quiet little town of a thousand people. I've still got some kin folks there. I didn't want to come to the city, but I had to work. I'd rather live in a real house in the country than in a crackerbox in the city. Out there I could play my country music without some fuddy-duddy telling me to turn it down. Country people have their heads screwed on better than city people."

Declan Jarry, 30
Maitre d'
Little Rock

"Integration has come a lot farther in Arkansas than in a lot of places. Here you live next door to people of different races. I work with them, I live with them. They're my friends, not my black friends or my Korean friends, just my friends. I drove a school bus during the '70s and I never knew any racial tension."

***Mary Steenburgen**, 34, an Academy Award-winning actress, grew up in North Little Rock. Last year she returned to her hometown to produce* End of the Line, *a film about railroad workers, which premieres this month.*

It's an extraordinary, magical place to live

USA TODAY: What are your early memories of North Little Rock?

STEENBURGEN: It's a very beautiful place to grow up. I loved the summers. The nights are warm, and there were woods behind our house, and a creek.

USA TODAY: What are the people like?

STEENBURGEN: The people are extraordinary. They're the most giving people I've ever encountered. There are educated, talented people there — and there are the country people, who are not as educated, but just as bright. Just as extraordinary. It's a magical place. Arkansas is one of the best-kept secrets in the world.

USA TODAY: How has your hometown changed?

STEENBURGEN: It's like a lot of places. There are more 7-Elevens. The woods behind our house are being bulldozed to make room for housing. That's inevitable. But it's not as transient as other places. They don't leave, because it's a good life.

USA TODAY: When did you leave?

STEENBURGEN: I left when I was 19 to go to New York's Neighborhood Playhouse. Leaving was kind of scary and wonderful at the same time. I had had a wonderful English teacher in high school who was sort of like a travel agent. So even though you couldn't afford to get on a plane and go somewhere, you went places through reading.

USA TODAY: Do people who aren't from Arkansas understand the state and its people?

STEENBURGEN: Unfortunately, a lot of people think of bigotry. But that was so many years ago, and there was a minority of people involved. The rest of the people were ashamed of what happened. We have a wonderful young governor — Bill Clinton — who is extremely concerned with the issue of civil rights. I think the stereotype that some people have about Arkansas is all wrong.

USA TODAY: What was it like to produce the movie *End of the Line* in your hometown?

STEENBURGEN: It was wonderful. Our budget was $3 million. Some people told us the movie couldn't be made for that. The reason I knew we could was because of the generosity of the people.

Topic: ARKANSAS

Diversity mixed with hill-country heritage

USA TODAY: How do the people in Arkansas see their state?

CLINTON: I believe there is a concern that we are known for two things that are no longer fully representative of what we are. The first is the barefoot hillbilly image. And the second is the racial crisis, which culminated in the Little Rock Central High School conflict in 1957.

USA TODAY: How should the USA view Arkansas?

CLINTON: The truth is that two major elements of our culture are the hill-country heritage and the heritage of the Delta, the farmers. But it's also true that we have a highly diversified economy and culture today.

USA TODAY: How is the business climate?

CLINTON: We've got some of the most impressive companies in the country headquartered in Arkansas. Wal-Mart Stores. A lot of big trucking companies. Tyson Foods in Springdale is the largest agricultural company in the country. Dillard Department Stores is the fastest growing department store chain in the country. Systematics is the largest data processing company serving banks in the country. We have a significant number of people in very sophisticated manufacturing operations. So Arkansas is a different state than it's perceived to be.

USA TODAY: How are you trying to change your image?

CLINTON: A few years ago, I supported an $800,000 campaign in *The Wall Street Journal* after a $60,000 research survey among major business executives. We asked major business executives, what's the biggest problem with Arkansas in terms of its business climate? And they said, "Well, it's not centrally located."

USA TODAY: And that's not quite true.

CLINTON: In fact, Western Arkansas is 200 miles from the geographic center of the USA. And we have the Mississippi River, the Arkansas River, transportation networks, an enormous number of business investments, and a lot of distribution centers.

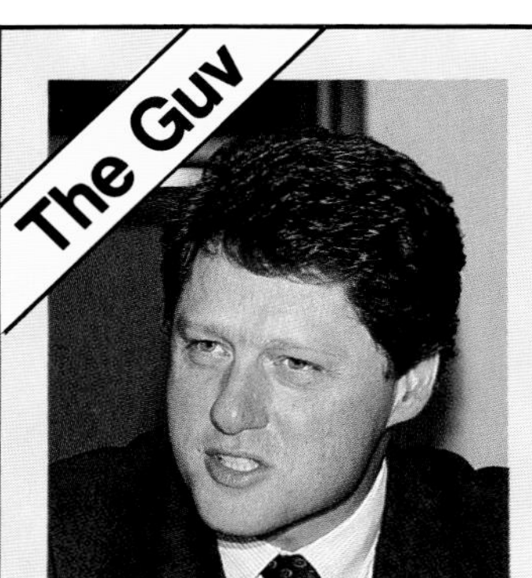

***William Clinton**, 40, a Democrat, was elected in 1978, lost his bid in 1980, and was re-elected in 1982, 1984 and 1986.*

USA TODAY: You were elected governor when you were 32 years old. When did you decide you wanted to be governor?

CLINTON: I didn't decide until about a year before I got elected. We got our first TV when I was 9, and I can remember people who spoke at the Republican and Democratic conventions when I was 10. I'd just sit there for hours, glued to the tube. I was probably the only 10-year-old in America lapping it up. I decided I wanted to be in politics when I was 16, because I was interested in public service.

USA TODAY: What's the most unpopular thing you did in your first term?

CLINTON: The most unpopular thing I did was to double the cost of car licenses, because we hadn't had a road program in 15 years. I tried to do it based on the value of the car, and I'd have been overwhelmingly re-elected if I hadn't done it. The car dealers beat me on that, because it made new cars more expensive. It was a disaster.

USA TODAY: You've got a full term ahead of you.

CLINTON: This is the most job security I've had since I went to work in a grocery store when I was 13. I've never had a job for four years. I haven't been able to hold down a job very well in my life, and it's nice.

California

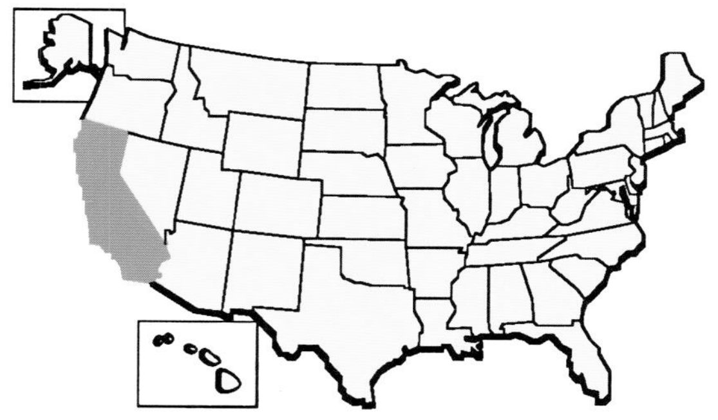

Visited: July 7-10, 1987
Featured in USA TODAY: July 13

"I still don't know what 'glamour' means. I know we had it when I started out in the '30s. We sure as hell don't have it now."

James Stewart
Actor
Beverly Hills, Calif.

California

No. 1 in people, pomp, possibilities, puzzlers

"*California, here I come . . . open up that Golden Gate . . .*"

Joseph Mayer wrote the song in 1924. Four million-plus people lived here then. They've been coming ever since. In 1987, California is:

■ People Center of the USA. 26,981,000 of them. More than 10 percent of all of us.

■ Glitter Center of the USA. Hollywood. Beverly Hills. Nob Hill.

■ Opportunity Center of the USA. For young and old. In its booming cities, rich valleys, majestic mountains.

■ Perhaps the problem center of the USA. Pernicious pollution over Los Angeles. Anguish over AIDS in San Francisco. Aliens crowding and crossing the border around San Diego. Tangled freeways. Water worries.

But hope is prevalent everywhere. Reach for the stars.

Stardom is Hollywood. Locked in concrete on the sidewalk at Mann's (formerly Grauman's) Chinese Theatre. Stars' footprints. Fingerprints. Hoofprints. Also on Hollywood Blvd., celebrities' names inside huge gold-edged stars. Blank stars for future names.

MISHA: Make me a star as big as Marilyn Monroe.

Millions have stood on that sidewalk and dreamed. Last week, **Misha Burkhalter**, 15, high school junior from the Sacramento suburb of Citrus Heights (pop. 98,800) was among them.

"One day I want to see my name in lights. I want to sign autographs. I want to be as big as **Marilyn Monroe**. I want to live in a fancy house and have a limousine and chauffeur."

If she makes it, she'll probably do what other stars have done. Move to nearby Beverly Hills (pop. 33,300). Richest city in the USA. "Average" home last year cost $552,965. Most expensive: $20 million. Cheapest: $250,000.

Beyond LaLa Land, there is real California:

■ Beautiful beaches. 840 miles of Pacific coastline. Top tourist attraction. 100 million tourists brought $31 billion last year.

■ Lush valleys. Fruits and vegetables. Crops brought in $14 billion last year. Plus $5.5 billion in wine sales.

■ Higher education's richest system. More than $4.4 billion spent last year. Second: New York, with $2.2 billion. 951,000 students in colleges and universities. Second: Texas with 524,000.

■ Huge industrial complexes. Defense spending: $30 billion last year. Construction: $31 billion. GNP in 1986: $546 billion. If it were a separate nation, California's economy would be the world's sixth largest.

Most of the action is clustered in the big three metro areas. Very different. Purely personal perceptions:

■ San Diego area (pop. 2,133,000). Gentle. Calm. Sedate. Sun and sea. Conservatism and patriotism. Ideal home for America's Cup.

■ Los Angeles area (pop. 12,738,000). Work hard. Play hard. Look good. Be healthy. Nothing else matters very much. Set trends, without trying to make statements.

■ San Francisco area (pop. 5,809,000). Some sophistication. Some serious students. Lots of yuppies and leftover hippies. Everything matters a lot. Make strong statements. Hope they'll set trends.

Most Californians play a lot. Those who don't, watch the players. More spectator sports than anywhere else in the USA.

Five Major League Baseball teams — most in any state. Four NFL football teams — most in any state. Four NBA basketball teams — most in any state. L.A. Lakers won 1987 NBA title. Pasadena's Rose Bowl hosted the 1987 Super Bowl. Oakland hosted the 1987 baseball All-Star Game.

AUTRY: Show biz did it all for Texas transplant.

Fun and games. Business and pleasure. Wonderful and weird. Success and stardom. Some experience it all. **Gene Autry** has. Age 79. Came from Texas in 1934.

Starred in 88 films. Sold 40 million records. Now owns the California Angels, a hotel in Palm Springs, a big ranch, four radio stations. Last week at his Anaheim Stadium, Autry commented about his adopted state:

"I don't think it's as crazy as everyone says. I've found just as many screwballs in Eastern cities."

That's Plain Talk from California.

Golden State

CALIFORNIA 1850 The Golden State

ENTERED USA: Sept. 9, 1850, 31st state

MOTTO: Eureka (I have found it)
POPULATION: 26,981,000; rank, 1st
LARGEST CITY: Los Angeles, pop. 3,096,668
CAPITAL: Sacramento, pop. 304,131
LAND: 156,299 square miles; rank, 3rd
POPULATION DENSITY: 172.6 per square mile; rank, 12th
RACIAL MIX: 76.2% white; 7.7% black; 5.3% Asian and Pacific islanders. Hispanic heritage: 19.2%.

Uniquely Calif.

GOLD MEDAL CITY: Los Angeles is the only city to have held the Summer Olympics twice in this century — 1932 and 1984.

CHINATOWN, USA: San Francisco's Chinatown is the largest Chinese quarter outside of Asia. 10,000 Chinese live in the 24-square-block area.

ON TRACK: San Francisco's cable cars are the USA's only moving national landmark.

WORLD CAPITALS: Gilroy is known as the Garlic Capital of the World. Other California capitals: Castroville, artichoke; Half Moon Bay, pumpkin; Santa Cruz, Brussels sprouts.

THE GRAPEVINE: California is the No. 1 wine supplier in the USA. 92.8% of the grapes grown in the USA are from the state.

BIRDWATCHERS: The entire town of Morro Bay is a designated bird sanctuary.

David Key, 36
Cellarmaster
Napa

"I enjoy the actual process of making wine. Some winemaking is art. It's more than just ordinary agriculture. Nobody writes books about 1948 apples."

Richard Little, 32
Doorman
Hollywood

"Hollywood is the country's stage. There's no stage where everyone can show their talents buried inside. They come here to show off. I started working here in hopes somebody would come by and discover me."

Gail Walter, 32
Bridge officer
San Rafael

"Golden Gate is the most beautiful bridge in the world. San Francisco is a unique city. The bridge makes it complete. It goes with the harbor and the islands and Alcatraz. People here love the bridge."

George Dom, 32
Instructor, Top Gun School
San Diego

"San Diego has the reputation of being the home of Navy fighters' best, although the guys who fly F14s or F18s on the East Coast would disagree. Duty here is regarded as the best flying you can do."

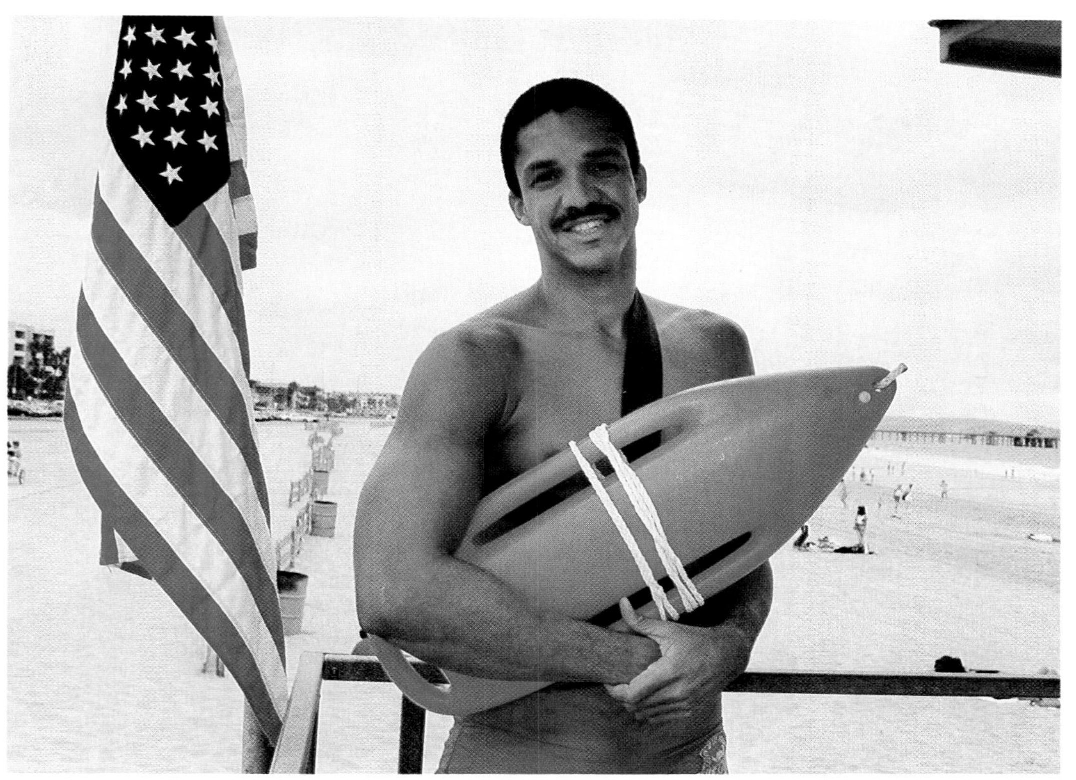

Voices
of California

Trec Shadid, 29
Lifeguard
Manhattan Beach

"This is a helluva story to behold. Some come to be seen, others come to see. On cloudy days, the activity is squelched, but on sunny ones, it's fiery alive. On Muscle Beach, you see everybody from businessmen to championship bodybuilders."

Susan Schafer, 38
Reptile care manager
San Diego

"Reptiles are the least-liked creatures in the zoo, but the most visited. The San Diego Visitors Bureau says we have sunshine 365 days a year, which isn't perfectly true. But it's close enough that the reptiles have a good time."

Carmen Bupara, 45
Legal assistant
Sacramento

"Ten years ago, you could walk down the street without bumping into each other. Now, there's people all over. Still, you can go 10 miles and get really out of town. I have relatives all over the country wishing they were here."

Pete Pavlukevich, 50
Cable car operator
San Francisco

"I've driven every cable car in the city. I love them. They're perfectly constructed — sturdy and durable. People in cars don't like to get caught behind us because we only go 9½ miles an hour. But we were here first. Some people swear at them; I swear by them."

Cindy Lee, 30
Family planning worker
Oakland

"This is the most integrated city in the country. There are a lot of mixed neighborhoods and there is a strong sense of community. I like the fact that Oakland has a bad reputation because nobody comes here. It's kind of like an underdog city. It's kind of like a secret."

James Stewart, 79, made his film debut in Murder Man *in 1935. Since then, he has appeared in more than 80 movies. He lives in Beverly Hills with his wife, Gloria, in the house they* bought *39 years ago.*

State's a lot more than just Hollywood

USA TODAY: When did you move to California?

STEWART: I came in 1935. I had started in the theater in New York. Hank Fonda and I shared a room in the Madison Hotel. All the big movie studios at that time had talent scouts; they offered him a contract, and he took them up on it. I stayed with more plays. I was doing *Divided by Three* and an MGM talent scout did a test of me and offered me a contract.

USA TODAY: When you arrived, what did you think of the Golden State?

STEWART: I never got out of this small area. Fonda and I rented a small house in Brentwood. I didn't know anything about California because we were working all the time. Our impression of California was Hollywood.

USA TODAY: Was Hollywood really as glamorous as its reputation?

STEWART: I still don't know what "glamour" means. I know we had it when I started out in the '30s. We sure as hell don't have it now.

USA TODAY: Would you encourage a young New York actor to come to Hollywood today?

STEWART: Stage experience for the actor is the finest experience you can get.

USA TODAY: Have you had a chance to see all of California by now?

STEWART: I've been in every part of the state. Our daughter is married to a banker — they live down the peninsula from San Francisco. That's a beautiful part of the state.

USA TODAY: What's your favorite spot in all of California?

STEWART: Beverly Hills is a nice place, a well-run city. We've been right here in the same house for 39 years. We still take the dogs for a walk. That's the way it is in small towns everywhere.

USA TODAY: Much of the rest of the world considers California a crazy place. What's the truth?

STEWART: That comes from the general idea of Hollywood. People connect California with Hollywood in some way.

Topic: CALIFORNIA

Land of opportunity — and creative outlets

USA TODAY: California's population continues to grow dramatically. What brings people to California?

DEUKMEJIAN: Opportunity. They see in California that you're accepted for who you are and what you are, that you don't necessarily have to have had a lot of long-established contacts. They also look at California as being a creative place where a lot of new ideas are started.

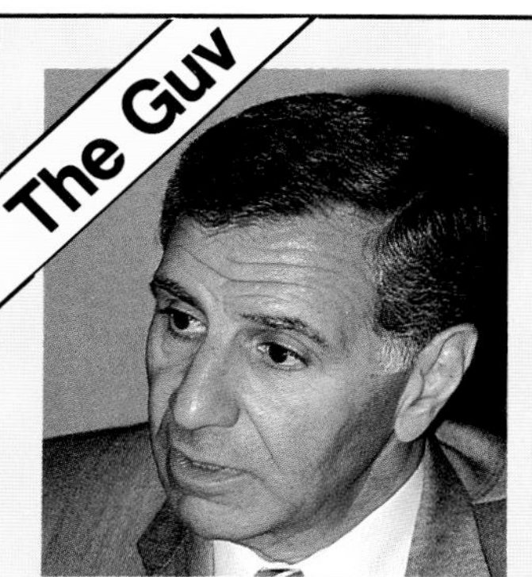

George Deukmejian, 59, a Republican, has been governor of California since 1982. He's a former state legislator and attorney general.

USA TODAY: You came here from New York. Were opportunities greater for you here?

DEUKMEJIAN: Much greater. I grew up in the Albany area. They had the same political machine there for 50 years. After I had passed the California bar and had been here a few years, I went into private practice in Long Beach. Four years later, I was elected to the state Assembly. That could never have happened in New York.

USA TODAY: California's lifestyle is world famous. How do you characterize it?

DEUKMEJIAN: I don't think you can generalize, because there is so much diversity. Whether you like to play golf, tennis, ski or swim, you can find it here. We've got areas where you can have snow, or you can be out in the desert area. We've got 1,000 miles of coastline, we've got areas that are rural, and we've got major urban centers, one of them the second largest city in the country. Just about any type of living condition that somebody might like to have or visit, you can find in California.

USA TODAY: What do you think California will look like 20 years from now?

DEUKMEJIAN: We'll continue to see an extension of the kind of diversity that we have in the population and economy.

USA TODAY: Do you expect continued population growth?

DEUKMEJIAN: We're continuing to see an increase in the number of ethnic communities within the state. They are making outstanding contributions.

USA TODAY: Sometimes people outside the state characterize you as boring and bland, but you were re-elected by a landslide. What do Californians know that others don't?

DEUKMEJIAN: I followed Jerry Brown, and he followed Ronald Reagan. There's a lot of comparisons. The press sometimes likes to be entertained, and I'm not necessarily entertaining.

USA TODAY: California probably has more celebrities per capita than anywhere else. Are you ever a little awestruck walking into a room where there are 100 household names?

DEUKMEJIAN: I enjoy meeting people, including celebrities. I wouldn't say I'm awestruck.

USA TODAY: Are Californians realistic about earthquakes?

DEUKMEJIAN: There's not much you can do to prevent them. But there's a great deal that can be done to try to cut down on injuries, deaths and destruction. The planning and training is good, but it could be increased.

USA TODAY: How is California preparing for growth?

DEUKMEJIAN: Californians recognize that there's going to be growth, but they want to make sure that it's done in such a way that the people will enjoy the high quality of life.

Colorado

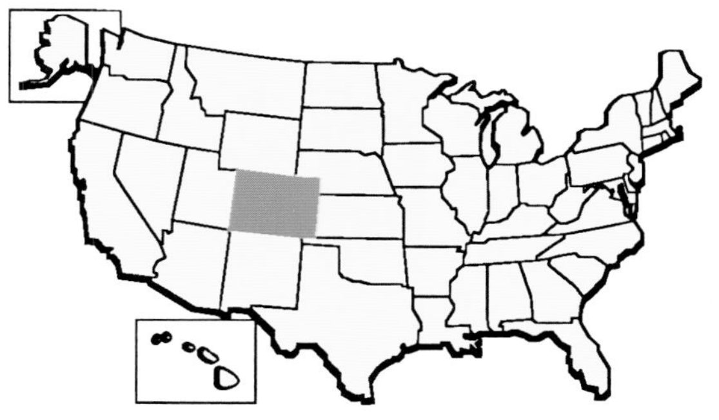

Visited: July 20-21, 1987
Featured in USA TODAY: July 24

"You feel like you're on top of the world. I'd never leave here. Everyone here is so high-spirited."

Sharri Shanklin
Telephone salesperson
Aurora, Colo.

Colorado

Rocky Mountain highs: Altitude and attitudes

"I've seen it rainin' fire in the sky . . . shadow from the starlight is softer than a lullaby . . . talk to God and listen to his casual reply . . . Rocky Mountain high in Colorado . . ."

DENVER: Writes, sings, lives high.

John Denver wrote it and sings it. Coloradoans live it. Visitors love it. Highs here:

■ No. 1 in altitude. Highest mean elevation in the USA. More than 1,000 peaks over 10,000 feet. Pikes Peak most famous, 14,110 feet.

■ No. 1 in highly educated. Highest percentage in USA of those over age 25 with four or more years of college.

■ No. 1 in the sky. The U.S. Air Force Academy at Colorado Springs trains our top military fliers. 4,500 men and women cadets there now.

■ No. 1 on skis. 9,453,359 ski lift tickets sold last season, more than in any other state. Affluence abounds at Aspen and Vail, two of the poshest places to plant a pole in the USA.

Altitude. Attitude. Ambition. Affluence. They add up to a state of high hopes.

"You feel like you're on top of the world. I'd never leave here. Everyone here is so high-spirited," says **Sharri Shanklin**, 19, telephone salesperson in the Denver suburb of Aurora (pop. 206,700).

That spirit grabs newcomers as well as natives. Colorado Springs (pop. 251,000) is temporarily home for hopeful medalists at the U.S. Olympic Training Center.

STALLWORTHS: Olympic-size dreams for father and daughter.

Cindy Stallworth, 16, is here from South Bend, Ind. A sprinter, she's training to try to qualify for the Olympic trials.

Says Cindy: "This is a sight. It doesn't look real. It reminds me of a framed picture. What a great place to train. I dream of winning the gold medal all the time."

Her father, **Charles Stallworth**, 37, is track coach at South Bend's Washington High School. He's with Cindy at the Olympic Track and Field Development Camp.

"I'm here only to assist in her dream," says the father-coach, who ran with Kentucky State's 1971 NCAA track-and-field champions but never realized his own Olympic dreams.

That urge to run, fly, ski takes many forms. One of the most intriguing is the annual Pikes Peak marathon. **Zebulon Pike** said no man could ever conquer this mountain. But now many men — and women — do.

This year's marathon is Aug. 23. Last year more than 500 men and 100 women ran the breathtaking 26.3 mile mountainous trail. The altitude changes by 7,600 feet. Temperatures rise and drop by 65 degrees.

Stanley Fox, 31, won last year in 3 hours, 40 minutes. Teaches first grade and kindergarten at Lake Elementary School in Gunnison (pop. 5,785). **Margie Loyd-Allison**, 38, a procurement analyst at Ford Aerospace in Colorado Springs, led the women in 4 hours, 55 minutes.

Says Loyd-Allison, "You don't take your eye off the trail for very long. But everything on the mountain is so quiet, peaceful, clean."

Off the slopes and trails and skyways, Coloradoans work at a variety of real jobs.

■ No. 1 — wholesale and retail trade. 314,000 people get their paychecks from service to others.

■ No. 2 — manufacturing. 191,000 employees. Aerospace and computers are big and growing.

■ No. 3 — tourism. 103,000 Coloradoans cater to 20 million visitors annually.

Since 1982, the Colorado economy has been flat. Oil and energy bust was devastating. In 1986, 3,000 more people left the state than moved in. But plans go on for more of everything.

Denver, state capital and biggest city (pop. 504,588), is a major air hub. Overcrowded Stapleton will get relief in the mid-1990s from a new airport, five times bigger. A $3 billion project covering more than 30 square miles.

Whatever else they do at work or play, Coloradoans have a great unifier in the Denver Broncos, 1987 Super Bowl runner-up. The Broncos play in Mile High Stadium. Their fan support is even higher. Last January, before the Broncos left for Pasadena and their Super Bowl loss to the Giants, fans organized a super sendoff.

Says Gov. **Roy R. Romer**, 58, first-term Democrat: "We're the only place in the country that could put 65,000 people in the stadium just to send the team off somewhere. The attitudes are amazing."

Amazing attitudes and altitudes. That's Plain Talk from Colorado.

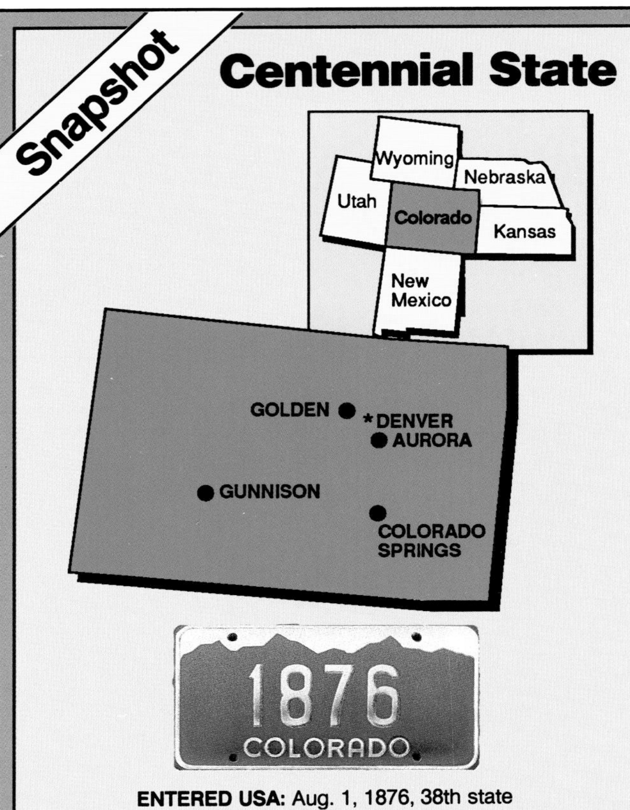

ENTERED USA: Aug. 1, 1876, 38th state

MOTTO: Nothing without providence
POPULATION: 3,267,000; rank, 27th
LARGEST CITY: Denver, pop. 504,588
CAPITAL: Denver
LAND: 103,595 square miles; rank, 8th
POPULATION DENSITY: 31.5 per square mile; rank, 37th
RACIAL MIX: 89.0% white; 3.5% black; 1.0% Asian and Pacific islanders; 0.6% American Indian. Hispanic heritage: 11.8%.

Uniquely Colo.

PURPLE MOUNTAINS MAJESTY: Katherine Lee Bates penned "America the Beautiful" after a trip to Colorado in 1893.

DUDE DEFINED: A "dude" is someone who comes from another area and pays for food, lodging and the use of a horse. Colorado has more than 40 dude ranches.

SILVER-BRICK ROAD: A path of silver bricks was laid when President Grant visited Central City's Teller House Hotel in 1873.

HANDS UP: Butch Cassidy made his first unauthorized bank withdrawal in Telluride.

MARBLE MEMORIAL: The largest single block of marble ever quarried in the world — 100 tons — was taken from the town of Marble. It marks the Tomb of the Unknown Soldier in Arlington Cemetery.

HOT STUFF: The world's largest open-air hot springs swimming pool — 405 feet long — is at Glenwood Springs.

Voices
of Colorado

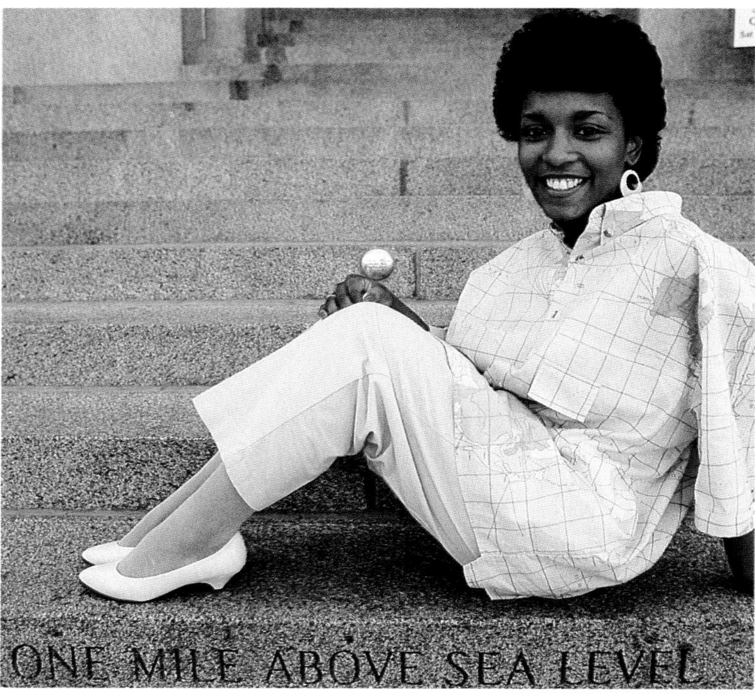

Sherri Shanklin, 19
Telephone saleswoman
Aurora

"When I first moved to Colorado, I slept for a week straight. I couldn't get used to the high altitude. I was exhausted. I'd wake up, take a shower, and go back to sleep. But I'm used to it now. Colorado is so high up you have to look down on other states."

Joyce Elmore, 18
Air Force Academy Cadet
Colorado Springs

"The Air Force Academy is really good about accepting women. I'm not intimidated. I want to be a fighter pilot. When I finish school, I want to be stationed in Spain. All my friends are behind me 100 percent. They think it's great to be with their best friend in a plane — as long as I don't fly the way I drive."

Mitch Biery, 23
Ski gear salesman
Denver

"I try to ski on slopes that are going to challenge me. If I'm going skiing, I'm going to ski hard. I figure if my legs aren't tired by the end of the day, I didn't get my money's worth. You've also got to be able to look cool. It's embarrassing if you're skiing under the lift and falling down all the time."

Doug Cogswell, 41
Hotel manager
Colorado Springs

"My son and I go fishing in the different canyons. Most of us never leave except maybe to visit families out of state in the off season. We live right here in vacationland and get to meet people from a lot of different backgrounds. It's sort of like heaven. I hate to sound hokey, but it's true."

Ed Feld, 43
Gondola operator
Aspen

"When you live in Aspen, you tend to have a lot of visitors. A lot of friends and relatives come to see you — anyone that likes to ski. I'm an avid skier, but I don't ski constantly. I've still got to do my laundry and go to the post office like everybody else."

Peter Grewe, 34
Guitarist
Vail

"Vail is a state of mind. People come here to relax, get out of the city and away from the concrete. It's a great place to create; that's why I'm here. Music and the mountains go together. A lot of the sources of aggravation just aren't here. There's not a stoplight in town."

Kathy Melies, 30
Airport flower
cart operator
Denver

"I love the Broncos. A couple of people I know dyed their hair orange. But it wasn't for me. It wouldn't go with my eyes."

William K. Coors, 71, was born in Golden, Colo., and still lives there. He is chairman of Adolph Coors Co., the USA's fifth largest brewery, and grandson of Adolph Coors Sr., who founded the brewery in 1873.

State is beautiful, come snow or shine

USA TODAY: Your grandfather, Adolph Coors Sr., founded the brewery in Golden. How many relatives are working for the company now?

COORS: Well, on a permanent basis, there are seven of us. My brother's five sons, my brother, and myself.

USA TODAY: What distinguishes Coloradoans from other Americans?

COORS: I think we're like everybody else. We love our state. But I don't think that distinguishes us from anybody else who loves their state. We like the mountains and the skiing. We like the lifestyle out here.

USA TODAY: What makes Colorado a good place to live and work?

COORS: I think primarily climate. It's dry. I went East to school for nine years. Of course, this was before air conditioning. And I can remember wondering when I got out there why people were dumb enough to live in a place like that and put up with that heat and humidity. That was back when I was about 14 years old. Then all of a sudden it dawned on me that they didn't know any better.

USA TODAY: What's your favorite spot in Colorado?

COORS: Probably Aspen. It's just a very, very delightful community. It's right up there in the hills and the mountains. I love to go up there and ski. And it's beautiful in the summertime. It's got all of the amenities you could ask for. It's no different than the other resort communities. Every one of them has got a lot going for it.

USA TODAY: What do you remember about growing up in Colorado?

COORS: Just sort of enjoying life. Things were not developed anywhere near the way they are today, and life was very, very simple. And I thought very, very delightful.

USA TODAY: How do you describe the state to people who have never been there?

COORS: One of the things I tell people about Colorado is that if you're going to spend the winter, you'd better enjoy winter sports. You have to want it to snow.

Topic: COLORADO

Athens of West applies new ideas in new ways

USA TODAY: What besides location brings so many people to Colorado?

ROMER: Our unique geography and beauty. It is a state that has been blessed with the plains, the mountains, the Western Slope. Another characteristic is the variety of economic life.

USA TODAY: Does that make Coloradoans different?

ROMER: There is a style about Colorado that is in part because of its beauty and its recreation. But if you come to Colorado, what do people do, they think about skiing, climbing mountains. It's outdoor. It's aggressive. It's not yuppie. It goes through a lot of spans.

USA TODAY: What effect does the economic variety have on the state?

ROMER: I view Colorado to be the Athens of the West potentially. Athens in the sense that it's a crossroads, not just of finance, commerce, industry, but Athens as a place where new ideas are applied in new ways. And that's what I think is exciting.

USA TODAY: Denver is the only major city planning a new airport. What impact will it have?

ROMER: It's a tremendously important thing. If I were in Japan and had one minute to give a pitch for Colorado, I'd say, look, the major hub airports of the United States are as follows: four on the East Coast, two on the West Coast, and three in the middle of the country. Denver is in the center. Then I'd say, why deal from the edge when you can deal from the center?

USA TODAY: Clean air is becoming a concern not only in Denver, but all the way down the Front Range. What can you do about it?

ROMER: One, we need to have better freeways. Secondly, we need rapid transit. Third, we need to do a more stringent job of emission control. Fourth, we need to consider converting coal-burning power plants to gas. Next, diesel. There is cleaner diesel available. They have it in

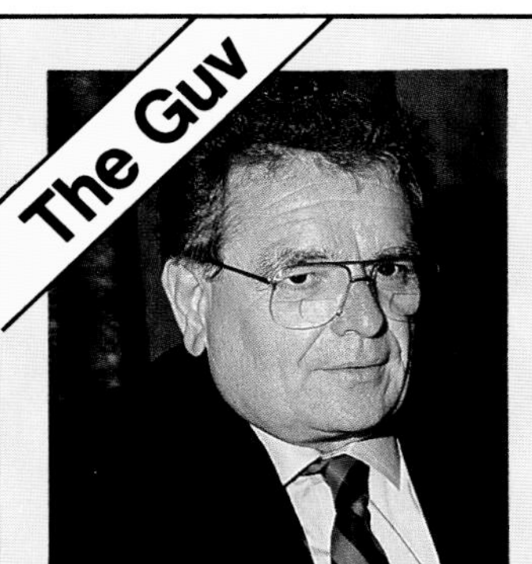

Roy Romer, 58, a Democrat, was elected governor last year. He's a former state treasurer and state legislator.

California. Costs a penny or two more. I think we have not yet come to terms with the restrictions on wood burning.

USA TODAY: What don't you like about your job?

ROMER: I worry about the trappings of public office. At a convention, you find these phalanxes of security, aides and officials. It drives me wild. I think people who are elected to office — Lincoln was my model — have got to maintain that sense of where they came from.

USA TODAY: Is that what Lincoln did?

ROMER: Lincoln did something which was absolutely magnificent: He conducted himself in such a way that everybody understood he was an approachable human being.

USA TODAY: Do you ski?

ROMER: I used to own and operate a ski area called Geneva Basin. I ski all over the state but I'm concerned about the price of lift tickets.

USA TODAY: Some would say ticket prices are none of a governor's business.

ROMER: I'm slow to intervene in the private sector. I'm in business in six locations in this state. I know how important it is for the government to keep its hands off. But we all have a lot at stake in terms of not getting an elitist reputation for tourism.

Connecticut

Visited: May 4-5, 1987
Featured in USA TODAY: May 11

"I have to get wealthy in this state. This is where the money is."

Roger Brimage
Construction worker
New Britain, Conn.

Connecticut

Yankee Doodle Dandy, money is here, handy

What's it like to live in the richest state in the USA?

Very nice if you're rich.

Pretty nice if you're at work trying to join the ranks of the rich. Most are.

Lonely if you're out of work. Not many are.

Connecticut characteristics:

■ Per person annual income, $19,208. Highest in the USA. National average: $14,461.

■ Unemployment, 3.8 percent. Lowest in the USA. National average: 6.3 percent.

Gov. **William A. O'Neill**, 56, who pushed to have *Yankee Doodle* named the state song, sums up the state of the state: "Jobs are going begging here."

Many of Connecticut's rich made their money here. Many more brought it here. Big bucks are hauled on U.S. Highway 1 from the streets of New York City and Westchester County to easy street in Greenwich, Darien, Westport.

The well-heeled made their money in a variety of ways and spend it that way.

Take **Paul Newman**, 62. Westport (pop. 25,290). Hollywood hero. Drives race cars for fun. Sells salad dressing, spaghetti sauce and other packaged foods. Now Newman's starting a Connecticut camp for children with cancer.

"I'm contributing money from my lunatic food companies. We had no resting place for the money. This (camp) will be the resting place," says Newman.

Actors, artists, writers are sprinkled heavily among bankers and brokers on Southern Connecticut's most affluent alleys. But some seek solace elsewhere.

William Manchester, 65, noted novelist, is one. He lives in Middletown (pop. 39,040). A working person's town. Sicilians hold most elective offices. Heavy Polish population.

"I learn a lot from people with other backgrounds. This enriches the society. I could never live in Darien or Greenwich. All affluent, white Anglo-Saxon Protestants. I would be one of them, but I would be very uneasy."

Highly rated and high-priced prep schools and universities dot Connecticut's countryside.

The acme of education here is Yale. Idealistic, ivory-towered, Ivy League. Yale's 10,448 students pay an average of $16,040 a year for their college education. The national average is $10,199.

The drama school, with its Yale Repertory Theatre, has high visibility. It produced not only Newman, but **Meryl Streep**, **Christopher Lloyd**, **Henry Winkler** and **Courtney B. Vance**, now starring in Broadway's *Fences*.

Two Yale theater graduate students hoping to follow in those footsteps are **Tom McGowan**, 27, and

YALE'S CYRINO, McGOWAN, PALMER: Classical, comedian, psychopath. All have high hopes.

Frank Palmer, 31.

McGowan currently stars in the university's Shakespearean play *Measure for Measure*. He plays Elbow, the stupid constable. "They train you to be versatile. But I'm passed off more in comical roles," says McGowan.

Palmer says, "I'm not pretty enough for L.A. but pretty enough for New York. I usually get typecast as the psychopath."

Yale became coeducational in 1969. Now, 43 percent of the undergraduates are women. **Monica Cyrino**, 25, came here from California to study classical literature. Says Cyrino:

"For what was supposed to be pretentious and snobby, Yale is pretty comfortable. There is that old-school, stoic-type person here. They have that intellectual sense of humor. They are clever and resourceful and appear never to be ruffled."

SILVERI: 'Ordinary guy,' no grudges.

The well-educated and well-off generally seem to be well thought of by Connecticut's working folks.

Joe Silveri, 72, is a retired factory worker in New Britain (pop. 73,840): "People think we're all rich. I'm just an ordinary guy. I worked in a factory. But I don't begrudge anybody. If they made it, they made it."

That's Plain Talk from Connecticut.

Snapshot

Nutmeg State

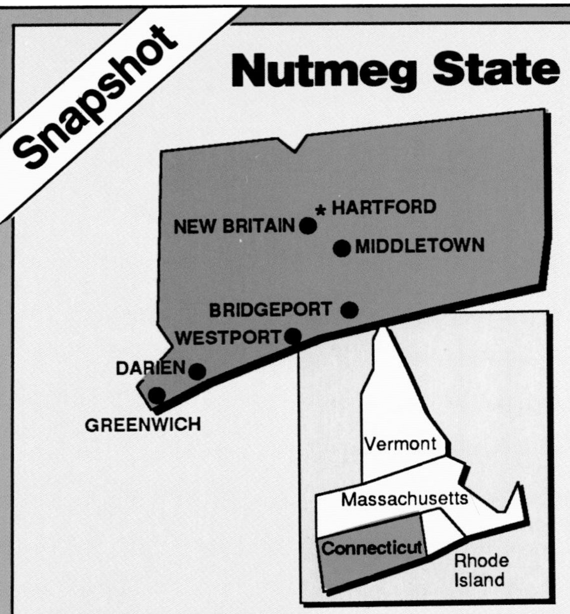

CONSTITUTION STATE
1788
CONNECTICUT

ENTERED USA: Jan. 9, 1788, 5th state

MOTTO: He who transplanted still sustains
POPULATION: 3,189,000; rank, 28th
LARGEST CITY: Bridgeport, pop. 142,140
CAPITAL: Hartford, pop. 135,720
LAND: 4,872 square miles; rank, 48th
POPULATION DENSITY: 654.6 per square mile; rank, 4th
RACIAL MIX: 90.1% white; 7% black; 0.6% Asian and Pacific islanders. Hispanic heritage: 4%.

Uniquely Conn.

WE THE PEOPLE: The first written constitution of a democratic government was Connecticut's Fundamental Orders of 1639. It based governmental authority on the consent of the people.

BY GEORGE: Wallpaper hung to welcome George Washington is still on the bedroom walls at the Webb House in Wethersfield.

NUCLEAR NAVY: The world's first nuclear-powered submarine was built in Groton. The USS Nautilus, launched in January 1955, is now a memorial at Groton.

CANDYLAND: The Bradley-Smith Co. began making lollipops in New Haven in 1908. Lollipop was intended to be a trademark name.

SCENE SETTER: Monte Cristo Cottage in New London was the boyhood home of playwright Eugene O'Neill and served as the setting for his play "Long Day's Journey into Night."

Voices
of Connecticut

Anthony Kovach, 69
Candy vendor
Torrington

"I was blessed with a good sense of direction. There's so much happiness in being blind if you go about it the right way. I'm too busy to feel sorry for myself. I'm too busy feeling sorry for other people. I don't know if I'll ever retire. I won't till I can't possibly toddle anymore. I love Torrington. I wouldn't leave. They'd only have to haul me back for burial. Why not save them the trip?"

Jill Leonard, 26
Store personnel director
Westport

"Most parents who have a family-owned business complain all the time. When we were growing up, we always heard my father saying how much he loved his job. I don't want to do anything but work here. It's so much fun. I can't believe the addiction I have for this store. I always want to be here."

Anthony Sala, 76
Owner, shoe repair shop/ex-shoemaker
East Hartford

"I make shoes now only for my family, sometimes. There's no pay and it takes too much time. Shoes made in factories are just as good, or better, than what we made by hand. It's a hard job. Kids don't want to learn. If I retired, I'd be in trouble. I talk with people everyday. I get up at 5:30 every morning. I have my customers. It's nice talking to the people, all kinds of people."

Bob Patterson, 55
Public relations
New Haven

"I got away from the concrete and cars of New York City and got into the grass, trees and birds of this country. I want to garden and do community service when I retire because I want to give something back. There's no real hoopla surrounding state pride. They innately love it."

Christine Peach, 41
Homemaker
Norwalk

"There's an awful lot of money here. So we attract people who think that's important in a place to live. Many of them want to live here because they think it's the right address. That's why some newcomers are seen as shallow. They seem to feel that this is the right place to live, but they really don't want to be here."

Jeffrey Northrop, 34
Yacht salesman
Westport

"The sea has always been important to Connecticut. It has always been a sea-going state. I don't think I have ever lived away from the sea. I come from a marine background. My father and grandfather were sailors. Boats are where I feel comfortable. When I was 7 years old we built rafts and went fishing. Now the kids just want to hang around in malls."

Roger Brimage, 21
Construction worker
New Britain

"Construction work around here is real good. I came up here from Mississippi, I learned my trade, and now I'm working. They're building houses every day, and I'm getting my share. I have to get wealthy in this state — this is where the money is."

***Paul Newman**, 62, who lives in Westport, Conn., won the best-acting Oscar for* The Color of Money *this year. His food business, Newman's Own, grossed $26 million last year. The profits go to charity.*

We'll give ill kids a break from hospital

USA TODAY: You're using profits from your food business — Newman's Own — to build a camp for seriously ill children. Why are you building it in Connecticut?

NEWMAN: Because I live here. You either get a sense of comfort or discomfort about a place, and I feel comfortable here. It's infested with rats and leeches and snapping turtles, but other than that, it's a terrific place.

USA TODAY: What's kept you and your wife, Joanne Woodward, here when you could live in Beverly Hills, closer to the film industry?

NEWMAN: We have a stream in back of our house, and I like to poke holes in the ice and go swimming and call my cardiologist. I suppose I live here for the way the leaves look in the fall. Don't laugh — that's legitimate.

USA TODAY: Have things changed much over the years?

NEWMAN: I miss the apple orchards and vegetable stands. I wouldn't have allowed the automobile to come in. I would have kept trolley cars going up and down Route 1 and only allowed a few select massage parlors. I tend to be irreverent and lewd, but I've chosen to stick around.

USA TODAY: Your children's camp is going to be built in the rural northeastern part of the state. Will the residents welcome it?

NEWMAN: We couldn't have done it without their cooperation. They moved a lot of mountains to expedite this thing.

USA TODAY: What will the camp look like?

NEWMAN: We're planning the camp so it looks like a turn-of-the-century mining camp. We've acquired the land, about 330 acres with a 47-acre lake. The Yale-New Haven medical community will provide the necessary medical staff, the consultants, the counselors, the whole seven yards. The Yale School of Architecture has designed the camp. That community has been fantastic.

USA TODAY: How are you raising the $10 million needed?

NEWMAN: The IRS lets us provide 50 percent of the total — we need help from the private sector.

Topic: CONNECTICUT

We want to spread the wealth around

USA TODAY: Some people picture Connecticut as a tax haven for the rich, or a suburb living in the shadows of New York City. Is that accurate?

O'NEILL: Connecticut is not in anyone's shadow. It's a leader in the nation in per capita income, and we probably have as many Fortune 500 companies as New York state does. As far as being a tax haven for the rich, I don't look at it that way. The state is doing so well that when you do live here, you've got a good chance to make a very good living in all walks of life.

USA TODAY: So, Connecticut is a relatively wealthy state?

O'NEILL: The wealthiest.

USA TODAY: In your State of the State address, you talked about spreading some of the wealth around. How do you intend to do that?

O'NEILL: By employing people. The only way I know to eliminate poverty is through jobs. I've tried to do everything I can to make sure there are jobs for people. The people have to be trained, and all those types of things are taking place in our core cities.

USA TODAY: Why is the job picture so uneven in the state?

O'NEILL: We have a low unemployment rate, and yet there are thousands of people in the core cities who don't have jobs. We're doing everything we can to reach them through vocational and technical training. There are McDonald's and such places around the Connecticut Turnpike that can't find anybody to work. They have to import workers from New York state.

USA TODAY: There are still homeless and hungry people here. Does the state's reputation for wealth and growth overshadow those needs?

O'NEILL: Not at all. We're spending more now for housing and we'll be spending more for shelters than ever before in the history of our state and, proportionately, probably far more than any other state in the union. So prosperity hasn't pushed those cares aside. It has allowed us to take care of those who do need help.

***William O'Neill**, 56, a Democrat, is serving his second term as governor. He's a former state representative and lieutenant governor.*

USA TODAY: Some think New Englanders are cold and aloof. Is that true?

O'NEILL: It's a feeling of being where it all began. They landed in Plymouth and in Virginia. At one time, New England was ready to break away from the country during the War of 1812. Fortunately for all of us who live here, it didn't. I like to say that we're all Connecticut Yankees, frugal and hardworking. Even though I'm Irish and my lieutenant governor's Italian, we're all Yankees when we live in Connecticut.

USA TODAY: When you want to get away for a weekend, where do you go?

O'NEILL: There's a spot about 23 miles from Hartford in the town of Easthampton, and in that town is a lake, and on that lake is a little house. That's our real house.

USA TODAY: What will be your legacy to Connecticut?

O'NEILL: I can't take all the credit — but I know if it were the other way around, I'd be getting the blame — that the state is in better economic shape than ever before. We've got money in the bank, bills paid, paying off state debt, rainy-day funds tucked away.

Delaware

Visited: Aug. 6-7, 1987
Featured in USA TODAY: Aug. 10

"I can just walk in and put down $50 and be incorporated. There's very little red tape. That's how Delaware makes its money — by making it easy for people to do business here."

Kelly Petit
Businessman
Dover, Del.

Delaware

Mighty Midget: Haven for banks, corporations

It's the legal home to more than half the Fortune 500 companies. Serves over 24 million credit card customers across the USA.

The Big Apple's biggest banks do business here. Bankers Trust. Citicorp. Chase Manhattan. Chemical. Manufacturers Hanover. Morgan. Marine Midland.

Very big business in a state that calls itself the "Small Wonder." Here's how small it is:

■ No. 47 in population. Only Alaska, Vermont and Wyoming have fewer people.

■ No. 49 in size. Only Rhode Island is smaller.

How has this tiny Tom Thumb, squeezed between Pennsylvania, New Jersey and Maryland, become such a titan in the business world?

"The blueprint was the financial center development act, adopted in 1981," says Gov. **Michael N. Castle**, 48, 1st-term Republican. Castle was Lt. Gov. at the time. The Guv was **Pierre S. du Pont IV**, now seeking the GOP presidential nomination.

"The initial concept was removing the usury (interest cap) laws and creating a bell-shaped tax curve for banks. Since then we've passed other banking legislation and it's clearly the catalyst for our low unemployment and strong economy. It's a complete win-win situation," Castle said.

The big banks pour money into the state coffer. In 1981, the bank franchise tax brought in only $2 million. This year, the state's take is a projected $39 million.

That has helped the state reduce its personal income tax four years in a row. It still has no sales tax.

9,000 well-paying new jobs have resulted from the banking boom.

Significant in a state with only 293,000 wage-earners. **Phyllis Levin**, 49, senior banking officer in Wilmington (pop. 69,500), is one who has benefited. She's proud of the industry and its image:

LEVIN: Banks known widely.

"We are known everywhere for our banks. My husband and I were in Acapulco and I was wearing my bank's T-shirt. A man from Texas came up and said 'I know your bank.' " One of the millions who send their credit card payments to Delaware.

While the pro-banking environment is new, the corporate colossi is historic. Delaware law for decades has lured corporations from across the USA to make this their legal home.

Gives managements more flexibility, from meetings to mergers. Other states have patterned laws after Delaware's, but the tradition and a court system with expertise in corporate law keeps the companies chartered here.

Individuals and small businesses benefit from that climate. **Kelly Petit**, 27, Dover, state capital (pop. 23,512) is starting a new business of refinishing linoleum countertops.

"I can just walk in and put down $50 and be incorporated. There's very little red tape. That's how Delaware makes its money — by making it easy for people to do business here."

PETIT: Red tape is eliminated.

Individuals also do business off the land and the sea.

■ Farms. 3,200 of them. Raised 196 million chickens last year.

■ Beaches. Entire 28 miles of seashore is public. Resorts draw heavily from Washington, Baltimore and Philadelphia.

Historically, big business here has meant Du Pont. Formally known as E.I. du Pont de Nemours. Founded by the family that came here from France in 1800.

Du Pont employs 23,800. Has made Delaware the chemical capital of the world. Revenues last year were $27.1 billion. Profits $1.5 billion. No. 14 on the list of the world's largest industrial corporations.

The du Pont families have about 2,000 living members. Most have been pillars in the Delaware community — economically, socially, politically. **Ben du Pont**, 23, is a mechanical engineer at the company's production plant in Wilmington. His father is Pete, the ex-Guv and presidential hopeful. Says Ben:

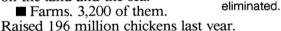

BEN du PONT: His family came here from France in 1800.

"Delaware is in a boom of boom times. There is so much prosperity. Property values have skyrocketed. I remember in the '70s there were parts of town (Wilmington) I wasn't supposed to be walking around in. Now, there are Cadillacs, BMWs, Mercedes parked out front in those neighborhoods."

That's Plain Talk from Delaware.

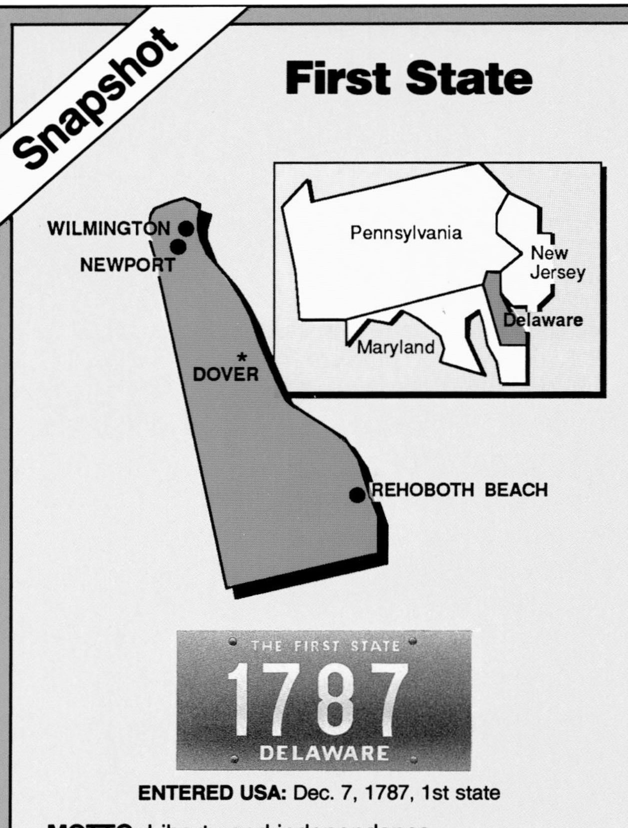

ENTERED USA: Dec. 7, 1787, 1st state

MOTTO: Liberty and independence
POPULATION: 633,000; rank, 47th
LARGEST CITY: Wilmington, pop. 69,500
CAPITAL: Dover, pop. 23,512
LAND: 1,932 square miles; rank, 49th
POPULATION DENSITY: 327.6 per square mile; rank, 7th
RACIAL MIX: 82.1% white; 16.1% black; 0.7% Asian and Pacific islanders. Hispanic heritage: 1.6%.

Uniquely Del.

CHICKEN CAPITAL: In 1923, Mrs. Wilmer Steele of Ocean View raised the USA's first commercial broiler chicken flock. Sussex County leads the USA in broiler chickens.

BEAUTY QUEEN: The first beauty pageant in the USA was at Rehoboth Beach in 1880. Myrtle Meriwether of Shinglehouse, Pa., was named "Miss United States."

RECORDING STAR: Dover-born mechanic and inventor Eldridge Johnson founded the Victor Talking Machine Company in 1901.

CHICKEN FIGHT: During the Revolutionary War, military units from Delaware were nicknamed Blue Hen Chickens for the fighting cocks they carried with them.

PEA SOUP: Pea Patch island gets its name from the legend that a shipload of peas emptied into the Delaware River and caused an island to form.

V. George Carey, 59
Chicken farmer/
state representative
Milford

"Delaware is the kind of place where a farmer's got a place in the legislature. I may not know the big words and the scientific terms, but I know that common sense is needed to take care of the state and the environment. There are other legislators who grow chickens, but I'm the only one who wears a chicken hat in the legislature. Chicken is a way of life here. It's Delaware's economy."

Eleanor Jordan, 60
Museum aide
New Castle

"I've always been a history buff. New Castle has charm. You have a feeling of the past. We have two signers of the Constitution who lived in this tiny town. We're living in a town that has not changed over the years."

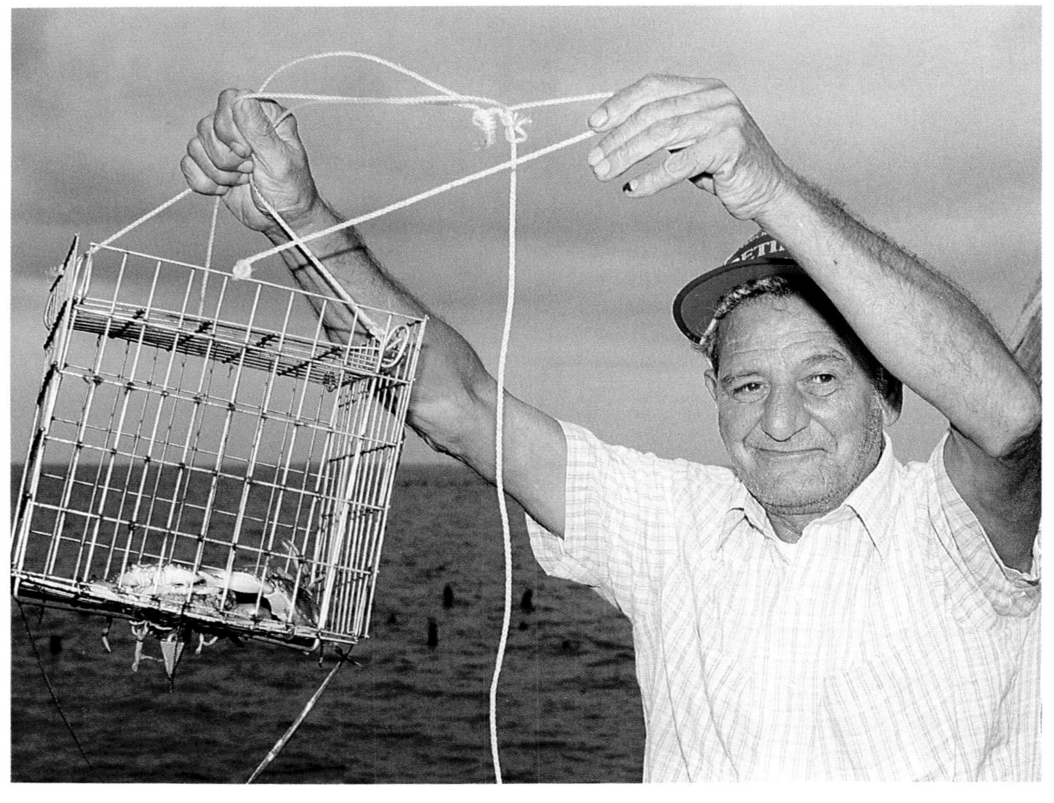

Voices
of Delaware

Henry Capasso, 64
Retired
Smyrna

"Delaware beaches have good crabbing. The crabs are large ones, too. You just buy a box net. Use chicken backs or breasts, cast it over. Then you wait for a crab to crawl in."

John Rago, 34
Executive assistant
Wilmington

"I like the rebirth of Wilmington. Having lived here most of my life, I knew a particular kind of Wilmington and I saw it deteriorate during a period in the '60s. And I've stayed in the city long enough to see it come back to life. Wilmington has an interesting mix of places and people — the professional, the worker, the blue-collar worker, the unemployed. They come from all sorts of ethnic backgrounds."

Randy Martin, 32
Builder
Dover

"Seafood is about all anyone around here eats. Seafood and beer. We can get crabs and shrimp year round. They get it every day off of the boats. If it isn't fresh, they throw it out. I cook out sometimes. I play the chef and eat it too. I do it all."

Barbara Ingersoll, 42
Interior designer
Rehoboth Beach

"I've been coming down to Rehoboth Beach since I was a child. I grew up in downtown Washington, and this has always been a breath of fresh air. This is freedom. It's natural. I can go crabbing with my friends, I can go sailing. There's great antiquing around. Here I can have everything."

Donna Keeler, 42
Clothing store owner
Smyrna

"My family has been in Smyrna for seven generations. We have roots to the Henrys, as in Patrick Henry. Delaware is changing. I used to be able to look outside my window as a little girl and see the rye fields. They looked like ocean waves. Now you see churches and schools. We're not so little anymore."

Dallas Green, 53, president and general manager of the Chicago Cubs, grew up in Newport, Del. Green and his wife, the former Sylvia Taylor, frequently return to Delaware.

No doubt about it, he'll be back someday

USA TODAY: What are your early memories of Delaware?

GREEN: The first thing that comes to mind is Krebs School. The principal there — Donald Richey — was the first guy to recognize that I had any sports talent, particularly in basketball. He used to let me sneak into Krebs at night to play basketball.

USA TODAY: What was it like growing up in the little town of Newport, Del.?

GREEN: Newport was a pretty active little sports town. We had a female baseball player long before it was fashionable. Gal by the name of Thelma Garvey; she was a helluva baseball player. Her brother, Bob Garvey, signed professionally, but only played a year or so.

USA TODAY: When you left Delaware on sports trips, did people tease you about the little state?

GREEN: Yeah. In 1952, our American Legion team won the state championship and went to West Virginia for a tournament. Half the teams there didn't even know where we were from. They used to say, "What state's Delaware in?"

USA TODAY: Even though you got a great career opportunity with the Chicago Cubs, was it tough to leave?

GREEN: Yes. I still find myself calling Delaware home and still say we're going home when we come back. That may not be fair to Chicago, because they've been tremendous to me and it is a beautiful city. I've been very happy there, but I kinda can't wait to get "home" and see my friends and family.

USA TODAY: Have you seen a lot of changes in Delaware?

GREEN With freeways and I-95, it has changed some. I've seen it grow. The push has been in the lower part of the state — Dover and further south. Going to Dover used to be a road trip. You were really going somewhere (from Newport) if you went to Dover and, of course, if you went as far as Rehoboth Beach, it was really a big deal. We watched that area grow and watched the farmland disappear.

USA TODAY: Do you plan to come back?

GREEN: No if, ands or buts about that. I plan to come back for good someday. It's home.

Topic: DELAWARE

A booming economy has lowered our taxes

USA TODAY: What's the image of the First State you would like to see projected?

CASTLE: I believe Delaware stands for excellence. When you look at the corporate climate here, at personal income and education levels, they're generally very high. Our greatest problem is just being unknown.

USA TODAY: But that is changing. Are you concerned about Delaware becoming too well known?

CASTLE: We do have some concerns about growth. Ecologically, it's a very difficult balance. We have bays, for example, that may not be any more than two or three feet deep in certain places. We have to worry about trailer parks and other development around them.

USA TODAY: Are you regulating the growth?

CASTLE: Recently, I've proposed quality-of-life plans. Counties would have to adopt land-use planning. If growth gets ahead of your highways, sewers and water, you're going to have a problem.

USA TODAY: How many times has Delaware reduced its personal income tax?

CASTLE: I don't know what the record is for income tax cuts, but Delaware reduced its personal income taxes four times in a row. In 1979, we were the highest in the country, about 20 percent. We took a big reduction in that year to 13 percent.

USA TODAY: Have the reductions hurt services?

CASTLE: They haven't. We had the highest increase in teacher salaries in the country last year. Also, we have increased economic development activity, which has brought in more people, more jobs. They, in turn, pay additional revenue, and that has produced the opportunity to reduce taxes again. That is true supply-side economics.

USA TODAY: What's ahead?

CASTLE: I understand it can't go on forever, but from where we started to where we are today, things have worked remarkably well.

Michael Castle, 48, a Republican, was elected governor in 1984. Castle is a former lieutenant governor and state legislator.

USA TODAY: It's difficult to come here without seeing the du Pont family influence. How are they regarded?

CASTLE: Fifteen years ago, there was a feeling that the du Pont family was controlling things, including the *News Journal* newspapers and the economy of the state. And that what the company didn't control, the family did control. The feeling now is that there is less control.

USA TODAY: Why?

CASTLE: There are fewer du Ponts on the board of the Du Pont company and fewer involved in the activities that run the state. Many are still involved but there is a feeling of acceptance now. A much more positive feeing than 20 years ago.

USA TODAY: What do tourists like about Delaware?

CASTLE: You're never farther than nine miles from salt water when you're in Delaware. Almost anything along the Brandywine, which is a very beautiful river. Our state parks are very pretty.

USA TODAY: What are your favorite spots?

CASTLE: I have always enjoyed the so-called Chateau Country of Delaware. Almost every week, I discover some new niche. There's a lot still to be discovered.

Florida

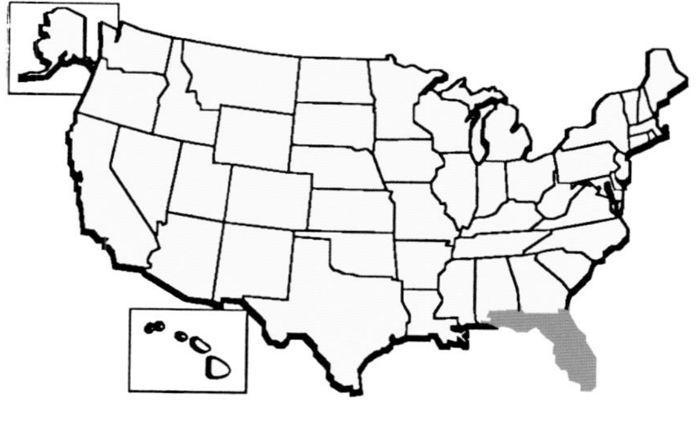

Visited: Sept. 1-7, 1987
Featured in USA TODAY: Sept. 8

"Our dream is the future."

Larry Koile
Space Center technician
Cocoa, Fla.

Florida

Gateway to the future: On earth, in heavens

Ponce de Leon came here in 1513 in search of the Fountain of Youth. Millions who followed him think they've found it. The Sunshine State.

Others leave here for sky-high searches. The universe. 132 men and women have rocketed from here to the moon or stars and back. One day soon, to Mars.

On earth and in the heavens, Florida spells future.

State No. 50 for the BusCapade. After 33,000 miles, the end of the road. It's also home. I live here. I love it. My heart has a very warm spot for my native state of South Dakota. But my head tells me Florida is where it's at.

Let me tell you a little about my adopted state. Keep in mind I'm prejudiced. So, take it with a grain of salt, the way others do when you brag about your home state or your hometown. We all do it. That's one of the beauties of life across the USA.

■ Florida people. 11,675,000 of us. When I first got sand in my shoes as a $95 a week reporter at *The Miami Herald* in 1954, there were only 3 million-plus. They come to stay at the rate of over 1,000 a day. 5th most populous state, behind California, New York, Texas, Pennsylvania. Projected to move into No. 4 this fall.

■ Visitors. Over 37 million last year. Yankees. Southerners. Midwesterners. Latins. Europeans.

Most head for the beaches. 1,350 miles of Florida oceanfront. More than the entire USA's West Coast.

Whether here to play or stay, attractions abound:

■ Disney World/Orlando (pop. 144,500). Mickey Mouse and the 22,000-acre Magic Kingdom are the No. 1 destination.

■ Miami-Miami Beach (pop. 484,800). Gateway to and from Latin America. The City of Miami (pop. 385,900) is over 60 percent Hispanic.

■ Tampa-St. Petersburg (pop. 527,500). Has an image as a retirement haven. The senior citizens are anything but retiring. Active. Affluent.

■ Jacksonville (pop. 586,900). Gateway from Georgia and the Northeast. "We're a baby San Francisco, " says **Trish Calhoun**, 41, antique dealer.

Some of those places sound a little like your home state. But one place in Florida is unique. Only one in the USA. Spaceport USA.

The Space Age began here July 24, 1950. A makeshift missile called Bumper 8 soared to an altitude of 10 miles.

Since then 2,411 rockets have been launched from what is now known as the Kennedy Space Center.

■ 56 "manned" missions. 132 astronauts. Nine women. Two politicians. Seven foreigners.

■ **Alan Shepard**, our first to pierce the space barrier. **John Glenn**, our first to orbit the earth. **Neil Armstrong**, first to step on the moon. **Bob Crippen**, first space shuttle pilot. **Sally Ride**, our first woman in space. All living legends here.

■ 10 dead space heroes. The Challenger Seven crew killed in a flight explosion on Jan. 28, 1986. The Apollo 1 crew, killed in a launch pad fire Jan. 27, 1967.

Despite those failures, the focus here is on the successes — past and future.

Says **Mike Parrish**, 31, site-test conductor, excitedly: "Everybody here wants to reach for the stars."

Larry Koile, 56, lead payload technician, puts it simply: "Our dream is the future."

The BusCateers toured the Space Center on Saturday. Sunday night they celebrated the conclusion of the BusCapade with 300 earth people and space people in Cocoa Beach (pop. 10,926). At Pumpkin Center, overgrown oceanfront log cabin that is my home. About 12 miles in line of sight from the launch pads to the universe. A few blocks from where USA TODAY was researched and conceived.

How did it all feel?

Exciting? Sure. Rewarding? Yes. But even more challenging. And compelling. Big dreams come easy on this vision-packed piece of the earth. Launch pad for the nation's space program. Launch pad for the Nation's Newspaper. And there are more dreams and launches to come.

That's Plain Talk from Florida.

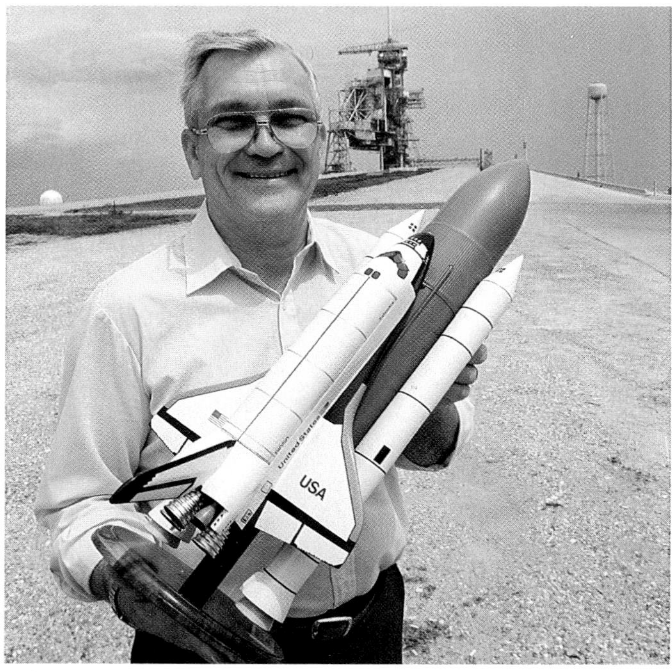

KOILE: 'I've worked on every shuttle that's gone up.'

Sunshine State

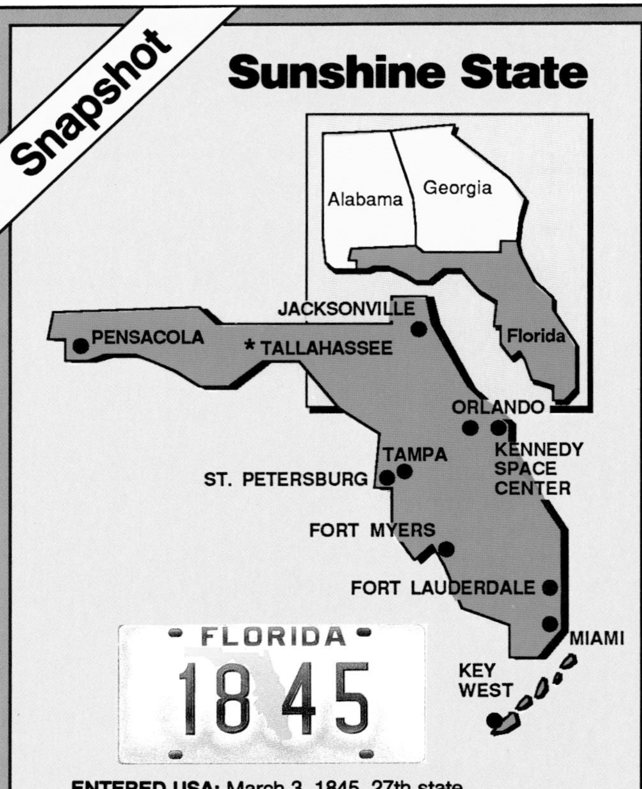

ENTERED USA: March 3, 1845, 27th state

MOTTO: In God we trust
POPULATION: 11,675,000; rank, 5th
LARGEST CITY: Jacksonville, pop. 586,900
CAPITAL: Tallahassee, pop. 112,258
LAND: 54,153 square miles; rank, 26th
POPULATION DENSITY: 215.6 per square mile; rank, 10th
RACIAL MIX: 84.0% white; 13.8% black; 0.6% Asian and Pacific islanders. Hispanic heritage: 8.8%.

Uniquely Fla.

NATIVE SONG: Stephen Foster, author of "Old Folks At Home," Florida's official state song, never lived in the state. The Pittsburgh, Pa., resident never saw the Suwannee River — he just thought it fit well in the song's lyrics.

NO THANKS: Thomas Edison offered to install electricity in his hometown of Fort Myers, but the town politely refused, fearing it would keep residents' cattle awake at night.

MANGO MARKET: Florida is the only place in the continental USA producing mangos.

COOL IDEA: Dr. John Gorrie, called the father of modern air conditioning, invented the first artificial ice-making machine in Apalachicola in 1849.

STONE WALK: The Walk of Fame at Rollins College in Winter Park contains 800 inscribed stones brought from the homes and birthplaces of famous people.

Voices

of Florida

Elizabeth Hoffman, 66
Retired
St. Petersburg Beach

"Who wants to see old people sitting on a bench? I'm pretty old, and I don't sit on benches. Retired used to mean giving up. Now it means keeping active. I play golf, bowl and do aerobics three times a week. I ride my bike every morning. I love to ride at the beach and see everything."

Pat Walsh, 32
Blue Angels pilot
Pensacola

"The Blue Angels are the ambassadors of good will for the Navy. It's not just flying, but it's landing and meeting the people. To put a tear in an old veteran's eye, to be a role model and inspire children — I feel like Santa Claus for an hour."

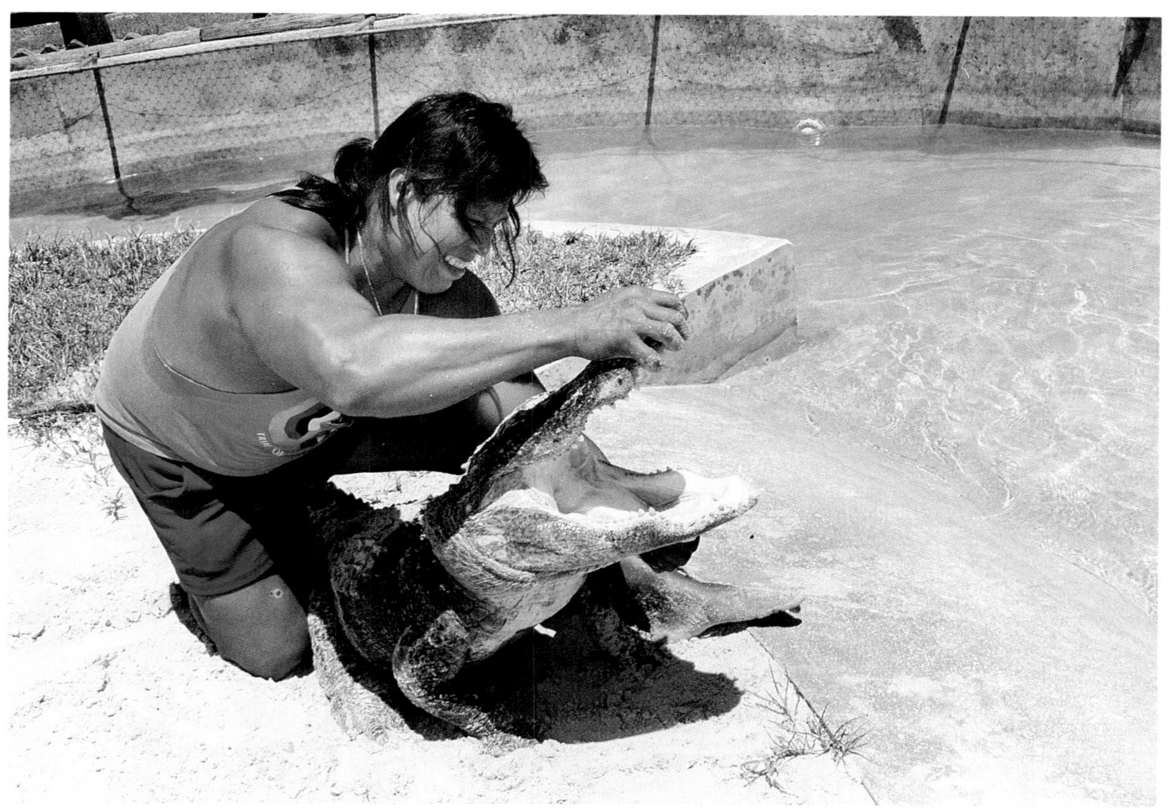

Bo Jim, 41
Alligator wrestler
Ochopee

"Alligators look lazy and sluggish, but when they want to, they can move real fast. You have to be careful. I know that I can't make any mistakes. Even though I've been wrestling for seven years, I've found that you can't rush. I did that once and I got hurt."

Barbara King, 30
Clothing store owner
Orlando

"This area is growing like wildfire. Since Disney and the other tourist attractions came, changes have occurred at a steady pace. New people are bringing in new business, and new ideas are pouring in. Orlando was kind of backward. Now, it's moving forward at breakneck speed."

Craig Leskiewicz, 22
Hotel manager
Fort Lauderdale

"I'm originally from Canada and the warm weather brought me here. I was sick of the cold. When people think of Fort Lauderdale, they obviously think of spring break. Those two months of spring are a zoo. The strip is wall-to-wall bodies. You can't walk on the beach. You just dive in, and where you land is where you stay."

Vicente Menendez, 47
AFL-CIO official
Hialeah

"Miami is a great city, a great melting pot. Almost every country in the world is represented here. We have Latins, blacks, Anglos. It all works together. It's definitely a plus for the economy of Dade County. To me, one of the greatest gifts of life is to be able to live with people from other countries and to learn and comprehend their backgrounds. You pick the best from each culture."

Marjorie Starnes-Stephens, 50
Lawyer
Fort Myers

"I live on a river with a beautiful view of the sunsets. My husband flies a World War II amphibious plane that lands on the water near his fishing shack. On our first date, he taxied up to my door in his plane."

Jimmy Buffett, 40, is a singer/songwriter born in Mobile, Ala. He "discovered" Key West in 1972. Florida inspired some of his biggest hits, including Margaritaville.

There's still room to be away from it all

USA TODAY: What was your first impression of Key West?

BUFFETT: It was November, 85 degrees, and everybody was swimming. I said, "This looks like the kind of place I ought to consider living in."

USA TODAY: Are you settled down?

BUFFETT: I don't know if I'll ever grow up and settle down. I'm 40 and didn't think I'd live this long, but I have.

USA TODAY: Was your big hit, *Margaritaville*, inspired by Key West?

BUFFETT: I remember coming back one weekend, and it was the first time they had a really huge tourist boom. The Winnebagos came down, people in checkered shorts and white legs were walking around downtown. That got me inspired.

USA TODAY: Your 1986 album is titled *Floridays.* What is your ideal Floriday?

BUFFETT: I like sunrise over the flats when I'm out in my little skiff, fishing. That's the magic of Key West. About 30 miles west, you have nothing but unpopulated islands. That's about the prettiest place I know. There are still places in Florida where you can go and not see another person.

USA TODAY: What about Florida evenings?

BUFFETT: This is bad for my reputation, but I don't go out much anymore. So, my Florida evenings are spent watching the sunset, going out for a big Cuban meal and reading a good book.

USA TODAY: Why did you become involved in environmental issues?

BUFFETT: It's a fragile ecological system. People weren't taking responsibility for the impact of what they were doing. There's more to being a citizen of Florida than changing your drivers license and buying a house with a swimming pool.

USA TODAY: Are you also trying to preserve a certain atmosphere in Key West?

BUFFETT: I hope Key West maintains a kind of wildness for people in this generation, as it did for me 17 or 18 years ago. This town has given me a lot of good stories to write about. But I have a feeling the island takes care of itself.

Topic: FLORIDA

Natives value growth; some newcomers fear it

USA TODAY: You're a first-term Republican governor but, until four years ago, you were a prominent Democrat. What's the biggest difference between the two parties in Florida?

MARTINEZ: We differ on the approach to issues. I always felt that the property tax was neither a sufficient nor equitable source of revenue for local government. Historically, Democrats have felt that local government should not use sales tax revenue, reserving it for state use.

USA TODAY: How do you differ on social policy from the Democrats?

MARTINEZ: I feel the state government shouldn't set up health clinics in schools, which is counter to the Democratic philosophy. We all recognize that every youngster needs an education, but the approach may be different. We're the second-highest dropout state in the nation, so it's obvious that up front, something's wrong.

USA TODAY: How would you fix these problems?

MARTINEZ: A lot of it is prioritizing budget expenditures. We ought to concentrate on public education, public health, public works, public safety. But when you look at what we have done over decades, we're into everything. We've got a lot of programs, but very few get served. We should begin to identify where it is that we can make a difference and add resources to that activity.

USA TODAY: Recently, Florida began taxing services, including advertising. Has that hurt the business climate?

MARTINEZ: They keep saying we lost $33 million in convention business. But in that same period the state of Florida would do over $3 billion worth of tourism and convention business. When you look at it that way, it's a loss, but look what's coming.

USA TODAY: That tax caused a few battles. Did anyone show signs of supporting the tax?

MARTINEZ: The advertisers continued the battle. Otherwise,

Bob Martinez, 52, a Republican, was elected governor in 1986. In 1979, he was elected mayor of Tampa and was re-elected in 1983.

it would have been over with. The lawyers would have liked it, the realtors would like it, everybody else would like it. But now nobody likes it.

USA TODAY: How would you describe the difference in attitude between a native of Florida and a newcomer?

MARTINEZ: The native Floridian may be more aggressive in supporting economic development. The newcomers are getting away from congestion and fear that Florida may end up like New York City or Chicago. The natives are looking at an expanded economy where they can make a profit.

USA TODAY: How will you handle the football rivalry between Florida and Florida State?

MARTINEZ: I'll probably do what all courageous governors do, which is to sit on both sides. One half on one side, one half on the other.

USA TODAY: Do you ever take your family to Disney World?

MARTINEZ: I'm about ready to start again with grandchildren. Our children got old enough and started going on their own. You cannot find a better postmark for a state than Disney. What Disney does is attract people to Florida, and once here, they may make other inquiries about Florida.

Georgia

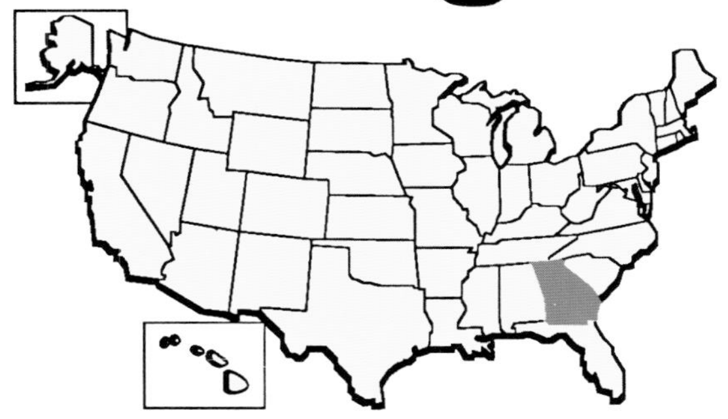

Visited: Aug. 26-29, 1987
Featured in USA TODAY: Aug. 31

"The only serious handicap Georgia ever had was the race issue. Once that was overcome there was a liberation in basic Southern philosophy."

Jimmy Carter
39th president of the USA
Plains, Ga.

Georgia

Going with the wind, this South has risen

On Sept. 27, 1864, Union General **William Tecumseh Sherman**'s troops took Atlanta and later burned the city.

On Nov. 15, Sherman's march to the sea began. Just 36 days later he arrived in Savannah, having devastated a 60-mile-wide strip of Georgia along the way. Sixteen weeks later the Civil War ended.

On Dec. 15, 1939, the USA first saw the epic motion picture of that war. *Gone With the Wind.*

In the 1980s, Atlanta and Georgia are going with the wind. Winds of change have fanned across the state. This piece of the South clearly has risen again.

Population, race relations, industry, incomes . . . even football fortunes . . . have been on the rise for a generation.

THE PREZ THE KING THE COACH
. . . Georgia heroes Carter, King, Dooley.

This generation's most talked about heroes here are:

■ **Jimmy Carter**, 62, the 39th president of the USA.

■ **Martin Luther King Jr.**, king of the civil rights movement of the '50s and '60s.

■ **Vince Dooley**, 54, Bulldog football coach at the University of Georgia. All three are credited with helping bring about racial harmony — if not total equality — in Georgia. And that single achievement probably has done more for the Peach State's progress than any other.

Dooley is so popular he's been urged often to run for governor or U.S. senator. But in their hearts, most Bulldog fans want him to continue his winning ways at the University in Athens (pop. 42,500).

Most remembered and revered Dooley protege of his generation is **Herschel Walker**, a black. Heisman trophy winner in 1982. Now with the Dallas Cowboys in the NFL.

"Herschel was a coach's dream," Dooley says simply.

King's life ended with an assassin's bullet in Memphis in 1968 when he was 39. But his dreams still live. Widow **Coretta Scott King** carries on. Selected for publication many of his most memorable quotes. They show his — and her — hope for their native state:

"I have a dream that one day on the red hills of Georgia the sons of former slaves and the sons of former slave owners will be able to sit down together at the table of brotherhood," King said in 1963. They have. Atlanta's Mayor **Andrew Young** is black. So was his predecessor, **Maynard Jackson.**

Jimmy and **Rosalynn Carter**, after four years in the Georgia statehouse and four years in the White House, are back where they began. Plains (pop. 651). No one has a better perspective on Georgia's past, present, future and its relationship to the rest of the USA.

President Jimmy states it simply: "The only serious handicap Georgia ever had was the race issue. Once that was overcome there was a liberation in basic Southern philosophy. That has now let us move forward."

Forward it has moved:

■ Population: 6,104,000. In 1966, it was 4,379,000.

■ Gross state product: $99.4 billion. In 1966, it was a little over $30 billion.

■ Passengers at Atlanta's Hartsfield Airport: 42.5 million. In 1966, 15.2 million.

While much economic and social progress has come in the Atlanta area, the other Georgia also has benefited. Gov. **Joe Frank Harris**, 2nd-term Democrat, said, "Atlanta is the catalyst for the whole state. The tentacles reach out and cause progress everywhere."

One rural area progressing is Ft. Valley (pop. 9,000). Peach and pecan country. Also home to the Blue Bird bus manufacturing company, which employs 1,500. Our BusCapade stopped there last week, to bring home both the bus and its driver, **Joel Driver**, 28, a native.

GUV AND JOEL: Homecoming for BusCapade's Driver.

Said **Terry Horton**, 51, Joel's former boss and Blue Bird's sales director: "You all have made a celebrity out of that country boy."

Responded Driver: "When the BusCateers checked into the Waldorf-Astoria in New York City I looked out the window and counted 37 taxicabs in one block. I shook my head and remembered there are no cabs in Ft. Valley. We've covered 33,000 miles and the USA is amazing. But I carried Georgia with me wherever we went."

That's Georgia pride and Plain Talk from the Peach State.

Snapshot

Peach State

North Carolina
Tennessee
South Carolina
Alabama
Georgia
Florida
ATHENS
ATLANTA
FT. VALLEY
PLAINS
SAVANNAH

• GEORGIA •
1788

ENTERED USA: Jan. 2, 1788, 4th state

MOTTO: Wisdom, justice, and moderation
POPULATION: 6,104,000; rank, 11th
LARGEST CITY: Atlanta, pop. 426,090
CAPITAL: Atlanta
LAND: 58,056 square miles; rank, 21st
POPULATION DENSITY: 105.1 per square mile; rank, 21st
RACIAL MIX: 72.3% white; 26.8% black; 0.4% Asian and Pacific islanders. Hispanic heritage: 1.1%.

Uniquely Ga.

TABLE TABOO: Gainesville has a rule prohibiting use of knives and forks while eating fried chicken. The Chamber of Commerce adopted it in 1961 to promote the "Poultry Capital of the World."

ACCIDENTAL APPELLATION: Ft. Valley was supposed to be named Fox Valley because it was a popular hunting area. The U.S. Post Office misread the application.

SHERMAN SWERVED: Madison retains much of its antebellum charm today because its homes were spared during Gen. Sherman's destructive March to the Sea in 1864. Sherman felt the city was too beautiful to burn.

ALLIGATOR LAND: The Okefenokee Swamp covers more than 600 square miles and includes more than 60 lakes. More than 50 species of reptiles live there.

FIRST RITES: The first baptism in what is now the USA took place in 1540 near the present site of Macon.

Voices
of Georgia

Sandy Styliano, 28
Photo shop manager
Savannah

"Only tourists do this. All the Yankees want to be Southern belles and Southern gentlemen — like Rhett Butler. They try to talk like Southerners, but they put too much into it."

T.E. Bowers, 67
Fruit vendor
Garden City

"Georgia peaches are supposed to be the best peaches that grow. They're sweet. You don't have to put sugar or cream on them. I think peaches are good for people, just raw. Just grab them and eat them. I've been to the doctor twice in my whole life."

John Roberson, 27
Site manager, Fort Jackson
Savannah

"We're here to show people the past and what it was like to be a soldier. The South fought on pure determination. I flunked history in school. Now I'm practically standing in the shoes of the Confederate soldiers."

Billy Carter, 50
Home builder/
ex-president's brother
Plains

"When I changed jobs, I told my wife, Sybil, we could live anywhere she wanted. She chose Plains. It's kind of quiet. Of course, it got to be a real madhouse when Jimmy was first elected president. I think it's gotten back to normal. It grew so fast, and then it shrunk smaller than it was. I like it this way."

Debbie Sparks, 23
Receptionist
Macon

"A lot of people think of Southern women as wearing long dresses and hats and sitting under a tree. That's not reality. That's just an image you try not to live up to. I think a lot of Southern women would like to stay home, but most of them are just average working women."

Jimmy Carter, 42
Gym manager/trainer
Augusta

"All everyone hears about Augusta is the Masters Golf Tournament. It's pandemonium time when that comes. Jobs open up everywhere. It brings in a lot of money for the city. But there are other things in Augusta. We've got a good medical school, and a lot of people are into power weight lifting. We're making a name for ourselves. . . . Yeah, everybody notices my name. I had a blast in '76."

Genna Crane, 23
Hotel clerk
Atlanta

"For a big city, Atlanta still has a smaller-town atmosphere. I've never seen a city this big that is that friendly. And it keeps growing. I don't see things slowing down. The airport makes everything so accessible. It also brings a lot of international visitors to the hotel. They always comment on how nice everyone is. Southern hospitality is definitely alive in Georgia."

Notables

Jimmy Carter, *62, is the only president elected from the Deep South. Elected in 1976, he lost to Ronald Reagan in 1980.* ***Rosalynn Carter****, 60, a Gannett Co. Inc. board member, married Carter in 1946. They live in Plains, Ga.*

Everyone is expected to do their share

USA TODAY: What's special about Plains that brought you back here?

CARTER: We have lived here most of our lives. Our parents, grandparents, great-grandparents and great-great-grandparents lived here, going back to the 1700s. It's where people look on us as Jimmy and Rosalynn.

USA TODAY: Do you enjoy the peace?

MRS. CARTER: I do. It's home. I think that's why we like Plains so much. It's a small town, yet we're close to Atlanta. It's convenient.

USA TODAY: What Georgian values do you think helped you in the White House?

CARTER: Georgia politics encompass conservative approaches to budgets and finance, strict accountability for public funds, a strong local government and a strong defense. And Georgia has always been progressive on social programs.

USA TODAY: What values are vintage Georgian?

CARTER: There's a basic work ethic. You're expected to do your share, have a productive life.

USA TODAY: Do you think people were surprised that a woman from Plains, Ga., had such an active role in the White House?

MRS. CARTER: Some people were surprised, but Jimmy and I have always worked together. In Plains, the men and women have always worked together.

CARTER: But the people did underestimate us because we were from the South, and I think there is a tendency among some people in the nation to underestimate Southerners.

USA TODAY: What surprises visitors to Georgia?

CARTER: Most people are surprised to see that Atlanta has been rebuilt after *Gone With The Wind*, that we have a very progressive attitude, both socially and technologically, that it's a confident state, and that the diversity that exists is our strength.

Topic: GEORGIA

Diverse state presents quilt of many patterns

USA TODAY: How has Georgia changed?

HARRIS: Twenty-three years ago, our budget was less than $500 million. Today our budget is over $10 billion per year. State government is a big business. If we were lined up on the Fortune 500 list of corporations, we'd probably be No. 72 or 73.

USA TODAY: Is it true that there are two Georgias, one made up of the thriving Atlanta area and the other of depressed rural areas?

HARRIS: That's been an emotional issue. Georgia is a very diverse state — a quilt of many patterns. Parts of Georgia are rural. And there are farming communities that never hope to be a city like Atlanta. And so, they're working for separate goals. If there are any barriers, they are disappearing.

USA TODAY: Why has Atlanta become the model for the New South?

HARRIS: Diversity would be the key, and then leadership and people working together. And the old Southern hospitality is still here. People catch it and bring it back when they return.

USA TODAY: What will Georgia be like in the future?

HARRIS: Projections show we'll still be one of the six fastest-growing states in the year 2000.

USA TODAY: How is that growth being controlled?

HARRIS: We have a growth strategy commission that's working right now. We're very conscious that unless we have orderly growth, we are not going to be able to serve some of the high-growth areas.

USA TODAY: During the recent racial incidents in Forsyth County, you said there's absolutely no place for bigotry in our society. Is Forsyth County an isolated case?

HARRIS: There are other Forsyth counties to some extent, not only in Georgia but all around the USA. It's a problem that exists wherever people are. People's attitudes have been changing for many years in the South. We've made probably more progress than any other state in the South in having a compatible relationship between the races.

Joe Frank Harris, 51, a Democrat, is serving his second term. Harris also served 18 years in the Georgia House of Representatives.

USA TODAY: Are there parts of the state that tourists have overlooked?

HARRIS: The state of Georgia is a well-kept secret. People think of Georgia as a corridor to Florida. But tourism is a $9 billion business for our state, and it's increasing tremendously. With the mountains in the North, and the lakes and streams in between, the farming area and on down to the coastal area, we've got everything to offer that anyone would like. We have some of the finest state parks.

USA TODAY: How do you feel about Georgia's future?

HARRIS: I like to feel Georgia's in a position almost like a locomotive going down a track. We're fueled up and moving. If we keep the fuel coming — and that comes from continuing the proper leadership with the state and the cities — then that locomotive will continue to move.

USA TODAY: What do you want Georgia's image to be?

HARRIS: As the place where the action is, where anything is possible and anything can happen if you're willing to work hard.

Hawaii

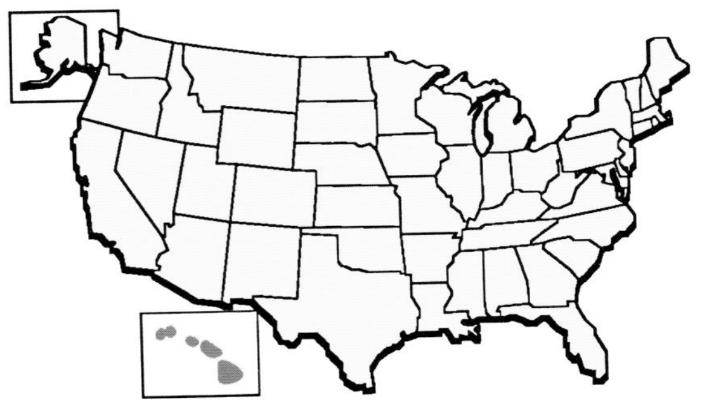

Visited by jet: June 26-30, 1987
Featured in USA TODAY: July 3

"The kids don't care about nationalities. They're not prejudiced. Prejudice isn't natural to children; it's taught. We don't teach it here."

Mary K. Dias
Program coordinator
at Palama Settlement
Honolulu, Hawaii

Hawaii

Paradise and paradox; sun, fun and memories

They call it the "Paradise of the Pacific." It is. Maybe of the world.

Sun. Fun. Leis. Luaus. Waikiki. Women. Men. Memories. Pearl Harbor. That's where it becomes a bit paradoxical:

■ 1941. Dec. 7. Japanese bomb Pearl Harbor. Their goal: Conquer Hawaii and the USA. Brought us into World War II. But we won. "Unconditional surrender" by the Japanese, Sept. 2, 1945.

■ 1987. Money is accomplishing for the Japanese much of what their military couldn't. Two-thirds of the major hotel properties here are owned by Japanese. They've invested $2.6 billion in Hawaii real estate and business. Nearly a million Japanese toured here last year.

Whether they came from East or West, reminiscing reigns at Pearl Harbor. More than 1.4 million tourists visited that historic site last year.

KINZLER: At Pearl Harbor with sunken Arizona.

Bob Kinzler, 65, was with the 27th Infantry Regiment based at Schofield Barracks on Pearl Harbor Day. Watched as 2,334 USA military comrades died in minutes. Now he's a tour guide.

"It seems ironic. They say that if the Japanese had only waited, they could have just come in and bought everything. Wouldn't have had to lose all those people. But I have no animosity toward them now. I've let bygones be bygones."

By and large, those bygones are forgiven if not forgotten. Hawaii of the 1980s is the melting pot of the USA, perhaps of the world. About 23 percent of the 1,062,000 who live here are of Japanese heritage. 27 percent are Caucasian. 18 percent are other Asian-Americans — Chinese, Filipinos, Koreans — or Samoans. Less than 20 percent are of chiefly Hawaiian ancestry. Very few pure natives.

Election results show this may be the most democratic — small "d" — state in the USA. All nationalities are represented at local and state office levels. Top officials:

■ Gov. **John Waihee**, 41, first-term Democrat, is the first native-born Hawaiian in that office. From Honokaa (pop. 1,555), on the big island of Hawaii.

■ Former Gov. **George Ariyoshi**, Waihee's predecessor, is Japanese.

■ Republican **Frank Fasi**, an Italian from Hartford, Conn., is mayor of Honolulu, largest city (pop. 805,266).

While they come from all over the world, most islanders are here for sun, fun and (hopefully) fortune. But the Aloha Spirit of warmth, love and patriotism prevails.

The Rev. **Kaleo Patterson**, 32, of the First Hawaiian Church in Kapaa (pop. 3,794) on the lush northern island of Kauai, says, "There is an ethnic richness because everyone who came here is sort of a foreigner. Hawaiian culture is a romantic culture."

DIAS: With mini melting pot.

Mary K. Dias, 36, is a program coordinator at Palama Settlement — for children of Hawaii's poorer or newer citizens. A mini melting pot. Says Mary:

"The kids don't care about nationalities. They're not prejudiced. Prejudice isn't natural to children; it's taught. We don't teach it here."

This July Fourth weekend has everyone waving the flag. So does Statehood Day, Aug. 21. Hawaii became the 50th state in 1959. The Guv, then a sixth-grader, recalls it emotionally: "Our teacher told us that now, for the first time, anybody in the classroom could become president of the United States. School was let out. Everybody was running around and cheering. It made us feel equal."

The statehood status brought about a boom in business and trade. Private and public leaders play heavily on Hawaii as the outpost for the USA on the Pacific Asian Rim. The economic future looks bright.

For most on the mainland, the image of Hawaii still is that in the newspaper and TV ads. Waikiki. Beautiful beaches. Beautiful women.

Sean Dowling, 26, lifeguard on Waikiki, gets paid to work in that environment. Says Sean:

"Girls are a good part of the job. There are usually 50 to 100 '9s' or '9½s' on my beach every day. One or two '10s.' The end of a good day for me is chasing those girls at night."

That's Plain Talk from Hawaii.

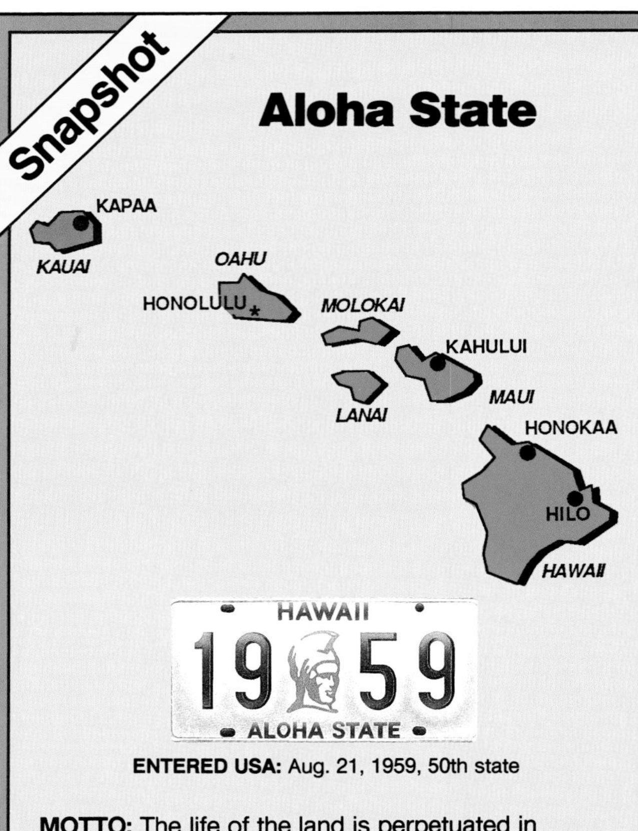

ENTERED USA: Aug. 21, 1959, 50th state

MOTTO: The life of the land is perpetuated in righteousness

POPULATION: 1,062,000; rank, 39th

LARGEST CITY: Honolulu, pop. 805,266

CAPITAL: Honolulu

LAND: 6,425 square miles; rank, 47th

POPULATION DENSITY: 165.3 per square mile; rank, 13th

RACIAL MIX: 60.5% Asian and Pacific islanders; 33.0% white; 1.8% black. Hispanic heritage: 7.4%.

Uniquely Hawaii

SEA AND SKI: It snows in Hawaii. Almost every year, the 13,000-foot summits of Mauna Kea and Mauna Loa are topped with snow in January and February.

ROOM ADDITION: Lava flowing into the ocean from Kilauea volcano has added about 20 acres to the Big Island since 1983.

ROYAL PAST: The only state in the USA with a royal background, Hawaii recognizes King Kamehameha I, who united all the islands in the early 19th century, with a state holiday on June 11.

POPULAR IMPORT: Pineapples were brought to Hawaii by visiting whalers in the 1800s. Lanai, the Pineapple Isle, is owned by Dole. Most of the 2,000 residents work at the company's pineapple plantation.

NAME CHANGE: The Hawaiian Islands were originally called the Sandwich Islands after the British Earl of Sandwich.

Voices
of Hawaii

Patrick Omo, 27
Maintenance man
Anahola, Hawaii

"I really love it here. I like the outdoor life. Hunting, fishing, wild boar. That's what's good about it here. This is paradise. Everyday as soon as I wake up, I think about paradise. Hawaiians are private people. They like to be by themselves. They share things with their family. That's what our style is. Aloha. We get mad. But we get happy again."

Mike Reilly, 15
Student
Kalapana, Hawaii

"We had to evacuate our house three days before Christmas because of the volcano. Our new house is up high where the lava can't get us, hopefully. When the lava hits the ocean, it explodes and makes new sand. I think I was the first person to make a castle out of the new sand. I love the volcano. It's exciting."

Andrea Fernandez, 26
Flower shop clerk
Kailua Kona, Hawaii

"The most popular flowers are plumeria. That's what most people will see when they get off the airplane. That's the traditional welcome lei. In Hawaii, leis are a form of saying, 'I appreciate you.' There's a lei for every occasion. We learn to make them from the time we're young. It comes innate in our culture. My auntie taught me how to make them."

Nan Decoite, 16
Student
Makawao, Maui

"In Hawaii, we get to stay kids longer. When I went to the mainland, I noticed how mature all the teen-agers are. I guess they see and experience things earlier. We do more outside things. I call up friends and we go to the beach. We paddle canoes in the ocean. I'm involved in 4-H where I am raising a steer."

Keoki Grace, 34
Mason
Kailua Kona, Hawaii

"I'm home-grown Hawaiian. I grew up in the water. Surfing looks easy, but when you get in there, it's a different story. You've got to respect the ocean. If you don't, you get hurt. The waves can crush you, and the undertow can get you. I like the big waves. They're more of a challenge. The bigger, the better."

Kaleo Patterson, 32
Minister
Kapaa, Kauai

"From the days of the missionaries, there's this sense of this place belonging to so many — Japanese, Chinese. There's the rainbow spirit. There's the aloha spirit. The Hawaiian culture is a romantic culture. People have adopted the Hawaiian ways. There's this immense cultural setting."

Vicki Shiroma, 24
Law student
Honolulu, Oahu

"I appreciate the weather every single day. It's too beautiful to take for granted. We always say, 'It's another beautiful day in Hawaii.' We never get tired of the sunshine. We don't miss wearing big, heavy sweaters. The high cost of living is the price we pay for paradise."

Don Ho, 56, is Hawaii's best-known entertainer of Hawaiian ancestry. Ho resigned from the U.S. Air Force to return to his native Oahu. He began a show business career that included a nightclub act, TV show and records.

Happy way of life is key to islands' lure

USA TODAY: A lot of tourists come to see your show. Is there anything you want them to learn about Hawaii or take away when they leave?

HO: Probably more than anything else, what they can take away is the spirit.

USA TODAY: How do you describe the spirit?

HO: It's like a free spirit, an independent spirit, a welcoming spirit. We say, "Hey, you're over here and we have a certain happy way of life here. Try to get caught up in it and everybody try to be positive."

USA TODAY: As a well-known entertainer, do you feel any responsibility as a role model for other Hawaiians?

HO: Only in maybe for them not to be afraid to set their sights a little bit higher than they might normally do. Set their sights for the moon. It behooves every young person in Hawaii to go to the mainland so that they can cope with the world. If you grew up over here, it's like growing up in a tunnel.

USA TODAY: What do you mean?

HO: It's not derogatory. It's like if you grew up in South Carolina and never left your hometown. Hawaii can be like the little isolated town in South Carolina; and that little town can be as much an island as this place is.

USA TODAY: Performing six nights a week is pretty demanding.

HO: Beats working. I like to tell people I retired two years ago, because this is not work really.

USA TODAY: Enjoy it?

HO: Immensely.

USA TODAY: There isn't anything else you'd rather be doing?

HO: Well, I'd rather be flying. I'd much rather be surfing. Or doing nothing.

USA TODAY: Were you ever tempted to live anywhere else?

HO: The temptation was to stay in the Air Force because I loved what I was doing. But somewhere along the line, you just say, "Hey, this is not for me." What I really missed was where I was brought up. I decided to go home and start over again.

Topic: HAWAII

Creative and exciting, we're the future's edge

USA TODAY: What image would you like people on the mainland to have of Hawaii?

WAIHEE: I like the image of Hawaii being a very exciting place; that there are a lot of things happening here; that America's future lies in the Pacific Asian Rim; and that Hawaii is the farthest outpost of the country. It's a kind of place where you could be creative, and it's creative in an East-West kind of crosscurrent.

USA TODAY: The Fourth of July weekend is coming up. Is that a big thing here? How does it compare to the islands' Statehood Day in August?

WAIHEE: Well, I think all of those holidays are important to Hawaii. For example, you can go down to Kailua this weekend and probably see a parade that would rival any in the nation. Statehood is important. It really peaked about two years ago, when we celebrated our 25th anniversary as a state. What makes Hawaii really special is the fact that a few years ago we started acknowledging the various ethnic groups for a year.

USA TODAY: How does that work?

WAIHEE: I think that we started with the Japanese migration to Hawaii. Then we celebrated the coming of the Filipinos. This year, we celebrate the "Year of the Hawaiians" and their contributions. We look forward to celebrating the Chinese, and so forth.

USA TODAY: People here wear aloha shirts at work. Do you think people would take Hawaii more seriously as a place to do business if that changed?

WAIHEE: Yes and no. I think there are people passing through who have a hard time looking at the Pacific and working. I studied easier in Michigan because I couldn't stand to go outside in the winter. The problem is that we don't have a Hawaiian business attire. The aloha shirt is too informal for many occasions; on the other hand, the coat and tie may be too formal, or too hot. I want to try to get together a sort of contest among the Hawaiians to come up with a business dress — something more than an aloha shirt, but not a coat and tie.

John D. Waihee III, 41, a Democrat, was elected last year. He is a former state representative.

USA TODAY: Weren't you wearing a Thai shirt around the Capitol last week?

WAIHEE: Yes, I brought it back from Thailand because it was so comfortable, and it is formal. And you know, why not?

USA TODAY: Is this a one-party state?

WAIHEE: Depends on your definition. This state has an awful lot of Democrats. The Democrats are everywhere. But you can see changes. We have two mayors who are Republicans; we have a Republican congresswoman.

USA TODAY: You went to school in Michigan. What differences stand out to you between mainlanders and islanders?

WAIHEE: When I was in Michigan, I knew a lot of people from the country. They were wonderful, just like the people I grew up with on the Big Island. But there was one essential difference, and that is the idea of vastness. I think it affects your thinking when you live on the continent.

USA TODAY: How so?

WAIHEE: There's so much. There's no sense of limitation. On an island, there's the isolation, and there's water on all sides of you all the time. So you get a sense that this is it. Therefore, it's a little bit more precious. This is a special place.

Idaho

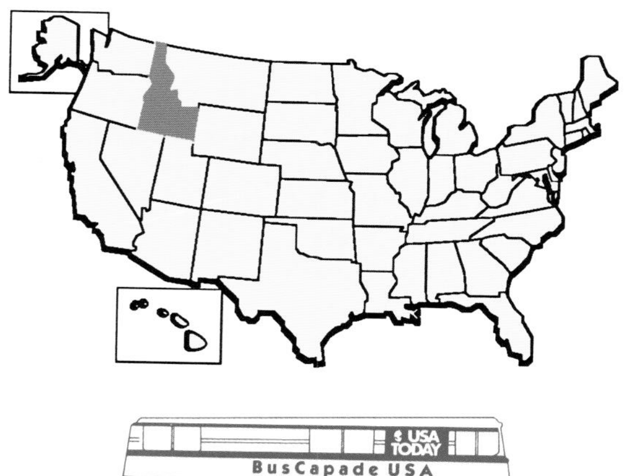

Visited: June 8-9, 1987
Featured in USA TODAY: June 12

"Be careful of imitations. Maine, for example. There's a lot of water in their potatoes."

Idaho Gov. Cecil Andrus

Idaho

Love those potatoes, but picky about people

This is meat and potatoes country. Make that potatoes and meat.

They grow more potatoes here than in any other state in the USA. Average Idahoan eats more of them, too.

"Mash 'em,
"Hash 'em,
"Bake 'em,
"Boil 'em."

Many an Idaho school team cheerleader has led yells like that. The state's No. 1 cheerleader, Gov. **Cecil Andrus**, 55, shares the spirit about spuds.

"I like mine baked, with a little salt, a lot of pepper and a little butter," says the third-term Democrat, who served as secretary of the interior in the Carter administration.

The Guv hucksters the baked Idaho potato as "high in protein, low in calories. Anywhere from 90 to 105. But be careful of imitations. Maine, for example. There's a lot of water in their potatoes."

ANSEL: Proud farmer grows good potatoes.

Statistics for 1986 from the state that carries a "Famous Potatoes" label on its license plate:

■ 8.7 billion pounds of potatoes grown.

■ About one out of every 10 wage earners in Idaho makes a living off the potato industry.

■ New products: Potato ice cream. Potato hand cream.

■ A "Potato King," worth an estimated $500 million. **J.R. Simplot**, 78. His potato-processing plants have sales of more than $1 billion a year. Based in Boise, state capital and largest city (pop. 107,188).

Despite its economic impact, the potato portrayal bothers some. Especially in cities in the west and north. Concerned about a "country bumpkin" image.

But potato producers are proud of the gracefully groomed and mechanically moistened farms in the east and south.

Ansel Haroldsen, 50, state Route 6 near Idaho Falls (pop. 39,734), is one of many moral Mormons on southeastern farms, still strongly oriented to Salt Lake City and Utah. "We grow good potatoes," Haroldsen says simply. "I know people who eat them three times a day."

Idaho's meat and potatoes preference in foods carries over to lifestyles generally. Unpretentious, but pleased and proud. Lovers of their land. Zealously guard their majestic mountains, deep canyons, meandering rivers, vast acres of wilderness. Growth-no growth is a touchy topic.

The Guv chooses his words carefully on that issue. "We're split. Some say pull up the drawbridge. Others want to grow, but are fussy. They want to pick and choose."

Some are more blunt about it. **Cecil Hobdey**, 64, bow-tied lawyer in Gooding (pop. 11,874), doesn't mince words:

"Our slogan is 'Don't Californicate Idaho.' We don't want that fringe faction."

Idaho has yielded two high-profile, modern-day daredevils. Both came from out of state.

■ **Evel Knievel**, motorcycle stunt man of the '70s. From Butte, Mont.

■ **Barbara Morgan**, teachernaut hopeful of the '80s. From Fresno, Calif.

Knievel, 48, attempted a mile-long motorcycle leap over the sinuous Snake River. Hyped it in advance with 62 press conferences across the USA.

Twenty thousand people were on hand and the nation tuned in when he revved up his bike at 3:44 p.m., Sept. 8, 1974. One thousand feet above the ramp, the parachute opened and Evel (real name: Robert) floated to the rocks below. He suffered minor bruises and major embarrassment. The site, near Twin Falls (pop. 26,209), is a tourist stop.

Morgan, 35, was the backup for **Christa McAuliffe**, Concord, N.H., teacher who died aboard the shuttle Challenger Jan. 28, 1986.

That program is on hold, but Barbara is ready. Not only does she want to fly the shuttle, but "I think we ought to go to Mars." While waiting, she teaches grade school in McCall (pop. 2,188).

Sun Valley gives Idaho its sparkle. First major Western ski resort. Built in 1936 by the late **W. Averell Harriman**, then chairman of Union Pacific railroad. Wanted to increase east-west rail travel. It did.

JACK: Ernest Hemingway son.

Ernest Hemingway loved Sun Valley and Idaho. He's buried in Ketchum (pop. 2,200). Son **Jack**, 63, lives there. He's the Idaho outdoorsman personified:

"I fish and hunt and look and photograph. When Sun Valley gets crowded, I go climb some hills. The few people you see in the woods are infinitely preferable to those in the cities."

That's Plain Talk from Idaho.

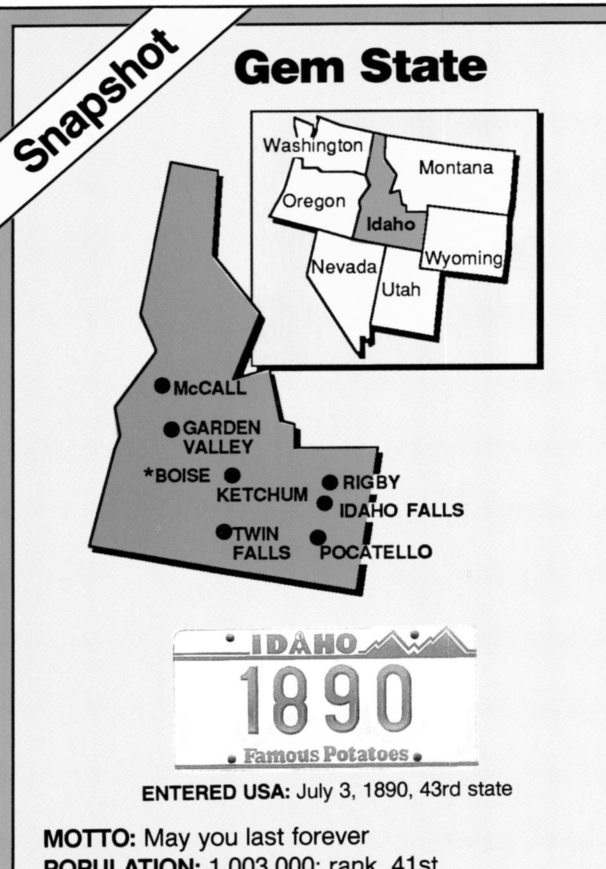

ENTERED USA: July 3, 1890, 43rd state

MOTTO: May you last forever
POPULATION: 1,003,000; rank, 41st
LARGEST CITY: Boise, pop. 107,188
CAPITAL: Boise
LAND: 82,413 square miles; rank, 11th
POPULATION DENSITY: 12.2 per square mile; rank, 44th
RACIAL MIX: 95.5% white; 1.1% American Indian; 0.6% Asian and Pacific islanders; 0.3% black. Hispanic heritage: 3.9%.

Uniquely Idaho

HORSE SENSE: Northern Idaho's Nez Perce Indians trained Appaloosa horses to be mounted from the right side, instead of the usual left. Reason: confuse horse thieves.

BANANA LIFT: The world's first ski chairlift began operation in December 1936 at Sun Valley. A Union Pacific engineer got the inspiration from a banana plantation in South America where he saw cables with hooks used to load bananas onto boats.

JUNIOR GENIUS: Philo Farnsworth, credited with inventing the TV tube in 1922 at age 16, drew his original designs while still in high school in Rigby.

SAILING HIGH: The St. Joe River is the highest navigable river in the world — 2,198 feet above sea level.

HOT WATER: Southern Idaho has more than 100 mineral springs. The waters of Warm Springs are 170 degrees Fahrenheit.

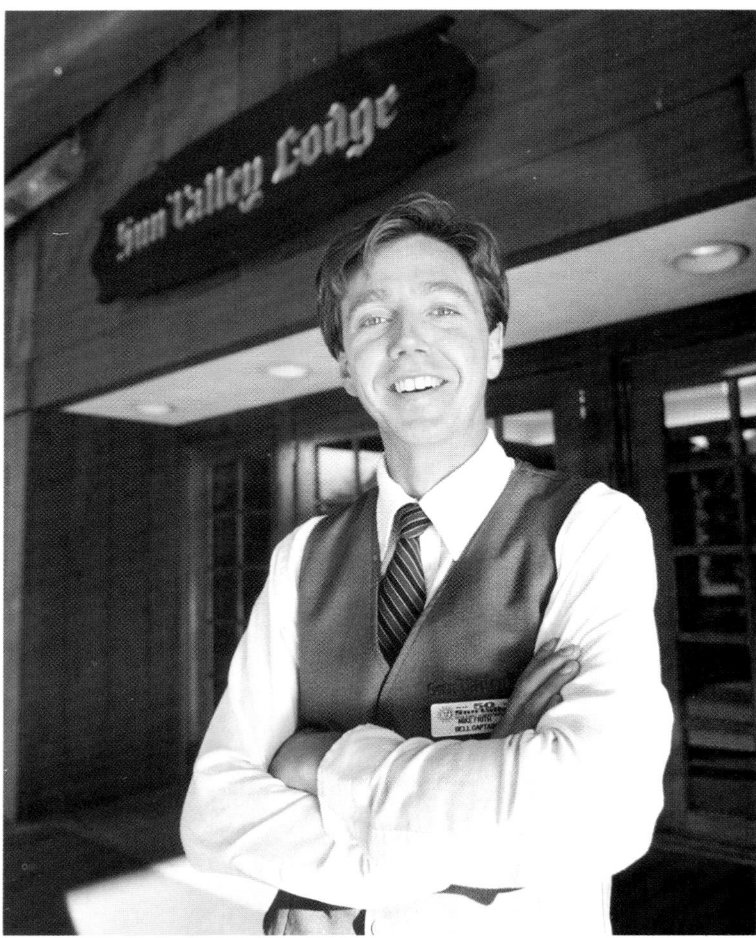

Mike Frith, 29
Bell captain, Sun Valley Lodge
Ketchum

"I ski about a hundred days a year. You can usually ski here into the summer if you hike up a mountain with your skis on your back. The outdoors is a major motivation for everyone that works here. There's a tremendous number of health nuts in Sun Valley. People ski, hike, camp, raft down rivers, ride mountain bicycles. They don't call it Sun Valley for nothing."

Dick Andersen, 40
Assistant manager,
Sun Valley Lodge
Ketchum

"To me Sun Valley is the hub of Idaho. There's a mystique to it. It's a combination of the geographic location and the people who come here and work here. The stars don't get bothered here. They can walk into a bar and people won't mob them. The winter brings people here and the summer keeps them here."

Voices
of Idaho

Rick Fehringer, 29, right, with brother Alan
Potato farmer
American Falls

"They call us spud farmers. I've been involved in it all my life. I took a welding course at Idaho State University and decided that in farming I could be my own boss. I personally think Idaho has the best tasting potatoes. Honestly I do. My personal preference of potatoes is french fries. French fries over baked potatoes anyday."

Diane Westerberg, 28
Secretary
Boise

"I'm a potato farmer's daughter. I used to pull boards. The trucks loaded up with potatoes would pull up to the storage bins, and I'd pull the boards out so the potatoes would fall down the sides. We worked to get food in our mouths, not for paychecks. We had meat and potatoes twice a day. I still love potatoes, but I do like rice once in a while."

Don Weilmunster, 56
Rancher
Garden Valley

"On a ranch, you're on your own. You don't have anyone else looking after you. The breaks you get are the breaks you make. I come down to the city to see the asphalt, but usually I'm up in the mountains breathing air that you can't see."

Angie Williams, 18
Student
Pocatello

"It's really small here. My cousins from Pittsburgh thought Pocatello was a farm instead of a city. They thought it was one big potato farm. Well, I've never even seen a potato field! For a while, I felt like this city was dying. A lot of the industries closed down. But we're coming back. Some of the stores are offering rent-free space just so people come in."

Britta Mabott, 12
Student
Boise

"Idaho is cool. Every summer my family goes up to the mountains and lives off the stuff we catch. We have fish for breakfast and dinner. I go hunting ducks with my Dad. Last season I had one shot, but I missed because the duck turned away."

***Barbara Morgan**, 35, of McCall, Idaho, is the second "teachernaut." The first, Christa McAuliffe, perished in the Challenger disaster.*

When NASA says 'Go,' I'll be ready

USA TODAY: What do tourists like about McCall?

MORGAN: It's beautiful. I can look out my window and see a lake and snow-capped mountains. I live in the middle of a huge forest on the edge of a lake.

USA TODAY: How would you describe Idahoans?

MORGAN: I hate to put labels on people. But I would say people here are self-reliant and optimistic, and even though our economy is down, we're looking forward to the future.

USA TODAY: What are your duties with the space program?

MORGAN: I've done a lot of speaking at schools and to different education, professional, and civic groups, and government agencies. What I'm most interested in is education and our future.

USA TODAY: Are students receiving the kind of education that will equip them to be a part of the nation's role in space?

MORGAN: We need to elevate the status of knowledge and learning.

USA TODAY: In what ways?

MORGAN: Teachers should be allowed to be professionals. A teaching degree should be a graduate degree. You should have teaching materials. Sometimes I have trouble finding chalk for my classroom.

USA TODAY: How have your students dealt with the Challenger accident that killed your predecessor, Christa McAuliffe?

MORGAN: It's very sad. We go on and look toward the future.

USA TODAY: When will you go up in space?

MORGAN: NASA will send a teacher when it is ready, and when my shuttle commander says, "Come on, let's go," I'll be ready.

USA TODAY: What are your thoughts as you prepare for your journey into space?

MORGAN: I hope many of us get an opportunity to leave this Earth and have a view of Earth from space. It's human nature to live and learn and explore. People in Idaho are explorers, and we can't wait until the shuttle starts flying again.

Topic: IDAHO

Growing, competing and bouncing back

USA TODAY: What has changed in Idaho since you first served as governor in 1971?

ANDRUS: Our population has gone up from 670,000 to well over a million. And we had somewhat of an exodus during the depression that parts of America have been struggling through. That has stabilized and bottomed out. We have a little plant coming into the Coeur d'Alene area. We've got one down in the southeast. We've got a reasonably large addition to an existing business here. The atmosphere has changed.

USA TODAY: How has Idaho responded to the changes?

ANDRUS: Idaho is more aware of the competitive nature of the world and what we have to do to perpetuate ourselves. Our basic economy now has gone through some very devastating times and we are now out there competing with the rest of them. We're the 11th largest in size geographically within the 50 states. We've got 82,000 square miles and roughly 53 million acres.

USA TODAY: Any difference in outlook in the regions?

ANDRUS: The southeast would be more conservative philosophically. I don't mean monetarily. You could take a test anywhere in the state and find that people are fiscally responsible. In the northern corner, they might be a little more relaxed in their lifestyle than you would find in the southeastern corner or in the Boise area.

USA TODAY: What made you decide to run for governor again?

ANDRUS: John Evans, my predecessor, was not going to run. The list of Democrats who could be elected was very short. I refused to accept the doldrums that the economy was in. I said we had to make an investment in the state.

USA TODAY: You said in your State of the State that Idaho is perceived to be a haven for white supremacists. How have you tried to remedy that?

ANDRUS: The attorney general — a Republican — and I drew up a bill that we thought was very tight and would give us the right of confiscation of their property — like you do with a drug dealer. The one way to really drive them out was, if they violated the law, to confiscate their property.

***Cecil Andrus**, 55, a Democrat, served two previous terms as governor, from 1971 to 1977, and was reelected in 1986. He also was U.S. secretary of the interior from 1977 to 1981.*

USA TODAY: But that bill wasn't passed.

ANDRUS: It failed because of lobbying efforts of the National Rifle Association and others. We did pass some legislation but it wasn't as strong.

USA TODAY: Idaho has a striking shape. Does it make sense?

ANDRUS: No. It shouldn't. The surveyors were supposed to go north and cut off a piece of Montana. We would have been rectangular. But the story goes that they were very drunk for days on end and got on the wrong ridge line.

USA TODAY: What difference would it have made if Idaho had that big chunk of Montana?

ANDRUS: Sizewise, it would have increased us by about 40 percent. Instead of being the 11th largest state, we probably would have been the third or fourth largest. Then with all the mountains, if you had stomped us out flat, we would have been bigger than Texas.

Illinois

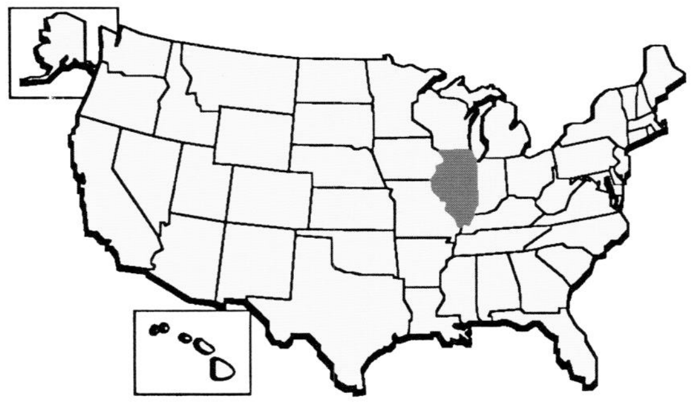

Visited: March 19-20, 1987
Featured in USA TODAY: March 23

"There's a lot of Lincoln's philosophy in use in this state. The ideas of freedom and equality will go on forever . . ."

Michael Zecher
Teacher
Auburn, Ill.

Illinois

Infighting in vogue in Land of Lincoln

Here in the Inland Empire, where **Abe Lincoln** warned against a "house divided" in 1858, divisiveness and discord are a way of life in 1987.

Old-timers tell outsiders not to take the infighting too seriously.

"It's all a game. Politicians here consider public fighting fun. In the end, or sometimes in the beginning, they all make deals with each other and everything works out," says **Thomas A. Reynolds Jr.**, 58, one of the area's veteran lawyers.

True, the fate of the nation is not at stake in the April 7 Chicago election, as it was in Lincoln's day. But some are sensitive about how the USA views the blatant black vs. white campaign.

WASHINGTON: Now Chicago's boss.

Black Mayor **Harold Washington** is expected to whip three whites — two other Democrats and a Republican.

Politics has always been a brawl and broil affair in Illinois. Upstate against downstate. Chicago northsiders against southsiders. But the bombination of the black-white division is new in this decade.

Many downstaters are fed up with the mercurial muckraking. "They should give Chicago to Wisconsin. Free of charge. But they wouldn't take it," says **Dan Moore**, 48, a painter and sandblaster in Morrisonville (pop. 1,208).

Others shrug and shake off the storms in the Windy City. "I don't muck with nobody who don't muck with me," says **Lon Pippin**, 78, a semi-retired truck driver and garageman in Kankakee (pop. 30,141).

Whatever their prejudices in politics, or sports — which is the other great divider or uniter here — most Illinoisans are clear about their heritage.

LINCOLN: Still center of Illinois pride.

Ask them what they are most proud of, the list is quick and short:

- Abraham Lincoln.
- **Richard Daley**.
- The Chicago Bears.

Downstate, these three generally are mentioned in that order. In Chicago, the list sometimes is reversed.

The Lincoln legacy lives above all else. Gov. **James Thompson** got a taste of it recently when a picture was published showing him with his feet up on his desk, which was once occupied by Lincoln.

"Did I get mail!" Thompson said. "Even though Lincoln probably had his feet on top of that desk more often than I have, nobody thought I had a right to do that."

Despite that political legacy, modern-day heroes are mostly from sports or entertainment.

- **Oprah Winfrey**, 33, the nationally syndicated TV talk show host making them forget **Phil Donahue**, who skipped to New York.
- **Michael Jordan**, No. 23 of the Chicago Bulls, whose 36.8 point average per game eases the pain of the Bulls' so-so record.
- **Harry Caray**, 70, beloved broadcaster of the Chicago Cubs games, recovering from a stroke suffered last month.

Except for Gov. Thompson, called "Big Jim" or "Papa Doc," politicians don't make the popularity list.

The mood of Illinois is as varied as its landscape.

Pragmatism prevails on the prairies, including the campus of the University of Illinois at Champaign-Urbana.

"Students here are real laid back. They are more concerned about getting a degree, getting a job, getting somewhere in the world than they are about changing the world," says **Erin Donahue**, 26.

In Chicago, the cynicism crops up. Cab driver **Dan Van Hecke**, who turned 44 on Sunday: "I'm going to start doing my income tax return around 3 a.m., when the street dies down. When I finish, I'm gonna find me a shrink. I'm probably the only cab driver in Chicago who pays income tax."

That's Plain Talk from Illinois.

POSITIVE ATTITUDE: We 'have an appreciation for quality,' says Peoria Mayor Jim Maloof, 67, holding a Stetson hat — a gift from the mayor of Peoria, Ariz. In rear is city hall, new civic center and sculpture *Sonar Tide*.

Snapshot

Prairie State

CHICAGO
KANKAKEE
DANVILLE
SPRINGFIELD
AUBURN
MORRISONVILLE
EAST ST. LOUIS
Minnesota
Michigan
Wisconsin
Iowa
Illinois
Ohio
Indiana
Kentucky
Missouri

illinois Land of Lincoln
1818

ENTERED USA: Dec. 3, 1818, 21st state

MOTTO: State sovereignty, national union
POPULATION: 11,553,000; rank, 6th
LARGEST CITY: Chicago, pop. 2,992,472
CAPITAL: Springfield, pop. 101,570
LAND: 55,645 square miles; rank, 24th
POPULATION DENSITY: 207.6 per square mile; rank, 11th
RACIAL MIX: 80.8% white; 14.7% black; 1.4% Asian and Pacific islanders. Hispanic heritage: 5.6%.

Uniquely Ill.

FIRESTARTER: According to legend, the Great Chicago Fire of 1871 started when Mrs. Patrick O'Leary's cow knocked over a lantern in a barn. The fire raged for 24 hours.

BAGEL BONANZA: Lender's, in Mattoon, is the largest bagel bakery in the USA. The 54,500-square-foot plant produces more than 1 million bagels a day.

CREDIT CHECK: In the early 1800s, the directors of the Shawneetown National Bank refused to give a loan to Chicago because they didn't think the town would amount to anything.

TOBACCO ROAD: The state's only cigarette manufacturing plant is at the penitentiary in Menard. Only customers: inmates.

TOWN HERO: Postville was renamed Lincoln in 1853 in honor of Abraham Lincoln. Lincoln himself christened the new town with the juice of an Illinois watermelon.

Voices
of Illinois

Michael Zecher, 23
Teacher
Auburn

"There's a lot of Lincoln's philosophy in use in this state. The ideas of freedom and equality will go on forever, and as long as those two ideas are alive, America will keep on going."

Tina Sipula, 33
Operator,
Clare House
of Hospitality
Bloomington

"What's unique about the shelter is that it's a home, not an institution. Treating each other with kindness and compassion is one of the things we have forgotten in our country."

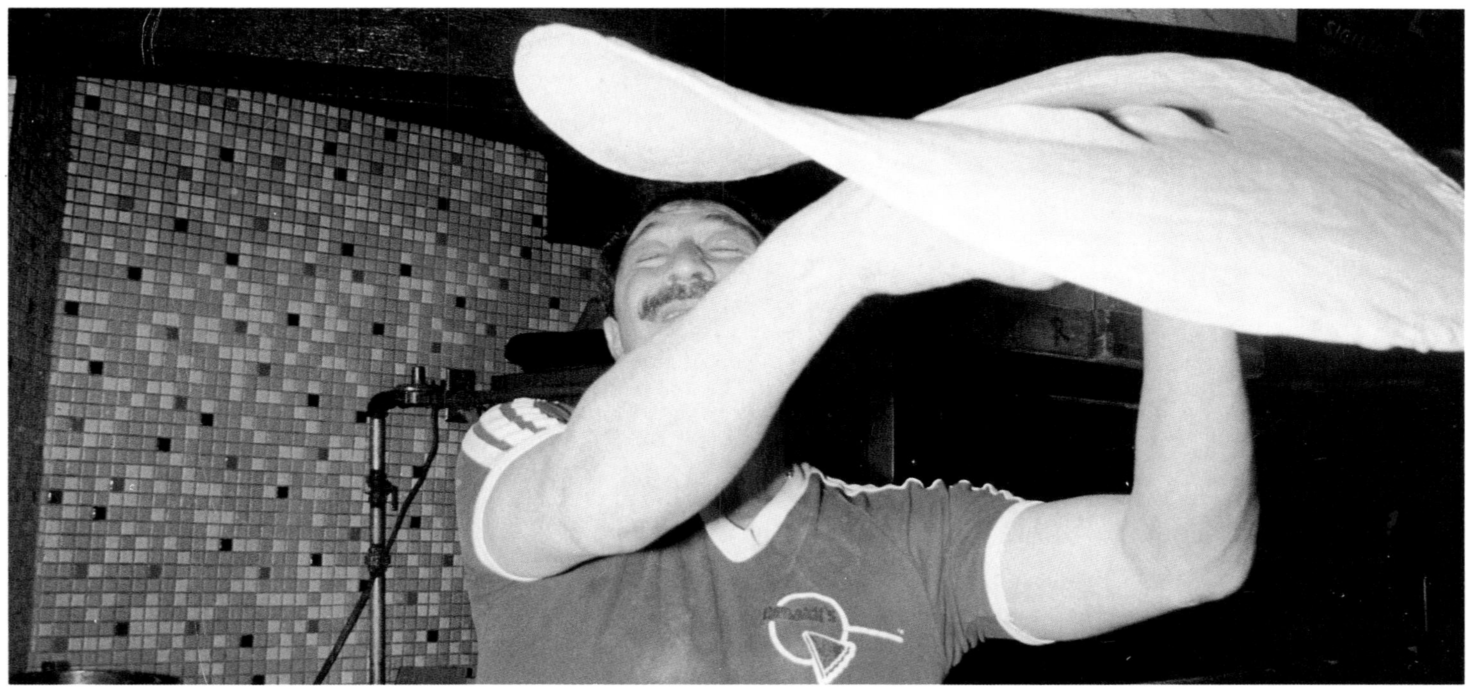

Frank Bruscianelli, 42
Pizza parlor owner
Chicago

"The activity is constant here. The city goes 24 hours a day. There are many fine pizza makers in Chicago. I don't think the Chicago taste is geared toward the fast-food type of product. I don't think Chicagoans mind a few minutes wait in order to get the quality product they expect. Chicagoans know pizza."

Scott Sanderson, 31
Pitcher, Chicago Cubs
Chicago

"A lot of people in Chicago have lived there for years and years. It's not like California where everyone comes from somewhere else. In the Midwest, there's more tradition and less turnover. Families grow up together for generations. There's a sense of loyalty."

Clare Sente, 24
Graduate student
Champaign

"There's Chicago, and there's Illinois. The suburbs look on the city as outsiders. It's kind of a source of amusement. By living in the suburbs, we have the best of both worlds. We have the name and recognition of Chicago, without the B.S. they have to put up with."

Mike Davis, 37
Teacher
New Lenox

"I grew up in a small town, and the town I now live in is not any bigger than the town I come from. The small towns contain the people that reflect the real Illinois. They retain the heritage of what Illinois was really like. Just about any small town in Illinois has something special about it. After talking to the people that live there you will learn what they hold special."

Hazel Morgan, 58
Welder
Danville

"I like a smaller town. I was born and raised in a town of 1,300, but I feel Danville has a lot to offer. I like the change of seasons here in the Midwest. Danville offers plenty of recreational activities, especially places to fish, my hobby."

Charlton Heston, 63, was born in Evanston, Ill., and lives now in Beverly Hills. He decided to be an actor at age 5. He's made more than 50 films, including The Ten Commandments *and* Ben Hur, *for which he won an Oscar.*

Midwest upbringing prepared me for life

USA TODAY: What was it like growing up in Wilmette, Ill.?

HESTON: I went to two excellent schools. New Trier High School was a marvelous school which gave me the beginnings of training as an actor. I went to Northwestern University on an acting scholarship from New Trier. So I really owe both schools a great deal and thus the state of Illinois.

USA TODAY: Did your childhood in Illinois prepare you for life as an actor?

HESTON: Certainly. Let's put it this way, growing up in the Midwest prepared me to be an adult human being, to be a man. Northwestern and New Trier prepared me to be an actor.

USA TODAY: Do you ever go back to Northwestern University?

HESTON: Yes, many times. And I met my wife there, so I really owe a lot to that place.

USA TODAY: So you have strong ties to Illinois?

HESTON: I think both of us also owe to Chicago our Midwestern identity. I'm very proud of being a Midwesterner.

USA TODAY: What are the people like there?

HESTON: I think they are indeed the backbone of America. You can come closer to defining an American by picking someone from Illinois or Missouri or Michigan or Kansas than you can from the East or West Coasts, which have become far more internationalized. It's perhaps appropriate that Illinois' most distinguished citizen is Abraham Lincoln. He comes from what New Yorkers and Angelenos call fly-over country.

USA TODAY: What are some of your favorite spots in Illinois?

HESTON: The lake is very impressive. I spent a great deal of time on the Lake Michigan beach with my wife. And the Chicago Art Institute.

USA TODAY: Everyone remembers you for your larger-than-life, heroic roles.

HESTON: I always challenge the description "larger-than-life." You can't describe Tom Jefferson and Cardinal Richelieu and Mark Antony and Michelangelo as larger-than-life because they lived.

Topic: ILLINOIS

Even without oceans, we still pull tourists

USA TODAY: Illinois spends more than any other state on tourism. Does it pay off?

THOMPSON: It has paid off for us. Our expenditures on tourism promotion will run about $15.5 million next year. That's more than Florida or California or New York.

USA TODAY: What is Illinois selling to tourists?

THOMPSON: We're a different kind of state, and we finally started to promote the difference. Nobody flies into Chicago to lie on the beach for two weeks. On the other hand, more people fly into Chicago to attend conventions and trade shows than to any other city in North America.

USA TODAY: And you're promoting other parts of the state?

THOMPSON: That's where we've really stepped up our efforts. In the past, the notion that the state would be putting up dollars to promote events in Rockford or Peoria would have been regarded as fanciful. But we've done that. We've succeeded.

USA TODAY: Does the rest of the state sometimes feel like a suburb of Chicago?

THOMPSON: There's always this downstate feeling that Chicago gets it all. We've got the cultural attractions. And we've worked hard to improve the underlying tourism infrastructure. So, we understand the dollars that are involved in business tours and the different attractions in Illinois, and we intend to be very vigorous in that.

USA TODAY: Can competition between regions go too far?

THOMPSON: People will always put their regions first. But I think there's a greater understanding that a dollar earned in Chicago pays taxes to Springfield, to support a school in Carbondale, and vice versa. Business and labor have been drawn closer together, and I think I played a part in that.

USA TODAY: You've been able to lure the Japanese here to do business. How about exporting Illinois products?

James R. Thompson, 51, a Republican, has been governor since 1976. Earlier, Thompson, a native of Chicago, taught at Northwestern University Law School and was a U.S. attorney.

THOMPSON: There has been an increase in exporting, but the great bulk of the work that we've done has been to bring manufacturing facilities here.

USA TODAY: Aside from an occasional Super Bowl victory, Illinois teams have not had a stellar record. Yet nearly everyone seems to be a sports fan.

THOMPSON: Absolutely.

USA TODAY: What does that tell us about Illinois?

THOMPSON: We're a great sports state. Yeah, we'd like to be winners all the time, but we can't. That doesn't mean we don't compete fiercely or enjoy the competition. Chicago is probably one of the few cities in the USA that is represented in every pro sport by a basically good team. But we're made to look like a cow town next to Indianapolis. Might as well say it, it's true.

USA TODAY: Are there any plans in the works to change that perception?

THOMPSON: I finally got the legislature to adopt a stadium authority that will build a new ballpark. The question of the Bears stadium needs to be settled, but so long as they insist they're going to build it in the private sector, I really don't have any say over that. But we ought to start catching up to Indianapolis.

Indiana

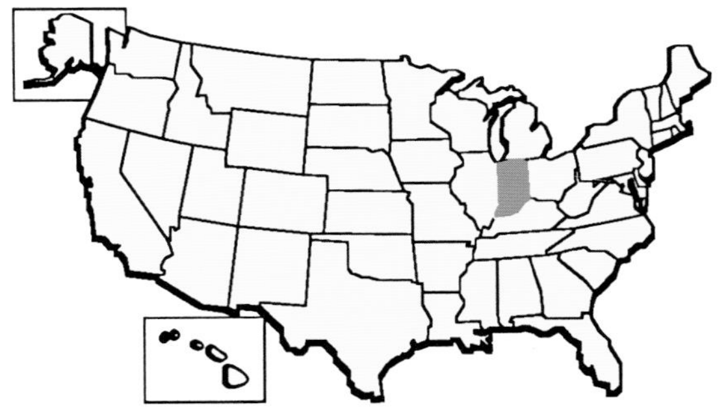

Visited: March 30-31, 1987
Featured in USA TODAY: April 3

"Basketball was invented in Springfield, Mass. But they really learned how to play it in Indiana."

Indiana Gov. Robert Orr

Indiana

Hoosiers are bouncing more than basketballs

Yes, basketball is king here.

But, it's not quite everything.

Yes, this week the real-life bouncing balls far outscored the make-believes in the movie *Hoosiers.*

But, on the same day that **Bobby Knight**'s national champions were wildly and worshipfully welcomed back to the Indiana University campus in Bloomington, the governor was quietly but almost as proudly dedicating a new General Motors plant in Anderson with GM boss **Roger Smith** on hand from Detroit.

Yes, Gov. **Robert D. Orr** and thousands of other Hoosiers were in New Orleans for Monday night's Indiana-Syracuse title game.

But, the governor took with him a group of state legislators and lobbied hard for his $400 million program called A-plus for Educational Excellence.

Yes, "Hoosier Culture," as they call it here, deserves its homespun image. It's the kind of no-frills lifestyle celebrated by Seymour-native **John Mellencamp** in his hit song, *Small Town.*

But, there is nothing monotonous or visionless in the bounce-back efforts in these areas beyond basketball:

- Education.
- Industrial development.
- Tourism, lured by major sports events and marvelous meeting facilities.

Indianapolis, the capital and largest city, is a sports mecca. The Hoosier Dome, a 61,000-seat, covered center completed in 1984, is the tip-off.

The Hoosier Dome stole the NFL Colts from Baltimore. It will bring throngs of visitors from two continents for the Pan American Games this August.

The Hoosier Dome is what Gov. **James Thompson** of Illinois had in mind when he said "Indianapolis makes Chicago look like a cow town."

Not many years ago, Indianapolis had the cow town label and deserved it. "The dome has just changed the complexion completely," says its marketing VP, **Bob Bedell**, 39, a transplanted Hoosier huckster by way of New York and Washington.

Manufacture of the "Magnequench," an iron-based magnet material for use in electric motors, at GM's new Anderson plant is only the latest industrial prize.

Last month, Lafayette, home of Purdue University, was picked for a Japanese Fuji-Isuzu auto plant. Indiana is much more industrial than its image.

The education effort comes in a state which always wanted to be No. 1 in basketball, but for years seemed content to be rated No. 47 in public high school educational standards.

Bobby Knight, who is boosting the governor's program, says Indiana can be No. 1 in both.

The program is spearheaded by State Supt. **H. Dean Evans**, who was recruited last year from the prestigious Lilly Endowment.

But, back to basketball.

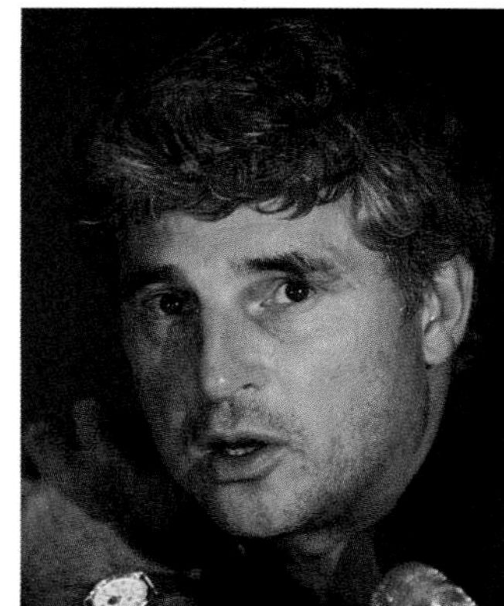

NO. 1: IU coach Bobby Knight says Indiana can be tops in education, too.

"Basketball was invented in Springfield, Mass. But they really learned how to play it in Indiana," says Gov. Orr.

Hoosier hysteria is not focused just on IU. There are two high school hot spots.

- Marion (pop. 35,874). The Giants won an unprecedented third straight state championship last weekend. This Saturday night, they play Kentucky's champs, Clay County, in the Mid-American Classic in Indianapolis for bragging rights between the fiercely competitive neighboring states.
- Noblesville (pop. 12,056). Their Indiana girl's state champs play Kentucky's king, Laurel County, in the same classic Saturday afternoon.

GIANTS FANS: Raising rafters for Marion at state finals.

In Bloomington, Marion and Noblesville, basketball really is the total talk of the town this week.

Jim Mantz, 42, a Bloomington auto mechanic: "Around here, you can tell when a baby is born. If it's a boy, a basketball hoop is stuck up on the garage the next day."

Mary Dennison, 34, a Marion hotel checkout clerk: "I think it makes sense that Coach (**Bill**) **Green** doesn't let the players have girlfriends. It keeps their minds on the game."

That's Plain Talk from Indiana.

Snapshot

Hoosier State

Michigan
Wisconsin
LAFAYETTE MARION
NOBLESVILLE
INDIANAPOLIS *
Indiana
Ohio
Illinois
Kentucky
BLOOMINGTON

ENTERED USA: Dec. 11, 1816, 19th state

MOTTO: The Crossroads of America
POPULATION: 5,504,000; rank, 14th
LARGEST CITY: Indianapolis, pop. 710,280
CAPITAL: Indianapolis
LAND: 35,932 square miles; rank, 38th
POPULATION DENSITY: 153.2 per square mile; rank, 15th
RACIAL MIX: 91.2% white; 7.6% black; 0.4% Asian and Pacific islanders. Hispanic heritage: 1.6%.

Uniquely Ind.

TOP POPPER: Indiana is the USA's top popcorn producer, growing about 148 million pounds, one-fourth of the national total.

SPORTS HERO: The first high school athlete to appear on the cover of "Sports Illustrated" magazine was Rick Mount, star at Lebanon High School and Mr. Basketball in 1966.

MUSIC REVOLUTION: Production of the first compact audio disc in the USA began at Terre Haute, Sept. 21, 1984, at Digital Audio Disc Corp.

FOOT DOCTOR: The USA's most famous arch support was invented in 1905 by LaPorte native Dr. William M. Scholl.

DUCK SOUP: Indiana is the USA's No. 1 supplier of duck feet. The state exports its supply to the Far East, where it is a delicacy.

THE KING: The last public performance by Elvis Presley was in Market Square Arena, Indianapolis, June 26, 1977.

Voices

of Indiana

Julia Carson, 49
State senator/clothing store owner
Indianapolis

"Indianapolis no longer has the image of a sleepy city. The whole amateur sports image has put the city on the map. It's a convention mecca. People come here and they want to come back."

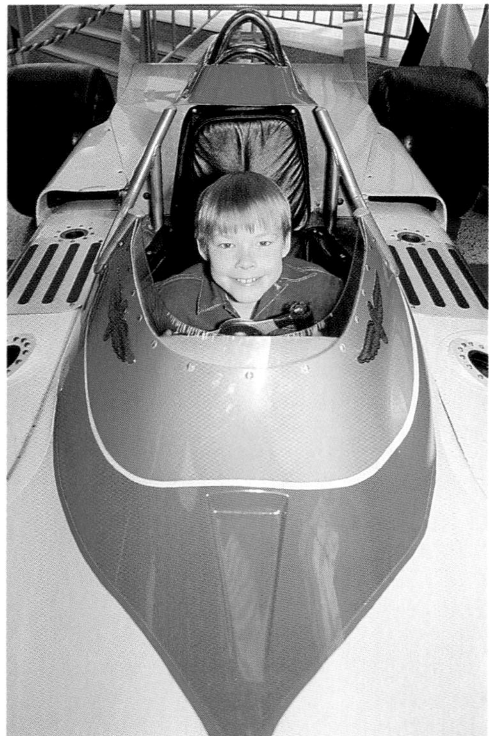

Roger Myers, 11
Sixth-grader
Camby

"I think the Indianapolis 500 is pretty neat. I like to see crashes, but I don't like to see people get hurt in them. I like fast cars. It's a neat race and it's in the main city of Indiana. Our town is country-like. You don't have to hear real loud cars. We can go swimming in the back yard."

Marcie Webb, 20
Computer operator
Richmond

"I like living in a small town. I like knowing everybody, and there is not too much trouble here. I'm more comfortable when I am aware of everything and I know what is going on. I feel safe and comfortable in my small town. I love working in the antique business. I'm learning things everyday. I don't collect anything in particular yet."

Christopher Mobely, 26
Graduate student, Purdue University
East Chicago

"Life in Indiana is at a slower pace. The people are conservative, but straightforward. You know where you stand. If they like you, you know it. If they don't like you, you know that, too."

Ann Woolman, 26
Public relations manager,
Indianapolis Project
Indianapolis

"Indianapolis citizens are very enthusiastic and very committed to their city. There is lots of volunteerism in the city. There is an unusual spirit of cooperation between the citizens and the government and the private sector. The city has done a major turnaround in the last 5 to 10 years."

Glenn Ryan, 61
Rose grower
Pershing

"I've been here all my life. I've never wanted to leave. It's not a big state, but I like it. The people in Indiana are the best there are in the world. They're agreeable and they try to help you. It's the Hoosier state. I used to follow sports quite a bit. But my favorite thing to do is stay around home and visit my grandchildren."

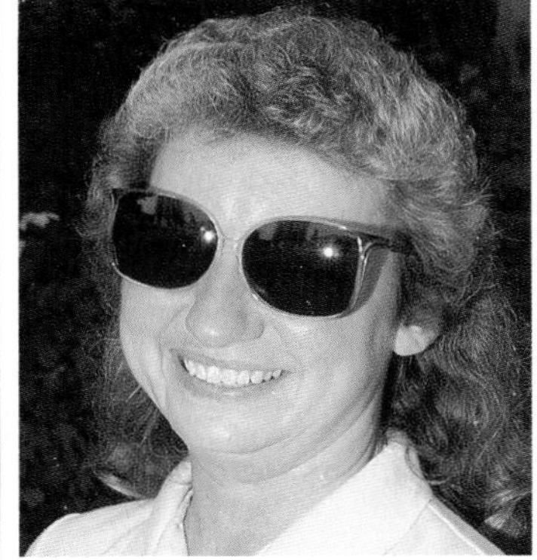

Edith Grenard, 35
Bank teller
Lafayette

"There's so much variety here with the seasons, and you're not overwhelmed with people. It's really comfortable. There's a lot of opportunity — high pay rates and a good chance for advancement. In Lafayette especially, there's the opportunity to go to Purdue without paying out-of-state tuition. It's great to live near a university."

Tom Carnegie, 67
Chief announcer,
Indy 500
Indianapolis

"Of the true Hoosier, I would say basketball is their first love and then the Speedway is No. 2. The 500 appeals to all ages. It captures and reaches out and grabs them and stays with them throughout their lives."

Jane Pauley, 36, is co-host of NBC's Today show. She joined Today in 1976 after working as a reporter in Chicago and Indianapolis, her hometown.

We're not neurotic; we use common sense

USA TODAY: You grew up in Indianapolis. How often do you get home?

PAULEY: Probably once a year, minimum. My parents are retired and spend a good part of the cold-weather months in Florida, so that cuts back on how often I get home.

USA TODAY: What is different about someone with Midwestern roots?

PAULEY: My perspective on New York City was that there was the USA, and then there was New York City. This was somewhere in the vicinity of London, Paris and Rome. Same solar system, but different planets. I always felt that all Americans were alike, and the quintessential American was from the Middle West, from the middle class — the middle.

USA TODAY: How do people see Midwesterners?

PAULEY: While people might look at us as plain, bland and colorless, they also know we are not neurotic, that we are not flaky, that we have a lot of common sense and a certain healthy, positive quality that, for someone in my business, is very effective.

USA TODAY: How about Indianapolis?

PAULEY: Big-city people tend to think of Indianapolis as cows and chickens roaming freely through the street. That hasn't been true in this century!

USA TODAY: What was it like, being on television in your hometown?

PAULEY: Television is television. You don't know if there's an audience of 1,000 or a hundred million. You're still sitting there all by yourself in a studio, hoping you're not making a fool of yourself.

USA TODAY: How can being a star of NBC's *Today* be compared with working on local television?

PAULEY: That was pretty big time, when you're just out of college as I was. Indianapolis was something like the 13th or the 15th largest television market in the country. That's very big.

USA TODAY: You recently celebrated 10 years on *Today*. How much of that Midwestern perseverance has guided you through?

PAULEY: My boss sometimes says the reason that Jane has been successful so long is that she never stopped being the girl from Indianapolis.

Topic: INDIANA

We showed the rest how to play basketball

USA TODAY: Everybody's talking basketball this week. Indiana University won the NCAA tournament, and people are flocking to the movie *Hoosiers*. How does it feel?

ORR: Well, it feels good, obviously. It's one of those heady moments, but the spotlight is on the team which worked very hard for a long, long time. Coach Bobby Knight made the difference.

USA TODAY: Lots of folks think Coach Knight ought to run for president. Do you think he ought to get into politics?

ORR: He'd be an interesting personage for politics. (Laughter) Most politicians aren't known for being as utterly candid as Bobby Knight, although it's refreshing. But I don't think Bobby Knight's likely to move in that direction.

USA TODAY: How important is basketball to Indiana?

ORR: Temporarily, we stop and rejoice with basketball. It happened this year with Indiana University. It could have been Purdue. It could have been Notre Dame. All of them are very good teams. Basketball was invented in Springfield, Mass. But they really learned how to play it in Indiana.

USA TODAY: Has Indiana changed much from the way it was in the '50s, the period in which *Hoosiers* takes place?

ORR: Farming is not as dominant as it was then. This state, while it has always been a major industrial state, has become much more industrial.

USA TODAY: How has education changed in Indiana?

ORR: School is quite different from 25 years ago. We had a different culture about education. Discipline was more conventional. The relationship with the family had a lot to do with it. There weren't many single-parent families in 1954. But we're on the verge of turning education into something a whole lot more important than it's ever been.

USA TODAY: Your plan to improve schools is having a rocky time in the Legislature.

Robert Orr, 69, a Republican, was elected governor in 1980 and was re-elected in 1984.

ORR: It's landmark legislation. We are changing the way schools will function. We are increasing the state contribution to school budgets from one-third to two-thirds. This introduces accountability.

USA TODAY: How so?

ORR: This requires evaluation of individual schools, measurement of the performance of students. It provides a mechanism to rate schools on results instead of on the basis of their assets, size of the auditorium, the number of books in the library.

USA TODAY: Indiana is the largest steel-producing state but foreign manufacturers subsidize the low cost of steel. What does this mean for Indiana?

ORR: We've got to encourage more deals like the joint venture between Nippon Steel and Inland Steel. And there are other ways ingenuity can help us be more productive and lower costs to be competitive. The problem is, we will employ less people.

USA TODAY: How would you like to be remembered?

ORR: I'd like to be remembered as having spent enough time thinking about the future. I have greatly enjoyed taking a look at China. It is bound to make a huge difference in the future of this world as it finally gets its act together. I'd like to see the country become a part of that.

Iowa

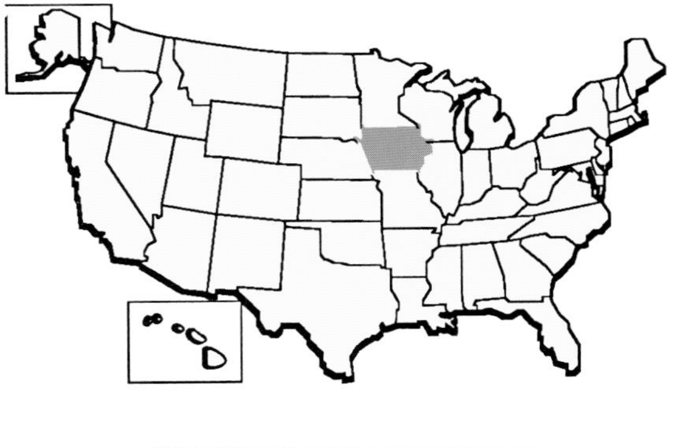

Visited: June 22-24, 1987
Featured in USA TODAY: June 26

"It's the heart of the country. Our doors always used to be open. We would feed anybody who came to the door. It's neighborly and friendly."

Abigail Van Buren
Author of "Dear Abby"
Grew up in Sioux City, Iowa

Iowa

Pigs and tall corn, pols and straight talk

"*This little piggy went to market; this little piggy stayed home . . .*"

That little ditty has been a favorite toe-tapper for parents with their kids since it first appeared in print in the 1740s (in a Mother Goose rhyme). In Iowa, it's more than a rhyme. More pigs go to market here than anywhere else in the USA.

■ 19 million Iowa pigs were butchered last year.

■ Average price: $123.75. A $2.6 billion business.

To feed and fatten all those porkers takes lots of corn. And the tall-corn state produces it.

■ 1.6 billion bushels harvested last year.

■ A $2.2 billion business.

Despite the corn and pig and farm image, only about 12 percent of Iowa's wage earners are on the farm. Ten years ago, Iowa had 130,000 farms. Now it has 109,000. But the same number of acres — 34 million — are still being worked.

DALE CLAUSSEN: Both little piggies will go to market.

The family farms are fewer, but bigger. Like the Claussens' near Le Claire (pop. 2,899) in extreme Eastern Iowa. **Arnold**, 55, and sons **Dale**, 31, **Tom**, 26, and **Kent**, 18, farm 2,000 acres.

"Farming is a business that takes a lot of dollars and a lot of strategy," says Dale. "The key to the farm crisis is to keep diversified. We raise soybeans, corn, hogs, cattle. That way you can hope to make a little profit off something."

Adds **Howard Postma**, 55, near Sanborn (pop. 1,398) in Northwest Iowa, "The Iowa farmer isn't a clodhopper anymore. With modern technology, I'm farming as much land as my dad and three uncles did, and I'm playing golf on the side."

Many farmers who failed have switched to city or suburban life. Iowa cities are growing. Des Moines is an example. State capital and largest city (pop. 190,832). The Des Moines metropolitan area has enjoyed nearly 10 percent growth since the '70s.

Insurance is big. More than 7 percent of Iowa wage earners work for the 251 Iowa-based insurance companies. You can buy protection against hog cholera, hailstorms, tornadoes, rickets.

Some big names in manufacturing make it very big in small Iowa towns:

■ Maytag. Annual sales of $1.7 billion. Headquartered in Newton (pop. 15,292).

■ Winnebago. Annual sales of $424 million. Located in Forest City (pop. 4,270).

Iowa's unemployment rate has dropped to 4.2 percent. The national average is 6.3 percent.

"We've gone from asking for help for the Heartland to offering hope for the Heartland," says Gov. **Terry E. Branstad**, 40, second-term Republican.

Two years out of every four, Iowa imports the full lineup of presidential hopefuls. The party caucuses are still eight months away. Feb. 8, 1988. But announced and unannounced candidates and their followers are crisscrossing cities and cornfields. Most Iowans love the limelight.

They also are proud of the fact that their choice is usually the USA's choice. In 1976, '80, '84, Iowa Democrats picked Carter, Carter, Mondale. So did the national Democrats. Iowa Republicans chose Ford, Bush, Reagan. They missed only on Bush.

"Iowa forces candidates to go out and meet the people, in the living rooms or barns. We want real answers to real questions. You can't win the caucus with glibness," says **Jeanne Hedican**, 41, a Des Moines mother of four.

Iowa exports more than pigs and corn. Some famous names in entertainment, sports, politics and the press grew up in the Hawkeye State. **John Wayne**. **Donna Reed**. **Glen Miller**. **George Gallup**. **Herbert Hoover**. **Bob Feller**. **Wyatt Earp**. **Ann Landers**. **Abigail Van Buren**.

CARR: Optimist shuns cynicism.

Ann and Abby were the Friedman twins in Sioux City (pop. 82,003). Now they are the most widely read advice columnists in the USA. Write out of Chicago and California. Have fond Iowa memories.

Says Abby: "It's the heart of the country. Our doors always used to be open. We would feed anybody who came to the door. It's neighborly and friendly."

That upbeat mood prevails. **Ken Carr**, 36, computer engineer in Mason City (pop. 30,144) describes it:

"It shows up in the schoolkids' faces. When you see a dad at the 4th of July parade with his boy on his shoulders — what else is there? We were brought up to be patriotic. This is what we go to war to protect. To us, it's easier to be optimistic than cynical."

That's Plain Talk from Iowa.

Snapshot

Hawkeye State

Minnesota
Wisconsin
South Dakota
Nebraska
Iowa
Illinois
Missouri
FOREST CITY
SANBORN
MASON CITY
SIOUX CITY
CEDAR RAPIDS
NEWTON
LE CLAIRE
★ DES MOINES

IOWA
1846

ENTERED USA: Dec. 28, 1846, 29th state

MOTTO: Our liberties we prize and our rights we will maintain

POPULATION: 2,851,000; rank, 29th

LARGEST CITY: Des Moines, pop. 190,832

CAPITAL: Des Moines

LAND: 55,965 square miles; rank, 23rd

POPULATION DENSITY: 50.9 per square mile; rank, 33rd

RACIAL MIX: 97.4% white; 1.4% black; 0.4% Asian and Pacific islanders. Hispanic heritage: 0.9%.

Uniquely Iowa

GOVERNMENT GOLD: The 275-foot high dome of the state capitol in Des Moines is gilded in 23-carat gold leaf 1/250,000th-inch thick.

76 TROMBONES: "The Music Man" was written by Meredith Wilson, a Mason City native who used his hometown for inspiration.

POPULATION SHIFT: 130 years ago, only 5 percent of Iowans lived in town. Today, 58 percent do.

BEST BYTES: The first digital computer was developed in 1939 at Iowa State University by mathematician J.V. Atanasoff.

OLD FASHIONED: The largest settlement of Amish west of the Mississippi is at Kalona. Highway signs caution motorists to watch for buggies.

PITCHFORK COUPLE: Stone City is home to Grant Wood's "American Gothic" painting.

Voices
of Iowa

Howard Postma, 55
Farmer
Sanborn

"There's more to life than the dollar bill. That's why you farm. There's so much satisfaction out here that I couldn't put a price on it. Getting your crop hailed out or blown out is all just part of farming. You want to throw in the towel, but you get back up and try again. We're some of the best farmers in the world."

Elaine Smith
Student
Ames

"I came here expecting to meet a lot of people with stereotypes about blacks. I haven't met anyone so narrow-minded that they couldn't see things from the other side. I had serious stereotypes about Iowa before I got here, but the folks were so friendly and nice I had to reform my ideas. If you're open-minded, you can learn. That goes both ways."

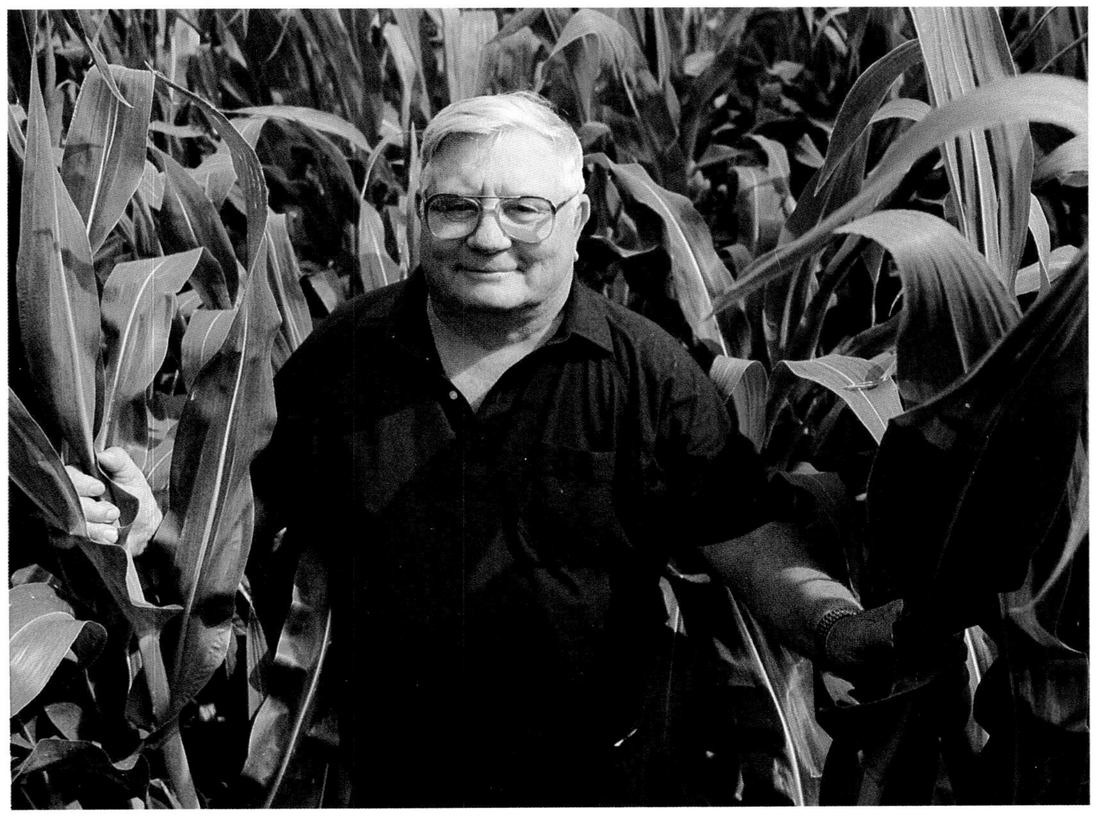

David Birkestrand, 67
Farmer
Cambridge

"Technology has changed farming. The machines came in about the time I graduated high school. That was a good day. Picking corn by hand was hard physical work. It was probably healthy, but I don't know if I want to be that healthy. Farming is a family occupation. You work with your family side by side for hours at a time. You have to talk to each other. You're forced to get to know each other."

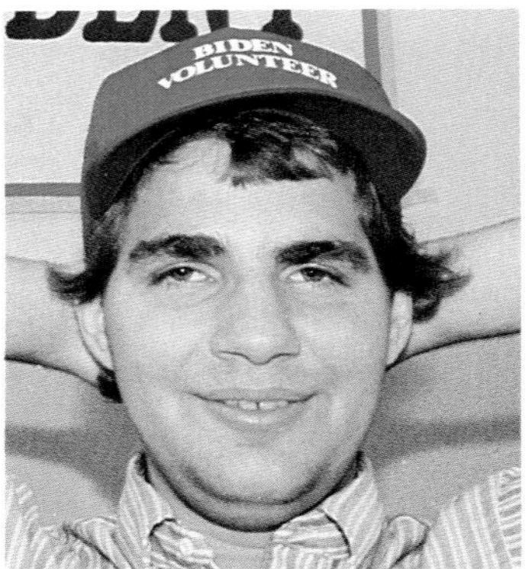

Mike Lux, 27
Campaign aide
Des Moines

"Running for president has to be one of the most humbling processes that could be imagined. Candidates have to go to all sorts of little events, to pig farms and sale barns. That's probably not a bad thing. Campaigning in Iowa is a lot of fun. There are probably more parades here per capita than anywhere else."

Carla McCullough, 26
Student
Iowa City

"It's important that people watch us to see what happens with the political caucuses here. Iowa provides a good sampling because the attitudes are commonplace. We're pretty much in the middle — not a lot of poverty, not a lot of wealth. We're mostly middle-class, level-headed people."

Jackie Mace, 21
Pet groomer
Silvia

"I grew up around a farm with dust flying in my face. I'd go into our cornfield, pick an ear, wash it off with a hose, peel it and eat it right there. Now the farm crisis has turned into a vicious cycle. When the farmers have problems, the manufacturing companies lay people off. It just tears the families apart. But the people are keeping a good attitude."

Jim Jackson, 18
Student
Klemme

"I had 13 people in my senior class. I got to know everybody. I got to participate in all kinds of activities. I'm a terrible basketball player, but they had to let me play. The community centers on the school. Everybody shows up for the games and plays even if they don't have kids in the school."

Abigail Van Buren, 68, was born in Sioux City, Iowa. She has written an advice column, "Dear Abby," for 31 years. It appears in 1,300 newspapers with a combined readership of 90 million. Her twin sister is Ann Landers.

Childhood hometown has really grown up

USA TODAY: How long were you in Sioux City?

VAN BUREN: I was born and raised in Iowa and was educated at Morningside College, a fine Methodist college. I left Sioux City in 1939 after I married. We moved to Minneapolis.

USA TODAY: What memories do you have?

VAN BUREN: I still have very proud memories of Sioux City. I can remember lovingly walking to school with snow coming up to my hips. My twin sister and I would be walking, holding hands, and literally lose track of each other.

USA TODAY: How were the summers?

VAN BUREN: Summer was so hot we dragged our mattress out on the lawn and slept there. Our doors always used to be open. We were never concerned about being burglarized.

USA TODAY: How has Iowa changed?

VAN BUREN: Sioux City has changed a great deal. It really has grown up. It's a metropolis. Lots of old landmarks are gone, but some of the same people are still there. The character of the town remains the same because it's not merely buildings, it's people.

USA TODAY: Do you go back to Iowa to visit?

VAN BUREN: I went back for my 50th high school reunion in 1986. It was good to see the old gang. I miss the people.

USA TODAY: Did growing up in Iowa, in what you call the USA's heartland, help prepare you to listen to people's problems?

VAN BUREN: Yes, it did. Living in a community like Sioux City made me a more trusting person. I could believe people. Other people from big cities are a little less trusting, more suspicious.

USA TODAY: Is Iowa misunderstood?

VAN BUREN: It certainly is. The impression is that it's a state full of country folk, rubes and hicks. Particularly among people from the coasts.

USA TODAY: How do people treat you when you go back for a visit?

VAN BUREN: Like a celebrity. But, no, my celebrity status has never hurt me. Anyone who wants can say hello, take a picture or get my autograph.

Topic: IOWA

Here is where the dream still works

USA TODAY: Many people think of *The Music Man* when they think of Iowa. That image of River City — small town, caring people — does that kind of town still exist in Iowa?

BRANSTAD: Absolutely. There are literally hundreds of communities in Iowa like Lake Mills, where I'm from, or Mason City, which is a little bigger. People really care about each other, and about their community.

USA TODAY: Aren't many Iowans concerned that these small towns will disappear?

BRANSTAD: That's why it's so essential that we aggressively work on rural development, and diversification, and providing job opportunities. Communities like Osceola, Mt. Pleasant and Lake Mills have been very successful.

USA TODAY: If diversification is the way for a small town to survive, does that mean giving up on the family farms?

BRANSTAD: No. In fact, that actually can be a very important part of maintaining the family farm. In most families today, unlike 30, 40 years ago, both spouses are working. One works on the farm maybe full time, and the other works in town. I really think that job opportunities and diversification in these rural communities can be the way to help stabilize the family farm.

USA TODAY: Are farms in Iowa doing better now?

BRANSTAD: Because of farm foreclosures, we were asking for help in the heartland. Now we're offering hope. And there are some very hopeful things happening. Land prices bottomed out. Livestock prices have improved significantly. So the farm situation is improving modestly.

USA TODAY: What about other sectors of your economy?

BRANSTAD: We're up 36,000 people employed in Iowa now from where we were a year ago. Our unemployment trust fund has got its highest balance of all time. When I came into office, we had over a $100 million deficit in our unemployment trust fund. It's now up to almost a $200 million balance.

Terry Branstad, 40, a Republican, was elected to a second term in 1986.

USA TODAY: You had Homecoming '86, a statewide celebration, last year. What was that all about?

BRANSTAD: We asked people to come back, see what's happening in Iowa, and renew pride in local communities. That was so successful that this year, we began the Iowa Ambassadors. This is what we call the Ambassador Creed: "Iowa is the America that you grew up believing in. It is faith, hope, and caring about each other. It is freedom, but through hard work and integrity. It is the belief that the future will be better than today if we make it that way. Iowa is a place where the dream still works, and it is our challenge as ambassadors to tell the world about it."

USA TODAY: Tell us how you view the Iowa caucus. Is it fair for a state the size of Iowa to have such an impact on the national political picture?

BRANSTAD: Iowa is the perfect place to start the presidential-selection process. We're in the heartland.

USA TODAY: How does rubbing up against all of these national figures wear with you? How long can a bright young Republican resist —

BRANSTAD: Forever. I have no interest in Washington, D.C., and I've been there enough to know how much better I like living in Iowa. My ambition is here at the state level.

Kansas

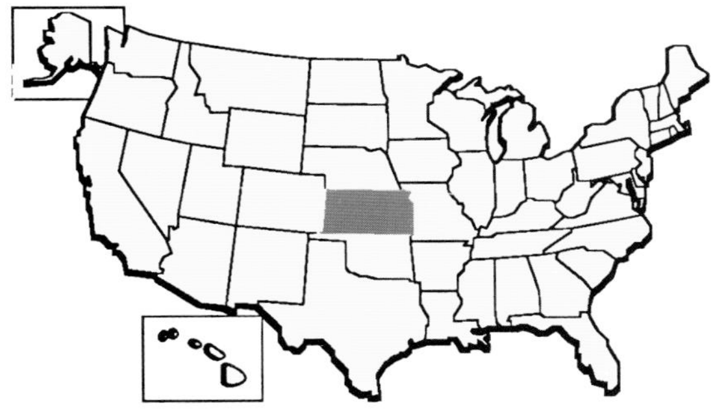

Visited: July 21-23, 1987
Featured in USA TODAY: July 27

"I've never planted a wheat crop failure. I've harvested a few, but never planted any."

Bob Bacon
Farmer
Hutchinson, Kan.

Kansas

Home on the range: No discouraging words

It's the foodbasket of the USA. No. 1 wheat producer. No. 1 in beef. Kansas farmers feed a lot of us. How are they doing?

OK. Same as they have for more than a century. Homesteaders **Brewster Higley** and **Dan Kelly** put it to words and music in 1873. Now the official state song:

Home, home on the range,
Where the deer and the antelope play,
Where seldom is heard a discouraging word,
And the skies are not cloudy all day.

Every few years, we worry about our heartland farmers. They worry less than we do. Of course, a few farms fail or fold. But nearly all survive. Many thrive. Seldom is heard a discouraging word.

■ 1933. Dust bowl days. Depth of the Depression. **Alf Landon**, 45, new Republican governor of Kansas. Drove his Ford Model A across the prairie. Encouraged farmers and bankers to hang in there. With some Democratic New Deal help, most made it.

LANDON: Still feisty, still fighting at 99.

Today, Alf Landon is just 45 days shy of his 100th birthday. Behind him: His 1936 presidential campaign. Nearly a century at home on the range. Do family farmers have a future?

"Of course they do! They've been through most of this before. Most of them grew up in it. There is a good future ahead of them. If I didn't think that, I'd be in pretty bad shape. So would everybody else."

■ 1987. Gov. **John M. (Mike) Hayden**, 44, 1st-term Republican. Grew up on the family farm near Atwood (pop. 1,665). Is there a future for the family farmer?

"Of course. The family farm has changed. It used to be very labor-intensive. Now, it's capital-intensive. My brother works as much land in one afternoon with one machine as it used to take my dad, uncle and me with three machines 20 years ago."

There will be a few fewer family farms, but bigger ones, the Guv says. Facts bear him out:

■ About 70,000 farms in Kansas today. 10 years ago, there were 79,000. Many on those 9,000 sold out, found work in town or retired.

■ Today's average farm is 684 acres. 10 years ago, it was 627.

For many in the USA, the vision of Kansas is that in the movie *The Wizard of Oz.* Runaway Dorothy and her dog, Toto. Released in 1939, the film has been seen more than any other, including *Gone With the Wind.*

No one is certain where the fictional Dorothy was from. But when she clicked her ruby-red slippers and recited "there's no place like home," Kansans in Liberal (pop. 14,911) say she ended up back there.

Real or make-believe, Kansans like it at home on the range. Seldom is heard a discouraging word. Listen to **Bob Bacon**, 62, and his wife, **Juanita**, 57. Farm 400 acres near Hutchinson (pop. 40,284). Been doing it for 35 years.

"I've never planted a wheat crop failure. I've harvested a few, but never planted any," says Bob.

BACONS: Happiness at home on the range at Hutchinson.

"Farmers are the greatest 'next year' people in the world. Next year, we'll have a bumper crop. Next year, prices will go up. If it is a bumper crop, you get such a feeling of accomplishment. To make something from nothing. It's like an artist who paints a beautiful picture."

Juanita echoes and adds to the futuristic melody:

"There's so much pride. First you see little green shoots. Then a big green carpet. Now, this beautiful, golden waving wheat. It makes you want to sing *The Star-Spangled Banner.*"

Seldom is heard a discouraging word.

That's Plain Talk from Kansas.

Snapshot

Sunflower State

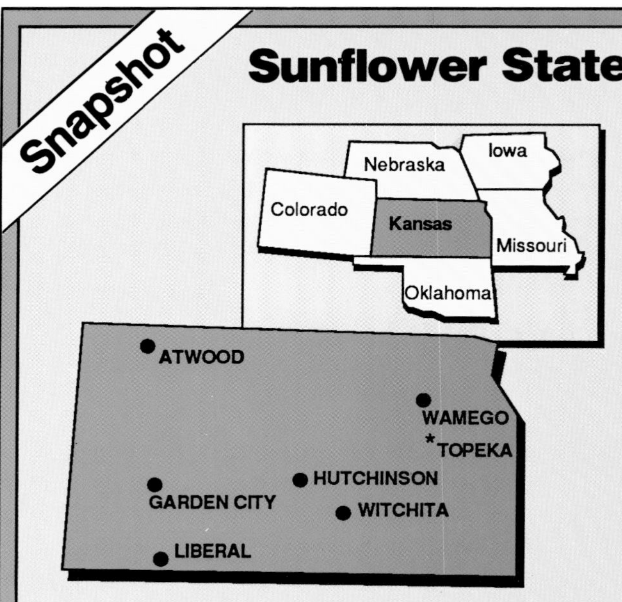

ENTERED USA: Jan. 29, 1861, 34th state

MOTTO: To the stars through difficulties
POPULATION: 2,461,000; rank: 32nd
LARGEST CITY: Wichita, pop. 283,496
CAPITAL: Topeka, pop. 118,945
LAND: 81,781 square miles; rank, 13th
POPULATION DENSITY: 30.1 per square mile; rank, 38th
RACIAL MIX: 91.7% white; 5.3% black; 0.6% Asian and Pacific islanders. Hispanic heritage: 2.7%.

Uniquely Kan.

SOFT TOUCH: At the Kansas State University College of Veterinary Medicine in Manhattan, horses are placed on waterbeds during surgery.

GUN RUNNERS: The Beecher Bible and Rifle Church in Wamego was used during the Civil War to store and smuggle rifles that came in boxes marked "Bibles."

SALT OF THE EARTH: Kansas contains enough salt reserves to supply the USA's needs for the next 375,000 years. The world's largest salt deposit is at Hutchinson. It yields 44.1 million tons per year.

PROFESSOR BOONE: Daniel Boone was sent to Kansas in 1825 to teach white agriculture to the Indians.

FOX CHASE: The only military fox hunt in the U.S. armed forces is held annually at Fort Leavenworth. It dates back to 1929.

Stan Harder, 40
Museum curator
Wichita

"When I came back to Wichita after growing up in metro L.A., I found it was the biggest little town I had ever seen. There's a certain feeling about Midwestern towns. Kansas isn't glitzy, much to our great advantage. We're kind of like whole-wheat bread. Just wholesome and basic."

Howard Tice, 45
Executive director
Wheat Growers
Association
Hutchinson

"You won't find an 'average' wheat farmer in Kansas. They're eternally optimistic. 'Things are going to get better,' they always say. They are persistent, hearty and neighborly. There was one farmer who couldn't get his wheat cut because of an accident. So about 30 farmers got together and cut his wheat."

Voices

of Kansas

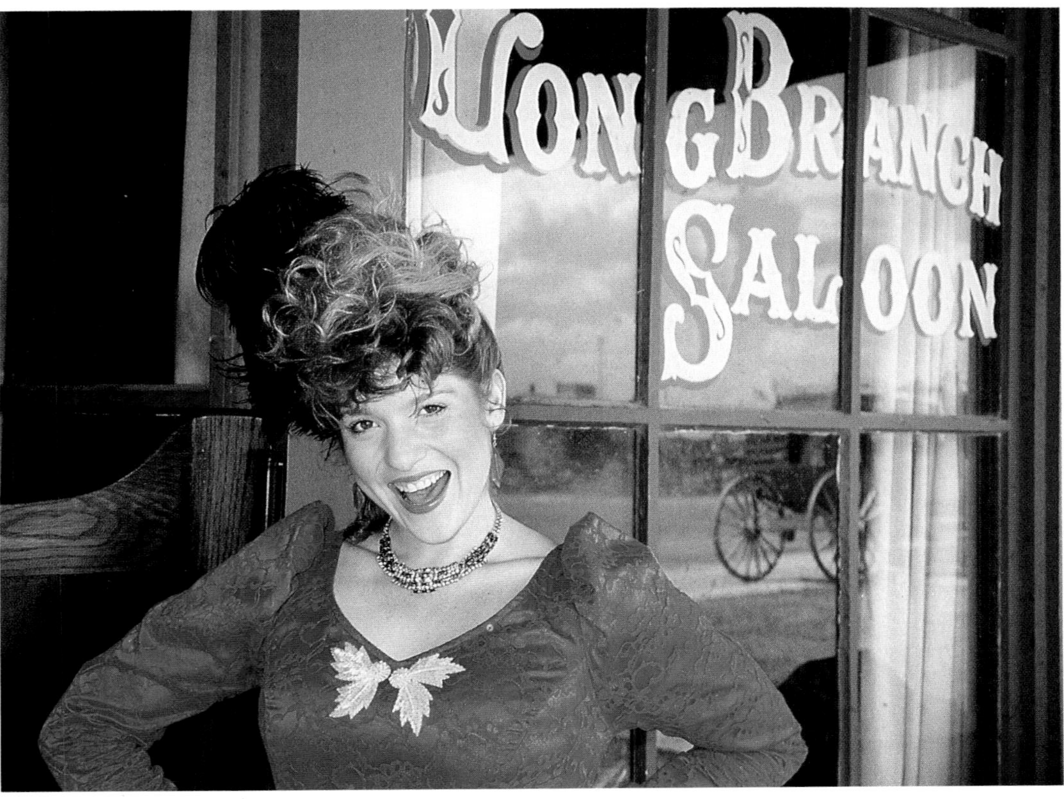

Roberta Scott, 23
Museum worker
Dodge City

"People are glad to see Miss Kitty here in Dodge. That's where she belongs. Dodge City is like a legend. The excitement of the westerns, the good guys and the bad guys. This is where it all happened. We have that tradition to carry on."

Lawrence Kelly, 36
On disability leave
Topeka

"When I was a senior, in 1969, Topeka High got its first black cheerleaders even though blacks had played sports for a long time. That was a breakthrough. But we're making progress in racial tension — blacks and whites. It affects everyone. That's why we're making progress."

Mary Rice, 23
Student
Kansas City

"There are no mountains or oceans in Kansas. We don't always have to be doing something — our social life revolves more around other people than activities. It's less materialistic. You don't have to own a pair of skis or a Porsche to have fun here."

Kristi Heinz, 24
Student
Lawrence

"There are more BMWs here than horses. I admire the farmers, I eat the food, but I don't get all excited when the crop comes in. I'm a city girl. The minds of the students here aren't on the Future Farmers of America — they want to be the future millionaires of America."

John Kraus, 66
Farmer
Hays

"People reflect the type of country they grow up in. Out here, we roll with the punches. You learn to take what comes and know that it won't get the best of you. Not many of the farmers around here went out of business. We live in a rural area, one of the reservoirs of conservatism. We don't believe in getting into more debt than we can handle."

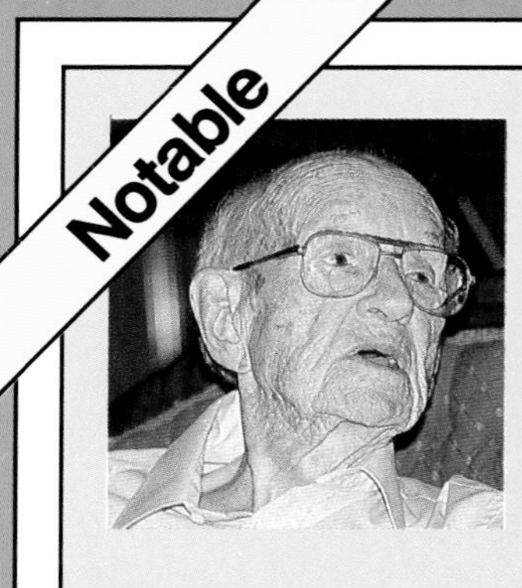

Alf Landon, 99, was governor of Kansas from 1933 to 1937. He ran for president against Franklin Roosevelt in 1936. Landon remains an avid follower of politics and sports.

I just take my life one day at a time

USA TODAY: Is President Reagan doing a good job for us?

LANDON: Of course, he is. He's doing a splendid job.

USA TODAY: Have you got any ideas about the 1988 presidential election?

LANDON: I don't know of anyone who can explain what's going to happen a year from now.

USA TODAY: Are you looking forward to voting for a Republican one more time for president?

LANDON: Of course! That means I would be 101 years old.

USA TODAY: When you were governor of Kansas, you helped out the Kansas economy with money allotted by Franklin Roosevelt's New Deal. Did you have any idea that you would be running against him in the 1936 presidential election?

LANDON: No, I didn't think so. I think he did, though. He called a meeting in Des Moines about the economy, and he put me at the head table with him.

USA TODAY: Did you like Roosevelt?

LANDON: Yes, we had a nice visit. Everybody was watching us to see whether we were going to be fighting before we got through. I remember I yelled a little too loud about something and there was a dead silence. They thought that what was coming was what they were looking for. It was all friendly.

USA TODAY: While you were governor, you apparently got along real well with the Democrats and a Democratic president.

LANDON: Yes, I did. I had been a Bull Mooser. I started in politics for Teddy Roosevelt.

USA TODAY: Are you still a great sports fan?

LANDON: I watch the Royals on TV. About the time I think they're gonna win it, it seems they hit a soft spot or something.

USA TODAY: How do you relax?

LANDON: I go out on the front porch if it's cool. I walk out to the stone wall and back nearly every day (about a mile). I enjoy that walk very much. The doctor says keep it up. I know I'm adding a little bit to my life. One day at a time.

Topic: KANSAS

We go around the world to sell our products

USA TODAY: Many people think of *The Wizard of Oz* when they think of Kansas. Is that the right image?

HAYDEN: That's an image that a lot of outsiders have of our state. It's not an image that most Kansans ever entertain in their own minds, because, of course, they live here every day.

USA TODAY: But like the movie says, "There's no place like home."

HAYDEN: That's exactly right. And to most of our 2.3 million people, that's absolutely true.

USA TODAY: How is Kansas different today from what it was 50 years ago?

HAYDEN: We find ourselves today not only very much involved in national affairs, but international affairs. Kansas — being the largest producer of wheat in the nation and the No. 1 state in production of red meat — finds that we've got to sell that red meat in the other 49 states and abroad. And we have to sell 70 percent of our farm commodities overseas in order for our farmers to find prosperity.

USA TODAY: Are you actively courting any overseas markets?

HAYDEN: We recently received a trade delegation of the Taiwanese. They bought in excess of $30 million worth of corn. We just sent our lieutenant governor to the People's Republic of China to work out how we might buy products and commodities from them and how they might buy from us.

USA TODAY: In the last election, Kansas voters surprised some of the nation with what they said about the lottery, parimutuel betting and liquor. Is there a changing view here?

HAYDEN: There is a changing face of Kansas. It is true that we have liquor by the drink now, for the first time in 108 years. But we had liquor by the drink before; you just needed a club card — and virtually anybody who wanted one could get one.

USA TODAY: So the voters were sending a message?

Mike Hayden, 43, a Republican, was elected in 1986.

HAYDEN: They see what's happening nationwide. Kansas is in line with the majority of the states. One thing people were saying on liquor by the drink was, "We have liquor by the drink. We might as well tax it."

USA TODAY: Kansas is known for its farm tradition. What's happening to the family farm? Is it disappearing?

HAYDEN: There's no doubt because of technology the number of family farms will be diminished. They already have. We lose on the average between 1,000 and 2,000 farms a year in Kansas. And we've been doing that for a long, long time. The face of the family farm is going to change significantly.

USA TODAY: You grew up in a rural community. How did that affect your values?

HAYDEN: You develop very strong traditional values. Your family is very close-knit, and you learn to depend on each other. There's a tremendous sense of community in a small town.

USA TODAY: How would you describe it?

HAYDEN: For example, in my family, I have a grandmother who is on a school board, a mother who was on the school board, a father who is a county commissioner and who is a municipal judge. There are only so many people, and everybody has a piece of the rock.

Kentucky

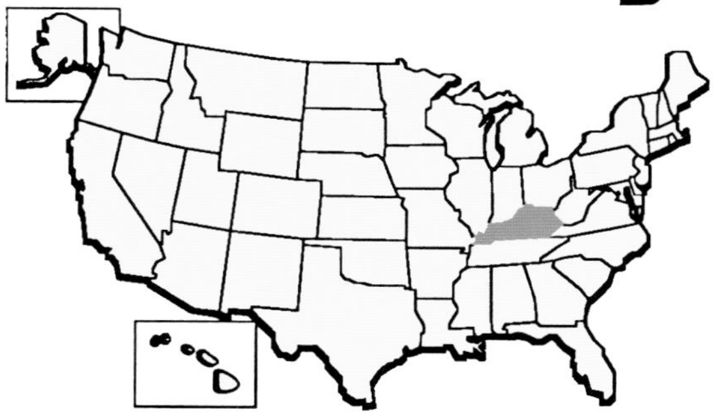

Visited: March 31-April 2, 1987
Featured in USA TODAY: April 6

"Here, the ups are the uppest and the downs are the downest."

Alice Chandler
Owner/breeder of horses
Mill Ridge Farm, Ky.

Kentucky

Horse talk: The Guv, the Queen and Ralph

Two reigning regal ladies — one from Kentucky, USA, one from the UK — will have a private lunch at 1 p.m. today in London.

■ Her Royal Highness, **Queen Elizabeth II**, 60, born to the lavish luxury of European royalty, whose horses and carriages glitter with gold.

■ Gov. **Martha Layne Collins**, 50, born in Bagdad, Ky., (pop. 220), where her earliest luxury was a Jersey calf she named Sunshine and showed at 4-H club events.

"I'm sure we'll talk about horses," Gov. Collins told the BusCapade news team just hours before her departure for London.

Horse talk, of course, is the universal language of the Bluegrass State. The queen understands. The British royal family owns horses in Kentucky and has visited here.

Except for that common interest, the backgrounds and lifestyles of the two lady leaders are as diverse as Kentuckians themselves.

The individual ruggedness of the first settlers who followed **Daniel Boone** from Tennessee through the Cumberland Gap 200 years ago is still there, from Middlesboro to Paducah.

So is the aristocratic sophistication of British ancestors in many a mansion overlooking the Ohio River around Louisville.

"Here, the ups are the uppest and the downs are the downest," says **Alice Chandler**, 61, of Mill Ridge Farm near Lexington.

UPPEST:

■ Old Money. It preserves many of the marvelously manicured farms with grand antebellum homes and white plank fences in the Bluegrass region.

■ New Money. Arab royal families are buying old Kentucky homes and turning them into showplaces. Many Kentuckians are contrarians and don't cotton to the foreign influx of dollars or people.

■ Old thoroughbreds. Fans flock to see them. Out to stud or out to pasture. John Henry, biggest money-winning horse of all time, at Kentucky Horse Park near Lexington. Secretariat at Claiborne Farms. Triple Crown winner Seattle Slew at Three Chimney Farms.

■ New thoroughbreds. Hope is eternally high among owners of colts and fillies. Highest at Friday's Keeneland track opening were **Roy** and **Helen Payne**, whose 2-year-old Main Blue won the blue ribbon in its first race ever.

"We didn't really push her and she led wire-to-wire," exulted Helen.

Next start for Main Blue: The WHAS stakes race for 2-year-olds on Derby Day, May 2, at Churchill Downs. Helen's highest hope: Main Blue as their first Derby entrant a year from now.

■ Heart research. The noted heart surgeon Dr. **William DeVries** has brought world renown to himself and to Louisville's Humana Hospital.

ROY PAYNE: Would like filly Main Blue to wear a crown.

■ Industrial development. Toyota's new $800 million plant north of Lexington will create 3,000 new jobs.

DOWNEST:

■ Tobacco farmers, bourbon distillers, coal miners and Louisville Cardinal basketball fans.

IN BETWEEN:

■ **Ralph Wade**, 60, had been a butcher for 22 years at A&P before that giant food chain went belly up in many markets. Now he and his wife, **Lillian**, 57, own and run Ralph's Market, just off exit 35 at I-64 in Shelbyville (pop. 24,800).

Lillian grills and sells up to 500 Ralphburgers a day. That's a juicy 5-ounce hamburger, everything on it, including Lillian's famous homemade green tomato ketchup.

The hours are long, 6 a.m. to 7:30 p.m. "He (Ralph) gives me Saturday and Monday off," Lillian says. "Saturdays, I wash, iron, clean the house. Mondays, I play with our 4-year-old granddaughter, Kathie."

Ralph himself sneaks away only every Thursday afternoon. "I go to the races then, of course. That's the surest way to make or lose some money. I enjoy it either way."

That's Plain Talk from Kentucky.

HOME OF THE RALPHBURGER: Lillian and Ralph Wade grill and sell, but still have time for fun.

Snapshot

Bluegrass State

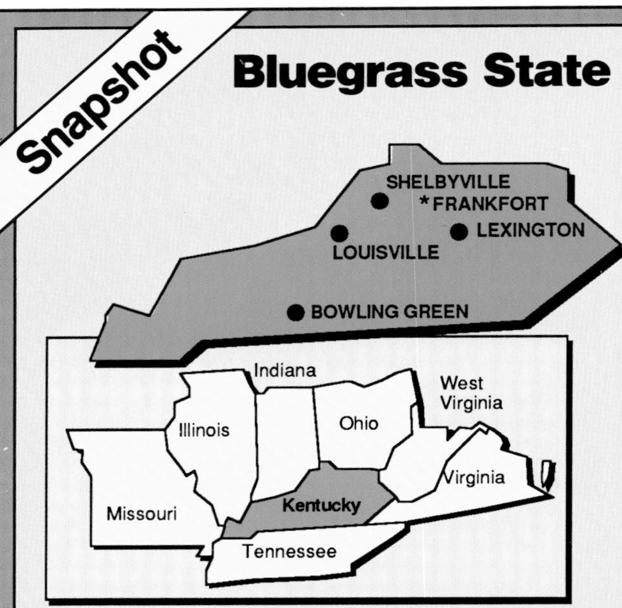

ENTERED USA: June 1, 1792, 15th state

MOTTO: United we stand, divided we fall
POPULATION: 3,728,000
LARGEST CITY: Louisville, pop. 289,843
CAPITAL: Frankfort, pop. 25,973
LAND: 39,669 square miles; rank, 37th
POPULATION DENSITY: 94 per square mile; rank, 23rd
RACIAL MIX: 92.3% white; 7.1% black; 0.3% Asian and Pacific islanders. Hispanic heritage: 0.7%.

Uniquely Ky.

NOT REALLY BLUE: Bluegrass is actually green. In the spring, it produces bluish-purple buds that make it appear blue.

COAL CAPITAL: Kentucky is the nation's largest coal producer. 1985 production: 150 million tons, worth an estimated $4.2 billion.

KEEPING COOL: The State Fair, held in Louisville each August, is the USA's largest air-conditioned fair, with more than 700,000 square feet of inter-connecting buildings.

BREWING BAPTIST: Bourbon whiskey was developed in Scott County in 1789 by the Rev. Elijah Craig, a Baptist minister. Kentucky produces 1 million barrels a year, about 85 percent of the nation's whiskey.

OVER THE MOONBOW: A combination of moonlight and mist at Cumberland Falls produces a rainbow-like spectrum called a "moonbow." It's the only one in the Western Hemisphere.

Voices
of Kentucky

Susie Barber, 40
Owner of flower/herb business
Springfield

"I give tours and lectures on the magic of flowers, the language of flowers in Shakespeare's time, all the folklore and all the healing qualities of herbs and flowers. The hats are just one of our designs. It's a design that has really caught the inspiration and love of Kentucky because it reflects so much femininity and the Old South kind of thing. In Kentucky, there's a tremendous amount of appreciation for nostalgia, the sentimentality that I love."

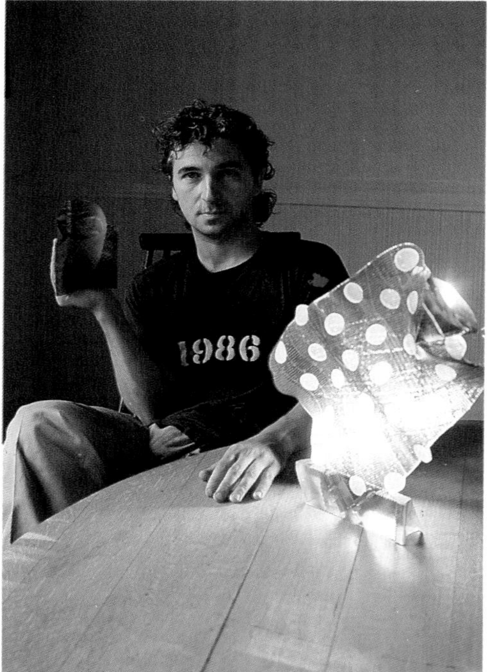

Fred di Frenzi, 33
Glass artist
Middletown

"It works out nice being in the area that you can kind of be to yourself and develop your ideas, then travel to the metropolitan areas to get the work out . . . I think this teacher I had in graduate school had a nice analogy about making art in a rural area. He made the analogy to a farmer. He grows his stuff here, and then gets it out to the marketplace and sells it."

Fred Haupt, 42
Assistant trainer
Churchill Downs
Louisville

"A horse will kick you or bite you. I got kicked in the leg last week. It didn't feel good. They get to playing with the other horses, and they get to thinking you can take it, too. You can't. A horse that weighs 900 or 1,000 pounds can hurt you just joking around."

Betty Johnson, 70
Director of nursing home
Louisville

"Kentucky is home. Having worked in the whole area of social problems and having been exposed to some of the largest cities — Chicago, Miami, Atlanta — I felt overwhelmed sometimes about the size of their problems. Louisville still to me seems somewhat manageable. It seems that we are small enough still to define our problems and work at them in a more orderly way."

Lou Muller, 66
Retired
Bullitt County

"I like to spend as much time in the woods being along the streams as possible. Kentucky has streams and thank goodness we have a lot of good wooded areas. I love the forest. I like to squirrel hunt, quail hunt and hunt turkeys in the spring. The last couple years is the first time we've had a gobbler season in Kentucky. You can only shoot gobblers, wild turkey. That's the male."

Faye Piercy, 54
Machine operator
South Louisville

"I've visited a lot of other states, but I don't think there's any place like Kentucky. We have almost everything. We don't have an ocean, but we have lots of lakes and state parks. We use the lake, and fish. There's a lot of hunting for the men. Most of my family lives in Kentucky. It's a beautiful place."

Tony Terry, 28
Publicity associate
Churchill Downs
Louisville

"I don't think that there's an owner who would put a horse in the race and not bet on it. You'd feel horrible to have a horse going off at 99-to-1 and not even put a dollar or two on it. Horses are like people. They're not always at their best. Some days they don't feel like racing. Unfortunately, that day can fall on Derby Day."

Notable

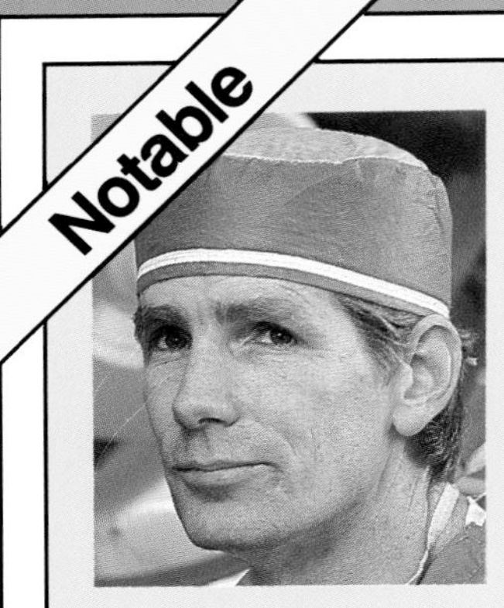

William DeVries, 43, implanted the first Jarvik-7 artificial heart in 1982. Since then, Dr. DeVries has performed the surgery on three more patients at Humana Hospital-Audubon in Louisville.

Import happy in new Kentucky home

USA TODAY: You were among the most famous physicians in the world when you were lured to Kentucky from Utah. What was it like?

DeVRIES: It was incredible. My daughter is 6 foot 5, and the Ballard High School basketball team knew that Adrie was coming. Her name was on the front page of the newspaper. When we came here, I took my entire family of seven children out to eat, and someone came up to my wife and said, "We're so happy to have you here in Kentucky." Then she said, "You're probably wondering how I knew who you were," and my wife said, "Well, probably because you've seen him in *Time* and *Newsweek*." And the lady said, "No, we recognized your daughter from the front page."

USA TODAY: That must have made your daughter feel good. What about you?

DeVRIES: I realized what kind of a place I was in, and it was incredibly refreshing — that people think athletics mean so much. I think the sports adoration that we go through is incredible. It's helped my daughter — she loves school. She's at Penn State.

USA TODAY: How does practicing medicine in Kentucky differ from Utah?

DeVRIES: I came from an academic practice in Utah to a private practice group here in Kentucky. One of the things that I was interested in was whether all the doctors who would participate in the project would be well-certified and be able to carry on the way they're supposed to. The people in Louisville were of very high caliber. The quality of medicine in this city is as good as anywhere in the world.

USA TODAY: How is your program of artificial heart implantation going?

DeVRIES: We're solidly in the middle of it. We've taken first Barney Clark, then Billy Schroeder, Murray Haydon. When we first started, the scientific community was kind of, "Well, let's see how this thing goes." Now, they've gotten excited about it. Last year, over 50 implants were performed in the world.

USA TODAY: What will happen in this field over the next 20 years?

DeVRIES: You're going to find as many as 40,000 people in the United States a year who can have this to keep them alive.

Topic: KENTUCKY

We're trying to open our doors to the world

USA TODAY: Your bags are packed for Europe, where you will open an economic development office for Kentucky. You'll also meet with Queen Elizabeth. What will you talk about?

COLLINS: We have a common interest in horses. She's been here twice. She's bought horses here in Kentucky. I'm sure we'll talk horses. We're obviously interested in working with a lot of people in London and England and seeing that the lines of communication are kept open.

The Guv

Martha Layne Collins, 50, *a Democrat, was elected governor in 1983.*

USA TODAY: People often connect Kentucky with tobacco and bourbon, yet many are quitting smoking and drinking. How does that affect your economy?

COLLINS: Our industries have felt some of the controversy and some of the changes. There's still a demand for both of those products, and as the world market opens up even more, there will be more of a demand. We're looking for diversity.

USA TODAY: The new Toyota plant will bring in $800 million to the state and add about 3,000 new jobs. Still, you're being criticized for giving the Japanese too much. Is that fair criticism?

COLLINS: As a result of the Toyota package, we've already brought in 14 other auto-related companies, to the tune of $370 million worth of investments and 2,700 new jobs. There was a little bit of fear at first.

USA TODAY: What sort of fear?

COLLINS: Maybe it is the fear of the unknown, or of change. Kentucky is a great commonwealth, with good people and many resources. It's a laid-back state. That's why we've been trying to change things a little bit.

USA TODAY: What is the next step in your career?

COLLINS: I try not to burn bridges or close doors, but right now, I don't have any plans to run for another public office.

USA TODAY: As Kentucky's first female governor, what has your tenure meant for women, especially politicians?

COLLINS: I hope that I've done a good job and opened some doors. I hope I haven't done anything that would discredit women. It was very important to me to be successful, for the state, but also to see to it that I was a good role model so that other women would have opportunities.

USA TODAY: Your election had very little support from women's-rights groups. Why?

COLLINS: I don't always agree with them. And I don't always do what they expect. I think all issues are women's issues.

USA TODAY: Kentucky seems to be a state in touch with its past. Is that true?

COLLINS: Very much so. We feel strongly about traditions, our culture and our heritage. We're very talented in crafts, and we're turning it into an industry.

USA TODAY: What do you see in Kentucky's future?

COLLINS: I want to stress that while we're working foreign investment, we're also working domestic investment. We've created a record number of jobs, almost 70,000. Most came from existing businesses expanding.

USA TODAY: What else should we know about Kentucky?

COLLINS: We're trying to promote our medical advancements. We're looking at electronics. We're looking at everything.

Louisiana

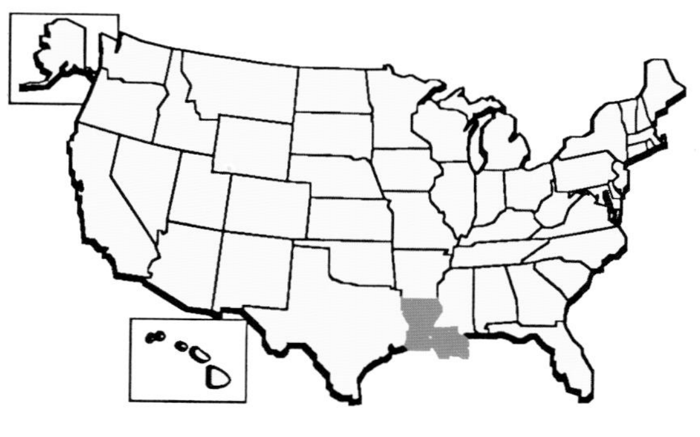

Visited: April 13-14, 1987
Featured in USA TODAY: April 17

"Politics plays the role in Louisiana that TV wrestling does in the rest of the nation. It is fixed. It is flamboyant. It is surreal. It is our spectator sport."

Eugene Schlossberger
Professor, Louisiana State University
Baton Rouge, La.

Louisiana

All that jazz, cajolery causes some to fret

"Call me colorful, controversial, brash ... anything but modest," Louisiana Gov. **Edwin W. Edwards** told the BusCateers over lunch at the governor's mansion.

"Cajun Casanova" to his admirers. Undefeated in 15 runs for public office. Four terms in the U.S. Congress. Three terms as governor.

"Fast Eddie" to his adversaries. Eight grand jury investigations. Indicted for fraud and racketeering. But, jury-tried and acquitted.

In many ways, Edwards, 59 — and his friends and foes — flaunt the clashing contrasts in this state that anchored the Louisiana Purchase of 1803.

When President **Thomas Jefferson** made a deal to pay **Napoleon** $15 million for what ultimately became 15 states of the USA, the French and Spanish already had spent 150 years here.

Cajun and Creole culture reigned in Southern Louisiana then as it does now.

■ Hot and heavy food. Hard-drinking. Free-living. But, church-going (mostly Roman Catholic).

Religion and raunch coexist because they ignore each other, says maitre d' **Fred Vesa**, 43, at Cafe Sbisa in New Orleans. Nuns and naked women both abound.

Up north, in Alexandria and Monroe and Shreveport, ancestors of another sort came from Alabama and Georgia and Tennessee.

■ Hard-working. Straight-laced. Some say rednecks. Also church-going (mostly Protestant).

There, folks fret about all that New Orleans jazz and cajolery.

"We aim not to be a burden," says Mayor **Elton Pody**, 49, of Ruston (pop. 20,585). His parish has only 6.8 percent unemployment; the state average is 14.3 percent.

Rustonians think that if South Louisiana thought less about sin and more about survival it would be better off.

To most of the USA, Louisiana means Bourbon Street. Mardi Gras. Revelry. Sports spectaculars. Jazz.

Those whose fame and fortune depends on that image work hard to embellish it. Sexist and racist jokes are commonplace.

"The only way I could lose this next election is if I was caught in bed with a dead woman or a live boy," says Gov. Edwards.

"Don't call it Dixieland. Dixieland is just a white man's adaptation. This is REAL New Orleans jazz," stresses **Jane Botsworth**, 43, manager of Preservation Hall. There, black musicians pack in jazz-junkies seven nights a week.

Visitors line up for Cajun cooking, the original version of what's now hot in New York and across the USA. You can't really duplicate that at home. But you can fix your own "Cajun Martini." Hostess Carrie Lea Pierson, 27, at K-Paul's, tells you how:

"Cut fresh jalapenos into gin or vodka. Add pickled green tomatoes. Chill and serve." Try not to choke.

HOT CORNER: Bent over in New Orleans.

Baton Rouge is where north and south Louisiana meet.

On the campus of Louisiana State University, students and faculty are amused by the flashing and clashing lifestyles statewide. Some choose sides. Many just "spectate."

Says philosophy Professor **Eugene Schlossberger**, 35, who came to LSU from Swarthmore College in Pennsylvania last August:

"Politics plays the role in Louisiana that TV wrestling does in the rest of the nation. It is fixed. It is flamboyant. It is surreal. It is our spectator sport."

That's Plain Talk from Louisiana.

PRESERVATION HALL: Playing to jazz-junkies.

Snapshot

Pelican State

Arkansas
Mississippi
Texas
Louisiana
RUSTON
BATON ROUGE
NEW ORLEANS

BAYOU STATE
1812
LOUISIANA

ENTERED USA: April 20, 1812, 18th state

MOTTO: Union, justice, and confidence
POPULATION: 4,501,000; rank, 18th
LARGEST CITY: New Orleans, pop. 559,101
CAPITAL: Baton Rouge, pop. 368,571
LAND: 44,521 square miles; rank, 33rd
POPULATION DENSITY: 101.1 per square mile; rank, 22nd
RACIAL MIX: 69.2% white; 29.4% black; 0.6% Asian and Pacific islanders. Hispanic heritage: 2.4%.

Uniquely La.

GROUND FLOOR: The dead are buried above ground in New Orleans because the ground is too damp for interment. Louisiana leads the states in annual rainfall — 57.34 inches.

OVERCOOKED: Louisiana chefs are famous for burning fish. The dish called blackened redfish is now popular nationwide.

LONG RIDE: The world's longest over-water highway bridge is Lake Pontchartrain Causeway at 24 miles.

GANGSTER TRAP: Bonnie Parker and Clyde Barrow were killed in an ambush on a rural North Louisiana road in 1934.

NO REINDEER: Parents in South Louisiana tell their children that Santa Claus travels in the bayous in a canoe. Residents light bonfires to guide him.

BACK ROADS: Every state has a north-south interstate except Louisiana. However, Interstate 49 is under construction.

Voices

of Louisiana

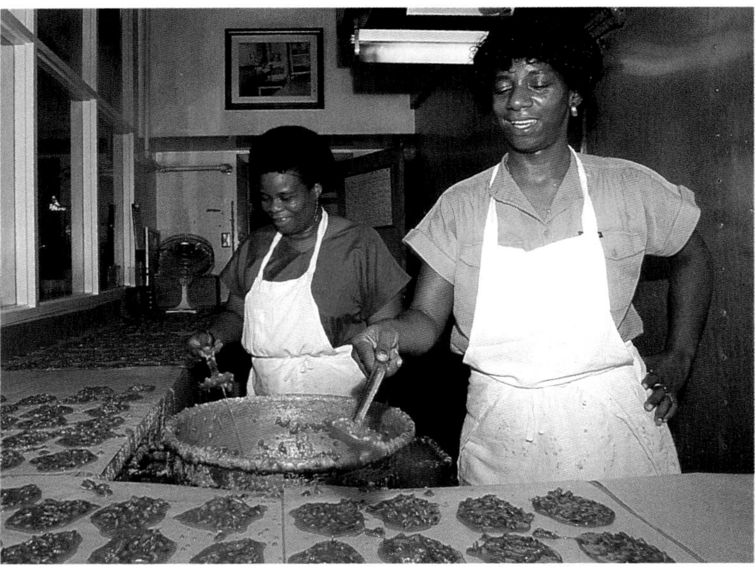

Mary Watson, 43, left (with Carla Alfonse)
Cook in candy shop
New Orleans

"You can find the best of everything in New Orleans. We have famous cooking, pretty sightseeing and the people are very sweet. People in Louisiana like to eat because the food is very hot and spicy. We like hot stuff. We have the best gumbo, the best cooks, the best entertainment, the best restaurants and lots of seafood. The best cooks are in New Orleans because they're from New Orleans."

Spencer Washington, 51
Cab driver
New Orleans

"Louisiana is a Catholic state. But I don't see religion and New Orleans' fun as a conflict. Yes, this city has a lot of variety that enhances what adults like to do, but it isn't necessarily 'sin city.' You just have to control your way of living. If you know your limit is two drinks, why drink five? Lust and overindulgence are the sins."

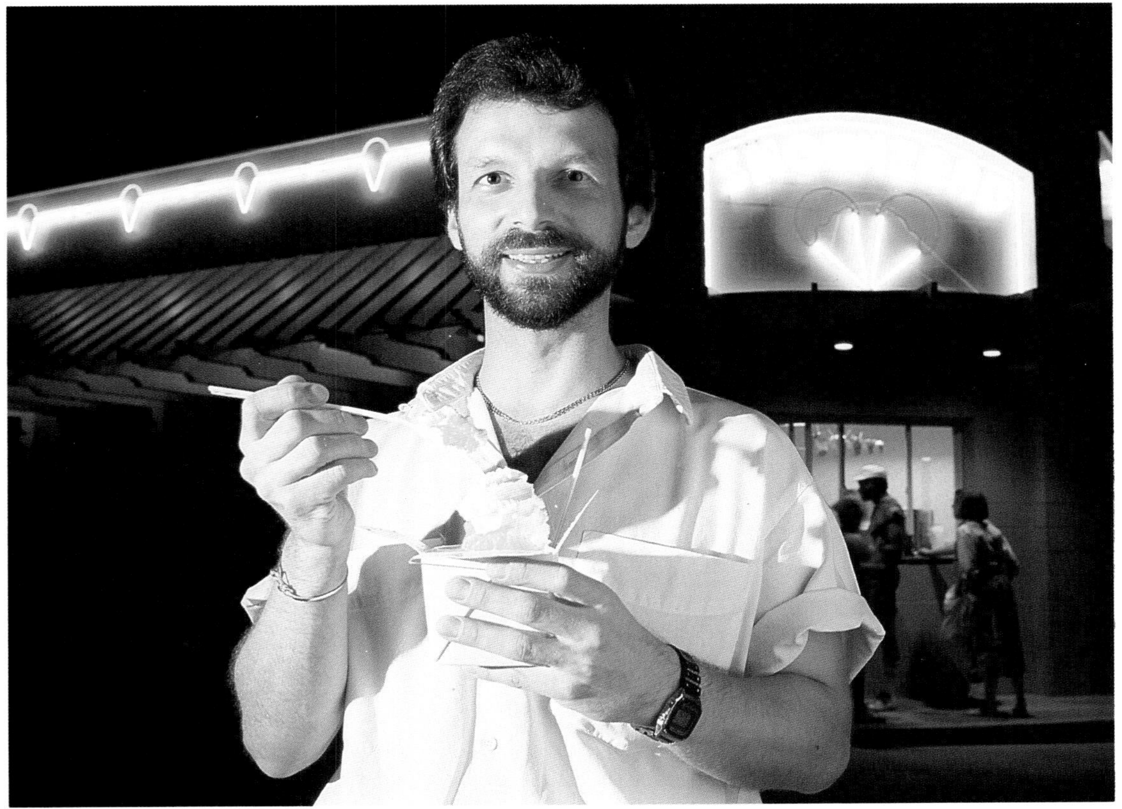

Ronnie Sciortino, 34
Businessman/
snowball shop owner
New Orleans

"The extreme heat and humidity make snowballs very popular in New Orleans. The snowball season starts just after Mardi Gras and runs through the hurricane season. When things get tough economically, many people set up a snowball business because it requires very little capital. This area has about 500 stands, which keeps the block ice business profitable."

Margena Johnson, 40
Metal finisher
Minden

"Louisiana is one of the friendliest states in the South. It's a wonderful place to raise a family. If the fast life is too fast for you, we have a more slow, easygoing life. When I speak of the fast life, I am talking about the Mardi Gras, the fun of partying and dancing, everything you would find in New Orleans."

Martha Garrett, 26
Deputy court clerk
West Monroe

"We don't live a rushed life; we take things easy. It's a relaxed pace. We do what we have to do and get it done when it needs to be done, but we don't rush anything. It's the atmosphere. You can't help but relax. It's a beautiful state that has a lot of history, especially in the southern part. The old houses built in the 1700s and 1800s are just magnificent. Everything you heard about the South being genteel is true in Louisiana."

Eddie Bradford, 27
Mechanic
Bossier City

"The city I live in is not too big. In larger cities the people have a protective shield around them, where they're afraid to even get to know their neighbors. When I moved to this neighborhood, I met the neighbors the second day. They all came by to introduce themselves to me."

Bill Racca, 63
Crawfish boiler
Baton Rouge

"They don't cook up yonder like we do down here. Some of the best cooks in the world are the old Cajuns. I know because my mother's one of them. She's 87 years old and she can make a meal with nothing."

***Paul Prudhomme**, 46, is owner and chef at K-Paul's Louisiana Kitchen in New Orleans. He is the author of* Chef Paul Prudhomme's Louisiana Kitchen.

Creole or Cajun, the food is exciting

USA TODAY: You were born in Opelousas, La., the youngest of 13 children in a family of sharecroppers. How did you get started cooking?

PRUDHOMME: It was my job at home. When my last sister got married, I was 7 years old. Someone had to help my mother. I would help her go in the field and get potatoes, and go in the yard and get a chicken, bring in wood so she could cook, help her can, help her make sausages. I did that until I was 12, 13 years old. And then we moved away from the country, and my interest turned to cooking for taste.

USA TODAY: When did you go into business?

PRUDHOMME: When I was 17, I had my own restaurant, which was a dismal failure. Three failed after that. And K-Paul's is No. 8.

USA TODAY: Is Cajun cooking your specialty?

PRUDHOMME: I'm a Cajun person, but the specialties are called Louisiana cooking. There are two kinds of food in Louisiana. There's Creole food, which is New Orleans food — it's more sophisticated. And there's Cajun food — that's country food, the food of the people. We do both.

USA TODAY: What are your best dishes?

PRUDHOMME: We usually try to put something blackened on the menu. We like to do blackened tuna, because it's actually better than blackened redfish. And blackened prime rib is just incredible.

USA TODAY: What does "blackened" mean?

PRUDHOMME: It means cooked at a very high temperature, just until the outside caramelizes. The black crust is sweet, kind of bitter and kind of smoky. It's just exciting to eat.

USA TODAY: Why do they say that Louisiana has the best food in America?

PRUDHOMME: The people are attuned to food. They like to eat, and they are great cooks. We have a lot of summertime for people to grow things. And the fishing boats are back early, so we can get absolutely fresh ingredients.

USA TODAY: People literally stand in the rain for hours to get into K-Paul's. Why?

PRUDHOMME: All we do is put the best food we can in front of you.

Topic: LOUISIANA

Attitude, atmosphere make our state great

USA TODAY: You are proposing a casino and a lottery for Louisiana. Is that a popular issue in the state?

EDWARDS: I'm not saying that people are marching in the streets for it. But the economy of New Orleans is so bad, and the people believe it would bring in needed revenue.

USA TODAY: Won't Christian groups raise a ruckus about the moral issues?

EDWARDS: They already have. I don't mind them fighting it, because they have a moral reason for fighting it. What bothers me is the business community and publishers and editors who ought to have a long-range view of Louisiana's economy and not concern themselves with what fundamentalist religious groups are expounding.

USA TODAY: Louisiana's economy is suffering from a drop in oil revenues. Can tourism counter that?

EDWARDS: We have 275,000 unemployed people. I'm willing to promote a casino in New Orleans because it would create thousands of jobs.

USA TODAY: What is the image of Louisiana to the rest of the nation?

EDWARDS: We're 21st in tourist spending in the nation, which is better than the national average. We have a joy for living, an understanding of each other and a willingness to get along.

USA TODAY: Why do you stand out as a governor?

EDWARDS: Because I'm different. I say things I shouldn't say, in joking. And I'm controversial. It takes a peculiar sort of fellow to come out for casino gambling.

USA TODAY: You also have a reputation for being very popular with the ladies. Is that deserved?

EDWARDS: How did I earn it? By being nice to them. Like I'm popular with the poor people, and old people, black people. About 96 percent of the blacks in Louisiana vote for me every time I run, and will this time, because I'm sensitive to their needs. I brought them into government. It's just like with women. This state has more women in policy-making positions in government than any state in the nation. Two-thirds of the people that I appoint in policy-making positions are women. And I flirt a lot.

***Edwin Edwards**, 59, a Democrat, has won election three times as governor — 1972, 1975 and 1983.*

USA TODAY: Are you a family man?

EDWARDS: I've been married to the same woman for 38 years. We've never had any legal or emotional problems.

USA TODAY: Cajun is a ubiquitous word here. What is the word's origin?

EDWARDS: It's a contraction of the word Acadian. The Acadians came from Acadia, a province in Nova Scotia, about 215 years ago. They came down here to get away from British rule and because they wouldn't give up allegiance to the French king and the Catholic religion.

USA TODAY: Why is the spotlight on Cajuns?

EDWARDS: I was the first Cajun in 100 years to be elected governor. Cajuns had been looked down upon as a disadvantaged, non-productive, uneducated people. I made it a campaign issue. After that, they started teaching French in schools again, and Cajun culture took on a new emphasis. Cajun food began to take on a new national image.

Maine

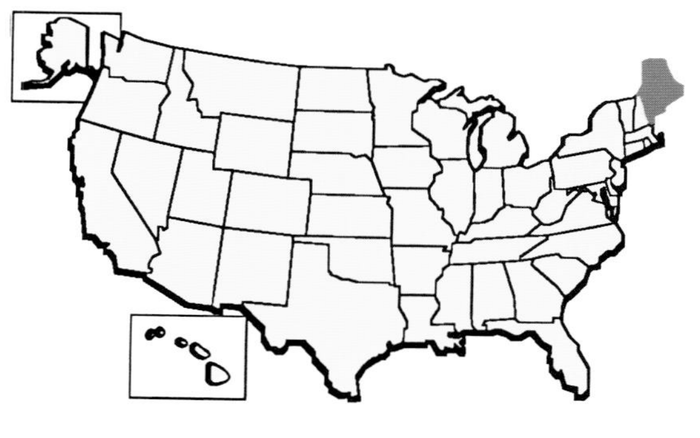

Visited: May 20-22, 1987
Featured in USA TODAY: May 29

"We're very independent. We are very warm people, but it takes us a little time."

Margaret Chase Smith
Four-term U.S. senator
Skowhegan, Maine

Maine

Lobster, 'THE lady,' woodpiles and canoes

Lobster. It's king here. 19.6 million pounds last year. No. 1 producer in the USA. Shipped around the world.

Another first: **Margaret Chase Smith**, 89. First woman to be elected to both the U.S. House of Representatives and the U.S. Senate. "THE Lady from Maine," she was called during her 33 years in Washington.

Now retired, she's back where she was born. Skowhegan (pop. 6,571). Still wearing a rose, her trademark during four U.S. Senate terms (1949-73).

What keeps her going?

"I work closely with younger people. I like to have dialogues with them to keep up with the times," says this worldly woman whose first job was in the local five-and-dime store at age 13. She earned 10 cents an hour.

In addition to THE lady and the lobsters, main impressions from Maine:

It's big by New England standards. Rugged. But clean. Litter is a four-letter word.

Status symbols:

■ Neatly stacked woodpiles.

■ Canoes, more prized than Cadillacs in the lake country.

■ Clothes from L.L. Bean.

One of the USA's most popular retail and mail-order stores. Just off U.S. 1 in Freeport (pop. 1,822). L.L. Bean started in 1912 with invention of lightweight, waterproof, Maine hunting shoes. Now you can buy anything to outdoor-outfit yourself, or an army.

Open 24 hours a day, 365 days a year. 2,200 employees. Another 1,800 are added for the Christmas rush.

The parking lots are packed with Porsches and pickup trucks. Three million shoppers stopped in last year. Nine million packages were shipped out.

JENKINS: Sold on seafood.

"We ARE Maine to many," says L.L. Bean executive **Kilton Andrew**, 54. He tells of middle of the night phone calls from places such as California with questions about hunting, fishing, lobsters.

Back to King Lobster. Let **Charlie Jenkins**, 60, owner of C & D's Halfway Market, a take-out seafood place in Saco (pop. 12,921), tell you how to prepare it:

Never boil a lobster. You'll pour the flavor down the drain. Always steam, broil or bake it.

Gov. **John McKernan**, 39, first-term Republican, tells you how, or how *not*, to eat it: "It isn't Maine to eat lobster sitting at a table with a coat and tie on." Roll up your sleeves. Or eat it at the beach. Let the butter drip.

MAINE LOBSTERS: Broil them, *never* boil them; let the butter drip.

Maine's license plates say it is "Vacationland." Tourism is the state's second-biggest industry. Mainers welcome visitors, but don't want to be like them.

Pat Curtis, 49, used to run a little grocery store in Searsport (pop. 1,110). Laughs about folks who were "always hurrying through their vacations."

Nurse's aide **Adrian Montgomery**, 38, Blue Hill (pop. 700), agrees. "I've learned the more you hurry, the less you get done."

Native Mainers are family people. Big families.

"I have 80 first cousins, 13 or 14 aunts and uncles. Around Christmas, you either have to cut the list short or get a loan," says **Tom Hanley**, 32, Department of Education word processor in Augusta, the state capital (pop. 21,819).

Adds **Crystal Brown**, 40, women's clothing store supervisor in Wells (pop. 850): "We all come from big families. Cold winters make big families, I guess."

That's Plain Talk from Maine.

HANLEY, BROWN: They're part of big Maine families.

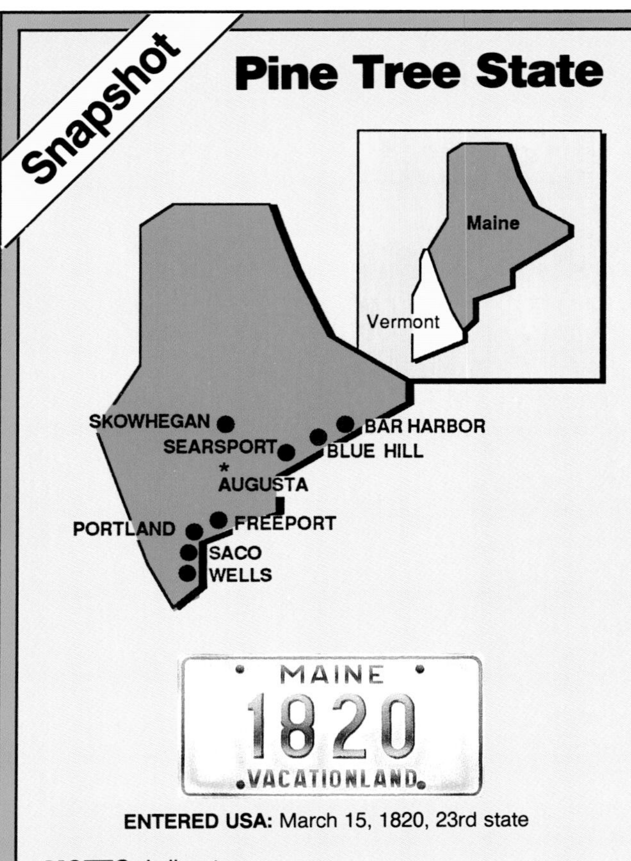

ENTERED USA: March 15, 1820, 23rd state

MOTTO: I direct
POPULATION: 1,174,000; rank, 38th
LARGEST CITY: Portland, pop. 61,803
CAPITAL: Augusta, pop. 21,819
LAND: 30,995 square miles; rank, 39th
POPULATION DENSITY: 37.9 per square mile; rank, 36th
RACIAL MIX: 98.7% white; 0.3% black; 0.3% Asian and Pacific islanders. Hispanic heritage: 0.4%.

Uniquely Maine

PACK 'EM IN: Maine leads the world in the production of canned sardines. More than 100 million cans are produced annually.

LOTSA LOBSTER: Maine lobstermen normally catch 80 to 90 percent of the nation's lobsters. The world's largest lobster boiler is in Rockland. The 24-foot-long boiler can steam 5,000 pounds an hour.

SUMMER STOCK: Lakeland Theater, the USA's first summer theater, opened in Madison in 1901.

GOOD KNIGHT: William Phipps of Phipps Point was the first resident of what now is the USA to be knighted at the English Court. He was honored in 1687 for returning treasure taken from sunken Spanish galleons.

EAR WEAR: In 1877, Chester Greenwood of Farmington invented the first pair of earmuffs by wiring together ear-shaped pieces of fur.

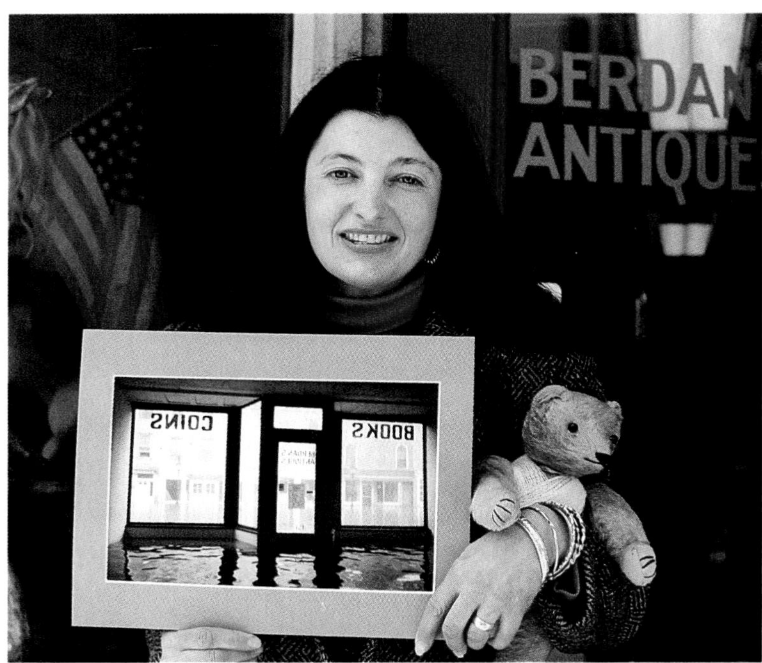

Betty Berdan
(with photo of April 1987 flood)
Antique dealer
Hallowell

"The water came up about a foot an hour. It was at a very angry, treacherous velocity. But everyone pulled together to help. All the churches had a collective dinner, with all the money going to flood victims. Hallowell had a tax increase, but they decided not to raise the taxes for waterfront street businesses until they get on their feet."

Thomas Peter, 27
Shipbuilder
Bath

"I could have gone to school in England, but there they work with computers. Here there's lots of fresh air. I work under a master boat builder. After this winter, I was ready to leave. I was living in a little house on a hill where I had to plow the driveway every day, sometimes twice."

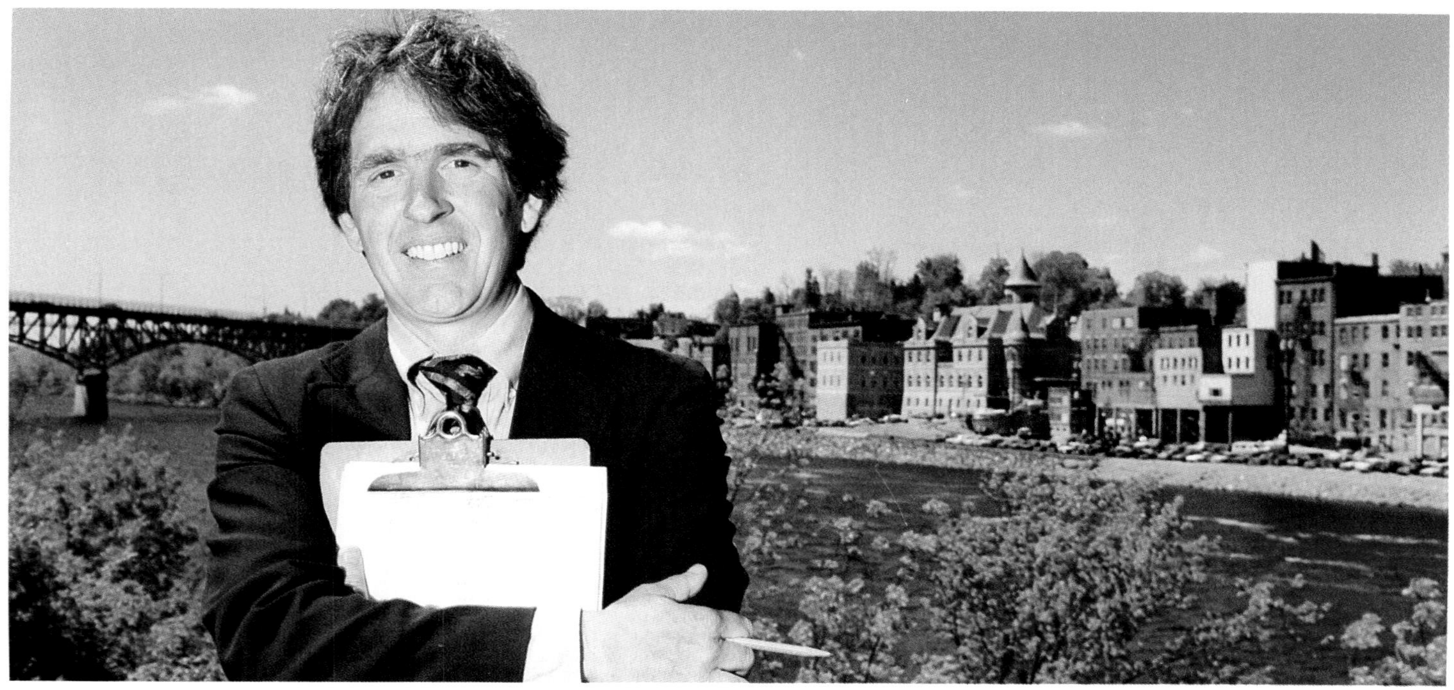

Voices
of Maine

Jay Adams, 41
Museum curator
Augusta

"My historical interest drives me at home and at work. For many of us, an early way of life is just a generation away. We live in an 1820 house that is on the register of historical sites. The new Augusta City Hall is being built directly behind the museum. How many towns build new city halls on historical sites? That's preservation and change all wrapped up into one."

Laurie Ledgard, 26
Reporter
Kennebunk

"I enjoy the stereotypical old Nor'easter lobsterman. You know, a scruffy old salt with an accent nobody can understand. You can't believe how intelligent, hard-working and dedicated they are to work and preserving their way of life. They always provide these wonderful personal pearls of wisdom."

Florence Callaghan, 65
Retired
Portland

"Everybody appreciates nature in Maine. It's all around us. It's in our bones. In Maine, we have time to look at the trees. We have a camp on a lake. Not a cottage — in Maine we're unpretentious."

Bob Ackerley, 42
Airport mechanic
East Yarmouth

"It's a calm, easy-going way of life here. When we have a 12-hour delay at the airport, Maine people still smile. I don't think I hear a car horn more than once a month, even with traffic jams. That's why the people live to be 80 or 90."

Ginny Foster, 33
Store owner
Bridgton

"You have to be pretty rugged to last up here. We burn 10 cords of wood a year. My husband splits it, and we all help lug it and stack it. We've already started on next year's wood. Maine people have the same talk, the same lingo. Ayuh, they do."

Notable

Margaret Chase Smith, *89, a Republican, was a U.S. senator from Maine for four terms. She was the first woman to win election to both the House and Senate. She returned to Skowhegan after her defeat in 1972.*

I ran for office as a person, not a woman

USA TODAY: You were born in Skowhegan and have seen more than 80 years of change in Maine. What are some of those changes?

SMITH: The textile mills are moving south, the shoe business is being ruined by foreign imports. The paper industry continues, of course, because we are a state of 31,000 square miles, and most of it is forest land. Tourism is very heavy up here. It's a short season. But winter sports bring a lot of people in.

USA TODAY: You have established a library in Skowhegan. What does it contain?

SMITH: I had 36 years at the Capitol, and all of my records, memorabilia and papers are there.

USA TODAY: What characteristics would best describe a native of Maine?

SMITH: We're very independent. We are very warm people, but it takes us a little time. We want to be sure that you're not seeking some particular favor. We're a very cooperative people, a very hearty and ambitious people.

USA TODAY: How difficult was it to launch a political career so long before the women's movement started?

SMITH: I am proud of what I did as a woman. But I didn't do it as a feminist. In fact, I moved over to the Senate in 1949 and, to be honest with you, I never was a "woman" candidate. And when I was elected in the Senate, I was one of two U.S. senators from Maine. I wasn't a "woman" senator.

USA TODAY: Does a woman have a good chance of finishing what you started by being elected president?

SMITH: I think of women differently than most people do. I think of women as being people. I hope that what I have done will do for women in the future what the pioneer women did for me and the people in my time period.

USA TODAY: When will we have a woman president?

SMITH: I can see no reason why a man or a woman, if qualified and desirous of being president, can't do it. I don't think it will be done right away, and I don't know that it will be done in this century. But it's coming very close.

Topic: MAINE

Pioneering spirit tends to change your values

USA TODAY: Shortly after you were inaugurated in January, you said, "It's time our children were no longer Maine's No. 1 export."

McKERNAN: Young people in the state, after they graduate, go to Massachusetts or Connecticut and find work. Then, years later, they come back. What really struck me is there's something about the uniqueness of Maine that really runs deep in people.

USA TODAY: What do most people think about Maine?

McKERNAN: They think of the natural beauty, the coast, the absolutely clean air, the freshness. And they also think of rural poverty. They don't realize what kind of opportunities there are, and that Portland is one of the best metropolitan areas in the country to live or work in.

USA TODAY: What would you like Maine's image to be?

McKERNAN: We want to get the word out that we have opportunity that's missing in some parts of this country. We are working to provide opportunities for people to not only invest, but also to address some of the shortcomings we have in parts of the state. We also must raise some aspirations in some of the northern and eastern parts of the state so that we can provide the skilled work force that people are going to need to make those kinds of investments.

USA TODAY: Maine is still very much pioneer country with a lot of open area. How does that affect people's lives?

McKERNAN: It changes your values. A woman from Massachusetts told me, "The difference is that when you live here, you don't have all the other activities that lure you out on Friday, Saturday nights, even during the middle of the week. Your life has a tendency to revolve around your children. And that brings a community together. But I don't want people to think this pioneering spirit means there are no amenities here.

The Guv

John McKernan, *39, a Republican, was elected in 1986. McKernan is a former U.S. representative.*

USA TODAY: Tourism is the second-largest industry in the state behind paper manufacturing. How does that translate into dollars?

McKERNAN: Four billion dollars — but we only spend a million dollars. There are 47 states in the country that spend more to advertise tourism than Maine.

USA TODAY: Why hasn't Maine spent more?

McKERNAN: Because there was a feeling that, well, we've got enough people here in July and August anyway. There are other things that we ought to be doing to help get people into the state and into areas other than along the coast between July and August. We have beautiful spring and summer seasons and an incredible fall, not to mention the winter. We hope to help some of the smaller businesses.

USA TODAY: Do you ever go white-water rafting?

McKERNAN: I've done white-water rafting. That is a good example of the kind of burgeoning little industry that we ought to be doing more to advertise. We ought to let the various rafting companies fight over who's going to get the lion's share of the business.

USA TODAY: Stephen King, the horror-novel author, may be one of Maine's most celebrated residents. Is that a blessing?

McKERNAN: He was a major supporter of my opponent. But we're trying to heal that.

Maryland

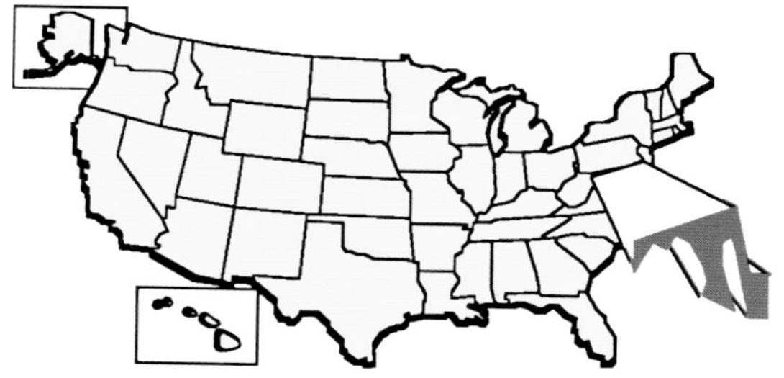

Visited: Aug. 11-12, 1987
Featured in USA TODAY: Aug. 14

"Marylanders don't use forks or knives to eat crabs. And they don't wear anything they'd wear to church on Sunday. It's great fun."

Brice Phillips
Restaurant owner
Ocean City, Md.

Maryland

Star-Spangled Banner marks miniature USA

It was a key battle of the War of 1812. **Francis Scott Key**, a young lawyer, watched aboard ship as the British shelled Fort McHenry all night.

He was inspired to pen *The Star-Spangled Banner*, as the 15-star flag fluttered in the light of the explosions. More than 100 years later — in 1931 — it was adopted as the national anthem.

KEY: Inspired at Fort McHenry.

Folks in Maryland think that very appropriate. They consider their state a miniature of the nation. "America in miniature," says a slogan. Of course, they mean "USA in miniature."

They point out Maryland, although 42nd state in size, has a little bit of nearly everything found across the USA. Seashore, mountains, farmers, fishermen. A little coal. A little tobacco. Some snow. Some sizzle. A few ships. A few thoroughbreds.

It also has a lot of some things. Seafood. Chesapeake Bay has its share of pollution problems, but it still produces much of our oyster and crab. Last year's harvest:

- 58 million pounds of hard-shell and soft-shell crabs. No. 1 in USA.
- 9 million pounds of oysters. No. 2 in the USA.

CRAB-KING PHILLIPS: Flavorful and fun food.

The crab capital has a crab king. **Brice Phillips**, 65. A landmark and legend in Ocean City (pop. 4,946). In 1956, he and his wife, **Shirley**, 65, turned a tar paper crab shack into a seafood restaurant.

Now, the family has a string of seven along the seashore. Crab-crazies line up around the block nightly in the summertime. Over 6,000 are served daily in one restaurant alone.

Says Phillips: "Chesapeake Bay gives seafood a better flavor. It's not the size of the crabs, it's the flavor. We steam them in 25-gallon pots. We dump two or three dozen on the table, add some corn on the cob and beer. Marylanders don't use forks or knives to eat crabs. And they don't wear anything they'd wear to church on Sunday. It's great fun."

The state that gave us the national anthem during a sea battle also is home to the nation's Naval Academy. Established at Annapolis (pop. 33,600) in 1845. Began admitting women in 1975. Currently trains 4,667 midshipmen and women.

The class of '88 includes **Bill Conley**, 22, from Boston and **Dawn Bennett**, 21, from Baltimore.

Says Bennett: "It's still a little hard for the women to get integrated. But if you perform as well as a guy, you do get equal recognition. The thing that attracted me was the uniform and all the discipline."

While Annapolis has the academy and the state capital, Baltimore is the hub. Largest city (pop. 763,570). A decade or two ago it had a reputation as one of our most decadent major markets. Now it's earned the label of the Comeback City.

Shops, restaurants and aquarium of Inner Harbor now attract millions of visitors to what was a rundown, rat-infested row of waterfront warehouses.

Frank Hopkins, 44, owns a souvenir shop at Inner Harbor. "I've seen the pride come back," says Hopkins, abrim with pride himself.

Much of the credit for the comeback goes to **William Donald Schaefer**, 65. Now the 1st-term Democratic governor. Mayor of Baltimore from 1971 to 1986. Outspoken. Controversial. Some call him a loner. Nearly all acknowledge he's a doer.

Says the mayor-turned-guv: "I have a theory about mayors and governors. Don't sit around the office. When you go out on the streets and into the country, your department heads can't fool you. If you don't know what's going on out there, they'll tell you all about the big bridge they're building but you won't know they didn't fix the potholes in the streets next to the bridge."

That's Plain Talk from Maryland.

DAWN BENNETT and BILL CONLEY: In Annapolis Naval Academy class of '88.

Snapshot

Free State

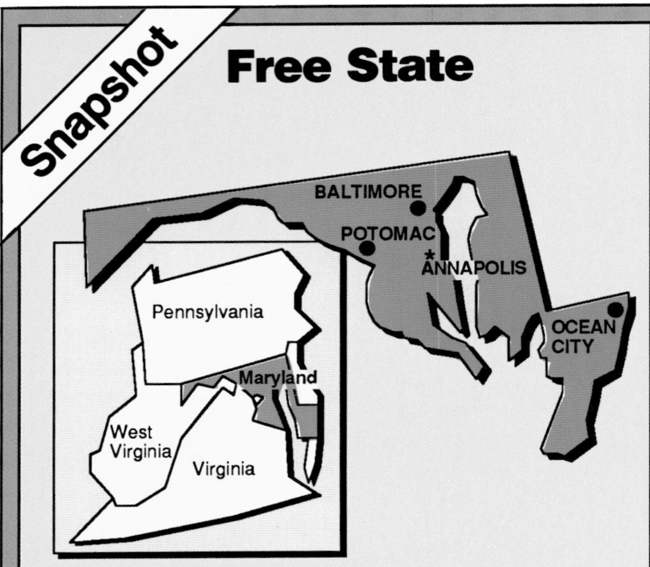

ENTERED USA: April 28, 1788, 7th state

MOTTO: Manly deeds, womanly words
POPULATION: 4,463,000; rank, 20th
LARGEST CITY: Baltimore, pop. 763,570
CAPITAL: Annapolis, pop. 33,600
LAND: 9,837 square miles; rank, 42nd
POPULATION DENSITY: 453.7 per square mile; rank, 5th
RACIAL MIX: 74.9% white; 22.7% black; 1.5% Asian and Pacific islanders. Hispanic heritage: 1.5%.

Uniquely Md.

SHINING ARMOR: Jousting is recognized as the official state sport.

CABIN FEVER: Uncle Tom's Cabin, immortalized by Harriet Beecher Stowe, is still standing as part of a private house in Bethesda.

SHORE-TO-SHORE SERVICE: The Oxford to Bellevue Ferry on the Eastern Shore is said to be the oldest continuous free-running ferry route in the USA. It has run daily since the 1700s.

SPIRITUAL GUIDANCE: The Fuld brothers of Baltimore invented the ouija board in 1892.

WILD HORSES: The free-roaming Assateague ponies are descendants of horses that swam ashore from a wrecked Spanish galleon in the 17th century.

SCOREBOARD: The USA's first sports magazine was Baltimore's "American Turf Register and Sporting Magazine," published in 1829.

Voices
of Maryland

Mary Wiley, 24
Jockey
Laurel

"The day of The Preakness, the air is filled with electricity. This is the sport of kings. For a rider and a horse to communicate on the track like we do is unbelievable. The horse is putting out. The jock is putting out. We're together as one as we come down to the money. To feel the horses thundering by . . . it's beautiful."

Jim Shriver, 59
Postal carrier/farmer
Westminster

"I'm a rural carrier, and I farm part time. Farming is sort of a lonely occupation. Delivering mail you get to see people to chat with them. Sooner or later everybody gets to know their mailman — or 'mail person.'"

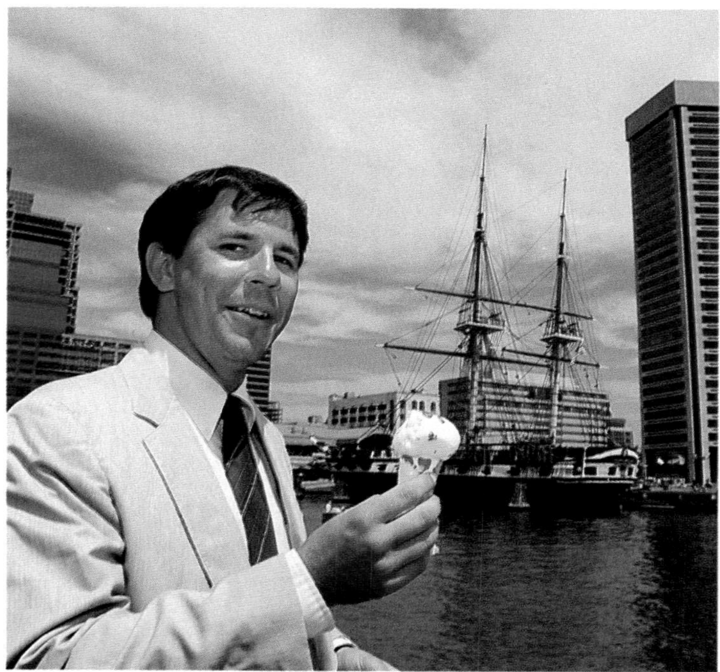

Don Geaslen, 29
Accountant
Millersville

"Baltimore is on the upswing of the pendulum. When I came here seven years ago, it was the older city you read about in the papers, in the process of making a turnaround. We've made it."

Kyle Culpepper, 29
Sportswear salesman
Baltimore

"Eating crabs at Harborplace is one of my favorite pastimes. I like the environment of the harbor. It gets crowded, but it's not hustle and bustle. It's relaxing being near the water."

William Lutz, 44
Carpenter
Wheaton

"Everything goes a little bit deeper in Maryland. You run across somebody who's really from here, and they'll know a little bit about the history and want to talk about it. I was born and raised in Montgomery County. That makes me neutral. I like the Redskins, but I'll bet against them to stir up a little something. It gets boring if five people are all rooting for the same team."

Vivian Wierenga, 75
Retired
Annapolis

"This is a big boat town. It's changed from a tiny little fishing village to a suburb of Washington. They come over here and bring their boats. They're nice people, just too many of them. My husband taught at the Naval Academy, and I taught at a public school. We're civilian, but it's nice because of the structure setup. If they know you're from the Navy, they know you're all right. You can get into any club."

Brian Workinger, 28
Computer program assistant
Gaithersburg

"I think the Chesapeake Bay is something we have to strive to protect. I think nature may be losing ground to man. There's still good crab, but you don't get as many today as you used to. We're trying to determine what shape we'll be in 10 years down the road. We're becoming more aware of problems we've had and are taking steps to combat them."

Jeanine Waterfield, 24
Teacher
Ocean City

"I teach in the winter time and waitress here in the summer. I can't imagine doing anything else in the summer. My mother thinks I'm a beach bum. It's go as you are in Ocean City. You can go on the beach all morning long, take five minutes to get ready for work, go in with your hair wet. That's beach life."

Sugar Ray Leonard, 31, who lives in Potomac, Md., is world middleweight champion. Last April, he scored a 12-round split decision over previous champion Marvin Hagler, who hadn't lost a fight in 11 years.

He rates residents champs for caring

USA TODAY: As a boxer, did you get a lot of support from Palmer Park, the community where you grew up?

LEONARD: I did get a lot of support. In fact, when we needed money to travel to national tournaments, people from area businesses would donate X amount of dollars. It was great support.

USA TODAY: When you come home to Maryland, what do you look forward to most?

LEONARD: My mother and father live in this area. I come back to Potomac and play tennis with my brothers and friends. My wife says I have an obsession with tennis.

USA TODAY: What are Maryland's strengths?

LEONARD: I think of caring. People are appreciative and more apt to do things for other people.

USA TODAY: What sort of things have the state and your community done to honor you?

LEONARD: They've gone all out to show their appreciation and acknowledge my accomplishments.

USA TODAY: What sort of business ventures do you have in Maryland?

LEONARD: I just signed up with Mutual Broadcasting, so I have a radio show. I've also formed a career management team to assist professional boxers.

USA TODAY: You were out at the Olympic Festival. Who impressed you out there?

LEONARD: There were a couple kids really. Andrew Maynard. I think he's from Virginia. There's a kid, Robert Bow, a heavyweight.

USA TODAY: Do you think people in Maryland want to see Ray in the ring again?

LEONARD: I don't know. I think probably just the ones that made money on me.

USA TODAY: Do you see yourself there again?

LEONARD: I doubt very seriously. I'm quite busy nowadays. Call me in three years.

USA TODAY: What do Maryland people think about Marvin Hagler?

LEONARD: Who? (laughs)

Topic: MARYLAND

Traveling in our state is a mini-tour of USA

USA TODAY: Some say Maryland is this nation in miniature. What does that mean?

SCHAEFER: We've got a big metropolitan area, an ocean, farm land, and little villages. There are places just bursting with energy. Baltimore has good museums and an aquarium, and a lot of things tourists can see. Mountains out in Western Maryland. Ducks flying all over the place. So anything in the United States is right here.

USA TODAY: The Chesapeake Bay is a recreational and economic treasure, but it has pollution problems.

SCHAEFER: We can save the bay. I need a million people — a million people of the 5 million people in this state committed to saving the bay.

USA TODAY: What's an example of something an individual can do to help save the bay?

SCHAEFER: A sponge crab is a female crab that has a sponge on the bottom of its eggs. I would never keep a sponge crab under any circumstances. I would put it back so it could lay eggs. I am very meticulous in never catching or keeping a fish that isn't right.

USA TODAY: Your approach is credited with revitalizing Baltimore when you were mayor. What lessons did you learn there that other large cities need to learn?

SCHAEFER: Go to the neighborhoods and work with people in the communities. Build strong neighborhood organizations. Let people do things for people. The mayors don't spend time in the communities. They don't organize. The second thing is a very close association with the business community. The city couldn't have moved forward if we didn't have cooperation from the business community. The third thing is brain power.

USA TODAY: While you were mayor, the Baltimore Colts left for Indianapolis. Will NFL football return to Baltimore?

SCHAEFER: We've got a good chance. When the owner pulled the team out, all the NFL owners were embarrassed. They felt there was some moral obligation to put a team back, but as time goes on and ownership changes, the moral obligation gives way to the bottom line.

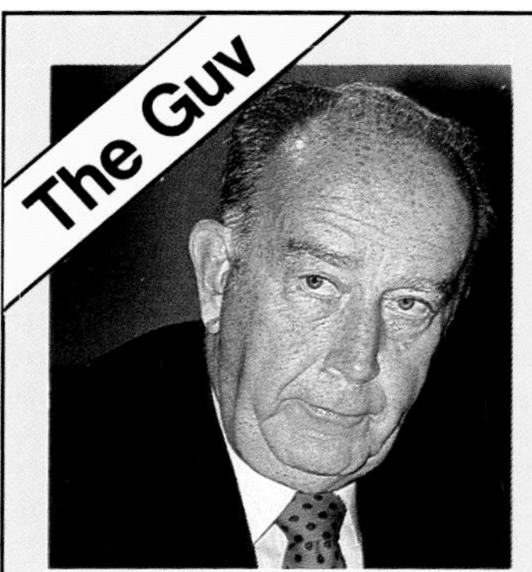

William Donald Schaefer, 65, a Democrat, was elected last year. He was mayor of Baltimore 15 years.

USA TODAY: Now that you are governor, what are your priorities?

SCHAEFER: Everything is my priority. I think if I concentrate on one priority, I make a mistake. What are my priorities? Economic development, the Chesapeake Bay, environment, prisons, mental institutions, mental health. All those are very important.

USA TODAY: Which is the better job, mayor or governor?

SCHAEFER: Mayor.

USA TODAY: Will you enjoy being governor as much?

SCHAEFER: No.

USA TODAY: Why is that? What's different about the job?

SCHAEFER: As mayor, you're right with people. You belong to somebody. Walk along the street, and senior citizens know you're going to do something for them. Kids know you are going to try to do something. Black people know you're going to try to do something, or at least they're going to be able to talk to you. They write you letters. They get on talk shows and blast you. Once in a while someone says something kind, and you almost drop dead.

Massachusetts

Visited: May 12-13, 1987
Featured in USA TODAY: May 18

"Coming here puts people in touch with their own pasts. . . . They realize that most of their ancestors traveled here like this, too. It helps people to realize that we all have a lot in common."

Steve Kocur
Site supervisor at Plymouth Rock
North Dartmouth, Mass.

Massachusetts

Presidents and poets, redcoats and Red Sox

Heavy history has unfolded for more than 350 years. History is revered here.

"Ask more than what we are going to do. Ask what we have already done" . . . from Gov. **Michael S. Dukakis**' presidential campaign kickoff three weeks ago.

History:

■ 1620. The Pilgrims landed at Plymouth Rock — by mistake. They were headed for the Virginia territory south of New York.

■ 1775. April 18. **Paul Revere** and **William Dawes** awaited the prearranged lantern signal in Boston's Old North Church. "One if by land." They jumped on horses, spread the word, "The British are coming!"

The next morning "the shot heard 'round the world" was fired as Minutemen confronted the redcoats at Lexington and Concord. The war of the Revolution had begun. And it was won.

"You can't come to Boston and not feel patriotic. You get a tingling all over," says Oklahoma restaurant supplier **Chuck Gresham**, 41, visiting here last week from Tulsa with his wife.

From the beginning, Massachusetts has been a preacher and teacher to the rest of the USA. It prides itself on giving us presidents and poets aplenty.

■ **John F. Kennedy**, 1961-63. **Calvin Coolidge**, 1923-29. **John Quincy Adams**, 1825-29. **John Adams**, 1797-1801.

Kennedy is not only the most recent, but the most revered.

The place the Kennedy torch burns brightest is the John F. Kennedy Presidential Library and Museum.

CAROLINE: Studies law at Columbia University.

"The library is designed to encourage visitors and especially young people, who cannot remember what occurred in the 1960s, to feel a sense of participation in those times," says **Caroline Kennedy Schlossberg**, 29, the president's daughter, now a law student in New York.

■ Poets and authors. **Ralph Waldo Emerson** wrote here. So did **Henry David Thoreau**. **Nathaniel Hawthorne**. **Henry Wadsworth Longfellow**. **John Updike** still does.

Much of modern Massachusetts history is being written by scientists and business people. From America's Revolution to computer revolution. Hi-tech highways stretch from Boston to Newton to Framingham and beyond. Paved with computer chips.

■ Digital Equipment. 1986 sales: $7.6 billion. Employs 94,700.

■ Wang Laboratories. 1986 sales: $2.6 billion. Employs 30,000.

■ Data General. 1986 sales: $1.24 billion. Employs 16,535.

Universities are ubiquitous. Most of the presidents and poets of the past — and money-makers of the present — passed through the once ivy-covered halls of Harvard.

FAJARD: Grew from 'obnoxious organism.'

Most uppity of the uppity Ivy League. But the ivy is gone. Harvard has stripped the vines from its buildings to slow damage to its walls. But the other traditions live.

"It's remarkable how the Harvard label blows people away," says **Andres Fajard**, 24, a senior social studies major from Palo Alto, Calif. Thinking back four years, he adds, "There is no more obnoxious organism on Earth than a Harvard freshman."

Patty Minehart, 25, graduate student at Cambridge's MIT, who watches Harvardians come and go, adds, "People here are intelligent and humane. If they could learn to be polite, they would be perfect."

Sports and entertainment play well here. TV's *St. Elsewhere*, *Spenser: For Hire* and *Cheers* are set against Boston's brick and cobblestone.

The Celtics, 1986 NBA champs, moved past Milwaukee Sunday, a step closer to repeating. The Red Sox hope to wipe out their 1986 World Series woes.

Even in sports, some take a sophisticated satirical point of view.

Dan Greaney, 22, former Harvard Lampoon editor and now junior journalist on the BusCapade, describes the Boston sports scene this way:

"The Celtics almost always win. The Red Sox always almost win."

Read it again slowly if you didn't get it. Don't be embarrassed. Most of us have to hear those Harvard quips at least twice before they take.

That's Plain Talk from Massachusetts.

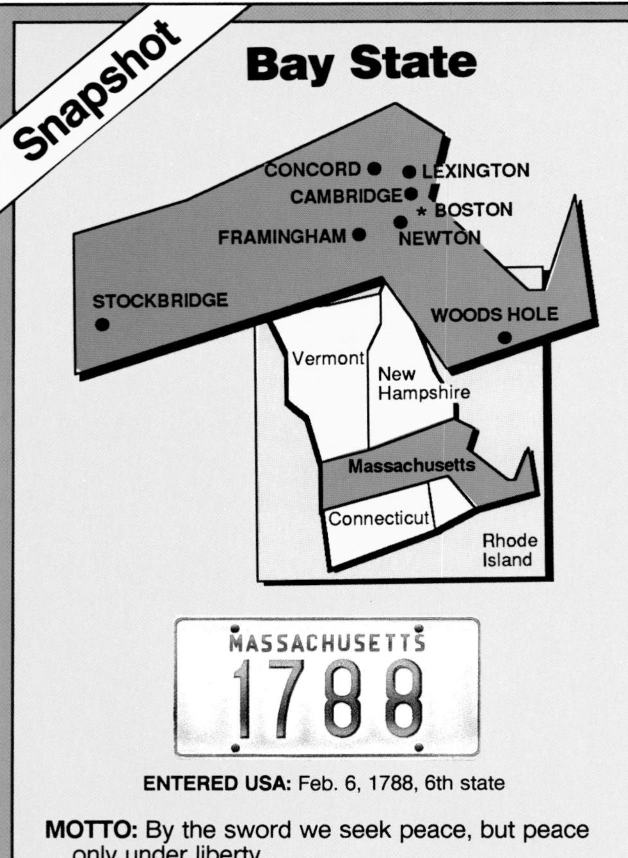

ENTERED USA: Feb. 6, 1788, 6th state

MOTTO: By the sword we seek peace, but peace only under liberty
POPULATION: 5,832,000; rank, 12th
LARGEST CITY: Boston, pop. 570,519
CAPITAL: Boston
LAND: 7,824 square miles; rank, 45th
POPULATION DENSITY: 745.4 per square mile; rank, 3rd
RACIAL MIX: 93.5% white; 3.9% black; 0.9% Asian and Pacific islanders. Hispanic heritage: 2.5%.

Uniquely Mass.

FIRE PREVENTION: In 1638, Massachusetts passed the USA's first no-smoking ordinance. It prohibited the smoking of tobacco outdoors. Reason: prevent fires.

COOKIE CUTTERS: The chocolate chip cookie was invented at the Tollhouse Inn in Whitman. The fig newton was named for Newton, a Boston suburb.

PICTURESQUE: The Berkshire town of Stockbridge was home to artist Norman Rockwell, famed for "The Saturday Evening Post" covers.

WHALE OF A TALE: Herman Melville wrote "Moby Dick" while at Arrowhead.

PREMIER BUS BOY: French Prime Minister Jacques Chirac worked as a busboy at a Howard Johnson's while attending Harvard.

MERRY CHRISTMAS: The first USA-printed Christmas card was made in Roxbury in 1874.

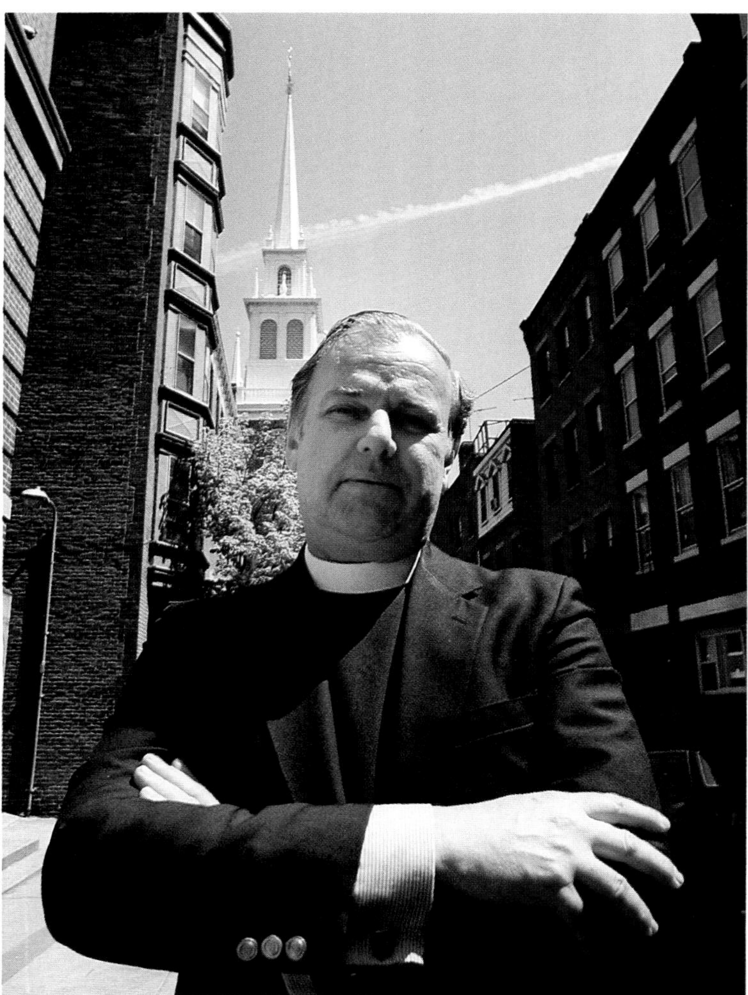

Robert Golledge, 54
Vicar, Old North Church
Boston

"Massachusetts is both a historic state and one that combines a variety of scenic things, from seacoast to mountains and hills, and urban centers to lots of country. Having everything so close, to have the opportunity to move from one to the other, gives you that rhythm that makes life particularly pleasant. Boston is a neat combination of the old and the new."

Danell Tomasella, 30
Student
Arlington

"There is a sense of origins here. You don't necessarily have to be into history to appreciate that history."

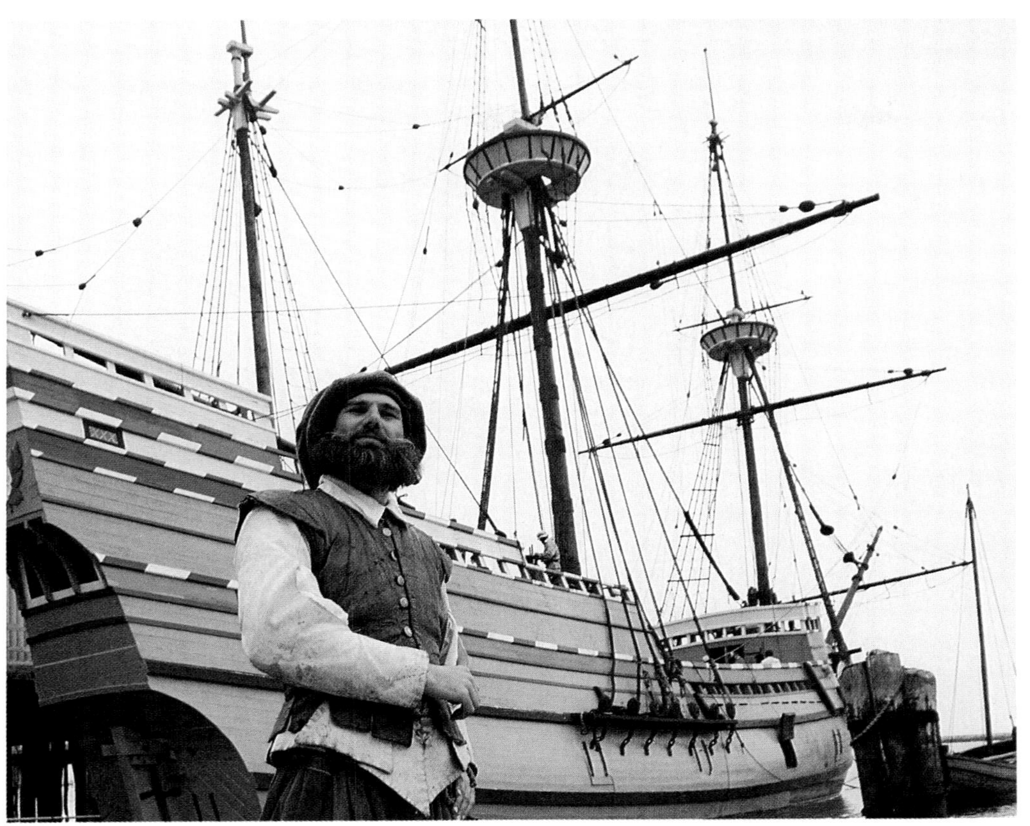

Voices
of Massachusetts

Steve Kocur, 30
Site supervisor,
Plymouth Rock
North Dartmouth

"Coming here puts people in touch with their own pasts. Even if they are not recent immigrants, they realize that most of their ancestors traveled here like this, too. It helps people realize that we all have a lot in common."

Arthur Ferreira, 57
Salvation Army Major
Brockton

"This state has clout because of the people who have come from here. Take Tip O'Neill and the Kennedys, for example. Some people around here don't like them, but you can't deny what they have done for the state."

Charles Cummiff, 30
Fisherman
Woods Hole

"It's like Coney Island here (along the Cape). It's all people trying to make too much money too fast. Just wait for the day when we have to pump in water for people to drink. Tell me then what people will say."

Joanna Revelas, 25
Editor
Boston

"The Sox may lose in the end, but the fans are diehard. You don't know what it's like to have a broken heart until you've become a Sox fan."

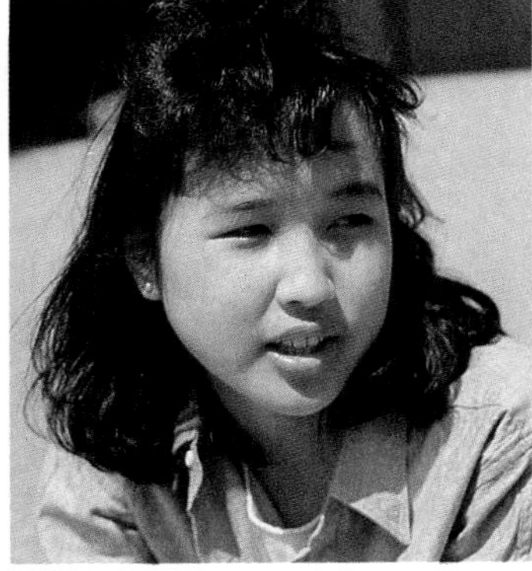

Andrea Li, 19
Student, MIT
Cambridge

"People say students here just study, do nothing, are 'nerdly.' But I was shocked when I first came here. The work is tough. But the parties are pretty wild. There are so many schools here. It's really a student sort of city. Boston's nice. It's kind of quaint."

Dick Gregory, 54, a resident of Plymouth, Mass., is a civil rights activist, nutritionist and author. He has protested against world hunger since the 1960s.

Here, it's like living in a picture post card

USA TODAY: You moved from Chicago to Plymouth, Mass., in 1973. Why?

GREGORY: With 10 children, I was trying to find an area that had fairly clean air where they could run and see nature and that was close enough to a major airport — because I travel all the time.

USA TODAY: How did your family take it?

GREGORY: They really resented leaving Chicago. I didn't realize that when you barge out of a polluted, overcrowded city that's crime-ridden with dope addicts, that when they got on the farm, they were scared of butterflies and chipmunks.

USA TODAY: Not really?

GREGORY: I came home one day, and they'd all checked into a hotel in town because a chipmunk was in the kitchen. The first day we were here, my wife, Lil, cried for two days.

USA TODAY: Are you sorry you moved?

GREGORY: In all my years on this planet, it's the best decision I ever made. Because the children changed. You could see them loosen up. We were so far away from a grocery store you could control the eating. And we didn't put a television in. It really forced them to get to know one another.

USA TODAY: How would you describe Plymouth?

GREGORY: The town is almost like living in a post card. Millions of people come every year to see where America got started. The most interesting day in Plymouth is Thanksgiving. You can come and see the Plymouth Rock and people dressed like Pilgrims. Then up on top of the hill across the street are Indians talking about how bad white folks are. Then at 5 o'clock they feed the Indians the traditional Thanksgiving meal. Plymouth Rock is small — about three feet wide. I had people throw bigger rocks at me when I was a child.

USA TODAY: What do you do to relax?

GREGORY: The biggest surprise to me is that, having been born and raised in ghettos, I was always running from home to someplace else. Beauty always seemed to be someplace else. It was — you know, you would take a vacation. Now, there's no reason to take a vacation because it's all there — at home.

Topic: MASSACHUSETTS

Our economic strength is in our diversity

USA TODAY: How is your campaign for the Democratic presidential nomination going?

DUKAKIS: We're off to a good start. Obviously, it's going to take at least three months to put the outline of a national campaign together, and this is going to be a 50-state campaign.

USA TODAY: What issues will you focus on?

DUKAKIS: I'm going to try to run a very positive campaign and emphasize the economic issues. I'm very deeply concerned about major foreign policy issues. I also believe strongly in partnerships between Washington, the states, business and labor. That's the way we've done it in Massachusetts, and it's worked.

USA TODAY: How do you think your campaign will be received in the Midwest, which is undergoing severe farm and manufacturing crises?

DUKAKIS: I am the governor of a state which 12 years ago was an absolute basket case, economically and financially. Today it is one of the great economic success stories. It's an industrial state, but we have some farming.

USA TODAY: Massachusetts' Employment Training program has received praise nationally for preparing welfare recipients for jobs. Is this a national blueprint?

DUKAKIS: You can train people until you're blue in the face. But if there aren't any jobs out there, you can't do much. We hope to get national welfare reform legislation — which is very much like ET — out of Congress this year.

USA TODAY: How else would you help regions with severe economic problems right now?

DUKAKIS: You can pull any region out of the economic doldrums if you work hard at it, if you put in some public resources and you bring the private sector in with you and go to work.

USA TODAY: Is that how it worked in Massachusetts?

DUKAKIS: Southeastern Massachusetts has been chronically depressed since the 1930s. The unemployment rate was 14 percent. I went down there in 1983 and said, "Folks, we're going to put together a regional development effort." Today, we've got a labor shortage in South Massachusetts.

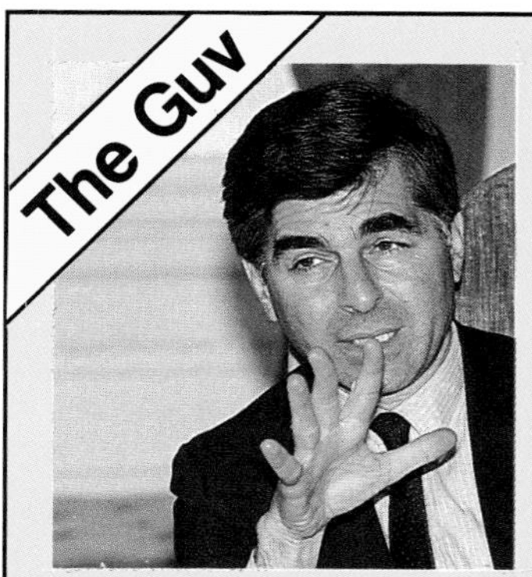

Michael Dukakis, 53, a Democrat, was first elected governor in 1975. He was elected again in 1982 and 1986.

USA TODAY: Hasn't hi-tech industry been a major factor in your economic growth?

DUKAKIS: Hi-tech is very important to us, but in terms of employment, it's maybe 10 percent of the total economy. Tourism employs many more people. Diversity is our great strength.

USA TODAY: Do you think the press is overzealous in its coverage of presidential candidates?

DUKAKIS: When you run for the presidency, you've got to assume that you're going to be the subject of intensive scrutiny.

USA TODAY: Gary Hart's aides asked him, "Is there anything that we should know?" Did your aides ask you?

DUKAKIS: No, I don't think they ever have, probably because after 25 years in this business, and in my ninth year as a governor, what you see is what you get. I'm not a very complicated guy. I love what I'm doing. I love my family. I've been blessed to live in a state that's been very supportive of me most of the time. And when it wasn't, it was my own fault.

Michigan

Visited: March 25-28, 1987
Featured in USA TODAY: March 30

"We're a center of high technology, and great public institutions, great public universities. We're a state of ideas."

Michigan Gov. James Blanchard

Michigan

Motown to Mackinac: Fired up, but fidgety

This state of Michigan, celebrating its 150th birthday, is like an old fighter back in the ring to regain his championship.

Fitting for a state that gave us **Joe Louis** in the 1930s, Michiganians — or Michiganders, for those who prefer that — in 1987 are fired up and ready to fight for their future. Because they have lost as well as won their share of fights, they're also a bit fidgety.

You sense a sort of "nervous high." Historically, hope and hopelessness have been close cousins here.

Memories of two recent examples keep Michigan folks a bit off balance.

■ Chrysler's near-collapse and $3.5 billion bailout in 1979.

■ The state government's near-bankruptcy and record $1.7 billion deficit in 1983.

Both those fights were won dramatically. But the sweet tastes of victory also left some scars and keep some people scared.

Chrysler's comeback made Bossman **Lee Iacocca** the folk hero. Especially for those who bought Chrysler stock at around $2 a share in '79 and have watched it zoom to $55. But the fact that one of the three big auto companies nearly went belly-up is always on the minds in Michigan.

Gov. **James Blanchard** gritted his teeth when he inherited the dreadful deficit in '83, and raised income taxes (temporarily). In 1986, the state had a cash surplus of more than $150 million. There's a huge relief the state is back in the black, but it's mixed with uneasiness about a repeat.

MAYOR YOUNG: In front of statue *Spirit of Detroit*, part of city's rebirth.

The "nervous high" state of mind certainly describes Detroit (pop. 1,088,973).

There, a business power group called "Detroit Renaissance" works with Mayor **Coleman Young** on major area programs and projects. Originally set up with a strong push from **Henry Ford II**, the group is now chaired by General Motors boss **Roger Smith**.

The RenCen board, as it's called locally, last week reviewed and rode on the mayor's People Mover, a fancy elevated train that will open for business in August and loop the three-mile downtown area. The group reviewed plans for an ambitious Theatre District development downtown.

"The challenge is to get all these horses running in the right direction. Because you've sure got a lot of them running around," GM's Smith said. Fired up, but fidgety.

Outstate, the nervousness seems a little lower, the highs a little higher, the fight for survival and success more often won.

HAPPY IN MICHIGAN: Nelsons in front of gas station-grocery store.

■ In Thompson (pop. 100), on the shore of Lake Michigan, 100 miles west of Mackinac, **Jack Nelson** and his wife, **Candy,** both 42, own and run Thompson Outpost. They sell gasoline and groceries, rent out cabins, dispense fish bait and fish stories.

"The spirit that built the country exists here. If someone gets stuck in a ditch, you pull them out and don't expect to be paid," says Nelson.

■ In Turkeyville, USA, near Marshall (pop. 7,201) in South Central Michigan, **Wayne** and **Marjorie Cornwell** started raising turkeys and serving turkey dinners in a 26-seat, one-room restaurant in 1942. Now, the Cornwell family carves and serves 15,000 turkeys to 500,000 visitors annually, in a huge barnwood dining room. Cornwell says his business is no "turkey." He's not nervous about the future.

■ In Ann Arbor, home of the University of Michigan, **Tom Monaghan** was renting a room for $6 a week in 1961. He decided to go into the pizza business.

Today, his Domino's Pizza chain has 3,800 outlets in 50 states and seven foreign countries.

Multi-millionaire Monaghan, who celebrated his 50th birthday last week, says:

"If you're starting out from scratch, you have to look far down the road. You have to be patient and wait until the cows start giving milk before you start spending it."

That's Plain Talk from Michigan.

Snapshot

Wolverine State

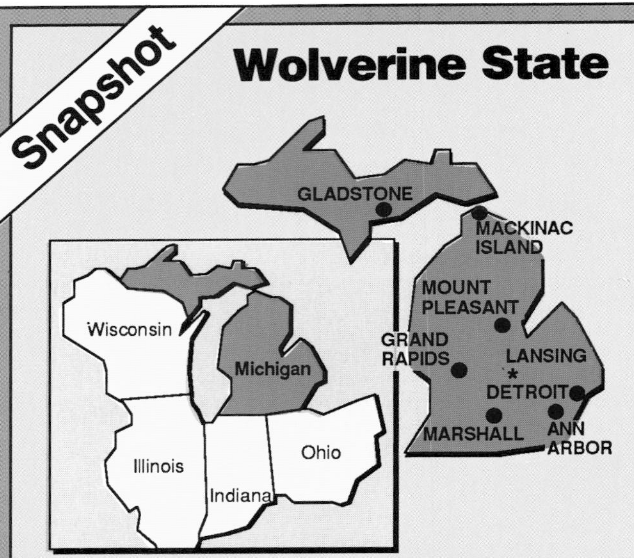

MICHIGAN
1837
GREAT LAKES

ENTERED USA: Jan. 26, 1837, 26th state

MOTTO: If you seek a pleasant peninsula, look around you

POPULATION: 9,145,000; rank, 8th

LARGEST CITY: Detroit, pop. 1,088,973

CAPITAL: Lansing, pop. 127,972

LAND: 56,954 square miles; rank, 22nd

POPULATION DENSITY: 160.6 per square mile; rank, 14th

RACIAL MIX: 85.0% white; 12.9% black; 0.6% Asian and Pacific islanders. Hispanic heritage: 1.8%.

Uniquely Mich.

CARS ABANDONED: In the state that has the motor capital of the world, there is a place where cars are forbidden: the summer resort island of Mackinac, founded before cars were commonplace. Mode of transportation: horse-drawn carriages and wagons, bicycles or foot.

FAMOUS FALLS: Tahquamenon Falls was immortalized in Longfellow's "Song of Hiawatha."

ROSE BOWL: The University of Michigan Wolverines won the first Rose Bowl in 1902, beating Stanford 49-0. They've won 4 times since then. Michigan State has won twice.

HI-YO, SILVER: "The Lone Ranger" radio program originated in Detroit in 1933.

LEISURE TIME: Michigan has more registered pleasure boats — 722,793 — and more public golf courses — 565-plus — than any other state.

Tom Whitfield, 56
Cab driver
Detroit

"As a cab driver, you can make ends meet between jobs and during layoffs. With a regular job, you have to wait for payday. With this job, you don't. And some of the people you meet are interesting and fun. I like this city."

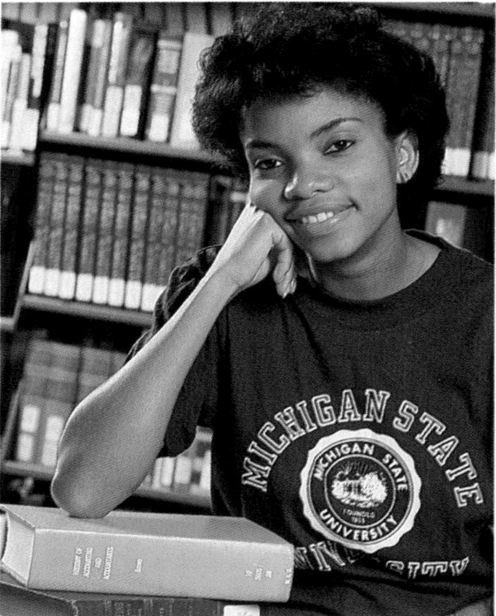

Karla Gardner, 21
Student
University
Of Michigan
Huntington Woods

"Michigan is very diverse. There's so much to get involved in. But most of all, I think it was the people, the whole atmosphere, that made me say, yeah, I'm gonna be a Spartan."

Voices
of Michigan

Jesse Kidd, 37
Autoworker
Detroit

"I'm very proud of the product we build here and I'm glad to be a part of that process. The best thing I like about Detroit is the people. Together they have great strength and I see sometime in the not-so-distant future that strength pulling the people together. That's Detroit pride."

Tom Vranich, 36
Sales representative
Mount Pleasant

"The state has been too dependent on the auto industry. People are getting the idea that the auto industry has responded to the foreign competition. I drive a Volkswagen, but I'll probably buy an American car as my next car. I think the American car industry is coming back."

Charles Symon, 74
Writer
Gladstone

"The Upper Peninsula has a mystique of its own. Most people who live here don't want to see it grow. They like the sparse living and having the timber around them."

Jelena Krstovic, 32
Book editor
Ann Arbor

"There is a lot of diversity in the people who live in the state. Ann Arbor is a place that has a lot of energy and a lot of things going on. There is a good mixture of people and the city offers a lot of things that a much larger city offers, but it's still a small town. I lived in New York before coming to Michigan, and I think the people here are much friendlier, more approachable and warmer in general than the people on the East Coast."

Linda Bateson, 39
Teacher
Midland

"My family and I do a lot of camping. You can take off and find many wide open spaces. You can climb mountains, drive through sand dunes, watch power boat races. I like the climate because you can ski in the winter time, and look for a lake to cool down in during the summertime. In the fall, the leaves change colors in the trees, and in the spring, Michigan is wonderful from all the green springing up signaling new life."

Thomas Monaghan, 50, whose childhood was spent in foster homes and orphanages in Michigan, grew up to become the founder of Domino's Pizza and owner of the Detroit Tigers.

I can't stop at just one slice of pizza

USA TODAY: Is it still possible for someone to take an idea and build it into a major business like Domino's?

MONAGHAN: I think so. I don't think a day goes by when I don't spot an opportunity for a new business. Things are changing; needs are being created.

USA TODAY: What else does it take?

MONAGHAN: I think you have to have a low standard of living and be patient. I think you have to think big. No matter how hard you work, if you don't have the dream that you're going toward, you're just swimming upstream.

USA TODAY: If you were starting out today, what would you do?

MONAGHAN: There's a million opportunities in real estate. I'm focused on the pizza business. There's more potential here than I could ever spend.

USA TODAY: How often do you eat pizza?

MONAGHAN: About twice a week. I eat too much of it. I can't eat one slice. I eat six or eight slices.

USA TODAY: What's your favorite?

MONAGHAN: Pepperoni is the most important ingredient. I like lots of pepperoni, fresh sausage, onions, extra cheese. Sometimes I like bacon. And I like a little jalapeno pepper.

USA TODAY: Do tastes differ across the USA?

MONAGHAN: In the Midwest, you can never sell pepperoni. Everywhere else in the country, it's No. 1. On the West Coast, you see a lot of pineapple. Jalapeno peppers are big in Texas.

USA TODAY: What's your prediction for the Tigers this year?

MONAGHAN: I just don't know. We lost Lance Parrish. Jack Morris isn't doing much this spring, and now he's making a million dollars more than last year. We have some old guys; I don't know how much longer they can produce. We have the ability to win, but we have the ability to fall flat on our face.

USA TODAY: If you had to pick one, Domino's or the Tigers, which would it be?

MONAGHAN: Domino's. That's my life. I'm a pizza man.

Topic: MICHIGAN

The key to our future is brains, not brawn

USA TODAY: Chrysler is planning to buy American Motors. What does that mean to Michigan?

BLANCHARD: It represents another milestone in Chrysler's remarkable comeback. Chrysler is very much committed to Michigan — they've invested $3 billion this last year.

USA TODAY: The Chrysler-AMC pact shows an automobile industry in transition. How is it changing within Michigan?

BLANCHARD: There will be more reorganization and automation. We will continue to see a reshaping and an incredible surge of new technologies in the industry for reasons of survival and competition.

USA TODAY: Why did GM pick Tennessee over Michigan for its Saturn plant?

BLANCHARD: General Motors has invested $9.5 billion in Michigan in the last four years. They put their Saturn headquarters in Troy, Mich., and their Saturn research and engineering center. The brain center and central nervous system are here. The assembly line will be in Tennessee. In the initial talks with us, GM indicated it wanted to create a whole new culture of management and labor attitudes.

USA TODAY: How do you feel about that?

BLANCHARD: There's some real wisdom there because the labor-management relations at GM are the worst of the Big Three. The size of the company just lends itself to bureaucratic problems, and it's hard for them to be flexible with the kind of size you're dealing with.

USA TODAY: In 1983, you told USA TODAY that Michigan was in a state of human emergency. Are you past that?

BLANCHARD: At that point, we had 17.3 percent unemployment. Now it's 8.5 percent. We were bankrupt. Now we're not only solvent, but have the strongest finances of any time in modern history. We've just finished four years of a massive investment in institutions designed to help people.

James Blanchard, 44, a Democrat, is serving his second term as governor. Blanchard was an assistant attorney general before serving four terms in the U.S. House of Representatives.

USA TODAY: Do graduates of Michigan universities stay in the state?

BLANCHARD: Now, yes. Two years ago, no. The percentages are up. I'd like to keep them all here. As a matter of fact, I'd like to draw the brain power from other states in here. Brain power, not brawn power, is the key to the future.

USA TODAY: What do you consider the best and the worst points about Michigan?

BLANCHARD: Michigan is one of the most beautiful states. We have more shoreline than Florida and California. We have more state-owned forest land than any state in the nation. We're a center of high technology, and great public institutions, great public universities. We're a state of ideas.

USA TODAY: That's the good. What about the bad?

BLANCHARD: Unemployment in some major urban areas leads to very serious social problems: crime, welfare, despair, ugly neighborhoods, racial strife. We have ideas and systems and programs to deal with them, but we're by no means on top. If we succeed, America succeeds. If we fail, America will fail. We're on the front line.

Minnesota

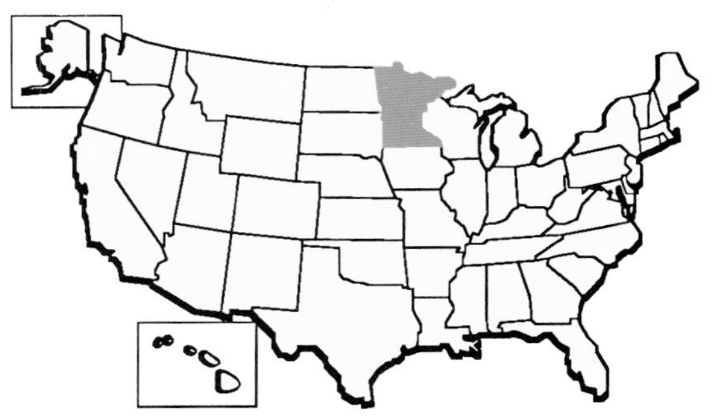

Visited: May 26-27, 1987
Featured in USA TODAY: June 1

"Without the cold weather, we'd be overrun. Literally."

Minnesota Gov. Rudy Perpich

Minnesota

Ice and fire: Pioneers in politics, pop, pain

It's called the land of 10,000 lakes. But state officials say there are actually 11,842.

Either way, that doesn't count **Garrison Keillor**'s make-believe Lake Wobegon from his popular *Prairie Home Companion* radio show, which exits the airwaves June 13.

All those real lakes lured 1.5 million Minnesotans to buy fishing licenses last year. Out of a population of just over 4 million.

Most are fair-weather fishermen. May to September. Like **Dan Seiler**, 25, an unemployed machinist, St. Cloud (pop. 42,566). He displayed a 3-lb. northern pike last weekend. That and the walleye are the prize catches. "I fish to kill time," Seiler said.

Many are more serious about it. Year round. From December to March, frozen lakes are dotted with thousands of flimsy or fancy huts. They house the hardiest anglers, who drop fishhooks through holes in the ice.

As far north as International Falls (pop. 5,611). The icebox of the USA. Its annual "Freeze Your Gizzard Blizzard Race" last January drew 200 runners. Ten kilometers at 28 degrees below zero.

"The human animal can adapt to any environment, unless he has a negative attitude," says **Tom Fairhurst**, 57, National Weather Service meteorologist at the frosty Falls.

Minnesota is much more than an icebox. Descendants of the Scandinavians and Germans who settled this north country have pioneered with fiery brands of politics and pop music. They've been pacesetters in social reform and health services:

■ The Mayo Clinic.

In Rochester (pop. 57,855). World-renowned. Treats 1.5 million patients a year from 150 countries.

Established in 1903 by the sons of **Dr. William W. Mayo**. Now the staff numbers 8,328. Has a reputation for personalized patient care.

"We're genuinely concerned about the patients. Not just the doctors, but the nurses, the attendants, the people who push the wheelchair. They're all local people. They don't make people like that in the big cities," says **Dr. Joseph M. Kiley**, 62, a 37-year internist at Mayo.

DR. KILEY: Mayo staff not 'big city.'

■ Pop music.

Bob Dylan grew up as Bobby Zimmerman in Hibbing (pop. 21,000). Turned folk music into a political movement with his protest songs in the '60s.

In the '80s, the prince of pop is **Prince**. Born Prince Roger Nelson in Minneapolis, June 7, 1958. Eccentric entertainer extraordinaire. Self-proclaimed Royal Badness of rock 'n' roll.

Many Minnesotans shun the controversial Prince. Others are proud of him as another cold weather pacesetter.

PRINCE: Image is Minneapolis' bad boy of rock 'n' roll.

Minnesotans are frustrated in one area where they used to shine. Sports.

■ The basketball Lakers, with big man **George Mikan**, brought NBA titles here in 1949, '50, '52, '53, '54. Yes, those are now the Los Angeles Lakers. Moved west in 1960.

■ The University of Minnesota's Golden Gophers. Under **Bernie Bierman**, won national collegiate football titles in 1934, '35, '36, '40, '41.

The golden era is long gone. But sports interest stays strong. The Twin Cities (Minneapolis, pop. 358,335 and St. Paul, pop. 270,230) are the USA's smallest market with a full complement of major pro teams. Baseball, football, hockey. Starting in 1989, once again basketball, as the newly franchised Timberwolves join the expanded NBA.

Politics has put its pioneers on pedestals. The Democrat-Farm-Labor coalition has the nation's attention.

Two of the past four Democratic presidential candidates were Minnesotans.

■ **Hubert Humphrey**, 1968. Within a whisker of whipping Nixon.

■ **Walter Mondale**, 1984. Routed by President Reagan.

Said Humphrey, "Minnesota is a special political place. It has a conservative base. But . . . has blossomed wild flowers of political, social and economic radicalism."

How do today's leaders feel about the pathfinders of the past?

HUMPHREY III: Follows dad's advice.

Hubert H. (Skip) Humphrey III, 44, is the state's attorney general. Home is New Hope (pop. 23,087). Generally considered to have hopes for the U.S. Senate or beyond. Says he accepts his late father's advice about the legacy:

"Don't deny it. Build on it."

That's Plain Talk from Minnesota.

Snapshot

North Star State

North Dakota
Minnesota
South Dakota
Wisconsin
Iowa
Nebraska
INTERNATIONAL FALLS
HIBBING
ST. CLOUD
MINNEAPOLIS
ST. PAUL
ROCHESTER

Minnesota
1858
10,000 lakes

ENTERED USA: May 11, 1858, 32nd state

MOTTO: The North Star
POPULATION: 4,214,000; rank, 21st
LARGEST CITY: Minneapolis, pop. 358,335
CAPITAL: St. Paul, pop. 270,230
LAND: 79,548 square miles; rank, 14th
POPULATION DENSITY: 53 per square mile; rank, 32nd
RACIAL MIX: 96.6% white; 1.3% black; 0.7% Asian and Pacific islanders. Hispanic heritage: 0.8%.

Uniquely Minn.

MINISOTA: The Dakota Sioux Indians named the region "minisota" — "land of sky-tinted waters."

PORT OF DEPARTURE: The port at Duluth ships more than 3 million tons of cargo each year, making it the largest inland fresh water port in the world.

FAVORITE FUNGUS: In 1984 the morel mushroom was designated the state fungus.

WATER BABIES: More than 95 percent of Minnesotans live within five miles of recreational waters. Skiers have been skimming on Lake Pepin in Lake City since 1922.

DESIGNER GAS: The town of Cloquet has the only gas station designed by architect Frank Lloyd Wright. It was designed in 1956 and opened for business in 1958.

NO FISH STORY: Lake Mille Lacs is considered a walleye factory. More than a half million pounds of the fish are caught annually.

Voices
of Minnesota

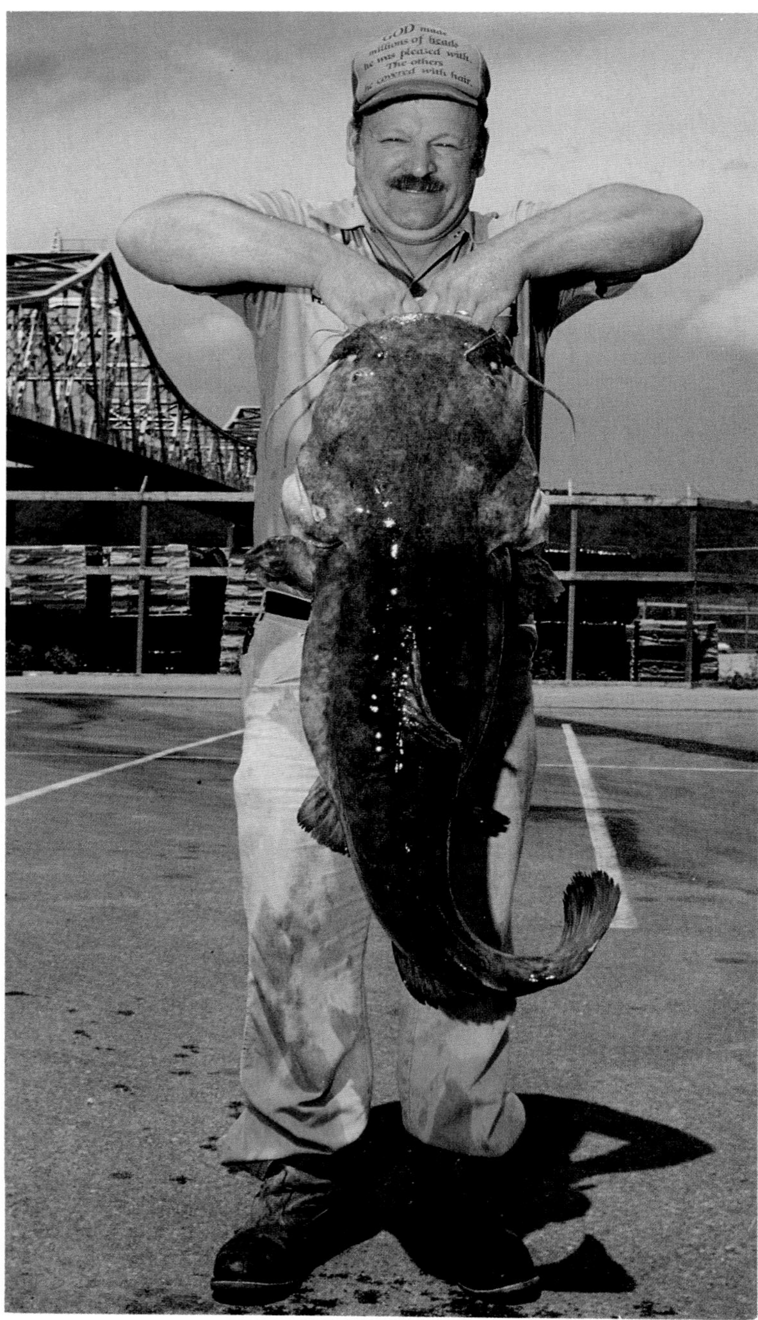

Bud Ramer, 50
Commercial fisherman
Winona

"I think it's great I can jump in my truck and be fishing in 15 minutes. I am always on the river with my pole in hand. I'm on the river every day. It's not like living someplace where you have just one lake. We take everything for granted here. Once you leave here, you can't wait to come back to fish. You really appreciate the state after you leave it for awhile."

Sandy Olson, 40
Executive assistant
Winona

"We're the Hawaii of Minnesota. Sure, we get down to 50 or 60 degrees below zero with the wind chill factor, but not a lot. Northern Minnesota has those temperatures more often. In 1965, we were known as the city that saved itself. The Mississippi flooded the entire city. It was going underwater. They closed the schools and everybody helped sandbag the dikes. If they didn't, we'd just be mud."

Mildred Elton, 72
Retired
Audubon

"We plant flowers every spring — marigolds, petunias and geraniums. We plant them, and then we can just watch them grow and bloom. Now and then we'll come back to weed and water. I'm a great-grandmother. I'm making one of my granddaughters a wedding dress. She's 25 and the dress is just as modern as can be. I guess sewing is my middle name."

Patty White, 21
Student
Minneapolis

"In the winter, it's bitter cold. People just wrap themselves up. No identity, just scarves wrapped all the way up their heads. In the summer, it's extremely hot. They call us the Minne-Apple because it's a smaller version of New York City. But ours is so clean, and it still has the nightlife."

Bill Haider, 28
Police officer
St. Paul

"Even though we're 'twin' cities, there is a difference. St. Paul is a city, but it's really a small town. St. Paul always gets underrated because Minneapolis gets all the glory. We're the capital, though. We live longer here. We stay younger, too. It's that deep freeze in the winter that's good for the complexion."

Earlene Brosh, 41
Bait shop owner
Glenwood

"If I had it my way, I'd go boating and fishing every day. But I've got to work. It's a good living. I get to see lots of different people. The people make it. But without the lakes, you don't have anything. Because of the lakes, the people have a reason to get together. Everybody has a stake in the lakes."

Jesse Longley, 21
Gift shop employee
Osseo

"There are a lot of great things in all the small towns. That's part of Minnesota. I grew up in the Iron Range. That region is similar to Lake Wobegon — it's very cold. People take their time and move about more slowly, especially in the winter. There are a lot of characters in small towns."

Charles Schulz, 64, was born in Minneapolis and grew up in St. Paul. He has been drawing the Peanuts *comic strip since 1950. It appears in 2,000-plus newspapers. He lives and works now in Santa Rosa, Calif.*

Midwest living gave me a broader view

USA TODAY: When did you realize you had a talent for drawing cartoons?

SCHULZ: Oh, when I was a little kid. I always liked the funny papers, and I always drew and read all of the different comics. It wasn't until I was in my early teens that I knew you could actually draw a comic strip and get paid for it.

USA TODAY: How did Minnesota shape your perspective as an artist?

SCHULZ: It was very important in that if you live either on the West Coast or in New York City, you're liable to have too narrow a view. Living in the Midwest gave a person more of a broad view of what was going on in the country — or maybe what was not going on — so that you didn't draw things that would not be of interest in other parts of the country.

USA TODAY: Your father was a barber in St. Paul for more than 45 years. Is that why Charlie Brown's father is also a barber?

SCHULZ: I don't think it's a coincidence. You can make your humor more authentic when you deal with something that you really understand.

USA TODAY: If you drew a cartoon image of your childhood, what would it include?

SCHULZ: It was not always that pleasant. We grew up in the Depression, but of course that didn't mean much to us kids. It's very difficult to be a little boy growing up when there are a lot of nasty kids around. I was just interested in playing sports. I had some good friends, and we had baseball teams and hockey teams. Probably the best thing that happened to me was when I learned how to play golf at 15.

USA TODAY: Are there any labels you would affix to Minnesota?

SCHULZ: It's a mistake to label Minnesota, for instance, as being backward, because Minnesota's a very progressive state, and the Twin Cities are beautiful. The whole state is very beautiful.

USA TODAY: You own the Redwood Empire Ice Arena in Santa Rosa, Calif., where you now live. Did you build it to remind you of Minnesota?

SCHULZ: We built it because my wife and I always said one of the things we missed about Minnesota was ice skating.

Topic: MINNESOTA

From politics to air, we're a clean state

USA TODAY: For many of us, the word "cold" immediately comes to mind when Minnesota is mentioned. Does that present an image problem for the state?

PERPICH: When people think of Minnesota, they think not only of cold, but clean water, clean air, clean environment, clean politics, clean government. People here do care about each other. So we have a very special quality of life in Minnesota. Without the cold weather, we'd be overrun. Literally.

USA TODAY: Your parents were Eastern Europeans. In fact, you spoke Croatian at home. Why did so many from that region settle in Minnesota?

PERPICH: People who left Eastern Europe did so because of political, economic, religious reasons. That's why I believe they're such good citizens. I remember my father and mother would get dressed up — they were laboring people, my mother worked in a laundry, my father in the mines — to go to vote. We used to laugh at that.

USA TODAY: How are cities like your hometown of Hibbing recovering from the downturn in the iron and steel industries?

PERPICH: It's stabilized. It's a very slow turnaround because we had about 14,000-plus jobs. The full-time equivalent now maybe would be about 4,000 jobs.

USA TODAY: What are some indications of a turnaround?

PERPICH: We don't have the people moving out like we did. People on the main streets say their businesses are improving.

USA TODAY: What's ahead for farmers?

PERPICH: There was a time, two years ago, when I really couldn't announce 24 hours in advance that I was going into one of those farm communities because the farmers would be there en masse. So some state programs — getting people off the land, giving them free tuition, classes — helped. At least they felt like someone cared. It even kept some people on the land who would have been off.

Rudy Perpich, 58, a Democrat, practiced dentistry until 1974. He was governor from 1976 to 1979 and was re-elected in 1982 and 1986.

USA TODAY: You've said more than 800 jobs are being created every week in Minnesota. Where are they coming from?

PERPICH: In the financial area, services. Manufacturing is doing somewhat better than the national average. Bankers say the farm situation is much better. Northeastern Minnesota is definitely better. The forest-products industry keeps expanding up there. And tourism's improving.

USA TODAY: In addition to the work ethic and the people, the lakes are perhaps your greatest treasure. Is acid rain taking a toll?

PERPICH: Yes, it is. We've been very active in fighting that, and we're making progress. It's a slow process because people are concerned about jobs on the other end. We're working on the federal level, also. Overall, the Conservation Foundation rated us No. 1 in environment.

USA TODAY: In terms of living quality?

PERPICH: Our laws, our regulations, our attitudes. Everything on the environment.

USA TODAY: Is this a state that takes its sports seriously?

PERPICH: Absolutely. I don't know if there's another state that has the programs that we do. It's just incredible.

Mississippi

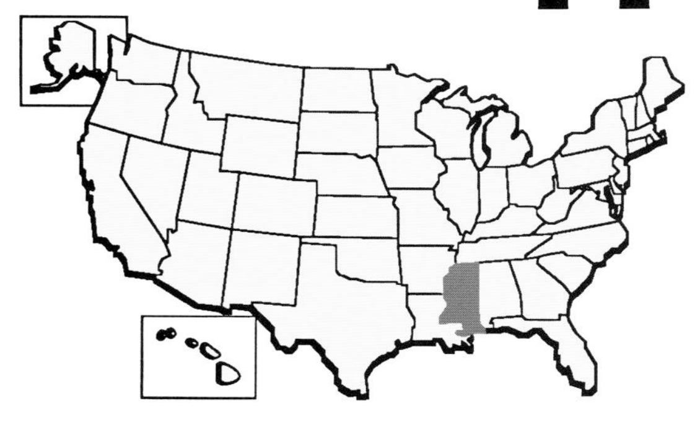

Visited: April 9-10, 1987
Featured in USA TODAY: April 13

"One builds on one's roots. I got the best in the world."

Leontyne Price
Opera superstar
Formerly of Laurel, Miss.

Mississippi

A state sweet and sad sticks to family, faith

In the Mississippi Blues Museum at Clarksdale (pop. 21,135) they crow about "The Crossroads."

That's where bluesman **Robert Johnson** supposedly sold his soul to the devil in exchange for musical genius. The deal was made at the intersection of highways 61 and 49 in the Northwest Delta.

Musical genius is glorified here — from blues to classical. The devil is not. The church controls this state. People pray and sing together. Faith and family are foremost.

Furry Lewis (1893-1981) put to music the Magnolia State's feelings in "Miss Becca's Blues:"

"Days be sweet and sad;
Times be good and bad;
Days all the same to me. . . ."

THE GOOD:

Mississippians have given a diverse group of leaders to the USA:

■ From Biloxi, **Jefferson Davis**, president of the Confederacy; current Washington, D.C., Mayor **Marion Barry**; former St. Louis pitcher **Dizzy Dean**; Chicago Bears running back **Walter Payton**; sportscaster **Red Barber**.

■ Four Miss Americas.

■ One of the most famous daughters came back last week. Opera superstar **Leontyne Price**, 60, filled the Jackson Municipal Auditorium in a symphony benefit Wednesday night.

PRICE: Diva from Laurel, Miss.

Thursday she went home to Laurel (pop. 21,897). "One builds on one's roots. I got the best in the world," said the Delta diva who won 18 Grammys and two Emmys.

THE BAD:

Mississippi's image still suffers from a rigid racist label acquired during the 1960s civil rights confrontations. But, most folks here insist the rest of the country has that all wrong.

"Our character is great. Our reputation is not as good," says Gov. **William A. Allain**, 59, a first-term Democrat.

Allain knows something personally about character assassination. A divorced Catholic, he was besmeared in his 1983 campaign. But he won, in a state overrun with Protestants and family people.

Coahoma County (Clarksdale) is anything but racist. It produced **Mike Espy**, 33, the first black U.S. representative from Mississippi since Reconstruction. Mayor **John Mayo**, 40, a Vietnam vet, is a McGovernite liberal. The home of playwright **Tennessee Williams**, Coahoma is an ethnic melting pot of Orientals, Jews, Hispanics, blacks, Anglo-Saxons. All gather at Chamoun's Lebanese food counter at lunchtime.

ESPY: Victorious for U.S. House.

THE SWEET:

Mississippians feel good about their faith — in their religion and generally in each other.

The saying is you're never more than a stone's throw from a church. There are 600,000 Southern Baptists; 400,000 members of black Baptist groups; 200,000 United Methodists. Thousands more church regulars in a state with only 2.6 million people.

"It's fabulous to be a minister in this state," says the Rev. **Mark Grisham**, 32, of the Jackson College of Ministry. He claims he has preached in 45 states. He's outspoken in mixing church and family matters. "God created Adam and Eve, not Adam and Steve," he admonished a town hall meeting Thursday night.

THE SAD:

The old in Mississippi long for the good old days, when families stayed together and the young never strayed far from home, but they don't expect those days to return.

In Merigold (pop. 475), two dozen women, average age 80, meet every Wednesday in a quilting bee at the United Methodist Church. They talk about children and grandchildren.

One is **Mrs. Evelyn Speakes**, 75, mother of former Reagan spokesman **Larry Speakes**. Larry left the White House for Wall Street in January, passing up business opportunities in Mississippi.

SPEAKES: White House to Wall Street.

"I really miss the children," Mrs. Speakes says sadly. A picture of a quilt that hung in Larry's White House office is a reminder to the stitching sisters.

Mrs. Taylor Collins, 78, is a retired 1st-grade teacher in Tunica (pop. 1,361), the county seat of the poorest county in the USA. She says, "This part of the Mississippi is so low down. So dead. I don't want to be here. But I don't think I'm going anywhere else except heaven."

That's Plain Talk from Mississippi.

Magnolia State

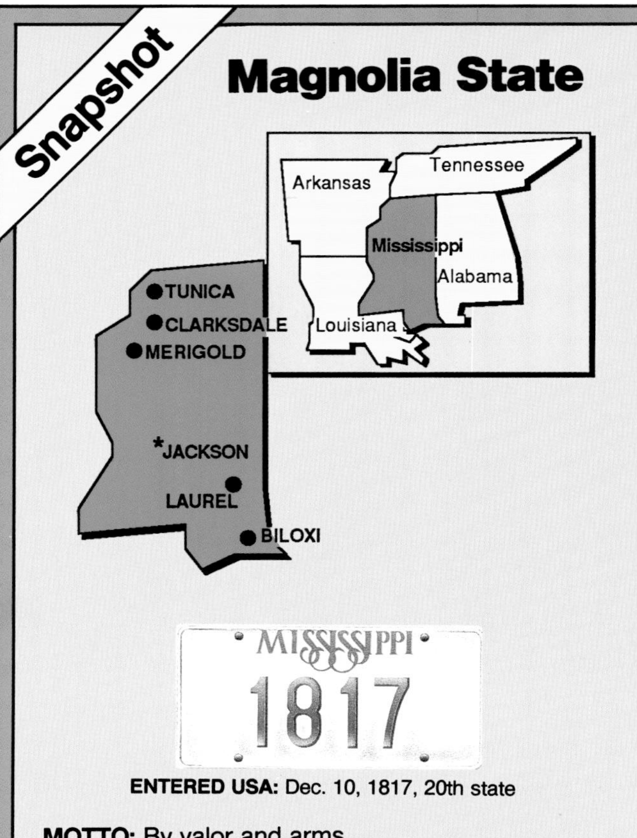

ENTERED USA: Dec. 10, 1817, 20th state

MOTTO: By valor and arms
POPULATION: 2,625,000; rank, 31st
LARGEST CITY: Jackson, pop. 208,810
CAPITAL: Jackson
LAND: 47,233 square miles; rank, 31st
POPULATION DENSITY: 55.6 per square mile; rank, 31st
RACIAL MIX: 64.1% white; 35.2% black; 0.3% Asian and Pacific islanders. Hispanic heritage: 1%.

Uniquely Miss.

NATION'S INNKEEPER: The world's first Holiday Inn franchise opened in Clarksdale June 14, 1954. All Holiday Inn managers train at Holiday Inn University at Olive Branch.

TEDDY BEAR: While on a hunting trip near Smedes in 1902, President Theodore Roosevelt refused to shoot a small black bear. The incident resulted in the creation of the "Teddy" bear.

CONFUSED: Cat Island was named by French discoverers who mistook raccoons for cats.

ODE TO BILLIE JOE: The Tallahatchie Bridge of Bobbie Gentry's famous ballad was torn down and replaced with a concrete structure in the 1950s.

FARM SCHOOL: The last public, residential, agricultural high school in the USA is the Forrest County Agricultural High School in Brooklyn, in Southeastern Mississippi.

Louise Chamoun, 50
(with husband, Chafik)
Owner of Lebanese diner
Clarksdale

"We moved here from Lebanon in 1954 with $300 in our pocket. Now we have a business. We've made it. We built a name and a life for ourselves and our family. We raised six kids here. People here don't care who you are or where you're from, as long as you have respect for yourself and them."

Betty Taylor, 34
(with children
Truitt and Laura)
Homemaker
Laurel

"I like small-town living. I think living in a small town is much better for bringing up children. People of Mississippi are among the friendliest anywhere. They'll do anything to help out other people and make them feel welcome. If there's a better place, I haven't found it."

Voices
of Mississippi

Tracy Williams, 27
Health physics technician
Fayette

"Fayette is a small community on the brink of developing. Jobs are hard to find if you don't have any particular trade. But the people don't let it get them down. The majority are trying to do something for themselves. They don't let the shortage of jobs change their attitude about life."

Andrew Halsell, 43
Maintenance worker
Hattiesburg

"We don't play a lot of Delta blues in Mississippi, but we do play a lot of down-home blues. The blues tell stories. They say the blues will get you down if you sing them long enough. But it satisfies me when I play the blues. It is a favorite thing to do in Mississippi. You can hear the blues nightclubs, concert fields and festivals across the state."

Charles Moore, 34
Teacher
Jackson

"We have hills, the Delta flat lands and a seashore. We have an abundance of resources. Even though many are untapped, they are still here. The opportunities are not as great as in some of the states, but Mississippi will have its chance. When other resources in the country are consumed, Mississippi will have its day."

James T. McMahon, 27
Off-shore oil driller
Purvis

"Purvis is a small town. I like that. Everybody knows everybody and you can tell who is in town by the vehicles you see. When I work, I'm tied down on one spot. I'm on an iron island where I can't go anywhere. When I get home, the pine trees are so pretty and you can just see the changes that have taken place after being out in the water so long. That's why I like the Mississippi outdoors so much. It's quiet and peaceful."

Glenda Coleman, 38
Self-employed jeweler
Hattiesburg

"I've been here a long time. There just aren't many opportunities for a job, that's why I'm self-employed. It's just not like a city. It seems like some people aren't ready for new ideas. But I stayed here because I want to raise my family. The city isn't a place to raise a family."

Susan Akin, 22, Miss America 1986, is from Meridian, Miss. Akin has appeared in 100 or more beauty pageants beginning at age 6 in her quest for the USA's top crown.

South wins pageants, but beauty is within

USA TODAY: You grew up in Meridian. What are some of your fondest memories of home?

AKIN: I've never been anywhere where the hospitality is as warm as it is in Mississippi. The people are laid back, and they don't live a rushed life.

USA TODAY: Are you a Southern belle?

AKIN: The first thing that comes to my mind is a very pretty woman in a big hoop skirt. We don't call each other a Southern belle. We don't say "Hey, Southern belle, how are you doing?"

USA TODAY: Why are there so many beauty queens from Mississippi?

AKIN: Mississippi always ranks high in the top 10, but only four Miss Americas were from Mississippi.

USA TODAY: The South always seems well represented among beauty pageant finalists.

AKIN: Eight of the top 10 Miss America finalists were from the South this past year. We have a lot of support behind the pageant system in the South.

USA TODAY: Are girls in the South taught that beauty is important?

AKIN: In Mississippi, they care about physical beauty. Real beauty comes from inside. People who are so carried away with their looks and their bodies — they're going to pass the world by and not enjoy it, because they're too wrapped up in themselves.

USA TODAY: You're doing a lot of shows with Bob Hope right now. Are you heading for a movie or a singing career?

AKIN: I'm going to try both. My love is country music, and I've been thinking about pursuing it.

USA TODAY: What did being Miss America mean to you?

AKIN: I was in pageants all my life. They helped me be who I am today, which is an outgoing person. I don't like some of the pageants that little girls are in — they have to pay an entry fee. Somebody's making money off these little girls. And I don't like pageants where the girls win all kinds of prizes — boats and cars and things. You're sort of being rewarded for your beauty and your body. The Miss America pageant rewards you for your talent and your intelligence.

Topic: MISSISSIPPI

We're working hard to improve our image

USA TODAY: What do you think the nation's perception of Mississippi is?

ALLAIN: Better than it used to be, not as good as we'd like for it to be.

USA TODAY: What do you think hurt your image?

ALLAIN: What's hurting not only Mississippi but Alabama and others is the 1960s, when we were going through the desegregation of our schools.

USA TODAY: How has the state changed since then?

ALLAIN: Today, we are a state that's moving from agriculture into other areas of economic development. We've got record employment. We've got trade missions going to Europe and to the Orient. We've still got some problems in our education system.

USA TODAY: Is education substandard in Mississippi?

ALLAIN: No. Mississippians are beginning to make a better showing on national tests. I think we're about 10th in the number of Rhodes scholars. We are improving education almost daily. We just tested schoolteachers; something like 98 percent or 90 percent of them passed.

USA TODAY: Then things are getting better for the state?

ALLAIN: No state's got enough employment, or enough money. No state's got all the things it wants. Twenty-one states this past year had to cut budgets. Mississippi didn't. So, we've got a lot of really good things going in this state.

USA TODAY: Mississippi has a well-known history of racial strife. How do blacks fare in this state now?

ALLAIN: We've got more elected black officials than any other state. I recently appointed the first black to the Mississippi Supreme Court. A number of our supervisors, local officials, are black. We've made a conscious effort to try to put black people and women on boards and commissions and to mirror the population. All of our boards and commissions reflect that today.

William Allain, 59, Democrat, a former state attorney general, has been governor since 1983.

USA TODAY: Are there any Southern issues that are different from issues elsewhere in the country?

ALLAIN: I doubt it. I know that a few of them might be more concerned with acid rain up in some parts of the country than we would be down here. We might be more concerned with where the nuclear waste is going than they would.

USA TODAY: What are the major issues of concern?

ALLAIN: The overriding issues would be the economy, education, what do we do about infant mortality in this country, and illiteracy in our state. I think most states are concerned about the same issues

USA TODAY: Many people today are concerned about the disintegration of the family. Is that a problem in Mississippi?

ALLAIN: I think the family has changed. Both parents now are working. They have to work, or they can't have the kind of things they want in life, so that leaves the child home in the afternoon with no parent. But I don't know whether we can ever go back to where you only had one parent working.

USA TODAY: What would you say are the favorite pastimes in Mississippi? What do people do?

ALLAIN: They hunt, fish, they go to ball games, just like most of the nation.

Missouri

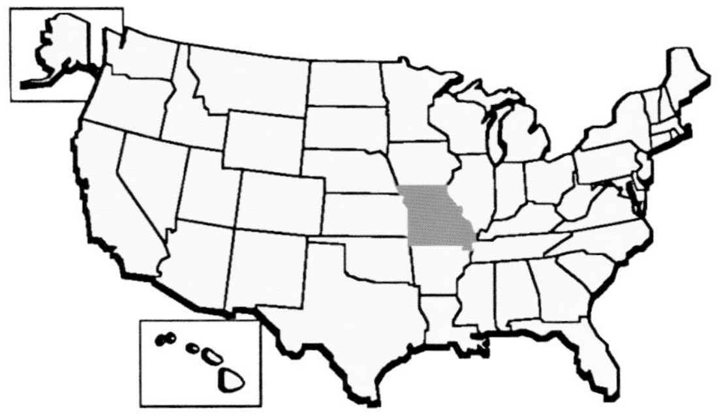

Visited: March 16-19, 1987
Featured in USA TODAY: March 20

"I don't expect no free ride from nobody."

Lynn Merrill
Farmer
Potosi, Mo.

Missouri

Show-Me staters love being in middle

People hereabouts are proud of being more middlemost than most of us — not just geographically, but philosophically, politically, economically and morally.

We began our 50-state BusCapade USA at the population center of the USA. That's near Potosi (pop. 2,558), about 60 miles southwest of St. Louis.

The tenaciousness of Potosians is more meaningful when you realize how tough times are here. The mining industry, once Potosi's No. 1 payroller, is dead. Unemployment is 23 percent, three times the Missouri or national average.

THE PEOPLE:

The folks like it here. They want to stay. They stick together. They help each other.

Angela Schlosser, 22 — her parents, **Ted** and **Beverly Kelderman**, run the Dutch Dairy ice cream store — is about to be graduated from college in St. Louis and wants to teach back in Potosi, where she went to school.

Lynn and **Rosemary Merrill**, both 53, own the 45 acres outside Potosi, where the USA's population center falls, according to the Census Bureau. They, their 10 cows, five cats and one dog live off the land.

Lynn worked 23 years in the Pea Ridge Lead Mine before it shut down in 1979. Since, he has trapped muskrats and coons and raised potatoes, corn, tomatoes and beets, which he sells in nearby towns. "I don't expect no free ride from nobody," Lynn said.

AT THE CENTER: Rosemary, left, and Lynn Merrill at their homesite near Potosi. Plaque in the USA TODAY vending box marks the USA's population center.

THE PLACES:

Across the "Show-Me State" — so dubbed by Congressman **Willard Vandiver** in 1899 — there is a balance and blending of thoughts and deeds, as well as population. Missouri — pronounced "Missourah" in the rural south and west, and "Missouree" in the urban east — entered the Union as a slave state in 1821. It remained in the Union in the Civil War.

Folks reminisce that their ancestors were caught in the middle in the 1860s. In 1987, that middleness reflects itself.

■ From St. Louis to Kansas City to St. Joe, Missouri proudly proclaims and practices its northern abolitionist view of equal rights for all.

■ But it still retains some of the privileged leisure society of the old South, especially in Springfield and Joplin and the Ozarks.

■ In spots, it is as shiny and brash and commercial — and sometimes as noisy and messy — as the industrial East.

■ Elsewhere it is pacified by the endless acres of peaceful pasture to the west.

QUOTABLES:

■ In St. Louis, bank vice president **B.A. "Todd" Parnell III**, 39: "Missourians are more tight-fisted. They don't flaunt their wealth the way it's flaunted on the coasts or was flaunted in Texas."

BANKER PARNELL: Missourians 'don't flaunt wealth.'

■ In Columbia, home of the University of Missouri, a surprising majority of journalism school students at a beer and pretzel bash called themselves conservatives. Said graduate student **Paul Raynis**, 21: "I want to make a hell of a lot of money but I want to spend it on some liberal causes. How do you define me?"

■ In Hannibal, home of the legendary **Mark Twain** and the fictional **Tom Sawyer**, **Huck Finn** and **Becky Thatcher**, **Becky Durand**, 26, a waitress at the Broadway Bar, said: "I know many guys named Tom, but I've never dated one. None ever asked me out, I guess. But if I were Becky and if Tom and I got lost in the cave, we'd get romantically involved. That's the only way to put it."

That's Plain Talk from Missouri.

Show-Me State

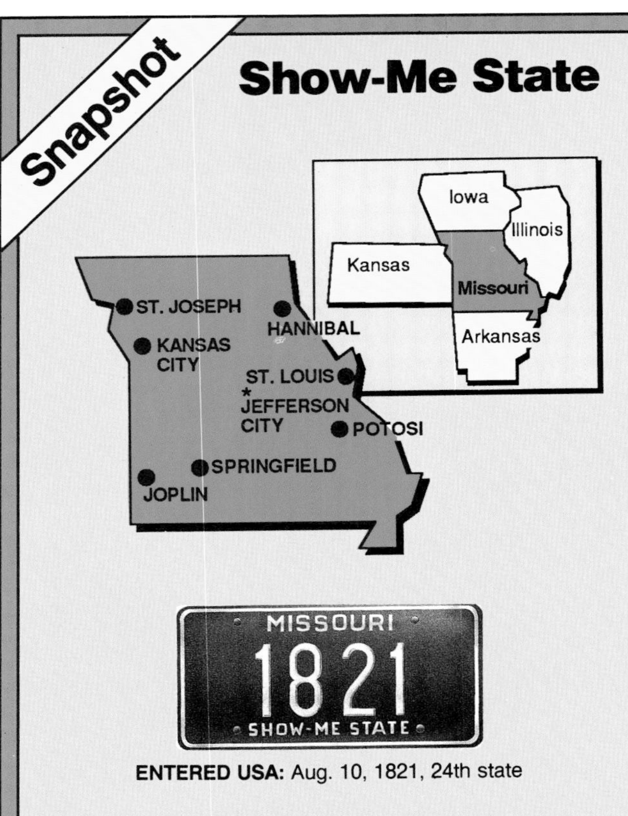

ENTERED USA: Aug. 10, 1821, 24th state

MOTTO: The welfare of the people shall be the supreme law

POPULATION: 5,066,000; rank, 15th

LARGEST CITY: Kansas City, pop. 443,075

CAPITAL: Jefferson City, pop. 35,600

LAND: 68,945 square miles; rank, 18th

POPULATION DENSITY: 73.5 per square mile; rank, 27th

RACIAL MIX: 88.4% white; 10.5% black; 0.5% Asian and Pacific islanders. Hispanic heritage: 1.1%.

Uniquely Mo.

EXPRESS MAIL: St. Joseph, in Northwest Missouri, was the starting point of the Pony Express trail, founded in 1860.

GOING UNDERGROUND: Missouri has the most known caves in the USA — 5,000. You can take guided tours of 23.

ATTENTION SHOPPERS: Kansas City's Country Club Plaza, built in the 1920s, was the USA's first suburban shopping center. It now offers 250 shops and restaurants.

GATEWAY TO THE WEST: The 630-foot-high Gateway Arch in St. Louis is the USA's tallest man-made national monument.

STARS UNDER THE STARS: The USA's two largest outdoor amphitheaters are in Missouri — the 12,000-seat Muny in St. Louis and the 8,500-seat Starlight in Kansas City.

CITY OF FOUNTAINS: Kansas City has more than 200 fountains. Only Rome has more.

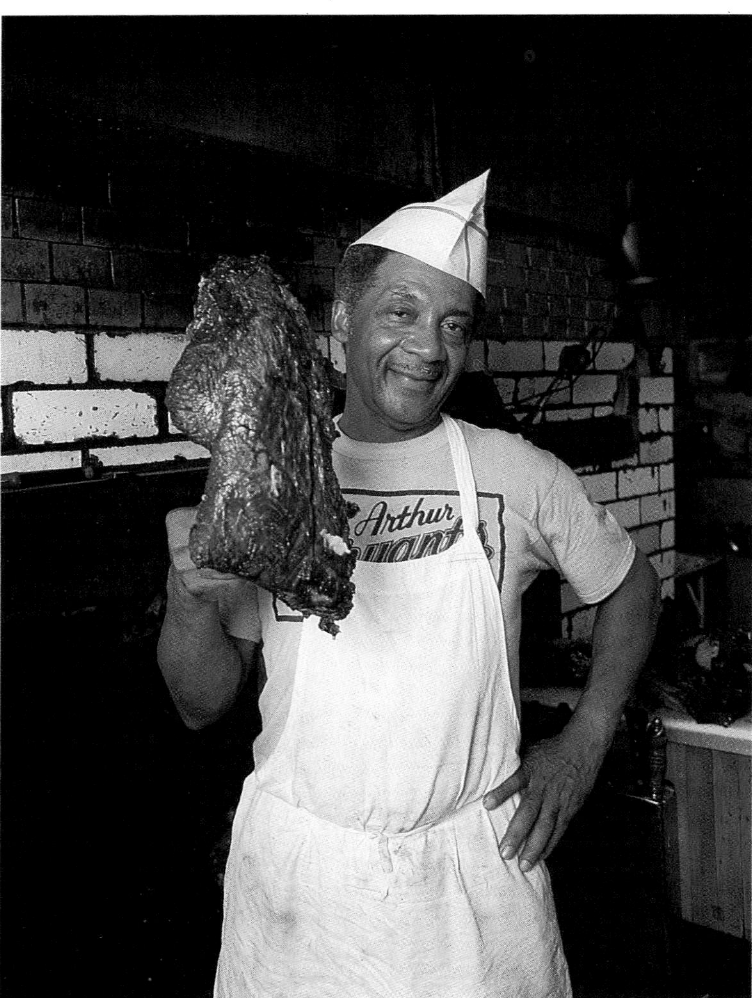

Woodrow Vacon, 66
Meat smoker at barbecue restaurant
Kansas City

"I take pride in what I'm doing. Some old fellows I know come in, see me back here cooking away, and say, 'The meat's got to be good if you're still cooking it.' Kansas City is an easy-going city for an easy-going guy like me. After all, life's what you make of it."

Sharon Burton, 35
Insurance company account manager
Manchester

"We have that big city effect of St. Louis, but we also have boating and fishing. Missouri is good for people who enjoy the outdoors. I like to be on the go. Flying is something I've always wanted to do. It's a great sensation. It's a feeling of freedom."

Voices
of Missouri

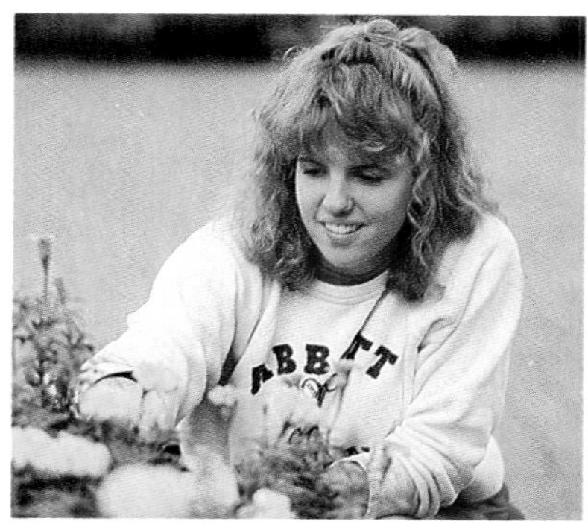

Jennifer Biery, 18
Gardener
Kansas City

"What I think is really funny is how out-of-town people still think of this as a cow town. And they come to learn that Kansas City is a beautiful city on the river bluffs, not stuck in the middle of some flat wheat field. It's not too big, but not too small, either."

Max Murry, 61
Stockyards owner
Springfield

"We're close to the big city, but still country. We're fortunate not to have the problems of the big city. I like my work, the challenge, new problems. It's very competitive. One thing we push is competition. If there's no competition, there's no encouragement to boost prices or business."

Frank Carver, 41
Line foreman
Florissant

"Missouri is centrally located. Everything is close and it's convenient for travel. It's a good place educationally, too. There are colleges around so that kids don't have to go out of the state. And I like the sports. We have all professional sports."

Joan Essen, 25
Customer service manager
Ballwin

"I like life in Missouri because it's a very progressive state. There's something for everybody — recreational as well as cultural. I enjoy St. Louis; it's a very sophisticated city. It feels like a small town, but it's a major metropolitan area. That's what I like about it."

Josie Powell
Cashier
Kansas City

"I've got everything here — my kids, all my family. Kansas City has been a good place to raise a family. The people are decent, the city is pretty clean, and there's always something to do. Plus, living is cheaper here than any other place I've been. My kids have had a good opportunity here."

Gene Price, 30
Welder
Potosi

"We can crab and complain and holler and murmur, but all in all, if we didn't like it here, we'd be gone. People here commute 100 or 150 miles a day to work, but they come back home at night. Times are hard, but people help out. They bust their hearts to do the best they can."

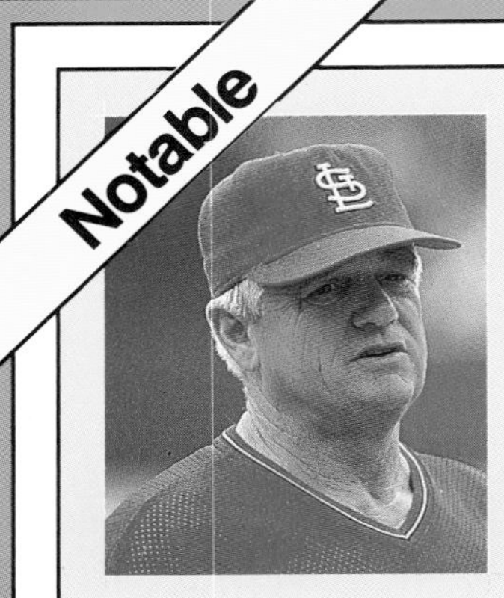

***Dorrel Norman (Whitey) Herzog**, 55, lives in Blue Springs, Mo. He has managed the St. Louis Cardinals since 1980. Previously, he managed Kansas City, winning three division championships.*

East, West of state are a hit with him

USA TODAY: Having grown up in New Athens, Ill., only about 35 miles from St. Louis, you must consider yourself a native of Missouri.

HERZOG: In 1958, I moved to Independence (Mo.) and I've lived in the area ever since. After I managed the Kansas City Royals and came back to St. Louis, it was like coming back to my second home.

USA TODAY: What are people in Missouri like?

HERZOG: Kansas City and St. Louis are very different. The people in St. Louis are more metropolitan. I guess when you talk baseball, people in St. Louis are well-educated fans because of the Cardinal tradition. But the people in Missouri are good people. They're Midwestern, friendly and very down-to-earth.

USA TODAY: Are you more comfortable here than you would be in New York or Los Angeles?

HERZOG: I don't know. I always dreamt when I was coaching the New York Mets or when I first signed with the Yankees (1949) that I would get to play there or manage there. I like to do a lot of outdoors stuff in the summer — fishing and golfing every day — it is more relaxing for me here.

USA TODAY: How was playing Kansas City in the all-Missouri World Series of 1985?

HERZOG: It sure didn't turn out the way we wanted it (the Cardinals lost in seven games), but I enjoyed it because I got to sleep in my own bed when we played in Kansas City. I thought it was great for the state. Really, though, it was kind of a dull World Series, mainly because we couldn't hit the baseball.

USA TODAY: Has Missouri changed much?

HERZOG: I don't think there has been a big population boom, but the super highways and everything make the whole state seem much smaller. We've got the Ozarks and great recreational areas, but so many people here go somewhere else. They've got one of the greatest playgrounds in the world right here.

USA TODAY: Is baseball special in St. Louis?

HERZOG: I would say it is. When I managed the Royals we didn't see many fans on the road. But the Cardinals — they're such a national team mainly because of the Gashouse Gang and the great tradition. Baseball in St. Louis is THE thing.

Topic: MISSOURI

We're probably the most pro-life state

USA TODAY: What makes Missourians unique?

ASHCROFT: There's a strong adherence to the work ethic in this state. This state has a set of family values and a respect for life that could make us the most pro-life voters in the USA. They are a relatively religious group of people. There is far more philosophical consensus in this state than there is political consensus.

USA TODAY: How does the nation perceive Missouri?

ASHCROFT: I don't think there is a national perception of Missouri. But Missouri is largely underrated. St. Louis, for instance, is thought to be a pretty old city but is underrated. It has excellent neighborhoods and outstanding civic features. St. Louis is one of the world's great cities.

USA TODAY: The Children's Budget Coalition reports one of every five children in Missouri lives in poverty, and their plight is getting worse. What are you doing to improve their lives?

ASHCROFT: If I have a dream for Missouri, it's this: Missouri would be a place where each person has the opportunity to reach his or her maximum God-given potential. If I have a second dream for Missouri, it would be a place where each person had a dream.

USA TODAY: How do you accomplish these dreams?

ASHCROFT: The best thing we can do to improve conditions in the state is to build opportunity. And we do that for children with education, and we do it by intervening for adults. For adults, we want to promote literacy.

USA TODAY: What types of programs are you proposing?

ASHCROFT: I have a proposal in welfare that I have dubbed "Learnfare." Basically, it says that if you don't have an education, and you're applying for welfare, you have to be willing to enroll in an educational program. The No. 1 barrier between people and work is a lack of education. So we're saying to people, we'll pay your day care, we'll give you an incidental fee, but we want you to become more employable. I think we have a reasonable shot of getting it through the Legislature.

***John Ashcroft**, 44, a Republican, was elected governor in 1984. He had served as state attorney general and state auditor and was on the business faculty at Southwest Missouri State University.*

USA TODAY: You said that Missourians tend to elect pro-life officials. Do they also favor capital punishment? Do you back the death penalty?

ASHCROFT: Yes, I do.

USA TODAY: Isn't that a contradiction?

ASHCROFT: Not at all. You save lives by implementing the death penalty. First of all, it's a deterrent. The person who is executed cannot commit additional crimes. If it prevents other crimes, you're saving lives. I'm talking about people who have committed murder.

USA TODAY: When you reflect on life in Missouri, what comes to mind?

ASHCROFT: I lived nine miles out of town on the river. I thought that was the way that most folks enjoyed it, standing with a foot in the convenience and challenge of the urban setting, but having the other foot in the rest and repose of the rural setting. I always liked to go down to the river, and just see whether the fish were biting before I went in for supper. It was a great life.

Montana

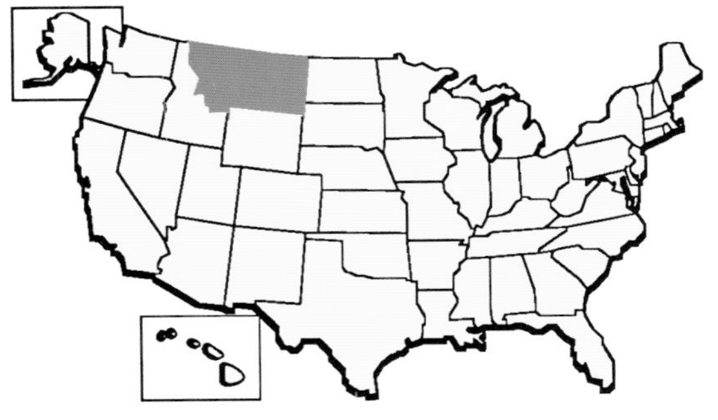

Visited: June 2-4, 1987
Featured in USA TODAY: June 8

"We run a real, honest-to-goodness ranch. All work and no income. Ranching is a way of life as much as a business. Nobody tells you what to do."

Jim Cox
Rancher
Winston, Mont.

Montana

'Big Sky,' tough guys, sprawling, neighborly

It's called "Big Sky" country. The license plate label. And true. The sky really does look bigger here. Even bigger than Texas.

Natives take it for granted. Visitors marvel at it, sunrise to sunset. Great Falls airport meteorologist **Tom King**, 23, explains it:

"It's the lack of humidity. There's just as much sky over Cleveland or along the coasts. But there humidity attracts pollution and you get haze. Here, it's dry and the sky is blue all the way to the horizon."

Horizon to horizon is a long way; 570 miles east to west. 4th-largest state, behind Alaska, Texas, California. Under that big sky live only 819,000 people. 44th in population.

Montana for many conjures up the image of the Marlboro man. Manly chic. Some left here with it. **Gary Cooper**, **Evel Knievel**, **Mike Mansfield**, **Peter Fonda**, hip author **Tom McGuane**.

JIM: Real-life Marlboro man.

Many are still here. **Jim Cox**, 67, ranches in Winston (pop. 30). "We run a real, honest-to-goodness ranch. All work and no income. Ranching is a way of life as much as a business. Nobody tells you what to do."

Ranges on the Great Plains east of the Rockies have their share of outdoor-loving women.

■ **Sue Morales**, 19, Hysham (pop. 449), has been riding and roping since she was 6.

SUE: Pint-size steer wrestler.

"I get up at 5 a.m. We round up cows, brand 'em, vaccine 'em, de-horn 'em. I sit on their necks while a guy grabs their back legs. You get dirty. When you're wrestling cows you sometimes sit on cowpiles." But the pint-size, 5-foot-2 teen-ager loves it.

■ **Jackie Wendell**, 39, a bartender in Helena, state capital (pop. 25,500), dresses the part. She serves up a favorite local drink — a "ditch." Whiskey and water. Derived from days when whiskey was drunk from the bottle and diluted with water from irrigation ditches.

Jackie carries a loaded Colt .45. "I wish I'd lived when it was really wild. I probably would have been an outlaw. Calamity Jane was fantastic. Women are naturally better with a gun than men. When I take a guy to the pistol range, he's so afraid of being showed up he usually messes up."

JACKIE: Her gun is loaded.

Montana is much more than cowboys, cowgirls or cowtowns. Even in the cities, folks seem friendly, neighborly.

"When people here ask, 'How are you?' they really want to know," says Gov. **Ted Schwinden**, 61. The 2nd-term Democrat grew up on a farm near Wolf Point (pop. 3,074).

Medium-size cities are sprawling:

■ Billings, largest (pop. 66,798). Trading and transportation center.

■ Great Falls (pop. 58,100), a farming center and home to Malmstrom AFB.

■ Missoula (pop. 35,600), home of the University.

Agriculture is still No. 1. Rapidly growing tourism is 2nd. Bumping up against neighboring Wyoming's popular Yellowstone Park helps.

Mining was big, collapsed in the '70s, now is coming back.

Butte (pop. 35,300) and nearby Anaconda (pop. 11,200) were big copper mining and smeltering centers. The environmentalists took on the corporations and won. Tough legislation was enacted to halt what was called "the rape of the Plains."

Anaconda's parent company, Atlantic Richfield, pulled out in 1980. Despite heavy job losses, most Montanans are proud they "reclaimed our land." Under strict regulation, coal mining continues, gold and silver is expanding.

"I'm an environmentalist, but I'm not a fanatic," says **Earl Hansen**, 64, Helena insurance agent. "I think we're proving you can have the best of both worlds."

George Dulmer, 63, retired rancher in Custer (pop. 250) sums up his world:

"Montanans are like John Wayne. We don't take no guff."

That's Plain Talk from Montana.

Snapshot

Treasure State

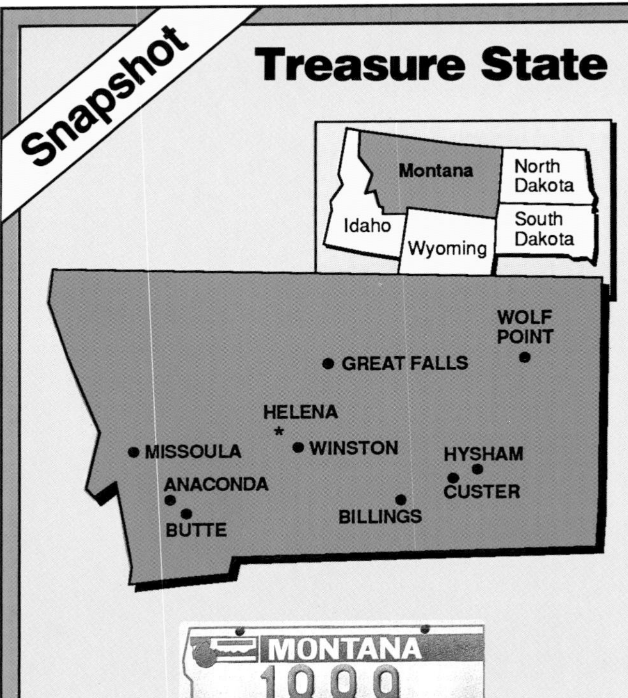

ENTERED USA: Nov. 8, 1889, 41st state

MOTTO: Gold and silver
POPULATION: 819,000; rank, 44th
LARGEST CITY: Billings, pop. 66,798
CAPITAL: Helena, pop. 25,500
LAND: 145,392 square miles; rank, 4th
POPULATION DENSITY: 5.6 per square mile; rank, 48th
RACIAL MIX: 94.1% white; 4.7% American Indian; 0.3% Asian and Pacific islanders; 0.2% black. Hispanic heritage: 1.3%.

Uniquely Mont.

NEST EGG: Dinosaur eggs were found near Red Lodge in 1931. Only other place in the world they've been found: Gobi Desert in East Asia.

TRENDSETTER: Jeannette Rankin of Missoula in 1916 became the first woman elected to the U.S. House of Representatives.

SNOW GOING: The first North American luge run was built in Lolo Hot Springs in 1965.

RICH HISTORY: In 1888, Helena was the richest city per capita in the USA with more than 750 millionaires. Source of wealth: gold mining at Last Chance Gulch.

BEHIND BARS: Montana's first jail was built by Henry Plummer when he was sheriff of Bannack in 1862. He was an outlaw on the side.

BEJEWELED: One of the crown jewels of England is a Yogo sapphire from Lewistown.

Voices
of Montana

Dewaine Carlsen, 38
Rodeo rider
Custer

"You have to practice about four to five hours a day and pay about $400 for rodeo entry fees. I've been stepped on by horses, bucked off. A nylon rope took about a half inch out of my forehead. It's like walking up to a poker table — maybe you win, maybe you don't. But I've been on a horse ever since I can remember. It's all I ever wanted to do."

Sue Quigley, 60
Owner, Frontier Town
Helena

"We did a lot of the things that the original pioneers did. My husband felled the trees and peeled the logs. He worked outside when it was 30 below zero. Pursuing a dream takes hard work and perseverance, but we never thought about quitting."

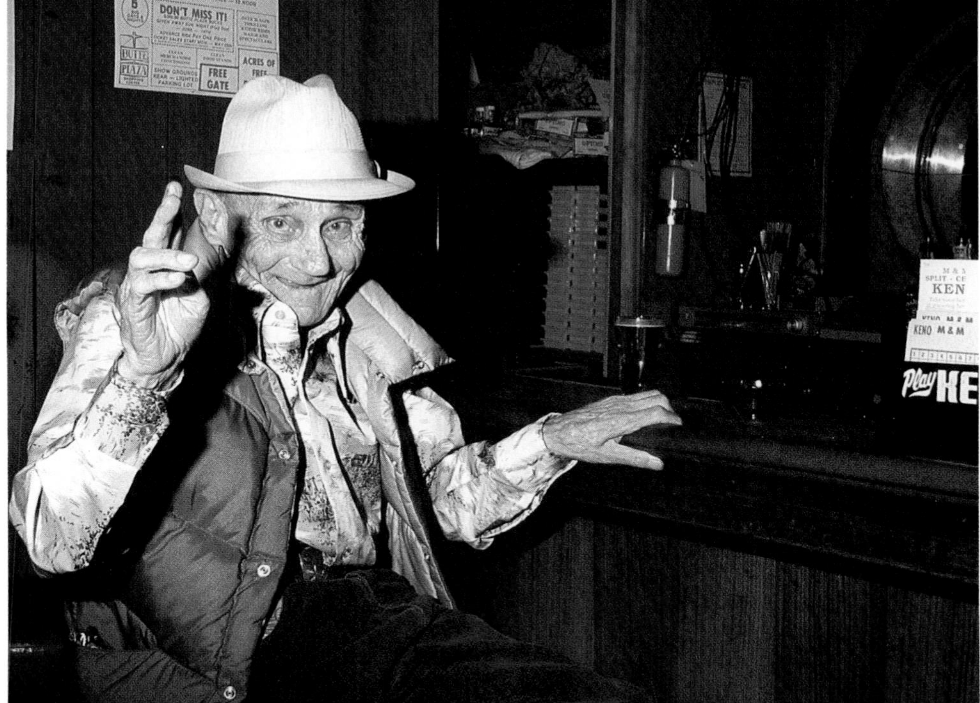

Hank Mougeot, 71
Retired miner
Butte

"I worked in the mines until I was 68 years old. It was awful hard. Pretty damn near got killed when a hanging rock fell down and plugged up the cave. We were trapped a whole day. Butte was pretty wild back then. If you carried a lunch bucket, you could walk into any bar, didn't have to carry no money 'cause they knew you were a miner. Get a glass of beer to drown the dust."

Ben Simpson, 25
Student
Bozeman

"You have to be attuned to the environment in Bozeman. We're surrounded by mountains. I think there's been some real valiant efforts at preservation, but we need to do more. The bears won't make a comeback if they get killed every time they wander near a house."

Melissa Morin-Smith, 25
Actress
Butte

"If you were asked what the most colorful town in Montana was, EVERYBODY would say Butte! Butte's not typical Montana. We've got the working class Irish Catholics. When you've got the Irish, who love to drink, don't mind working hard, you have a town with a strong base. Look, our mining dried up, but did we die? No! We pulled together and went on."

Dennis Schwartz, 43
Gutter installer
Glendive

"I was raised a cowboy. I still go to rodeos, but I'm too old to compete. I'll bet I haven't had a suit on for 10 years. Most working people here wear Levis. If you're a doctor or lawyer you may dress up. But if I go out, I wear a sports coat and Levis. It's accepted in Montana."

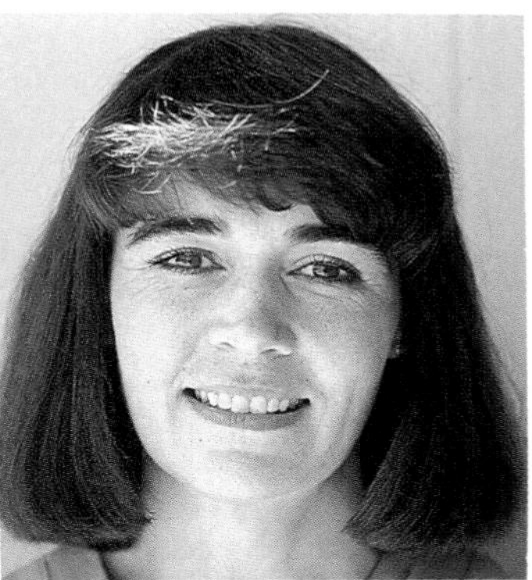

Melody Nansel, 35
Teacher
Miles City

"Everything is so spread out here, but that's why I stay — for the big sky and wide open spaces. After work, I have to drive 800 miles for a teachers' conference. It's not unusual to travel hundreds of miles. We're used to it. But we also don't have big city hassles. No clock-punchers here, just cow-punchers."

Notable

Brent Musburger, 47, owns a ranch near Big Timber, Mont. He has been a CBS sportscaster for 12 years. He anchors most CBS big sports events and is the network's No. 1 college football and college basketball announcer.

It is the greatest escape in the world

USA TODAY: What are your memories of growing up in Billings?

MUSBURGER: Montana was a tremendous place in the '40s and '50s to grow up in. It was rural, and you had a lot of space. A lot of ball fields.

USA TODAY: Did you play sports in Montana?

MUSBURGER: I played everything. My father started the Little League baseball program in Billings. Baseball was the favorite sport in Billings. And probably still is to this day.

USA TODAY: How about football and basketball?

MUSBURGER: I played some pick-up football games, and my father built a basketball court in the back yard. The Little League field was right down at the end of the street, and we'd go play down in there. So there was always a ball game going on someplace.

USA TODAY: Do you go back to visit?

MUSBURGER: We own a small ranch outside of Big Timber. And I still go out, at least for the month of July, and a couple of other times during the year. My mother operates it. My father passed away a couple years ago. But they were so very close to the land in Montana and had friends.

USA TODAY: What do you do when you go back?

MUSBURGER: It is the greatest escape in the world to go back to Montana and just disappear into the hills or go up into the mountains, or go fishing, or play golf.

USA TODAY: What do you find unique about the people of Montana?

MUSBURGER: They're iron-willed. If I had to compare Montanans with anybody, I would compare them with people from Maine. They're quite isolated where they are, they're very independent, very tough-minded people, and very opinionated. And they pay attention to what's going on in the rest of the country, too.

USA TODAY: Which Montanans are you most proud of?

MUSBURGER: A special hero of mine was Chet Huntley. I thought he was one of the great newscasters of all time. I loved his voice. Senator Mike Mansfield. He was somebody we looked up to.

Topic: MONTANA

Montanans in control of their own future

USA TODAY: Street signs with names like "Last Chance Gulch" echo the Old West tradition in Montana. How much of the Old West still lingers?

SCHWINDEN: There clearly are some Western influences. I moved here in 1969 from a small town in the eastern part of the state where our farm is, and I heard about a house. I took a look at it. I said, "What do you want for it?" The guy said "$28,500." I said, "That's a deal." We shook hands. You can still do that here.

USA TODAY: Is this "Marlboro country?"

SCHWINDEN: Nope. There is a lot of respect here for our heritage, for the people who settled this state, the cowboys, the ranchers. There's a strong Western tradition, no question. But I don't know what "Marlboro country" is.

USA TODAY: Montana will be celebrating its 100th birthday in 1989. Is that renewing people's interest in the past?

SCHWINDEN: We've gone through a very exciting process of self-examination. Montana's a state that is probably more known for its period of corporate domination, and once the people sort of seized control in the 1960s, they've been downright determined that they're going to shape their own future.

USA TODAY: How?

SCHWINDEN: We have, I think, the only new constitution in the last 20 years. We've completely reorganized the executive branch. Our strip-mine legislation is basically the parent of the federal legislation that was passed several years later.

USA TODAY: What do you see as being the most important issues in Montana in the next four or five years?

SCHWINDEN: The easy answer is jobs. We've gone through the shift from the basics into the service industries with, in many cases, lower wages. In some areas, we just didn't go through a transition — we saw industries fall right off the table with the

The Guv

Ted Schwinden, 61, a Democrat, was elected governor in 1980 and was re-elected in 1984. He served as lieutenant governor from 1977 until 1981.

collapse of oil prices a couple of years ago.

USA TODAY: Mining was in trouble. How is it doing now?

SCHWINDEN: Mining has turned around dramatically. There's a tendency to focus on coal production, which is flat or falling. But in the area of precious metals, we're seeing the most aggressive development.

USA TODAY: What about agriculture?

SCHWINDEN: In 1985, we had the worst agricultural year since the 1930s. In a state that produces 140 million to 180 million bushels of wheat, we didn't even make 50 million. This is a combination of drought, grasshoppers and a shrinking price.

USA TODAY: Montanans seem to have a high interest in the environment. What is the most important issue?

SCHWINDEN: It would depend on where you are in the state. People in some of our communities would say it is air pollution. Billings and Yellowstone County have one of the highest ambient pollution levels in the country. The biggest environmental challenge that we have is how we deal with the Clark Fork River. It is going to test our ability not only to protect the stream from further damage, but to find ways to deal with over 100 years of abuse.

Nebraska

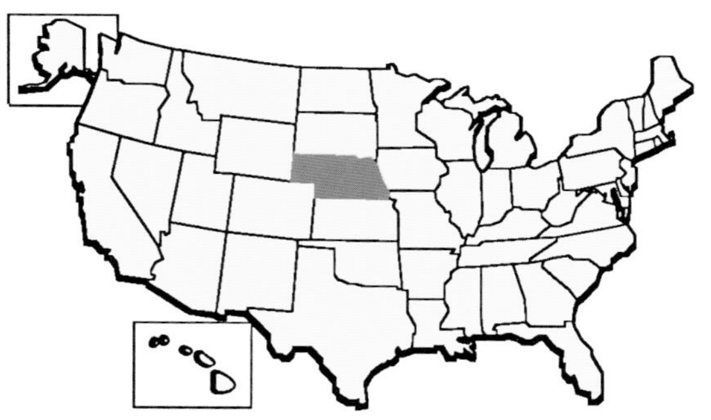

Visited: June 15-17, 1987
Featured in USA TODAY: June 19

"Any dope can sit and look at the seashore and be inspired because it shouts at you. So do the mountains. But the prairie only whispers. You must listen closely and never miss the message."

Father Val Peter
Executive director
Boys Town
Omaha, Neb.

Nebraska

Cornhusker equality: Boys Town, lady guv

The state motto is: "Equality before the law." Nebraskans practice it.

In politics:

■ One of the USA's three women governors. Elected last fall in the only gubernatorial race ever that had two women nominated by the two major political parties.

■ A unicameral legislature. One house. Only such in the USA.

In education:

■ 282 one-room, one-teacher schoolhouses, most in any state in the USA.

■ "Open enrollment" at Omaha's Central High. State's largest. A melting pot for 1,850 outstanding students.

In humanity:

■ Boys Town. Haven for 500 troubled teen and pre-teen boys and girls from across the USA.

Gov. **Kay Orr**, 48, first-term Republican, thinks last year's election demonstrated the "political maturity" of Nebraskans. She won in a race against Democrat **Helen Boosalis**, 67, former mayor of Lincoln (pop. 171,932).

She recalls how the national media flocked to cover the unusual race between two women.

But Nebraskans took it in stride. "To turn this agricultural state into a very productive state took men and women working together," says Gov. Orr. Nebraskans think of politicians as people — not of their sex or their political party affiliation.

The unicameral legislature, adopted in 1934, emphasizes the equality. No upper or lower house. Just one; everybody equal.

One-teacher, one-room schoolhouses still dot the prairies. Nebraska's 282 are more than a third of all (838) such remaining in the USA.

Nancy Bess, 32, has been the only schoolmarm for the past seven years in a one-roomer on Route 2, 14 miles from Crete (pop. 4,782). Nine students, grades kindergarten through eighth.

"They learn independence real fast. But they also learn to share and be patient. They learn that you can't always do what you want. They could hold their own in any high school."

That includes Central at Omaha (pop. 334,016). A marvelous mix of academically strong students is recruited there. A 128-year record of excellence.

"At a lot of schools the very bright or gifted student is left to flounder. We make sure we have special programs to challenge them," says Principal **Gaylord Moeller**, 57.

Biggest school of all, of course, is the University of Nebraska at Lincoln. 25,000 enrollment. And a 76,000-seat stadium that "Big Red" fans fill to overflowing every home football weekend.

The Huskers, perennial national college championship contenders, are the unifier in Nebraska. The state has no major pro team. Those who can't get inside the university stadium crowd around TV sets and radios from Omaha to Scottsbluff. Farm work stops and city shops are empty on those Saturday afternoons.

BANDERAS: Football makes prairie stars.

"Husker Power" signs are everywhere. Even in June. On a T-shirt across the massive chest of **Tom Banderas**, 22, 6-foot-2, 240-pound tight end. Says Banderas: "We run out and the crowd goes crazy. I know we'll win the national championship this fall." He'll be a senior. Says being a Husker is the closest thing to being a movie star on the prairie.

A real movie star put Nebraska's Boys Town on the map in 1938. **Spencer Tracy** won an Oscar for his role as founding **Father Flanagan** in the movie *Boys Town*. **Mickey Rooney** also starred.

Today, Boys Town teaches learning and living to 401 boys and 99 girls, ages 9-18. Housed in 60 "family homes" on a 1,300-acre site west of Omaha.

Has a reputation for taking in kids everybody else has given up on. The current enrollment is from 44 states.

Father Flanagan died in 1948. **Father Val Peter**, 53, is now executive director. He thinks the peaceful prairie environment is a key to the Boys Town record of success with the troubled or troublemakers. Says Father Peter:

"Any dope can sit and look at the seashore and be inspired because it shouts at you. So do the mountains. But the prairie only whispers. You must listen closely and never miss the message."

That's Plain Talk from Nebraska.

FATHER PETER: Listen to the 'prairie's whispers.'

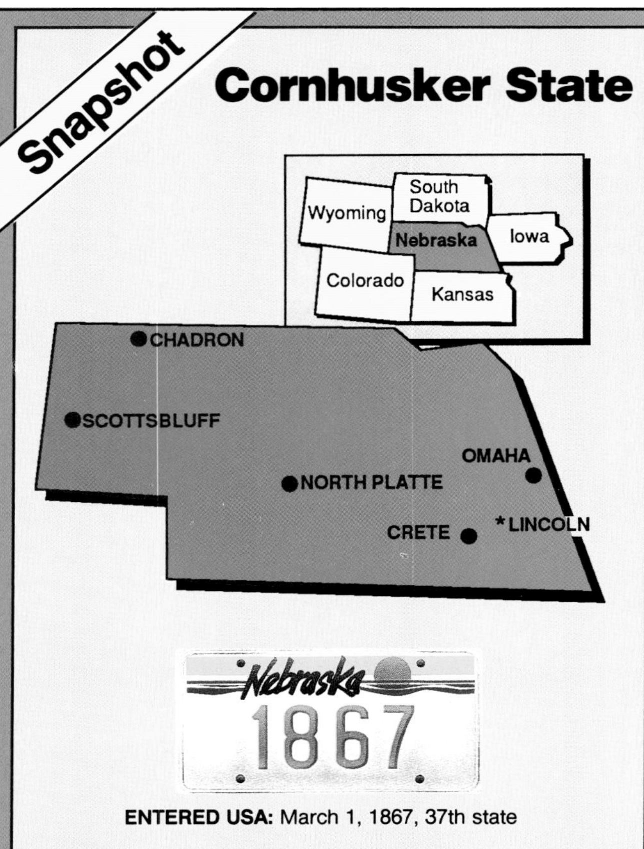

ENTERED USA: March 1, 1867, 37th state

MOTTO: Equality before the law
POPULATION: 1,598,000; rank, 36th
LARGEST CITY: Omaha, pop. 334,016
CAPITAL: Lincoln, pop. 171,932
LAND: 77,727 square miles; rank, 15th
POPULATION DENSITY: 20.6 per square mile; rank, 41st
RACIAL MIX: 94.9% white; 3.1% black; 0.4% Asian and Pacific islanders. Hispanic heritage: 1.8%.

Uniquely Neb.

WORLD WONDER: The American Institute of Architects ranks the Nebraska State Capitol as the 4th architectural wonder of the world. First: India's Taj Mahal.

ROUNDUP: The world's first rodeo was held at North Platte July 4, 1882, and starred its founder, Buffalo Bill Cody.

CITY ON WHEELS: Lincoln is home to the world's only roller skating museum.

GO BIG RED: The University of Nebraska's football team has ended the season ranked in either AP or UPI's Top Ten every year since 1970. On a football Saturday, Memorial Stadium becomes the state's third-largest city when 76,000 people fill the stands.

BUGEATERS: Before it was the Cornhusker State, Nebraska was called the Bugeating State. Reason: many bull bats, which eat bugs.

Brian Frahn, 22
Cattle rancher
Hemingford

"I don't feel cramped because my nearest neighbor is about two miles away. The ranching business has fallen hard. But prices of cattle are coming up. I took college for two years, and I couldn't sit down and study. I'd rather be outside."

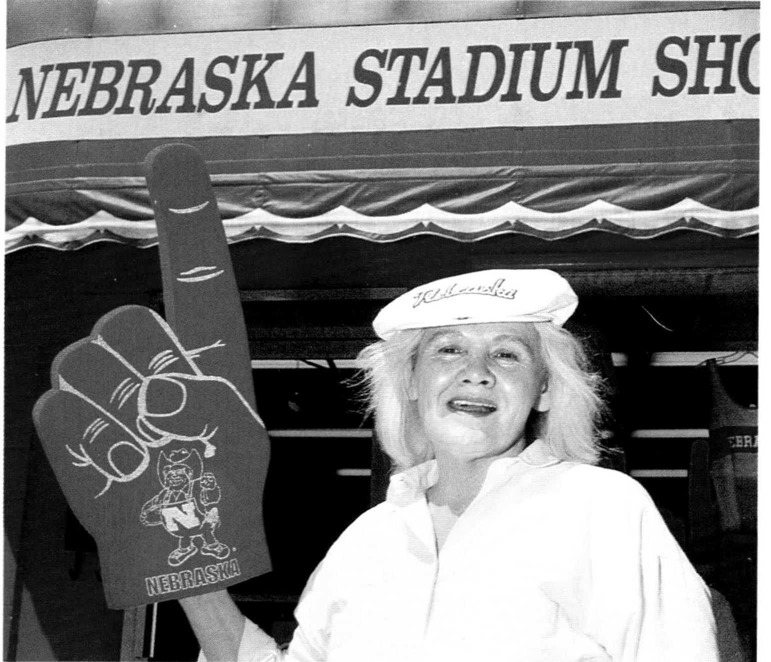

Loraine Livingston, 60
Shop manager
Lincoln

"We happen to have the nicest football players. They're nice boys and are such gentlemen. I guess you could say I'm 100 percent Husker. Make that 200 percent!"

Voices
of Nebraska

William Otto, 66
Farmer
Phillips

"When I was a kid, we'd shuck corn for three cents a bushel. If you got a hundred bushels a day you were darn lucky. You bet it was hard work. The young bucks today wouldn't shuck corn for three dollars a bushel. In the summer you can hear the corn crack as it grows. I used to plant with two horses and a two-row planter. It may have been a little rough, but the corn always came up."

Christine Curtis, 21
Student
Lincoln

"I'm not a huge football fan, but what I do like is that it makes so much money, they give some of it to promoting women's sports. I grew up with football Saturdays. Downtown is swarmed. Bars are swarmed before and after. The roar in the stadium is overwhelming."

Mimi Elsasser, 55
Retired
Omaha

"You really have to use your imagination when you drive through Nebraska. There are no mountains or oceans here. God ran out of everything when he got to Nebraska, except history. Thinking about those people tromping across the plain amazes me. The people who came through here had a lot of stamina."

Jim Blecha, 57
Construction worker
Chadron

"Nebraska is very much divided. The eastern edge of the Sand Hills separates the east from the west. The east has got most of the population with the cities. They consider us in the west to be rural, more country-bumpkin types. It's said they think we should belong to Wyoming. We're over 400 miles from our state capital and only 100 from Wyoming's."

Dub Covey, 57
Semi-retired
Omaha

"Nebraskans have a strong work ethic. They're hard-working people. It was strong, hard-working people who built this city. They worked in the packing houses, stockyards. Immigrants were the backbone of Omaha and that strong work ethic still exists."

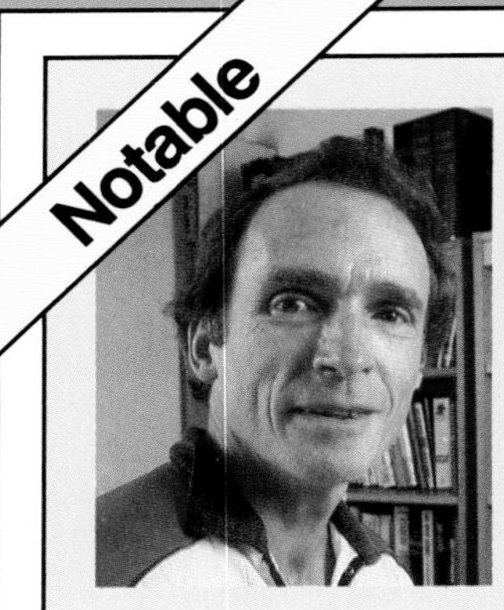

Dick Cavett, 50, was born in Gibbon, Neb., and his parents still live in Lincoln, Neb. Cavett hosts a syndicated radio show, Dick Cavett's Comedy Show.

Nebraskans big hits in show business

USA TODAY: Do you return home to Lincoln often to see your parents?

CAVETT: I've averaged once a year.

USA TODAY: Other than seeing relatives, what do you like best about returning home?

CAVETT: The beauty of the Great Plains. People who've never been West say there's more sky here. And one of the most beautiful areas of the world is the Sand Hills of Nebraska. You travel through dreamy, rolling, beautiful countryside, seeing cattle and isolated windmills, and quiet.

USA TODAY: What view do many Easterners have of Nebraska?

CAVETT: They say, "Let's see, that's somewhere near Oregon, isn't it?" The other reaction I always get is, "Oh my God, I drove across that state once — 650 miles of flat country." Ex-soldiers say, "I was stationed there during the war," because there was a Strategic Air Command there.

USA TODAY: Do you find people associate Nebraska with the Wild West?

CAVETT: Yeah, some people ask, "Didn't Buffalo Bill come from there?" or, "Are there still Indians roaming around?" You get that more in Europe, but occasionally still in America.

USA TODAY: Do you feel defensive about that?

CAVETT: I did, a little. I wouldn't have thought I would.

USA TODAY: Isn't it true that a lot of people believe that Midwestern roots are the best?

CAVETT: They're thought to be. It seems more people in show business come from Nebraska per capita than any other state.

USA TODAY: There's you, and Johnny Carson —

CAVETT: Marlon Brando, Fred Astaire, Darryl Zanuck, Sandy Dennis, Henry Fonda, James Coburn.

USA TODAY: Have you any feedback on how your radio comedy show is received back home in Nebraska?

CAVETT: A woman told my stepmother she thought the comedy show was keeping her husband alive. He was one of many farmers losing his farm.

Topic: NEBRASKA

Rich heritage came from a harsh land

USA TODAY: Do people across the USA have the right image of Nebraska?

ORR: It's a unique blend of the Midwest and the West, but I would like people in the USA to get to know us better, through our people, because that's our greatest asset. We've got extraordinarily friendly people.

USA TODAY: The 1986 governor's race attracted national attention because it featured two women opponents, neither of whom championed "women's issues." Wasn't that unusual?

ORR: Both candidates made every attempt to focus on what the state needed, such as economic development. We didn't want to be identified with the "women's issues." ERA and abortion were questions that could divert attention from things we felt were more important.

USA TODAY: You are opposed to abortion and the ERA?

ORR: That's correct.

USA TODAY: There are three women governors in the USA. Do you talk to each other or do much networking?

ORR: I haven't talked to any governors other than those here in the Midwest. There's simply not enough time. My biggest problem is making good use of my time.

USA TODAY: Why is Nebraska so renowned for having such passionate college football fans?

ORR: It's Nebraska's way of focusing attention on our state and saying to a national audience, "Here's Nebraska, and we have something we're very proud of in the state."

USA TODAY: How is Nebraska unique?

ORR: I often talk about our rich heritage, and I've always been intrigued by history. We were a little harsher with the land here than in Iowa or in Illinois, and when you get farther out west, it's range land. We have both the rolling hills of Iowa and the range land of the West. We've struggled to make it productive for us.

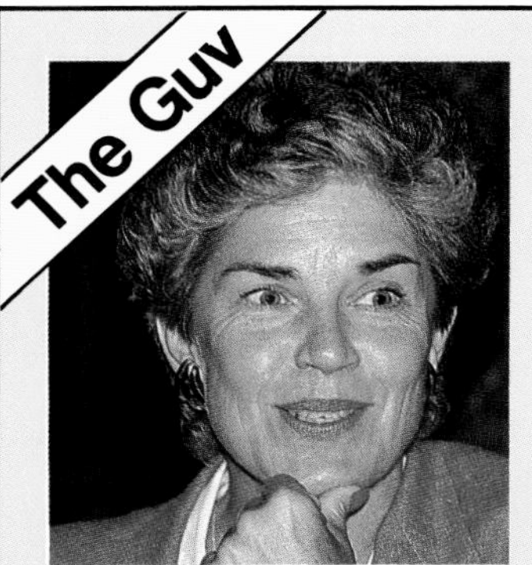

***Kay Orr**, 48, elected governor of Nebraska last fall, is the first woman Republican governor in the nation.*

USA TODAY: If you were to run again, would you rather run against a female or a male?

ORR: Here in Nebraska, it doesn't make any difference.

USA TODAY: Nebraska has more one-room schoolhouses than any other state.

ORR: Nebraskans are very proud of the education in those schools. They send forth young people well prepared. There are those who favor consolidation, who feel that it's long past due and that children ought to be exposed to more modern-day teaching tools and techniques. We'll be working for some common ground.

USA TODAY: Is the family farm surviving in this state?

ORR: I believe it is. Look at what's happened in agriculture in the Midwest. It's been rather dramatic, the amount of suffering that's gone on in agriculture. But there's been a decline in people on the family farms for more than 50 years. Now they're just getting more efficient.

USA TODAY: Do you have any interest in the national political picture?

ORR: In November of 1983, I was back in Washington and I got a phone call, would I meet Sen. Richard Lugar the next day. They wanted me to run for Senate. Some think that's a step up from being governor. I don't.

Nevada

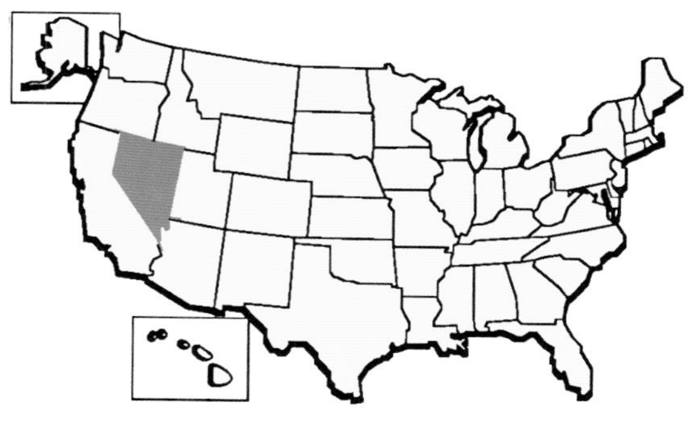

Visited: July 13-15, 1987
Featured in USA TODAY: July 17

"I don't mind this state being more honest than most. Gambling and prostitution goes on in other states. It's just more aboveboard here."

The Rev. Terry Coursey
Winnemucca, Nev.

Nevada

Adventurous, angelic subsist side by side

First state to legalize gambling. Only state with legalized prostitution. No. 1 in marriages per capita. No. 1 in divorces.

Saints and sinners and in-betweeners. Performers and preachers defending the unusual lifestyles.

Las Vegas (pop. 183,227) is called the City of Sin. Singer **Wayne Newton**, resident King of the Strip, says it isn't so.

"Vegas has taken a bum rap over the years. If you're sleazy and looking for that, you'll find it. You'll also find it in New York, Chicago, Los Angeles. We have more churches per capita than any city in the United States. And people who work in the casinos do their jobs and come home to their families. On their days off, they go to the park and play ball just like anywhere else."

Echoes the Rev. **Terry Coursey**, 39, who runs the Seventh-day Adventist church in Northern Nevada's Winnemucca (pop. 4,140).

"I don't mind this state being more honest than most. Gambling and prostitution goes on in other states. It's just more aboveboard here. As a result, churches are closer-knit than the ones I've known before."

Nevada numbers:

■ Gambling. A very big business. The take: $3.3 billion a year. One out of every five wage earners, more than 109,000, gets a paycheck from the gambling industry.

■ Prostitution: A pretty small business. 38 bordellos in the state. An average of 300 registered prostitutes.

Some point out that many more women than that practice the oldest profession illegally within a few blocks of the White House and *The Washington Post* building; at Times Square and near *The New York Times* building.

"If the national media would leave our prostitutes alone, I wouldn't even know they're here," says **Charles A. Hollis**, treasurer of the Church of Christ in Pahrump (pop. 1,000), 75 miles north of Vegas.

Prostitutes themselves mix unabashedly in the outside world. **Veronica Allen**, 23, sells her staples at the Mustang Ranch near Reno (pop. 108,000). She commutes to Sacramento state university, where she takes courses in marketing and advertising. **Debbie Brown**, 26, also a Mustanger, says:

"I'm trying to put together a down payment on a house and buy a second car. I'm going for the American dream."

You can make almost any type of sporting wager you want in the big casinos of Vegas and Reno. Some super Super Bowl odds:

■ To win: Seattle Seahawks, 4-1; San Francisco 49ers 5-1; New York Giants 5-1; Tampa Bay Buccaneers, 150-1; Indianapolis Colts, 150-1.

Away from the flashing lights of the casinos and the red lights of the bordellos, Nevada has much to offer the 26 million annual visitors.

Ski the Sierra. Snow-capped year-round. Sail, swim or fish the lakes that dot the valleys and the mountains. Lake Tahoe is the jewel. One of the USA's most scenic settings.

Barbara Himmelright, 47, homemaker in Incline Village (pop. 8,000) on Tahoe's north shore, describes the serenity:

"Tahoe is everything. It's impossible to be in a bad mood here. You'd have to have an ingrown toenail to be grouchy."

Many Nevada visitors bring families. Many come alone. Many come as couples. Quickie marriages are a big attraction. 109,020 marriages last year, in a state with 963,000 people. Most who get hitched are non-residents.

The Cupid Wedding Chapel in Vegas caters to those who want to tie the knot in a hurry. Night or day. No delay. No blood test. Low cost. $45 for the package. Includes the chapel, minister, background music and free limo service.

FREYA: Has beeper tie to Cupid.

Catherine Freya, 57, is a marrying minister there. Wears a beeper to respond to Cupid's call. "I've gotten beeped in the middle of picnics, family dinners, church services, garage sales. I just grab my robe and go."

Last Monday two Tacoma visitors tied the knot at the Candlelight Chapel in Las Vegas. **Johnny Summers**, 26, Army helicopter pilot, and **Elaine DeMaris**, 34, a bank loan officer. Says the new Mrs. Summers:

"He suggested we come to Las Vegas for fun and then he popped the question. This place is overwhelming. All the people, lights, slot machines. I've never gambled before. Of course, this (the marriage) is the biggest gamble."

That's Plain Talk from Nevada.

Snapshot

Sagebrush State

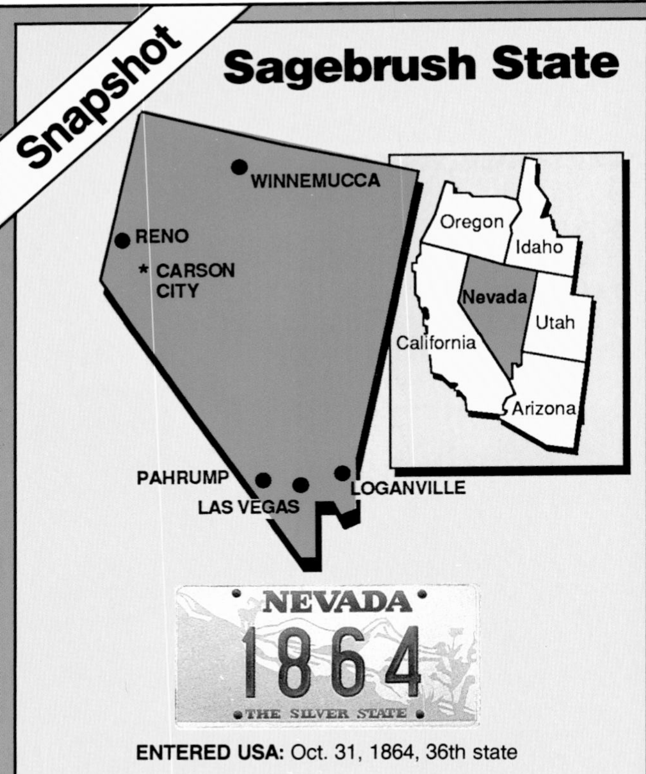

ENTERED USA: Oct. 31, 1864, 36th state

MOTTO: All for our country
POPULATION: 963,000; rank, 43rd
LARGEST CITY: Las Vegas, pop. 183,227
CAPITAL: Carson City, pop. 36,200
LAND: 109,893 square miles; rank, 7th
POPULATION DENSITY: 8.8 per square mile; rank, 47th
RACIAL MIX: 87.5% white; 6.4% black; 1.8% Asian and Pacific islanders; 1.6% American Indian. Hispanic heritage: 6.7%.

Uniquely Nev.

DRY RUN: Nevada has an annual rainfall of 3.73 inches — the driest in the USA.

GIDDY UP: Part of the 1,800-mile Pony Express mail route was along what is now Route 50 in Nevada. Riders were paid $25 a week and had to be under age 18.

MOTHER LODE: Virginia City's Comstock Lode was the world's largest and most important silver discovery. Founded in 1859, it has produced more than $1 billion in ore. After a long shutdown, it's being revived.

HANDS UP: Jarbridge was the site of the last USA stagecoach robbery. Year: 1916.

EARLY JOB: Writer Mark Twain worked a mining camp claim in Unionville in the 1860s.

HOVERING HOOVER: Hoover Dam is one of the seven man-made wonders of the modern world. Its 660-foot-thick base has enough concrete to build a two-lane highway from San Francisco to New York.

Jody Stewart, 22
Dealer
Reno

"People come here because they like the idea of making a fast dollar. It's the American way. The person that comes to my table is not expecting to make his fortune, but the thought of it is definitely in the back of his mind. I never gamble. I'm a poor college student, and it's a losing game."

Carol Piper Marshall, 45
Operator
Piper's Opera House
Virginia City

"I've never felt as comfortable in another part of the country as I do here. I love the dryness, the beautiful sunny days and the spaciousness of it. They're friendly here. I feel like I've come home."

Voices
of Nevada

Julian Albulet, 33
High wire artist
Las Vegas

"Las Vegas is THE party town. It's the most wild thing going on in the world. You've got all the big stars here. It's exciting and easy to get caught up in. I used to smoke and drink and gamble, but I gave it up. It's good to be square. Besides, I gamble every time I go up on the rope. But I know that 99 percent of the time I win."

Victor Stoffer, 43
Casino supervisor
Reno

"You see so much money that you lose what money is worth. It just doesn't mean anything to you. You have a tendency for not trying to save your money. You say, 'Let's just go out and spend it.' "

Joyce Benka, 29
Travel agency owner
Incline Village

"It's not really expensive up here. I don't think the cost of living is different than anywhere else, except maybe the groceries are a little bit high because it's a resort area. I bump into airline pilots and probably millionaires at the gym. Most of the people up here are pretty athletic so they're next to you in aerobics classes. In the summer, the Rolls Royces and Mercedes and Jaguars start coming out a lot."

Louie Reese, 40
Cab driver
Las Vegas

"I like the couples who are going to get married. Some are lovey-dovey, most are real nervous. I take them to get their license and then on to one of the chapels. After I get them married, I find out where they're staying and send them a bottle of champagne from their tip."

Ilon Webster, 76
Retired restaurant owner
Cactus Springs

"Desert living is different. One night, I was crossing the road to my house in the pitch-black and bumped into a mountain lion that was going through the trash can. I just stood there frozen, and finally it ran away. But I tell you, I'd rather run into a mountain lion than a thief from Las Vegas. Your chances are better."

*Entertainer **Wayne Newton**, 45, the "King of the Strip," has been a headliner in Las Vegas for the past 20 years. He is a single parent and lives with his daughter, Erin, 11.*

People here are the true pioneers

USA TODAY: You were born in Virginia and moved to Phoenix, Ariz., as a child. Why did you move to Las Vegas?

NEWTON: In 1959, my brother, Jerry, and I, opened at the Fremont Hotel as a singing duo. We were working so much there, and the weather was comparable to Phoenix's, so my asthmatic condition simmered down. Just plain healthwise, it made sense to move.

USA TODAY: What are your earliest memories of Nevada?

NEWTON: Before I ever saw Las Vegas, I thought the Flamingo Hotel was shaped like a big bird and the Dunes was a big pile of sand.

USA TODAY: What happened when you saw the real thing?

NEWTON: I was disappointed. It was really strange. I had to get a special permit to work because I was underage. So, between shows, I would have to go to the restaurant, or go outside and stand in the street, or go to my dressing room. I wasn't allowed to go to the casino.

USA TODAY: What comes to mind when you think about Nevada?

NEWTON: Nevada has a side to it that I don't think any other state can brag about. Lake Tahoe is the most beautiful lake in the world. The water is 99 percent pure, and there are places you can see 200, 300 feet down. Then you've got Mount Charleston, where you can snow-ski nine or 10 months a year, 20 minutes out of Vegas.

USA TODAY: What are your two homes like?

NEWTON: I have two ranches. I keep 210 Arabian show horses on the ranches. It's beautiful riding country — the last frontier for that kind of thing.

USA TODAY: What about the people in Nevada?

NEWTON: The people are very warm people, because basically they're all from somewhere else. I believe the people of Nevada to be the true pioneers of this country — the people who would have crossed the desert in the covered wagons. The things that make Nevada a great state are mining, cattle and gaming. These made up the early West.

Topic: NEVADA

We offer a lot besides gambling and tourism

USA TODAY: Many people think of gambling and prostitution when they think of your state. What else should they think of?

BRYAN: They should think of an extraordinary amount of diversity and scenery. This year, for the first time in our history, Nevada will have a national park — the Great Basin National Park in the eastern part of the state. In the southern part of the state, you've got the first of the state parks — the Valley of Fire. There's a tremendous recreational potential above and beyond our gaming and tourism.

USA TODAY: Do you feel the state has an image problem because of the gaming, legal prostitution, and quickie divorces?

BRYAN: The problem is that the image is primarily that which is perceived by people who have not been here, who do not know that Nevadans are a good people who value the work ethic, that they are fiercely independent, proud of their heritage, and that it is a state in which opportunity abounds.

USA TODAY: What kind of opportunities?

BRYAN: Someone can come to this state and, in a relatively short period of time, make his or her mark. People tend to accept you as you are, not for your family lineage or your last name. I think that's one of the great redeeming qualities.

USA TODAY: Does the state have gambling, prostitution, and speedy marriages and divorces because Nevadans have a "live and let live" attitude?

BRYAN: Some of the things which you refer to were born out of economic necessity. Nevada has been heavily dependent upon a single industry. Initially, it was mining. When the Comstock mines played out, the economic dislocation was severe. In the 1930s, we embarked upon this great social experiment. In the last decade, state after state has passed lotteries. As gaming in one form or another has been expanded, it suggests to us that Nevada's experiment has proved extremely successful.

***Richard Bryan**, 50, a Democrat, was elected governor in 1982 and was re-elected in 1986. He also served as state attorney general and a state legislator.*

USA TODAY: How much does Nevada depend on gaming?

BRYAN: Nevadans know that 45 percent of our general fund revenues come from gaming. It's a terribly important industry. I think, for the foreseeable future, it will be the largest single part of the economy. But, clearly, we ought to diversify.

USA TODAY: Is it difficult to attract new businesses?

BRYAN: Ask the person who has come to Nevada to establish a business. Those people are our most eloquent sales force. They have a business climate that is very favorable both in terms of tax structure and in terms of attitude of the community.

USA TODAY: Do you think you can keep the nation's high-level nuclear waste depository out of Nevada?

BRYAN: Yes. I get more encouraged as we move along.

USA TODAY: You grew up in Las Vegas. How do you compare the city of your youth to the city of today?

BRYAN: When I started school in Las Vegas, there were about 8,500 people. Things were happening in the community — new subdivisions going in, new hotels opening up. There was an excitement that captured us all. We haven't lost that feeling.

New Hampshire

Visited: May 13-14, 1987
Featured in USA TODAY: May 22

"My favorite story is about the old farmer in the North Country. Just before the 1980 primary, there were TV crews at his door, trying to find out whether he was going to vote for Ronald Reagan. His answer was, 'I'm not sure, I've only met him three times.' "

New Hampshire Gov. John Sununu

New Hampshire

No. 1 in political clout, 40th state in population

You probably laughed if you saw comedian **Pat Paulsen**, 59, in his jogging outfit declaring last week that once again he's running for president.

But they didn't laugh where he made his announcement — in the state capital of Concord (pop. 30,400). Or elsewhere in New Hampshire.

"We can see through the bull," says **Patricia Little**, 31, city clerk in Keene (pop. 21,449).

PAULSEN: Perennial Pat promises humor in presidential campaign.

They take their politics very seriously here. And well they should. Look at the record:

■ Since 1948, no presidential candidate has won the general election without carrying New Hampshire.

■ Since 1964, no Republican candidate has won the party nomination without scoring first in the Granite State.

■ Since 1972, only one Democrat (**Gary Hart** '84) has won New Hampshire's primary without winning the party nomination.

Is it fair that the state, which ranks 40th in population (1,027,000) and 44th in size, carries more clout than any other of the 50?

"I've just assumed that's the way God intended it to be," replies Gov. **John H. Sununu**, 47, third-term Republican.

God and the Legislature. New Hampshire's primary election law is automatic. It shall be first. If any other state moves its primary date ahead, New Hampshire automatically jumps in a week earlier. It's been first since 1952.

It's a matter of politics and pragmatism. Big bucks are brought in by the premiere primary.

Each candidate is permitted by federal law to spend about $450,000 in the state. Add that to the hordes of media people and political followers who move in and out for months, or years, before the primary.

New Hampshire knows how to tap those expense-account dollars:

■ A 7 percent tax on every hotel room and restaurant meal.

■ 17 cents a pack on cigarettes.

■ State liquor stores, with the whole markup from wholesale going into government coffers.

Shaping opinion for many in New Hampshire is *The Union Leader* of Manchester (pop. 94,937). State's largest city. State's largest newspaper (circ. 69,965).

The vitriolic voice of *The Union Leader* has crowned or crushed many a candidate:

■ Called **Eugene McCarthy** a "skunk's skunk."

■ **Ted Kennedy**: "Just plain stupid."

■ **Edmund Muskie**: Made him cry with a "Big Daddy's Jane" editorial lambasting his wife.

MUSKIE: Editorial brought him tears.

■ **George Bush**: "A spoon-fed little rich kid."

From 1946 to 1981, **William ("Wild Bill") Loeb** ruled *The Union Leader*. Since his death, his wheelchaired widow, **Nackey S.**, 63, has done the same. Different styles. But the Page One editorials, always decked in red, white and blue, have the same effect.

"He came out swinging. He used a sledgehammer. She does essentially the same thing, in a different manner," says **Tom Wreck**, 61, an aptly named security guard at *The Union Leader*. Her jabs are more like a sharp needle.

Who will *The Union Leader* bless or bruise in 1988?

"We haven't endorsed anybody yet," says Nackey. "We will when someone proves themselves worthy of the job. I'm not enthusiastic about anyone I've seen so far. . . . There might be some people in the boondocks that could become available."

CONCORD PRIDE: Wayne Devoid, 10, leads Boy Scouts in parade.

Back to the perennial Paulsen. He ran on the "Stag Party" ticket in 1968, as a Republican in 1972. This year, he'll run as a Democrat.

While most in New Hampshire resent his silliness in their business, some see the humor. Says **Tom Hansen**, 48, of Concord:

"We have so many clowns in the White House. Why not one that gets paid for it?"

That's Plain Talk from New Hampshire.

Snapshot

Granite State

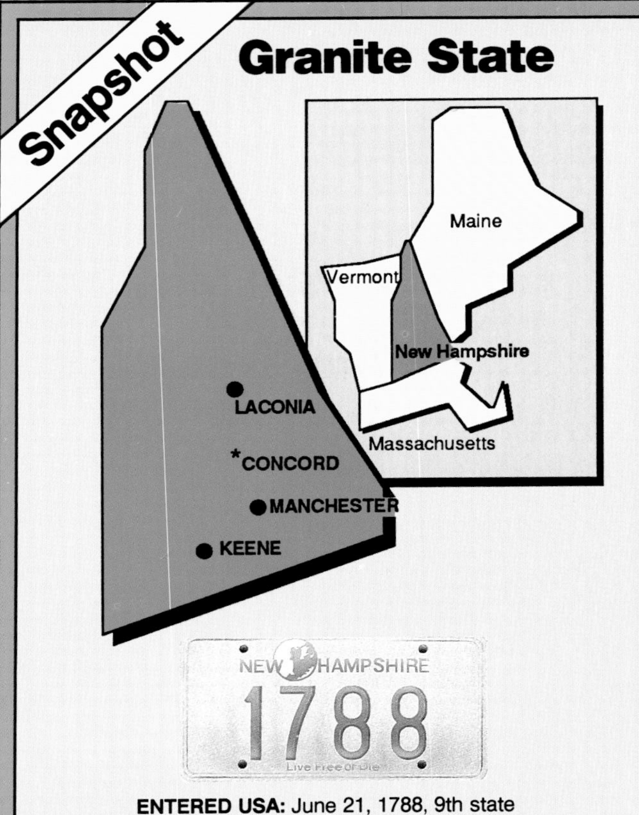

ENTERED USA: June 21, 1788, 9th state

MOTTO: Live free or die
POPULATION: 1,027,000; rank, 40th
LARGEST CITY: Manchester, pop. 94,937
CAPITAL: Concord, pop. 30,400
LAND: 8,993 square miles; rank, 44th
POPULATION DENSITY: 114.2 per square mile; rank, 19th
RACIAL MIX: 98.9% white; 0.4% black; 0.3% Asian and Pacific islanders. Hispanic heritage: 0.6%.

Uniquely N.H.

I DO: New Hampshire has the nation's lowest legal age for marriage. Girls can marry at age 13 with parental permission; boys must be at least 14.

LOTTO FEVER: The first state lottery was run by New Hampshire in 1963. Proceeds were earmarked for education.

PEAK WEATHER: The summit at Mount Washington holds the world's record for the highest recorded wind speed — 231 mph on April 12, 1934. The mountain also holds the USA record for the most snow in a single storm — 97.8 inches, February 24-28, 1969.

TINY TRADE: New Hampshire exports only two agricultural products — apples and maple syrup.

ROLE REVERSAL: 100 years ago, more than 80 percent of the land in New Hampshire was cleared of forest. Today, the reverse is true — more than 80 percent is wooded.

Gerry Gallup, 32
Student/custodian
Manchester

"New Hampshire is proud of having the first primary. I think New Hampshire is true to the old-fashioned New England standards. It's reluctant to change. Reluctant to be molded by the times. Most ideas are better if they've stood the test of time. You have a college-type atmosphere in New England, and they hold conservative views. They have close family ties. They tend to settle and stay in this area."

Bertha Lindsay, 89
Shaker eldress
Canterbury

"My parents died when I was 4 years old. My sister knew it was their wish to have me sent here. At 8 years old I came here. At 21 we have the right to choose whether we want to be a Shaker. I felt I could give as much here in this home as anywhere else. We took in needy children. We did charity work. I love the sisters. I've never regretted it."

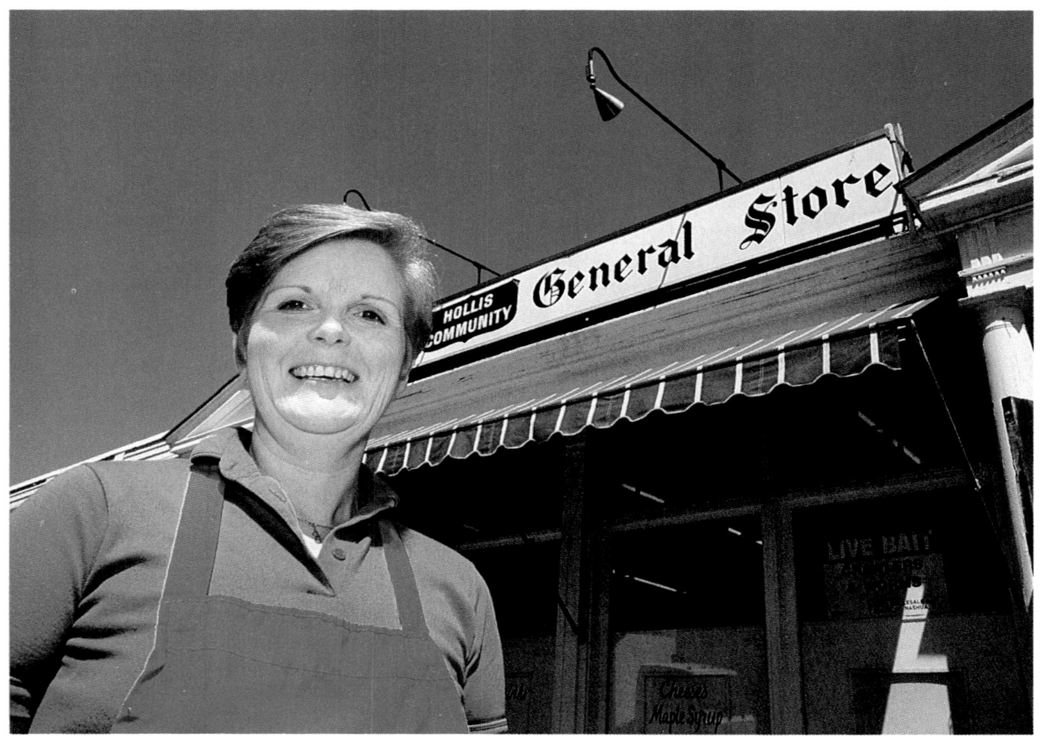

Voices
of New Hampshire

Jessie Smith, 44
Sales clerk
Hollis

"I love living in a small town. I feel like I belong here. Everybody says hello. Everybody goes to the dump on Saturday. It's a big social event. At election time, the politicians go to the dump to meet everybody and give out coffee and donuts."

Betsy Gagne, 36
Shop owner
Concord

"New Hampshire weeds out an awful lot of the also-rans. Those are the people who are casually thinking about running for president. They know if they can't make it here, they're out. And being a small state, politicians can travel the whole state and get to know people."

Tom Kingston, 21
Student
Laconia

"All there is in Northern New Hampshire is mills. Unless you want a mill job, you get out. There's not too much opportunity, so everyone moves south. It's just now starting to grow. We actually got a McDonald's. That's big time. I'm studying electrical construction and there is a 90 percent placement rate. The unemployment in this state is the lowest in the country."

Susan Brooks, 27
Homemaker
Randolph

"We feel privileged living here. When people are hiking around, it's great when you hear them say, 'You live here. You're so lucky.' I think New Englanders get the reputation as stoic because of all the tourism. Some people feel as if they are invading the territory and worry if they are exploiting the resources. It's tender ground when you live in an area where you live off and depend on natural resources."

Howard Fuller, 64
Electrician
Keene

"We're a quiet, church-oriented place. When I told a friend I was going away on vacation, he said, 'Why go away? You live in a Currier and Ives painting, with all the covered bridges.' We do live right in the middle of vacationland."

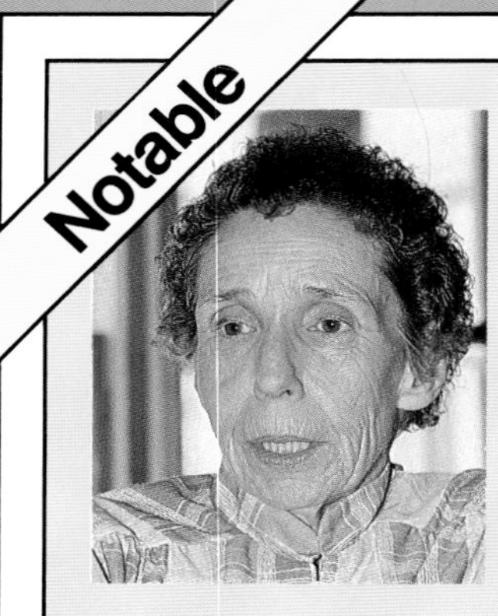

Nackey Loeb, 63, a resident of Goffstown, became publisher of The Union Leader *in Manchester in 1981, after the death of her husband, William.*

We want to make our readers think

USA TODAY: What impact does your newspaper, *The Union Leader*, have on the state?

LOEB: We have supported people who haven't made it, and we have supported various issues in the state that have not succeeded. We are an outspoken paper. Our main reason for being outspoken is that we want to make people think. We want to make people get involved.

USA TODAY: Do most of your readers agree with you?

LOEB: We print more letters in the paper than any other paper in the country. We allow people to spit in our eye, so to speak. If they disagree with us, they can tell us so in no uncertain terms. We want people to be involved and to be concerned. This is what the Founding Fathers had in mind when they established the government of this country, and I think that one of the dangers in this country is that a lot of people don't really care.

USA TODAY: What do you think of the cast of candidates for next year's primary election?

LOEB: There's a bunch of characters. Our editor-in-chief says that it's very simple — it's called the '88 primary because we're going to end up with 88 candidates! I don't think we have all the actors on the stage yet.

USA TODAY: What should people across the USA know about New Hampshire?

LOEB: One of our ex-governors once said New Hampshire is what the United States used to be and what the United States should be. People think of us as a bunch of yokels up here at times, but we have hi-tech industry, we have small manufacturing, large manufacturing, agriculture, big cities, small towns.

USA TODAY: What is your role at the newspaper?

LOEB: I poke my nose in everywhere.

USA TODAY: Ten years ago, you were in an auto accident that left you in a wheelchair. That doesn't seem to have stopped you.

LOEB: Actually, you know, this wheelchair business toughens you up. Makes you really more capable, because you've had to face something tough and beat it.

Topic: NEW HAMPSHIRE

Our character's rural, but we're hi-tech, too

USA TODAY: The one thing that everybody hears about in New Hampshire is presidential politics. What else should people know about the state?

SUNUNU: There's still a historic image in a lot of the country about the low taxes in this state. We are the only state with neither a sales nor income tax. A lot of folks still have the vision of New Hampshire as a rural state. Although we've done an excellent job in preserving the rural character of the state, it is really a very industrialized state. We have the highest percentage of hi-tech employment of any state in the country.

USA TODAY: You also have low unemployment and high growth.

SUNUNU: We're at about 2.5 percent unemployment. We've had the lowest unemployment in the country for the last five years. Over that period, the state's gone from about 26th in per capita income to eighth in the nation.

USA TODAY: Is there a negative side to low unemployment?

SUNUNU: The business community keeps telling me they can't find anybody to hire.

USA TODAY: How do you attract firms to New Hampshire?

SUNUNU: I'll go and spend time with them and encourage them to come up here. In the last few years, we have worked on the theory that if we get the fundamental manufacturer, their suppliers and peripheral services will follow.

USA TODAY: Do the voters of New Hampshire take their responsibility seriously?

SUNUNU: I don't think they cast their votes lightly. My favorite story is about the old farmer in the North Country. Just before the 1980 primary, there were TV crews at his door, trying to find out whether he was going to vote for Ronald Reagan. His answer was, "I'm not sure, I've only met him three times." The point is that the voters do get involved in trying to understand the differences among the candidates, and most hold off a commitment until the very end.

***John Sununu**, 47, a Republican, was elected governor in 1982 and re-elected in 1984 and 1986.*

USA TODAY: What do the Northeast states share?

SUNUNU: The governor of Texas, when I first got elected, very proudly told me that all six New England states could be tucked in one small corner of Texas. And I said, "That's probably true, but we were smart enough to divide in six and end up with 12 U.S. senators." We are small. We are compact. We have very much interdependent economies, and we share assets.

USA TODAY: How is New Hampshire recovering from the loss of Christa McAuliffe, the teacher who was killed in the Challenger accident?

SUNUNU: The people of New Hampshire were impacted at a very personal level. We have established a Christa McAuliffe sabbatical program for teachers. The Legislature is considering a memorial planetarium. People talk about her more frequently than you might expect. Most of the discussion is about building on what they felt was positive.

USA TODAY: Do you prefer the executive or the legislative branch?

SUNUNU: I ran for the U.S. Senate in 1980, and I lost in the primary by 2,000, 3,000 votes. In retrospect, I suspect I'm probably a heck of a lot happier as a governor where I can get more done than as a senator.

New Jersey

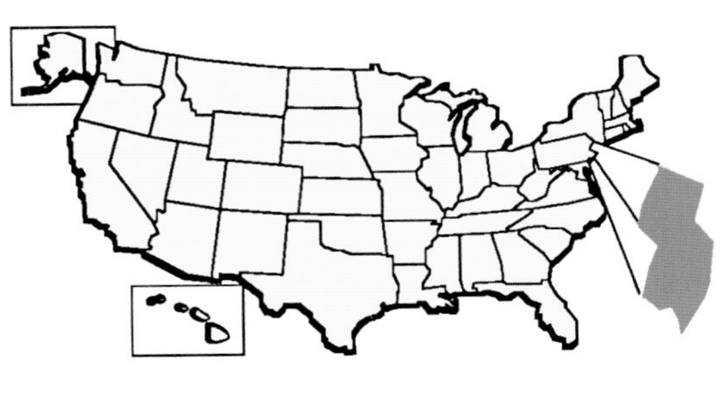

Visited: Aug. 4-6, 1987
Featured in USA TODAY: Aug. 7

"People from New York who used to laugh about Hoboken now can't afford a house there."

Richard McMullen
Insurance account manager
Union, N.J.

New Jersey

Shaded by N.Y., Pa., but humble no more

Benjamin Franklin called New Jersey "a valley of humility squeezed between two mountains of conceit." New York and Philadelphia.

That was 200 years ago. The mountains are still there, egos still sky-high. But the valley isn't as humble anymore.

Jerseyites have stopped laughing at all those old jokes about their state. They're cleaning up their act, including some of the dump yards of waste. Given us Super Bowl football kings. The Boss of entertainment. Flexed their business muscle. Beginning to beat their breast.

7.6 million of them. More people per square mile than any other state. 250,000 commute to the Big Apple and back every day. Another 100,000 to Philly.

Three top salesmen of the '80s sell Jersey in words and music. **Bruce Springsteen**, 37. The Boss. **Tom Kean**, 52. The Guv. **Malcolm Forbes**, 67. The Chairman.

Forbes — motorcyclist, balloonist, capitalist — commutes daily from his 40-acre estate near Bedminster (pop. 2,469) to his *Forbes* magazine headquarters in midtown Manhattan.

"You get the best of both worlds. . . . It enables me to enjoy all the perks of the most vital and alive city in the world, which New York is, and at the same time go home at night to a genuine country. It's one hell of an attractive combination."

SPRINGSTEEN: Sings songs of Jersey.

Gov. Kean, popular, urbane Republican, gets much credit for the economic turnaround since he was elected in 1981, reelected in 1985. Courted new corporations and citizens, many from the Empire State. Unhappy New York officials call him the "Pied Piper."

Kean denies he "steals" from his neighbors. Says nice things about them. "New York City is strong and Philadelphia is strong and we use them as assets. What we do to be successful is create the right climate."

Springsteen comes home often to Asbury Park (pop. 17,100). Sings worldwide of the Jersey Turnpike and Jersey girls, with understanding sympathy for the state's blue-collar workers. May need new lyrics to stay in tune with the growing white-collar crowd.

White-collar women are on the move. Many of them educated at Rutgers, 48,539-student state university with its main campus at New Brunswick (pop. 41,500). Or Princeton, park-like Ivy-League campus in the city of 12,000. **Brooke Shields** was among this year's grads.

Lynn Kurtz, 36, lives in Pennington (pop. 2,109) near Princeton. A childs-wear buyer who commutes to Manhattan.

KURTZ: Commuters from the Garden State have a new look.

"Years ago, I was always amused at the businessmen in the same dark suits. Like little robots. That's what a commuter was. That isn't so any more. There are many more women and it's far more aggressive."

But most Jerseyites make their living at home, in the factories and on the farms.

■ Manufacturing is the leader. Chemical production No. 1. Food processing No. 2. Electric machinery No. 3.

■ Tourism is growing dramatically. Atlantic City (pop. 37,700) is the USA's No. 1 resort destination. Nearly 30 million visitors in 1986. Casino gambling, legalized in 1978, is the draw.

Despite heavy urban concentrations, two-thirds of New Jersey is farms and woods. Nickname the "Garden State" applies. 8,300 working farms. Many thousands more back-yard gardens.

Tony Ciavaglia, 32, Emerson (pop. 7,793) has one. "If you don't have tomatoes growing in your back yard, you're not a real Jerseyite."

Whether they work in factories or on farms, commute to the mountains or stay in the valley, Jerseyites boast of what's happened to employment, incomes, real estate values.

Richard McMullen, 33, insurance company account manager in Union (pop. 50,100), says it:

"People from New York who used to laugh about Hoboken now can't afford a house there."

Humble no more. That's Plain Talk from New Jersey.

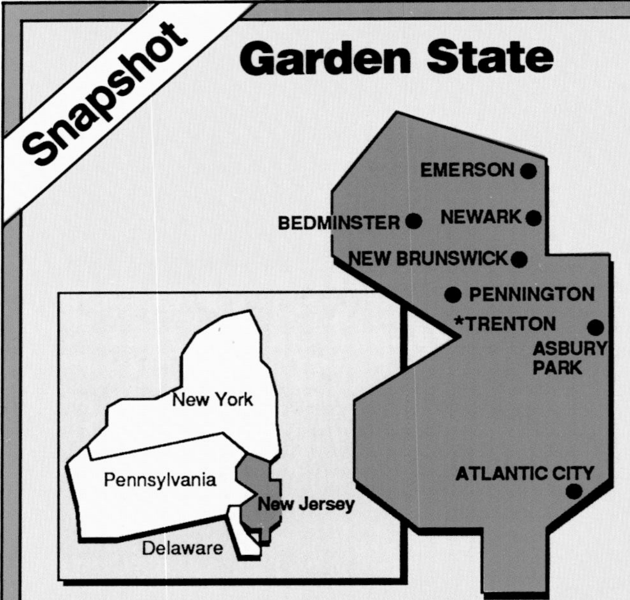

NEW JERSEY
17 87
GARDEN STATE

ENTERED USA: Dec. 18, 1787, 3rd state

MOTTO: Liberty and prosperity
POPULATION: 7,620,000; rank, 9th
LARGEST CITY: Newark, pop. 314,387
CAPITAL: Trenton, pop. 92,124
LAND: 7,468 square miles; rank, 46th
POPULATION DENSITY: 1,020.4 per square mile; rank, 1st
RACIAL MIX: 83.2% white; 12.6% black; 1.4% Asian and Pacific islanders. Hispanic heritage: 6.7%.

Uniquely N.J.

NOW SHOWING: The first motion pictures were shown in West Orange by Thomas Edison in 1889. First drive-in: a 10-acre plot in Camden built in June 1933.

ON THE BOARDWALK: Atlantic City opened as a resort in 1854, and built the USA's first boardwalk in 1870. The board game Monopoly takes its property names from Atlantic City streets and landmarks.

PLAY BALL: 600 pounds of mud from a Burlington County mudhole are shipped annually to the USA's Major League baseball teams, a practice that dates back at least 50 years. The mud is rubbed into new baseballs to take out the shine and slipperiness.

SULTAN OF SWOON: Hoboken native Frank Sinatra was singing at a New Jersey roadhouse for $15 a week in the early 1940s when Harry James signed him to play with his new orchestra.

Jerry Schneidman, 42
Teacher
The Bronx, N.Y.
Visiting Atlantic City

"I went into the casino with $25 and I came out with $25, and I'm happy with that. I don't come here expecting to win a jackpot. If I win, it's nice. If not, I consider it an entertainment fee. You come out here expecting to make a donation, but the idea of hitting a jackpot is always in the back of my mind."

Bill Falcon, 34
Bar manager
Asbury Park

"Bruce Springsteen comes in and hangs out all the time. He stops in to check out the new bands. People usually crowd around him, but they leave him alone. They just want to get close. When he plays, there are people standing on the stools, standing on the railings, waving their hands in the air. They go nuts."

Anne Lizzio, 65
Hardware store owner
Clayton

"I've lived here for 37 years. I read in the paper about New Jersey being one big toxic dump site, but I don't see it. We have some problems, because we are an industrial state. We have lots of chemical plants. But we are, after all, The Garden State. If you like fresh fruit and vegetables, you should definitely come to New Jersey."

Voices
of New Jersey

Jerome Premo, 44
Transit director
Westfield

"New Jersey is a good place to do business and to live. We're tired of being the brunt of jokes. We've got a booming economy. People are taking pride in what they do and where they live. I'm one of eight people in history to move from Southern California to New Jersey, and I'm glad I did."

Beth Coyle, 26
Fund-raiser
Bordentown

"The state is trying to get together. The middle class is willing to do things for the poor. We've had problems longer than other states, and we're handling them better. Half of the people I've heard talk bad about New Jersey have never been here."

James Keyes, 26
Engineer
Newark

"Newark is obviously on the upswing. New construction is going on. New condominiums are being developed. I moved to Newark because the services are great. They pick up the garbage, the streets are always clean. They trim the trees. People who have invested in Newark are going to make out like bandits."

Lisa Farber, 28
Graduate student
Princeton

"Princeton is like an island in the middle of New Jersey. It's not urban — it's more of a country club. The campus is wonderfully manicured and green. All the trees are labeled. It's an island of affluence. It's a very high-powered academic institution."

Leslie Walten, 50
Businessman
Flemington

"There's more industry moving out here from the city. You can tell by the housing boom that's going on. People are moving out of New York because it's more desirable in New Jersey. The cost of living is cheaper. The taxes are cheaper . . . in relationship to New York. I believe it is The Garden State. There are lots of pretty areas. It's never pictured as pretty, but it is."

Malcolm Forbes, 67, is chairman, editor, and sole stockholder of Forbes *magazine, which his father founded in 1917. A resident of Bedminster, N.J., he is one of the USA's wealthiest men, worth $500 million.*

Places are blooming as never before

USA TODAY: Were you born in New Jersey, and did you grow up there?

FORBES: My mother had come from Brooklyn. She went back there for my birth. Other than that, I've been a resident all my life, through prep school and Princeton University. And I've lived in Bedminster for 40 years.

USA TODAY: You say you've lived out of New Jersey for only a few days of your life. What do you find so enticing about the state?

FORBES: It's been good fortune for those of us who always knew how attractive New Jersey is that most people didn't and were put off by some of the cliches about the Mafia. So New Jersey has been unspoiled by overdiscovery.

USA TODAY: Is that still true?

FORBES: People have now discovered that New Jersey is a great place to headquarter a company and to live. There's a bigger traffic jam coming out of New York. It's almost as big a traffic jam of cars coming from New York to work in New Jersey as the other way around.

USA TODAY: Do you welcome the growth?

FORBES: It's a mixed blessing, but it's understandable. And places that had been going to seed are blooming as never before. I'm referring to the waterfront, and Hoboken, and Jersey City, all of which seemed to have a terminal waterfront illness and are now becoming prime and priceful real estate.

USA TODAY: What do you most enjoy about New Jersey?

FORBES: You get the best of both worlds. . . . It enables me to enjoy all the perks of the most vital and alive city in the world, which New York is, and at the same time go home at night to a genuine country. It's one hell of an attractive combination.

USA TODAY: Still room for the sports you enjoy, such as ballooning and motorcycling?

FORBES: Right. Every once in a while we get some crackpots who will propose laws outlawing helicopters, sky diving and hot-air balloons. New Jersey isn't about to hamstring the lifestyle and freedom that appeal to most Americans. There's always somebody who wants to hogtie somebody else.

Topic: NEW JERSEY

We have right climate for business, baseball

USA TODAY: New Jersey has long had an image problem.

KEAN: New Jersey had an image that wasn't in touch with reality, in part encouraged by some of our own citizens who laughed at the New Jersey jokes, who almost were apologetic about the state. This has always been a state with deep history. It's also a state with many natural resources.

USA TODAY: What are your favorite features of the state?

KEAN: You can drive for a couple hours, and you're in the mountains. The Northwest has ravines and canyons. It's a state that people think of as urbanized, yet almost two-thirds of New Jersey is farms and woods. We have more ethnic groups than any other state, except one. We have a farm economy, and we're in the top five in the number of farm products produced.

USA TODAY: At one time, New Jersey was considered anti-business. Is that still true?

KEAN: We've cut taxes. We now have a lower tax climate than most of our neighbors. That's an asset. When I came into office, we were thought to have a very anti-business climate. Officials thought of business as something that they taxed and regulated, and that was about it.

USA TODAY: Has that changed?

KEAN: We consider business an asset, something to be encouraged. I get personally involved with trying to get through to the companies that I think would be assets to come to New Jersey — but only when they're looking at other states.

USA TODAY: For years, New Jersey was a regional dumping ground for toxic waste and had a history of organized crime.

KEAN: On organized crime, we've had some of the strongest U.S. attorneys and some of the best attorneys general in recent years. I don't think anybody would make a statement anymore that New Jersey is a haven for organized crime.

Thomas Kean, 52, a Republican, is serving his second term as governor. Kean is a former teacher, reporter and state legislator.

USA TODAY: What about the toxic waste problem?

KEAN: We've got a toxic waste problem. We recognized it earlier than the rest of the country. We still have the best program in the country. My feeling is that New Jersey is a rich enough and intelligent enough state to get the problem solved. We've got more sites on the Superfund list. We expect to be the first state to clean up its toxic waste.

USA TODAY: Has casino gambling been good for the state?

KEAN: No question, it's created jobs. As people come to Atlantic City, they go see other parts of the state. But gambling has its problems. One-half of the attorney general's office works to keep it straight. I opposed it, but now that it's here, I want to make sure it works for everyone.

USA TODAY: New Jersey is looking for a baseball team. Will you get one?

KEAN: Yes. This is the greatest serious sports market in the country, where we're going to build a stadium.

USA TODAY: What does Bruce Springsteen mean to New Jersey?

KEAN: He's a symbol. Wherever he goes, he talks about the state. If we were Japanese, we'd make him a national treasure.

New Mexico

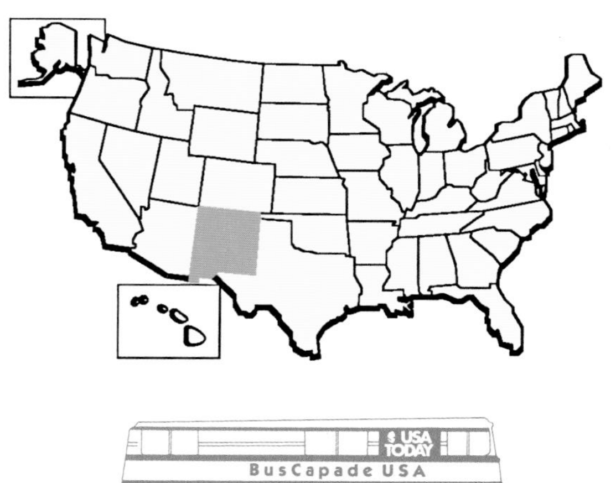

Visited: April 20-21, 1987
Featured in USA TODAY: April 24

"We're going to come out with an advertising campaign. We may start off by saying, 'Guess who just joined the 50? We're now in the United States.' "

New Mexico Gov. Garrey Carruthers

New Mexico

Beauty and THE bomb, avant-garde and ailing

They call it "the Land of Enchantment." It is. It is also the land of ambivalence. Curiously contrasting people and places.

■ The beauty. Mesmerizing blue skies add sparkle to majestic mountains. Sunsets paint surrealistic pictures of canyons and deserts.

■ THE bomb. The first A-bomb exploded on those deserts in 1945. In 1987, scientists work in secrecy at Los Alamos on more deadly bombs — and "star wars" defenses against them.

■ The ailing. An estimated 30 percent of more than 100,000 Indians who live on reservations have no electricity or running water. Education and employment are elusive.

HAGMAN: 'J.R.'s daughter.

■ The avant-garde. Santa Fe, the state capital (pop. 52,274), is home for the sophisticated and the chic. From New York. Texas. California. Laid-back and lavish at the same time.

A strange mix of ties draws or keeps men and women here.

Kristina Hagman, 29. Blonde. Beautiful. Daughter of **Larry Hagman**, the J.R. of *Dallas* fame. Her family heritage helped her to Hollywood by age 14. Her name was Heidi then.

She has abandoned acting and her name. The new Kristina took to the brush full time four years ago. Now she supports herself comfortably through the sale of sophisticated nude paintings that hang nationwide.

"You can have your own identity here. Tolerance and diversity are the key," Kristina says.

ERLICHMAN: Nixon's henchman.

John Erlichman, 62, President Nixon's chief adviser for domestic affairs. Caught in Watergate. After he got out of jail, he wanted out of the limelight.

"A friend told me about Santa Fe. How peaceful it is. People here respect your privacy. This is it. This is home," Erlichman says. He is working on his seventh book and lives off royalties.

Heather Smith, 31. Former gardener in Old Salem, N.C. She couldn't get along with her new boss, quit and headed west.

Now, she roams the Santa Fe shopping malls with bucket, brush and squeegee, looking for window-washing jobs.

"I ran into some unexpected expenses and now I'm broke. But I get enough work to make out," she said, sitting curbside savoring a dish of Dairy Queen.

Compare fashionable Santa Fe with Albuquerque, the state's largest city (pop. 350,575). *Forbes* magazine recently called Albuquerque "Wild West" and said it is the worst city in the USA for marriages.

Albuquerque Journal columnist **Jim Arnholz** reflected on that *Forbes* article this week. "What if it was right? What if we are cold, aloof, distant and in a quiet way, hostile?" Arnholz asked readers. He didn't answer the question.

Nearly all New Mexico has a Native American look. Gallup (pop. 18,161) is an Indian center. Navajos north. Pueblos south.

McArthur Halona, 36, wife, **Pam**, and four children live on the nearby Navajo reservation at Tohatchi, where he grew up. They came back from Provo, Utah, where he earned a college degree.

"This is where my people are. I want to help them," Halona says. But he worries that his children are disadvantaged and depressed by the austere lifestyle.

BLUE CORN: She loves Bill Cosby.

Blue Corn, 66, prominent Pueblo pottery maker, learned the craft from her grandmother. She works and lives in a comfortable adobe home. Raised 10 children there. Her favorite pastime is watching Bill Cosby's TV show.

"I wait for it every week. He has a nice, clean family. Cosby takes care of his family the way I like to take care of mine. He teaches them to be good," she says.

That's Plain Talk from New Mexico.

Snapshot

Land of Enchantment

Colorado
New Mexico
Arizona
Oklahoma
Texas

GALLUP
*SANTA FE
ALBUQUERQUE
LAS CRUCES

19 12
New Mexico
Land of Enchantment

ENTERED USA: Jan. 6, 1912, 47th state

MOTTO: It grows as it goes
POPULATION: 1,479,000; rank, 37th
LARGEST CITY: Albuquerque, pop. 350,575
CAPITAL: Santa Fe, pop. 52,274
LAND: 121,335 square miles; rank, 5th
POPULATION DENSITY: 12.2 per square mile; rank, 43rd
RACIAL MIX: 75.0% white; 8.1% American Indian; 1.8% black; 0.5% Asian and Pacific islanders. Hispanic heritage: 36.6%.

Uniquely N.M.

SNOWBALL: Santa Fe annually receives an average of 17 more inches of snow than Fairbanks, Alaska.

UP, UP AND AWAY: The Albuquerque International Balloon Fiesta is the largest gathering of hot air and gas balloons in the world. Balloons: almost 600 each fall.

CAPITAL CITY: Santa Fe is the USA's oldest state capital. The city was founded in 1610.

HISTORIC HIGH-RISE: Chaco Canyon is the site of the world's largest excavated pre-Columbian Indian ruins. Thirteen major ruins and more than 400 minor ruins are in the area. The "apartment houses" of Pueblo Bonito (pretty village) had about 800 rooms.

LONG AND WINDING ROAD: The oldest road in the USA runs from Santa Fe to Chihuahua, Mexico. It first served travelers in 1581. It is now Highway 85.

Voices

of New Mexico

Jim Davila, 31
Artist
Rio Rancho

"This area has everything. It's rich in history and culture. I love the rich colors of the traditional arts and crafts, and the colors of the landscape. I'm inspired by them."

Eliseo Rodriguez, 72 (with wife, Paula)
Artists
Santa Fe

"Santa Fe is friendly and historical. People are willing to help each other. We have the three cultures which seem to be getting along beautifully. Hospitality starts here. The art field in Santa Fe is open; it's an ideal environment. The subjects for an artist are all around."

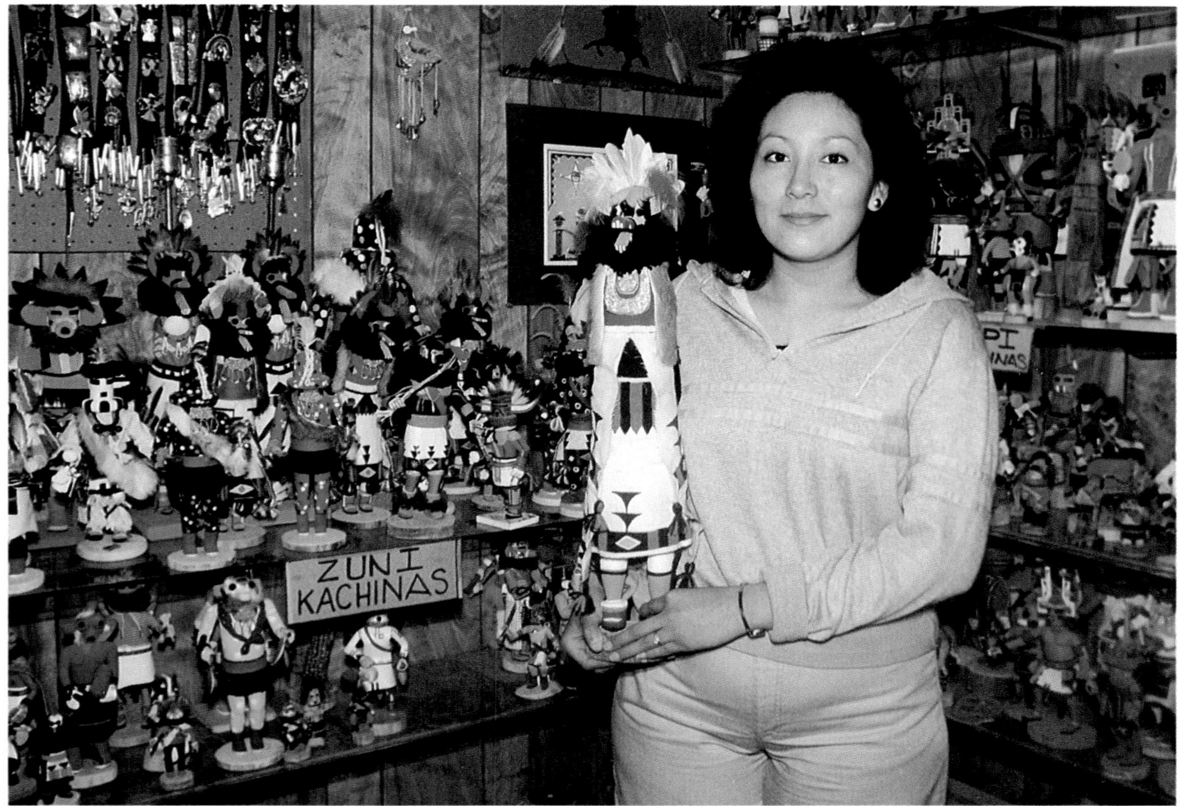

Pam Lee, 24
Jewelry store clerk
Zuni Pueblo

"The Zunis are really happy people. People who don't even know you will welcome you to their houses and give you a cup of coffee. They are into traditional things. My people (Tohono O'Odham Indians) have forgotten about traditional ways."

Diane Calabaza, 30
Artist
San Ildefonso Pueblo

"We try to stress keeping up the tradition, especially the dances and religion. Even people who have moved to the city will come back for our dances. They relate to the weather, to give us good rain for the crops. I know if I left the pueblo and went to the city, I'd get homesick and want to come back the very next day."

Catherine Hill, 35
Education consultant
Santa Fe

"We're finding a lot of the Easterners are coming because it's not as crowded. Santa Fe is city life, but it still has the atmosphere of being a very small town because it keeps its cultural setting. I see a big difference culturally in the northern part of the state compared to the southern part of the state. There is more stress on the Indian and Spanish up north. Most of the reservations are up north and on the Arizona border."

John Phillips, 30
Gas station attendant
Los Alamos

"Los Alamos could use more jobs outside the scientific fields. The bomb was built right here, but frankly I don't care. I was brought up with it, and I've become indifferent to it. My belief is that we have to defend ourselves. God gives us a spiritual armor, and our physical bodies have to be protected, too."

John Massengill, 34 (with daughter, Lauren, 6 months)
Businessman
Pojoaque

"We still have open space here. The air is clean. It's not as populated as other states and it's a fast-moving state. Year-round we have the best climate in the USA. Northern New Mexico offers everything we enjoy — mountains, wildlife, skiing and horses. I don't have any use for large cities . . . none whatsoever."

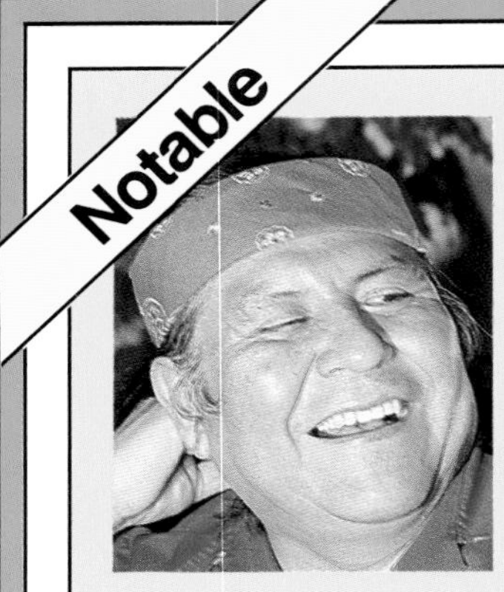

R.C. Gorman, 55, is an artist whose paintings of Indian women are known worldwide. He has lived in New Mexico for 13 years.

I paint what I see, not social statements

USA TODAY: Your paintings, lithographs, pottery and sculptures are all over New Mexico. Does your work convey any one message?

GORMAN: No, no message. I just paint. I've been painting since I was 3 years old, and at 3 years old, you don't start out thinking, "I'm going to present a message."

USA TODAY: You grew up on a Navajo Indian reservation. How did that affect your art?

GORMAN: In my case, at least, the Indian child had more opportunities to express himself, because we entertained ourselves. We created our own fun out of clay, and drawing on rocks and sand.

USA TODAY: Does New Mexico's beauty give you an advantage as an artist?

GORMAN: Everything that I paint is related to where I came from. In other words, I don't make it up, I don't copy magazines, or trends, or anybody.

USA TODAY: Does some of the pain Indians have suffered come through in your art?

GORMAN: As I said, I'm not trying to make any social statement. I don't think people will hang on the wall painful things. I'm very interested in a lot of causes. I help with a lot of causes. But I don't depict them in my paintings.

USA TODAY: Are you a role model for Indians?

GORMAN: For young people, yes. I'm very anti-alcohol, for instance. If somebody's going to use me as a role model, that to me would be more appealing than me just being an artist.

USA TODAY: Why do you mainly paint women?

GORMAN: Well, I can relate to Navajo women, because that's where I come from. I was raised by women, mostly. I was raised during the second World War, when all respectable men were in the war. I was surrounded by all these women, so it sort of rubbed off.

USA TODAY: Your father, Carl, is often called the master of contemporary Native-American artists. In what ways are you two similar?

GORMAN: There's no similarity whatsoever. I didn't learn anything from him. He likes to do horses. And I like to do women.

Topic: NEW MEXICO

We have everything, except enough people

USA TODAY: You've been in office 115 days. How do you like it so far?

CARRUTHERS: I love it. This is my first time ever in public office of this kind. This is the first time I ever ran for office.

USA TODAY: You weren't supposed to win the six-candidate primary or the general election. What happened?

CARRUTHERS: We deceived enough voters out there to get the job done. We are in a state that wanted something different. And, an old college professor is the best contrast.

USA TODAY: New Mexico has redesigned its prisons. Is it now riot and escape proof?

CARRUTHERS: In 1980, we had a horrible prison riot here — 33 people were killed. As a consequence, we designed and built new prisons. They're almost riot proof. About the biggest riot you can have is 18 to 22 people, because they're in pods.

USA TODAY: How are you coping with New Mexico's image problem?

CARRUTHERS: We're going to come out with an advertising campaign. We may start off by saying, "Guess who just joined the 50? We're now in the United States." We believe that New Mexico truly is the land of challenge. It's a beautiful state. The word we like to use is a union state.

USA TODAY: What does that mean?

CARRUTHERS: According to some sources, we have no dominant ethnic group here. The Hispanics are about 35 percent, native Americans 10 percent, blacks and other minorities, about 14 percent. You get a blanket of people in New Mexico, which leads to a unique character of the state.

USA TODAY: What are some of the state's best attributes?

CARRUTHERS: We have great artists, and we have some of the most diverse environment that you've ever seen. Two of the largest wilderness areas in the

Garrey Carruthers, 47, a Republican, became New Mexico's governor in January after a career in government and education.

USA are in this state — the Pecos and the Gila wilderness. We have about everything you could ask for here, except one: We don't have all that many people. We have about 1.5 million people.

USA TODAY: How are Indians faring in the state?

CARRUTHERS: Some of the highest unemployment in the state is on Indian reservations, and some of the highest suicide rates are on reservations — drug and alcohol abuse.

USA TODAY: The first nuclear bomb was tested here. At what stage is the nuclear research now?

CARRUTHERS: Now the emphasis is on the safe use of nuclear energy and economic development since we have a lot of resources here: coal, solar energy.

USA TODAY: Is the research important to the economy?

CARRUTHERS: It's very important to New Mexico. A major facility going in the White Sands project will affect the economy of Las Cruces, and El Paso.

USA TODAY: You used to be a professor. Did college politics prepare you for this?

CARRUTHERS: Campus politics are the toughest politics in the world. I launched my career at New Mexico State. The essence of politics is you must like people.

New York

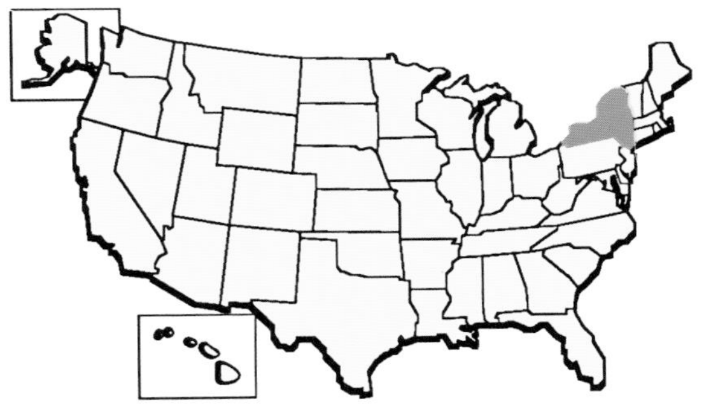

Visited: May 2-4, 1987
Featured in USA TODAY: May 8

"We walk faster, talk faster, think faster."

New York City Mayor Ed Koch

New York

Big Apple, big orchard, Empire State has it all

It's all here in the Big Apple. The best and the worst of New York state. Maybe the best and worst in the USA.

Our biggest city. Bold. Brash. Chic. Colossal. Sometimes chaotic.

7,201,300 people. Minorities in the majority. 25 percent black. 20 percent Jewish. 19 percent Hispanic.

What do the rest of us in the USA think about when we think Big Apple? Statue of Liberty. Times Square. Broadway. Wall Street. Yankee Stadium. Harlem. Best and worst. But coveted.

"I wanna be a part of it . . . New York, New York.
Start spreadin' the news, I'm leaving today
My little town blues . . . are melting away
I'll make a brand new start of it . . .
If I can make it there, I'd make it anywhere
New York, New York.

Bus stops in the Big Apple:

■ City Hall. Colorful **Ed Koch.** Mayor for 10 years. Mayor for life, he says. "Come back in 1997," he told BusCateers. "I'll be planning then for a real celebration in the year 2000."

What makes New Yorkers different? "We walk faster, talk faster, think faster," the mayor says, lickety-split.

■ Times Square. New and old hotels. Young and old hookers. "Here you live with sirens, horns, vagrants, bag ladies, drunks," says **John Loustau**, 43, math professor at Hunter College.

■ Wall Street. **Boesky** and real bankers. "I used to say 'I work on Wall Street' and people would say 'Wow!' Now people have a different attitude," says **Tim Bigley,** 24, a Citibank computer systems auditor.

■ Broadway. 6,140,000 tickets sold for the 1986-87 season. "Broadway weeds out the men from the boys. The women from the girls. The persons from the personettes," says **Lynn Redgrave**, 44, starring with **Mary Tyler Moore** in the play *Sweet Sue* at the Royale Theater.

LYNN REDGRAVE: 'Persons, personettes.'

■ Harlem. Crack and chaos amid community concern. **Antonio Colon**, 21, clothing salesman: "Crack is getting worse every year. They get into crack because they think it will solve their problems. But it gets into their brains."

Bus stops in the big orchard:

The Big Apple is nourished by a very big orchard all across the Empire State. Agriculture and culture. Education. Manufacturing. Money.

■ Buffalo (pop. 338,982). Second largest city. On the rebound with new jobs in banking, computers, insurance — to replace laid-off steelworkers and autoworkers. Mayor **James Griffin**, 57, refutes the reputation as a cold dingy city. "This year, we had less snow than anywhere in the Northeast."

UPBEAT, UPSTATE: 'Bubble Thing' inventor David Stein, 44, entertains outside Rochester's Memorial Art Gallery.

■ Rochester (pop. 242,562). Kodak. Xerox. Eastman School of Music. "New York City is like Baskin-Robbins with its many flavors. Rochester is like the local Gellato's, an ice cream store with fewer, but better flavors," says **Bonnie Lippa,** 38, fifth-grade teacher, at this week's opening of the $5.9 million Memorial Art Gallery addition.

■ Syracuse (pop. 164,219). More than 21,000 Syracuse University students. Their Orangemen came within five seconds of beating Indiana for the NCAA basketball title. "The spirit was overwhelming, on campus and in the city. Orange streamers in restaurants. Orange balloons on mailboxes. Wonderful," says **Maureen Lindner**, 22, public relations senior at SU.

■ Ithaca (pop. 28,732). "I can think of no more cosmopolitan small town in the USA," says British-born **Frank H.T. Rhodes**, president of Cornell University. Ivy League blend of city and country.

■ Saratoga Springs (pop. 23,906). Famous spas. Preserved Victorian architecture. The best in thoroughbred racing each August. Says **Linda Toohey**, 38, Chamber veep: "Something for everyone. Lovers of the arts, lovers of history, lovers of horses."

■ Albany (pop. 100,800). State capital. Gov. **Mario Cuomo**, 54, told the BusCateers:

"I love USA TODAY. Especially the 'battle page' — the editorial page. Two different points of view. It's the epitome of argument. I've talked to others about it, including *The New York Times*. They didn't receive it too well."

That's Plain Talk from New York.

Empire State

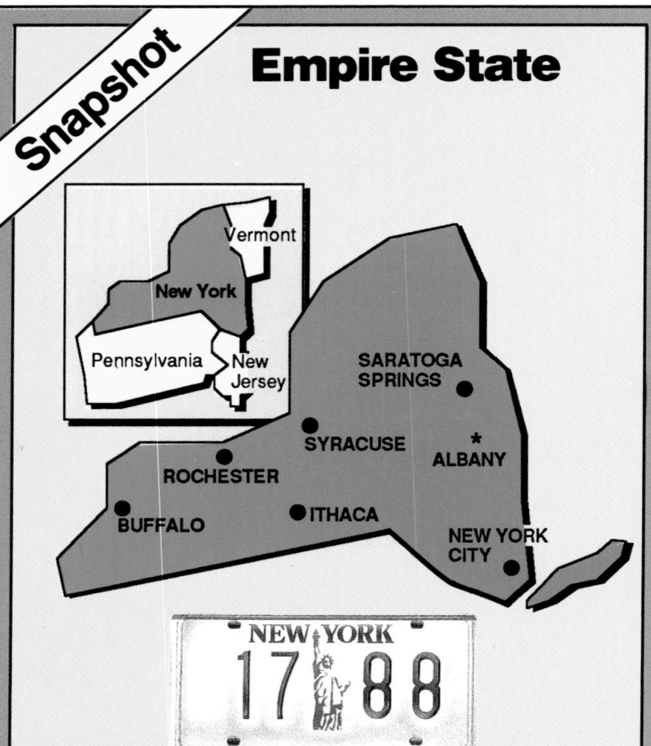

ENTERED USA: July 26, 1788, 11th state

MOTTO: Ever upward
POPULATION: 17,772,000; rank, 2nd
LARGEST CITY: New York City, pop. 7,201,300
CAPITAL: Albany, pop. 100,800
LAND: 47,377 square miles; rank, 30th
POPULATION DENSITY: 375 per square mile; rank, 6th
RACIAL MIX: 79.5% white; 13.68% black; 1.8% Asian and Pacific islanders. Hispanic heritage: 9.5%

Uniquely N.Y.

1,800-ISLAND SALAD DRESSING: There are actually more than 1,800 islands in the Thousand Islands — a 50-mile stretch of the St. Lawrence River. Thousand Island dressing originated there.

PATRIOT-PACKER: "Uncle Sam" was a meat-packer from Troy. During the War of 1812, Sam Wilson stamped "U.S. Beef" on his products; soldiers interpreted that as Uncle Sam. Wilson's caricature later came to personify the USA.

DIET BUSTERS: The first ice cream sundae was served in Ithaca in 1897; pie a la mode originated in Cambridge; potato chips were first served in Saratoga Springs.

DOWNWARD GUSHER: Every minute 40 million gallons of Niagara River water pour over the falls. That's enough to make 640 million cups of coffee.

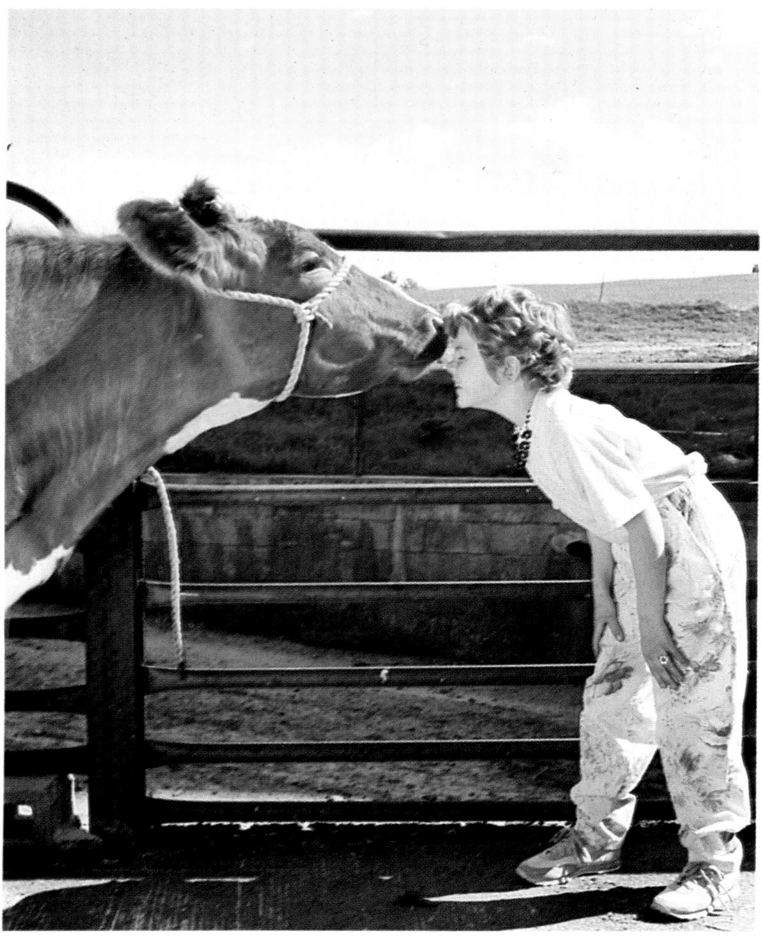

Jenny Kelsey, 7
Second-grader
Canastota

"Daddy's an all-the-time farmer. He milks cows, grows alfalfa, oats and sells baler twine and seed. The farm is different from the city. The city has sidewalks, but here there's lots of room. I want to be a worker here 'cause when I look at the men, they seem happy when they work. We can't be happy in the city. They only have out-fronts, out-backs and no sides."

James Fleming, 50
Police officer
New York City

"Everyone knows me down here. I'm a gun. You see a lot of things you won't see anywhere else. Greenwich Village is getting busier and busier and busier. If it's hot, the place is jammed. Weather makes a difference down here."

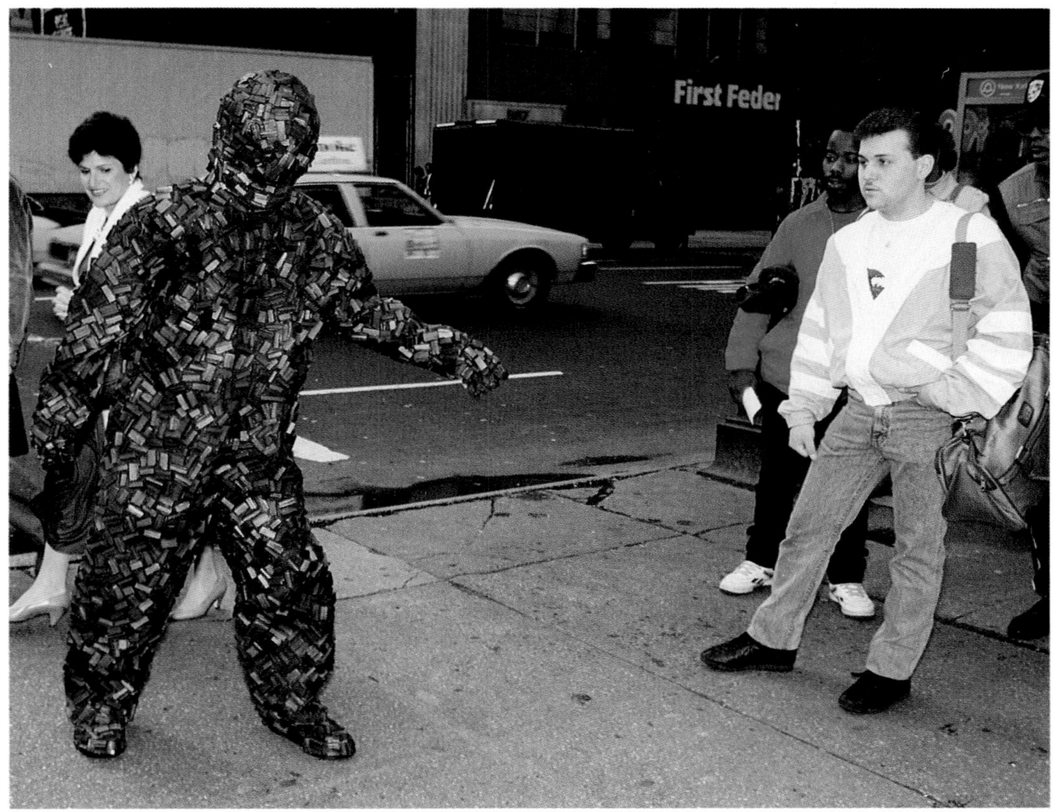

Voices
of New York

Harold Olejarz, 34
Sculptor/
limousine driver
New York City

"My major occupation is being an artist. Unfortunately, I do have to do other stuff to survive. I got frustrated with the New York art scene and trying to present my work to the public. If I wear it (sculpture suit), I can present my work anywhere. I install myself in museums and on the streets. I can bring art to different types of audiences, from Manhattan's Upper West Side to the grungy Times Square area."

Margaret Leahey, 58
Court clerk
Albany

"I enjoy the outdoors, the fresh air and green grass. I can't stand big city clutter. People consider New York City to be a state in itself. But those people look out their windows and see tall buildings. I can drive for 10 minutes and be in the mountains. That's the life for me."

Tom Sullivan, 42
Shoe store owner
Mechanicville

"In upstate, I sense there is a lot of resentment of New York City. A lot of it has to do with the tax structure and thinking that much of it goes to the city and not for things up here. When people ask me where I'm from, I say, 'New York.' They say, 'Oh, the city!' And I say, 'No, upstate.' Well, the interest definitely wanes."

Enock Milien, 31
Cab driver
New York City

"I came from Haiti to make my life better. It is better, but the work is harder. I have to work seven days a week to pay my rent. And then there's food. If you have kids and a wife, you have to work eight days a week."

Herbert Holman, 64
Subway conductor
The Bronx

"The transportation system is so vast, it makes you proud to be a part of it. We have breakdowns and delays, but those trains go back and forth all day long. I like my job. You meet some people who will aggravate you, but the average person is very nice."

Edward Koch, 64, is serving his third four-year term as mayor of New York. A former congressman, Koch has written two books: Mayor: An Autobiography *and* Politics.

Being a New Yorker is a state of mind

USA TODAY: What should visitors do to get a taste of the real New York City?

KOCH: They shouldn't hang around 42nd Street. They should visit the other boroughs as well as the many sights in Manhattan. That is the heart of the city. The wonderful place to see in Manhattan would be Soho — marvelous restaurants and marvelous stores. Wonderful bars.

USA TODAY: What is your favorite restaurant?

KOCH: I am a devotee of Chinese food, and for $20 or less the best dinner in the country is at Peking Duck. All you have to do is, A, be sure you order the Peking duck, and B, say that you want to eat what the mayor eats, and they'll take care of it.

USA TODAY: You've been in office almost 10 years. Your new budget proposal is $22.7 billion. What was it your first year in office?

KOCH: About $12 billion. When I came in in 1978, our budget, which was Abe Beam's last budget, was $1 billion in deficit. Today, we have a budget that has a $500 million surplus, and we have had half-a-billion dollar surpluses for the last four years, and several hundred million dollars even before that.

USA TODAY: Obviously, you think the city is in much better shape now.

KOCH: We had a city in 1978 that was on the edge of bankruptcy. Today it is the strongest city in America. When I came in, we had to reduce services to get rid of the billion-dollar deficit. We brought the police force back up to 33,600.

USA TODAY: Ten years from now, will you still be mayor?

KOCH: Ten years from now, I want you to come in, and I'm going to tell you about my next budget.

USA TODAY: What is a New Yorker?

KOCH: This is what's unique about the city: Only about 25 percent of the people in New York were born here — I'm one of that 25 percent. What does that establish? It establishes that you don't have to be born in New York to be a New Yorker. If you're here for any period of time, three months, six months, it becomes a state of mind. You either accept that you're a New Yorker or you'll never be a New Yorker.

Topic: NEW YORK

I'd like to be president, but this is it for me

USA TODAY: In February, you announced your decision not to run for president. Are you having second thoughts?

CUOMO: The statement was inevitable. Once I ran for governor again in '86 and won, I could not run for president.

USA TODAY: Why not?

CUOMO: I called two people regarded as truth-tellers and asked, "What do I have to do to run for the presidency?" They said, "You have to go to Iowa — 50 times." They said I could theoretically try to make a television appearance. Forget about that. Some Iowa farmer says, "This joker wants me to vote for him, but he's too busy to talk to me. He's in New York." That was it.

USA TODAY: What about the personal satisfaction of the job?

CUOMO: To be able to say I was the first Italian-American president in history — that would mean something to me. It meant something when I became the first Italian-American governor. I do regret that I don't have that opportunity.

USA TODAY: How do you manage to stay popular statewide despite the conflicting interests between New York City and upstate?

CUOMO: I don't think politics and making yourself popular is an elusive science. You've got to give people what they understand is right on the issues, and you have to be with the people.

USA TODAY: Is that why President Reagan is so popular?

CUOMO: Reagan does it by magic. He stands up there — so nice, so thoroughly non-menacing that his appearance on television is like being in your living room.

USA TODAY: Don't you share that magical quality?

CUOMO: That's not true in my case. I'm always running into situations like one I had at Tulane. This anthropologist turned to me and said, "You know, Gov. Cumo, Kemo, Cucumo, you know, you're not as ugly in person as you are on TV." I get that all the time, so I have to spend time with people.

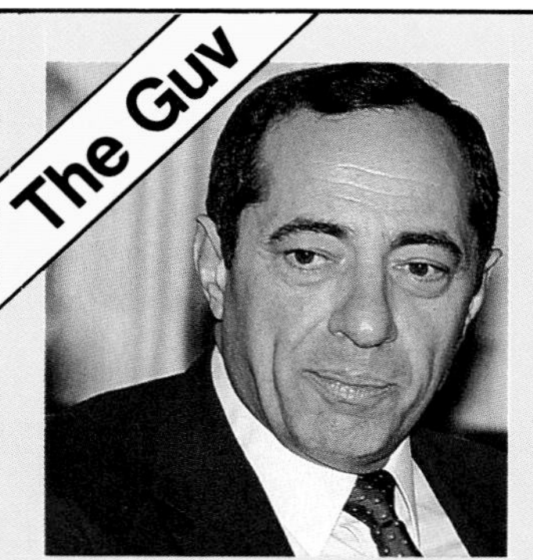

Mario Cuomo, 54, a Democrat, won a landslide victory for a second term last year.

USA TODAY: New York has been in the news lately because of political corruption.

CUOMO: I don't want to excuse us by spreading the blame to the rest of the country, but the truth is — Irangate, Washington, Chicago — it's universal. It's been more dramatic in New York City than in most places.

USA TODAY: What can be done about it?

CUOMO: The temptation of the politician is always to hunker down in a squall. But this one's not going to go away, this one should not go away until it's been dealt with.

USA TODAY: What can the people of New York expect from you 10 years from now?

CUOMO: My mother has this wonderful expression, "Between now and then a pope will be born." Everything happens between now and then. If 15 years ago someone had told me I'd be governor, I would have laughed.

USA TODAY: Why?

CUOMO: As a lawyer who regularly sued Wall Street firms for fun, it just didn't make any sense to think that you could actually get to be the governor of New York. Then I got devastated in two elections. Mayor Koch ate me for lunch in 1977, just awful. So, this notion that you can figure out the future, it's not like that. I love what I'm doing.

North Carolina

Visited: Aug. 19-20, 1987
Featured in USA TODAY: Aug. 24

"When I think of home, I think of a place where there's love, blue skies, clear water, nice people, safe streets and an air of congeniality."

Roberta Flack
Singer and composer
Formerly of Asheville, N.C.

North Carolina

Brains and basketball: High tech, high hopes

In the '60s, *The Andy Griffith Show* gave the USA its image of North Carolina. The CBS sitcom featured overalls and corn pone in the fictitious country town of Mayberry.

In the '80s, *The Andy Griffith Show* is gone. Overalls are giving way to white collars. High tech is the high hope.

But one thing hasn't changed. Carolinians still are bonkers over basketball. The same triangle that's now home to more Ph.D.s in science per square mile than anyplace else in the USA also has the highest hoop fever:

■ Chapel Hill (pop. 34,100). University of North Carolina.

■ Durham (pop. 161,900). Duke University.

■ Raleigh, capital, (pop. 181,300). North Carolina State.

Those three cage cahoots have played in the NCAA Final Four 17 times. UNC's Tar Heels won the national title twice. Ditto N.C. State's Wolfpack. Duke's Blue Devils have been the bridesmaid three times.

THE DEAN **COACH 'V'** **COACH 'K'**
... basketball bosses at UNC, N.C. State, Duke

UNC's Coach Dean Smith is the dean. Lifetime record: 611-175. Last year he was 32-4. Jim Valvano, Coach "V" at N.C. State, won the hearts of hoopsters when his Cinderella team took the NCAA title in '83. Duke's Mike Krzyzewski, Coach "K", gets added applause because every scholarship basketball player he has coached has graduated.

Basketballmania plays as well with some of the brainy undergraduates as it does with athletes and alumni.

Lisa Godwin, 19, zoology sophomore at Duke, puts her priorities in perspective: "Academics are really important to me. Ranks right up there with basketball."

At UNC, **Gina Lamb**, 20, radio-TV-movie junior, says, "One of my roommates came to study. One came to shop. I came for basketball."

Some students are as concerned with their state's image as with its basketball record. **Kevin Norris**, 25, graduate student in English at N.C. State:

"North Carolina is not just Andy Griffith and Jesse Helms. We're not all Baptists preaching fire and damnation. I don't have anything to do with brimstone. It's high tech now."

Research Triangle Park is the home to high tech. A non-profit foundation operated on behalf of the three major universities. The park:

■ Covers 6,700 acres.

■ Has 27,000 workers at businesses with a total annual payroll of more than $1 billion.

■ Has 35 major industrial research facilities, including IBM, Northern Telecom, Burroughs Wellcome.

Outside the triangle, other Carolina population centers are on the move. Charlotte (pop. 330,838), joins the NBA in 1988-89 with its expansion team, the Hornets. Greensboro (pop. 177,900) is a trade, distribution center for companies throughout the Carolinas and Virginia, including USA TODAY.

The magnificent mountains around Asheville (pop. 59,200) are the summer home for thousands of Floridians and others throughout the Southeast. The coastal area around Cape Hatteras draws more than its share of hurricane scares, but those who love the sand and surf and sea keep coming.

Despite high hopes over high tech, farming remains big in North Carolina. Many still earn their living off the land:

■ No. 1 in tobacco in the USA. 445 million pounds harvested last year. Kentucky is second, Tennessee third.

■ No. 1 in turkeys. Over 39 million grown last year. Minnesota is second, California third.

But tobacco is losing ground — literally. The acres planted are fewer than half what they were 10 years ago. So is the harvest. Anti-smoking sentiment has hit Carolina pocketbooks hard. But even some who have spent their lifetime growing 'bacca are philosophical.

VEASEY: Grows tobacco but doesn't smoke it.

Carl Veasey, 57, farms outside Durham: "I don't smoke, but my wife does a little. My daddy smoked all his life and was 80 when he died. His heart and lungs were the strongest things about him.

"I don't think someone should sit down at dinner and blow smoke all over everyone. That's common courtesy. But I don't know if the smoke really hurts someone else.

"All the politics and publicity about smoking is like someone coming into your home and taking the dinner plate from in front of you."

That's Plain Talk from North Carolina.

Snapshot

Tar Heel State

ENTERED USA: Nov. 21, 1789, 12th state

MOTTO: To be rather than to seem
POPULATION: 6,331,000; rank, 10th
LARGEST CITY: Charlotte, pop. 330,838
CAPITAL: Raleigh, pop. 181,300
LAND: 48,843 square miles; rank, 29th
POPULATION DENSITY: 129.6 per square mile; rank, 17th
RACIAL MIX: 75.8% white; 22.4% black; 0.4% Asian and Pacific islanders. Hispanic heritage: 1.0%.

Uniquely N.C.

HEAVY METAL: Gold and silver were first discovered in the USA in North Carolina. The first gold nugget was found in Cabarrus County in 1799 and the first silver lode was discovered in 1838 near Lexington. Charlotte once had 250 gold mines.

A DEEPER LOOK: The first X-ray photograph was made by Dr. Harry Lewis Smith of Davidson College, on Jan. 12, 1896.

JEWELER'S DELIGHT: Nicknamed "nature's samplecase," North Carolina is the only state that has the four most precious gems: diamonds, rubies, sapphires and emeralds.

YO HO, YO HO: The famed pirate Blackbeard, born Edward Teach, was slain at Ocracoke Island in 1718.

FIRST SCORE: The first Patriot victory of the American Revolution was at the battle of Moores Creek Bridge Feb. 27, 1776.

Voices
of North Carolina

Gil McElravy
Manager of tobacco shop
Mint Hill

"The state is diversified now. The economy is not dependent on its income from tobacco, yet it remains a source of great pride because we've had tobacco growers in this state for many years. It's the kind of pride you get from growing a good product. Like the fruit growers in Florida who take pride from growing oranges, we have the pride of growing good tobacco."

Chris Thompson, 24
Hang-gliding instructor
Nags Head

"My friend gave me a hang-gliding lesson and that was it. It's unlike anything else. Have you ever had a dream you were flying? That's the way it feels! You can't see the glider above you, and your legs are hanging out the bottom . . . no motor. It's just like being a bird."

Martha Walker, 28
Park ranger
Wright Brothers Memorial

"I got a job as park ranger three years ago after doing research on Wilbur and Orville. It changed the way I felt about flying. To think that two bicycle repairmen invented the entire science of aviation!"

Dorothy MacGill, 64
Retired
Charlotte

"What I like best is how civic-minded and involved the people are here. Jimmy Carter and his family came here for the Habitat for Humanity. The people in Charlotte built houses for the lower-income people. I think that's typical of Charlotte. Everyone pitches in."

James Graham, 42
Store owner
Alligator River

"People in Alabama or Mississippi think we're Northerners. People from Pennsylvania or New York think we're part of the Old South. I do think we fit more in the Southern states. I like the serenity of the Outer Banks of North Carolina. I live on the river in a small town. We've got one doctor and one lawyer."

Lisa Godwin, 19
Student
Durham

"It's very competitive to get into Duke. You not only have to be smart, you have to be ambitious. You have to work for it. And when basketball season rolls around, there's the reward. I'm a true Blue Devil. The Carolina game is the biggest basketball game here. People start camping out to get in a week before the game. I painted 'DUKE' across my face in blue eye shadow."

Cy Richardson, 17
Student
Chapel Hill

"I'm from a suburb of New York, but I have always wanted to go to the University of North Carolina. My mother is from North Carolina. When she was in high school, black people couldn't go here. She's real proud of me."

Roberta Flack, 47, a Grammy-winning singer/composer, was born in Asheville, N.C. At 15, she won a scholarship to Howard University in Washington, D.C. Flack gave up teaching to focus on her music. She lives in New York City.

Blue sky, clear water, an air of congeniality

USA TODAY: What are your early memories of North Carolina?

FLACK: I have vague memories of the house we lived in with my grandmother, my aunt and my uncle. There was a great big front porch and lots of cherry trees. We had a very large extended family.

USA TODAY: What images come to mind when you think of North Carolina?

FLACK: When I think of home, I think of a place where there's love, blue skies, clear water, nice people, safe streets and an air of congeniality. I'll always consider North Carolina my home.

USA TODAY: What is it like to go back?

FLACK: I went back to a town called Farmville to teach after I graduated from college. The school was kindergarten through 12th grade, with black students from all over. I tried to give them my love for music.

USA TODAY: What was it like to perform back in North Carolina?

FLACK: It was like going home. Years back, I went there for a Christmas tree lighting. I led the people in a couple of carols. They treated me like they had waited a long time for me to come home. That moment, in the square, when I flicked the switch to turn on the lights — it was precious. I'll never forget that feeling.

USA TODAY: How has Asheville changed?

FLACK: Asheville has changed for the better — it has a unique character. The buildings are better and stronger. Asheville is surrounded by mountains. It is a very clean city.

USA TODAY: What are the people like?

FLACK: The people are the warmest I've met anywhere in the world. When it comes to improving race relations between peoples of all colors, the people of North Carolina have worked hard at it. So many illustrious people have come from North Carolina — Billy Graham, Nina Simone, Thomas Wolfe.

USA TODAY: Would you want to live there permanently?

FLACK: Right now, I need a city like New York, Chicago or Los Angeles as a springboard. But I quite honestly am thinking of going back there to live.

Topic: NORTH CAROLINA

Tobacco plots, poultry barns dot landscape

USA TODAY: North Carolina was king of tobacco. But now smoking is widely believed to be a health hazard. How does that affect North Carolinians' pride about tobacco?

MARTIN: It affects the market and the tendency of Congress to look toward cigarettes as a revenue source. When they don't want to raise taxes on anything else, they'll raise them on cigarettes. We've seen some weakening of the market.

USA TODAY: What has hurt the most?

MARTIN: The farm markets have been growing, but we've been losing our share of markets overseas. That has hurt our production quotas more than anything else. North Carolina is still No. 1 in tobacco. In a way, it's a spiritual issue — it's so much an ingrown part of society in all of our rural communities. A couple of major cities, like Winston-Salem and Durham, are very heavily committed to it, because of cigarette manufacturing there.

USA TODAY: Are farmers managing to diversify?

MARTIN: In the first year of my administration, poultry passed tobacco as the No. 1 farm commodity. You'll see two distinctive features as you fly low over our state. You'll see the neat, orderly, small plots of tobacco, and these long turkey barns and chicken barns, usually two or three of them on an operation.

USA TODAY: A recent report rated North Carolina as a top leader in attracting corporations. What is the strategy?

MARTIN: We've offered a good business climate, a modest tax rate that is a uniform burden on everybody. We also provide — through our community college system — training at our expense. There is no extra charge for any business that retools and has to retrain people.

USA TODAY: You oppose a state holiday honoring Martin Luther King Jr. Why?

MARTIN: When I was in Congress, I voted for a holiday on

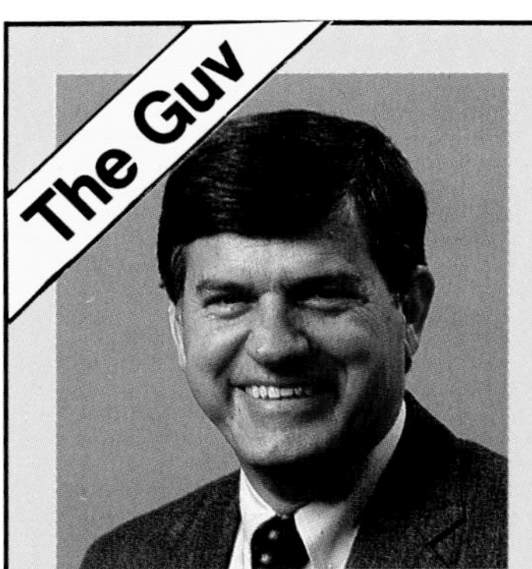

James Martin, 50, a Republican, was elected in 1984. Previously, he served six terms in the U.S. House of Representatives.

Sunday, which I thought would be an appropriate day. He was a minister of the gospel. I wasn't demeaning his importance or his contributions to society. It's just that I don't think we need more days off.

USA TODAY: Is there anyone you can think of who embodies the spirit of North Carolina?

MARTIN: I would say Billy Graham.

USA TODAY: Why?

MARTIN: Billy Graham epitomizes the kind of personal commitment and expression of deeply held beliefs that appeal to most North Carolinians.

USA TODAY: How do people feel about their fellow North Carolinian, TV evangelist Jim Bakker?

MARTIN: There's a high degree of embarrassment about that. Even his supporters feel a great deal of disillusionment.

USA TODAY: With so many strong basketball teams, how do you divide your loyalties?

MARTIN: Basketball is a major celebration in our state. Once I went to a game between Carolina and State. Both chancellors were there. At halftime, Chancellor Poulton said, "All right. We've seen you cheering for both sides. Are you for Carolina or are you for State?" And I said, "Yes." I haven't been in politics 20 years for nothing!

North Dakota

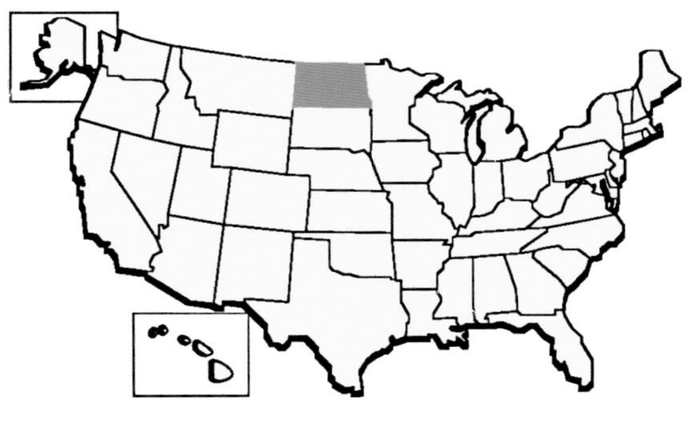

Visited: June 1-2, 1987
Featured in USA TODAY: June 5

"I like the quiet of North Dakota, the not having to worry about locking our doors. When you say you're from North Dakota, people know you're trustworthy."

Richard Muir
Parking lot attendant
Fargo, N.D.

North Dakota

Cowboy, Indian legacy: Plucky prairie populists

Cowboys and Indians is not a game here. They lived out the real thing in the 1800s.

The two most famous to ride and roam the North Dakota prairies:

■ "Rough Rider" **Teddy Roosevelt**.

■ Sioux Chief **Sitting Bull**.

Roosevelt came West in 1883 looking for adventure. Fresh out of Harvard, age 25. Spent much of the next 15 years here. Riding, ranching, fighting, investing. Became a local hero.

Left in 1898 to lead his "Rough Riders" to Cuba. Then, on to the governorship of New York and the White House, becoming the 26th president in 1901.

ROUGH RIDER: Roosevelt is most famous North Dakota cowboy.

Roosevelt roamed the western range around Medora (pop. 94). The town has a "Rough Rider" hotel. A "Bull Moose" newspaper. Tourists flock in from June to September.

Lorraine Tescher, 61, a Medora ranch wife, speaks of Teddy's legacy. "I admire him. When he came out here, lots of people called him 'Four Eyes' because he wore glasses. He knocked a couple of cowboys down and got their respect. He was a lot like people in North Dakota."

People in North Dakota include about 20,000 Native Americans, more than 3 percent of the population. Their hero is Sitting Bull, legendary and controversial Sioux chieftain and-or medicine man.

He's generally credited with firing up the Indians for their massacre of **George Custer**'s troops at the Battle of Little Big Horn in neighboring Montana. Some historians claim The Bull was back in camp with the women when the battle actually took place.

From such Cowboy-Indian history of the 1800s has come the preaching and practicing of populism in the 1900s.

Gov. **George A. Sinner**, 59, is often called "The Prairie Populist." "That's quite an honor. But, I don't think of myself as a populist. I am not terribly liberal," says the first-term Democratic guv.

Populism. Liberalism. Individualism. Call it what you wish, you'll find it on the farms and in the cities.

Fargo in the east is the largest city (pop. 65,721). It has North Dakota-style sophistication. Center for banking, medicine, education. The nearby lush Red River valley keeps beet and potato farmers prosperous.

In the middle is Bismarck, state capital (pop. 44,485). Surrounded by thousands of neatly fenced farms. Hundreds of tiny towns.

Flasher is one (pop. 410). Folks in Flasher pooled resources to buy a fire truck, an ambulance. Volunteers man both. "We don't wait for a federal loan to roll in," says Flasher's Mayor **Jerry Rhone**, 62, an insurance agent.

North Dakotans tax themselves to take care of themselves. In a special election in March, they approved a 33⅓ percent increase in their income tax rather than accept reduced services.

Neighbors in north and south present a sharp contrast.

■ Canada. A kissing cousin. A 1,474-acre International Peace Garden near Dunseith, N.D. (pop. 625), and Buissevain, Manitoba (pop. 1,628). People wander peacefully from country to country.

■ South Dakota. The two Dakotas are fierce rivals. In sports. Business. Life. Death.

Chief Sitting Bull is claimed by both. He spent time on the Standing Rock Indian Reservation, which straddles the Dakota border. When federal agents killed him in 1890, he was buried in Fort Yates, N.D. (pop. 771).

In April 1953, midnight riders from Mobridge, S.D. (pop. 4,174), raided the cemetery. Removed the remains and buried Sitting Bull on the sacred soil of South Dakota.

SITTING BULL: Trophy travels; did his bones?

North Dakota officials claim the raiders got the wrong bones, or just some of them. Now the official maps of both Dakotas mark Sitting Bull grave sites.

The ghoulish controversy led to the annual "Battle of Sitting Bull" football game between the Universities of North and South Dakota. A bigger-than-life carved oak bust of the Indian leader was donated by "SoDak Sports," a defunct weekly that a friend and I published from 1952-54.

The trophy travels back and forth with the winning team. UND has won it 18 times. USD 14. It's currently in the USD trophy case after last fall's 28 to 14 victory.

Says **Rob Bollinger**, 35, assistant football coach at UND, Grand Forks: "We've lost the game for the last five years and we're trying to rebuild. We want to be in the position where we have the firepower and numbers the Sioux had at the Little Big Horn."

That's Plain Talk from North Dakota.

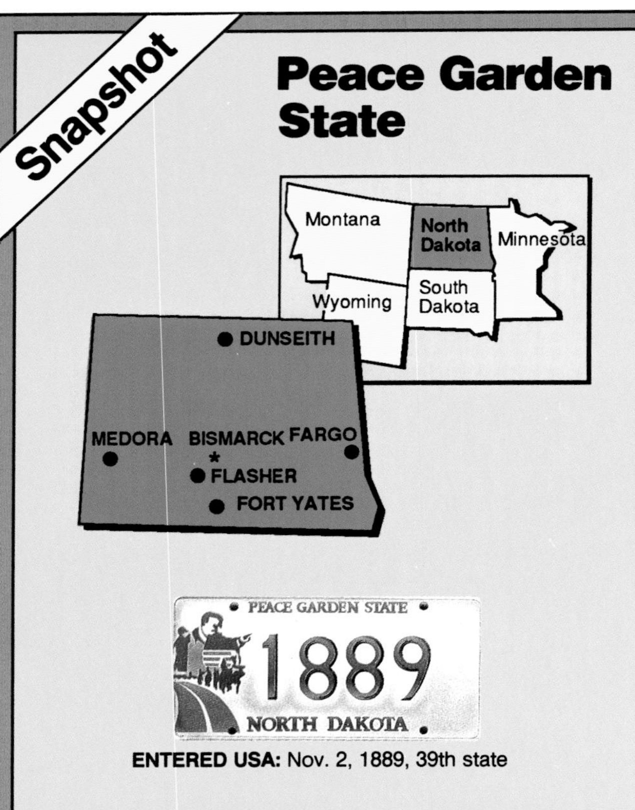

Peace Garden State

ENTERED USA: Nov. 2, 1889, 39th state

MOTTO: Liberty and union, now and forever: one and inseparable

POPULATION: 679,000; rank, 46th

LARGEST CITY: Fargo, pop. 65,721

CAPITAL: Bismarck, pop. 44,485

LAND: 70,665 square miles; rank, 17th

POPULATION DENSITY: 9.6 per square mile; rank, 45th

RACIAL MIX: 95.8% white; 3.1% American Indian; 0.4% black; 0.3% Asian and Pacific islanders. Hispanic heritage: 0.6%.

Uniquely N.D.

TRAFFIC JAM: In North Dakota, there are more motor vehicles than residents — 1,039.5 per 1,000 residents.

MAN-MADE BEACH: Lake Sakakawea, in Western North Dakota, is the largest man-made lake all in one state. It has more shoreline than California — 1,600 miles.

BATTLE BOUND: Gen. George Custer set out from Fort Lincoln on his ill-fated last campaign, the Battle of Little Big Horn, in 1874.

PADDLING UPSTREAM: The Red River, located in the Eastern Dakotas, is the only river in the USA that flows north.

JAZZ SINGER'S DEBUT: Al Jolson played his first solo role in Fargo's Grand Theater in the early 1900s.

LAND LOVERS: North Dakota is the most rural of all the states, with farms covering more than 90 percent of the land.

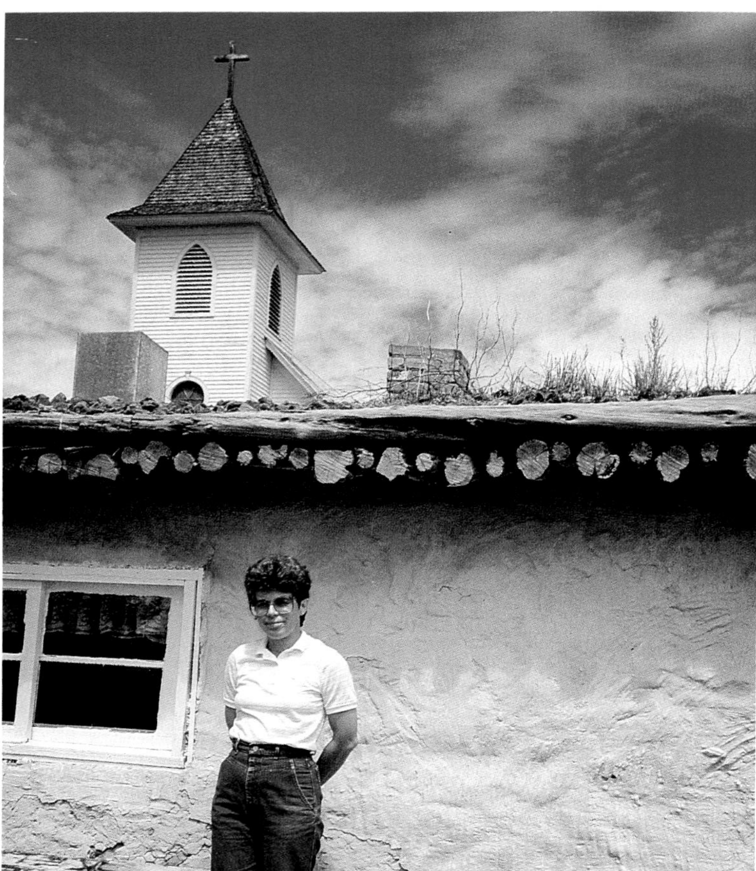

Lois Schwarzenberger, 41
Homemaker
Grassy Butte

"Growing up in a small North Dakota town is like belonging to one big family. We never worried about going on to somebody's property. The whole town was a playground. If you got into mischief downtown, somebody would pat you on the head and send you home as good as your parents would. When somebody has a big job to do around here, everybody gets together. It's faster and more fun that way. Our neighbors helped us build our garage and plant our trees. My husband helps them fix their pickup trucks, or do whatever needs to get done."

Jerry Rhone, 62
Mayor/insurance agent
Flasher

"You've got to learn to help yourself. If people here want something, they work for it. We don't wait for a federal loan to roll in."

Voices
of North Dakota

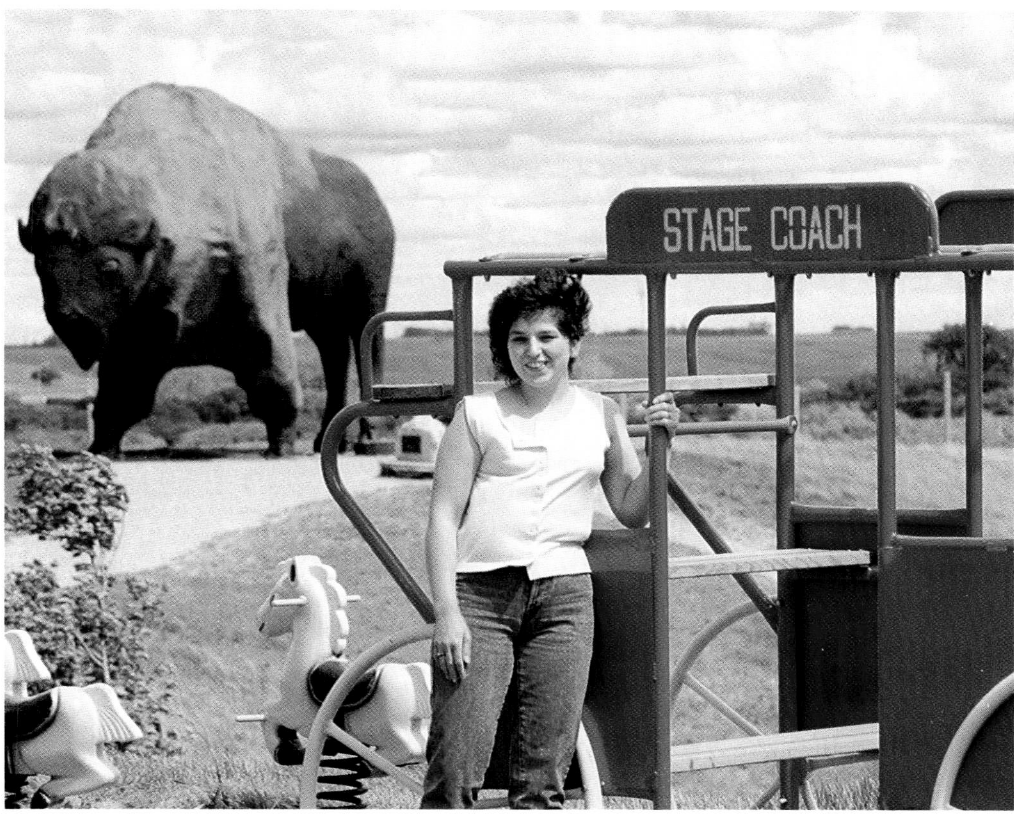

Kristy Ouren, 18
Laundry supervisor
Bismarck

"Me and my mom and dad went on a trip to Las Vegas. I noticed as you went farther away from North Dakota, the people weren't as friendly. On the way back, as you got closer to North Dakota, the people got friendlier."

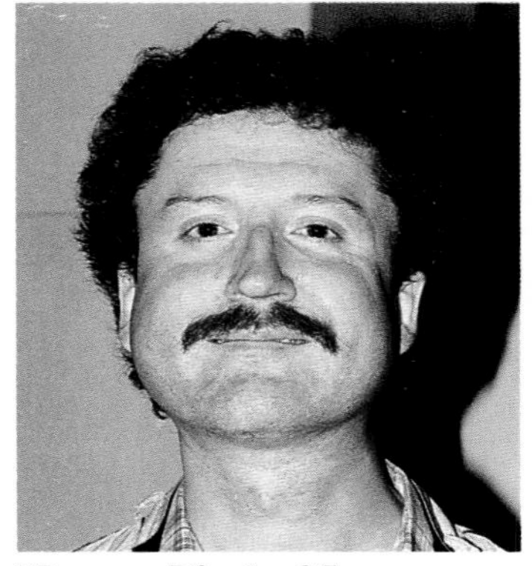

Harvey Ficek, 25
Legal assistant
Dickinson

"There's a good rural and city mix. The city depends on the farmers and the farmers depend on us. I do see a lot of farm foreclosures, but the attitude is that things are geting better. They went through a lot, and there is an upward trend. They're tough people with a lot of stick-to-it-iveness."

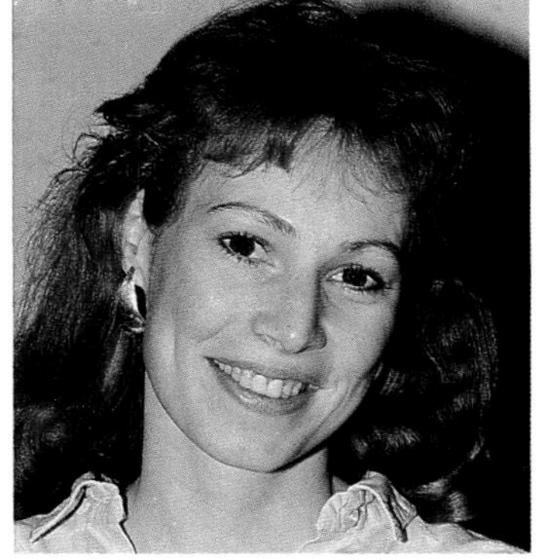

Carmen Connell, 30
Gift shop owner
Medora

"I'm third generation in this town. Growing up, I'd hear accounts of ancestors' pasts. I've inherited a diary that tells how my great grandfather drove Buffalo Bill's stagecoach and how my Grandmother Gertrude took care of Teddy Roosevelt's horse!"

Beeman Dockrey, 68
Horse trainer
Bismarck

"The people have a competitive spirit to survive. They say difficulty creates character. Well, they've got more character than they'd like, thank you. They survive because they stick together. If you're stranded or stuck in a storm, they help. They may speak broken English, with the Swedish or Norwegian elements, but it sure sounds good when you need help!"

Richard Muir, 37
Parking lot attendant
Fargo

"I like the quiet of North Dakota, the not having to worry about locking our doors. When you say you're from North Dakota, people know you're trustworthy. A lot of times you have to trust people. They're leaving the parking lot, and they say they don't have any money, but they'll come back and pay. In three years, I haven't had one that hasn't come back."

Notable

Angie Dickinson, 55, was born Angeline Brown in Kulm, N.D., but spent most of her early years in nearby Edgeley. She appeared in the TV series Police Woman *1974-78.*

Enjoyed growing up in a small town

USA TODAY: What are your memories of North Dakota?

DICKINSON: My first memory is playing in the streets with a wagon or a sled without fear of cars or kidnapping or dangers other kids have.

USA TODAY: What was it like in Edgeley, where you grew up?

DICKINSON: The land was totally flat, forever. There were no woods. It's fascinating to see; it's so bleak. But, of course, that was in very rough times — the '30s and '40s. Since then, they've planted trees, and I'm told it's very beautiful now.

USA TODAY: What did your folks do?

DICKINSON: We ran the weekly newspaper, the *Edgeley Mail*, and in Kulm they also had the paper, the *Kulm Messenger*.

USA TODAY: Did you ever do any reporting?

DICKINSON: My mother would let us make some of the calls. I remember her dialing one or two numbers and saying, "Any news today?" It was one of the many things I considered becoming when I grew up.

USA TODAY: Did you watch a lot of movies?

DICKINSON: There was one movie theater in town, and because we ran its ad, we got in free. So my two sisters and I saw every movie that came to town.

USA TODAY: Which stars were your favorites?

DICKINSON: Gary Cooper was my favorite, and Marlene Dietrich.

USA TODAY: When was the last time you visited home?

DICKINSON: I've never gotten back. I'd love to go back from an intense curiosity, and even more, to show my daughter (Nikki, 20, by ex-husband Burt Bacharach) where I was brought up. I know she'd be fascinated at the simplicity of it.

USA TODAY: What's your secret for remaining so youthful?

DICKINSON: My secret is trying to keep the age out of the papers (laughs). I try to keep the weight off, and a certain amount of exercise, and a very happy attitude.

Topic: NORTH DAKOTA

State boasts high level of education, low crime

USA TODAY: Fargo has been described as the least stressful place to live in the USA. Does that apply to the rest of North Dakota as well?

SINNER: No question about that. That's why the crime rate remains low. We're low on suicides. We're low on incidences of mental illness. Fargo is unusual in that it is the center of the largest metropolitan area. As small as it is, it's the largest one between Minneapolis and the West Coast, and has an incredible array of cultural activities.

The Guv

George A. Sinner, 59, a Democrat, was elected governor in 1984. He previously served in both the state House and Senate.

USA TODAY: How do you think most of the nation perceives North Dakota?

SINNER: The perception is that it's up there where it's cold. And probably that it's an agricultural state. The reality is that it's probably not nearly as cold as other states with a much higher humidity. It also has an uncommon culture and some of the most literate people in the USA.

USA TODAY: In what ways?

SINNER: It was the first state to have statewide public broadcasting with a central programming plan. It was the first state with regional mental health clinics. It maintains more nursing home beds per capita for the elderly than any state. It has the lowest crime rate of all the 50 states. The smallest percentage of its people are incarcerated.

USA TODAY: What about education?

SINNER: The most startling thing I have discovered is that we have more high school graduates per capita than any state in the nation. And send a higher percentage of them to college.

USA TODAY: Your state's economy has been badly hurt in oil and farming, two of your biggest sectors. How are North Dakotans dealing with that?

SINNER: In the near term, it's going to be pretty tough, but there are some good things showing up. The cattle industry has come back. Ranchers are getting pretty good prices for their feeder cattle. The oil industry crisis is over, provided we stop relying on OPEC, where they can completely manipulate the market.

USA TODAY: How is North Dakota's experiment with limited casino-style gambling going?

SINNER: It's done some good things. The modest approach that's been taken here recognizes that it's perfectly all right for people to engage in recreational gambling. But there are some risks, and if you're going to move into the area, you might want to do it on a gradual basis and feel your way along. That's essentially what we've done.

USA TODAY: Did you ever try your luck?

SINNER: I've played some blackjack. I'm a fair player.

USA TODAY: Why are some blue laws banning alcohol sales on Sunday still in effect?

SINNER: There are different reasons for different blue laws. If you're talking about Sunday marketing or Sunday business activity, you'll find a wide disparity of ideological thinking that supports the retention of that quiet time for society.

USA TODAY: What do you do to relax?

SINNER: I love to play tennis. I am, with reluctance, going on a two-week vacation as soon as you get out of here! We have a lake home in Minnesota. It's one we've had for years.

Ohio

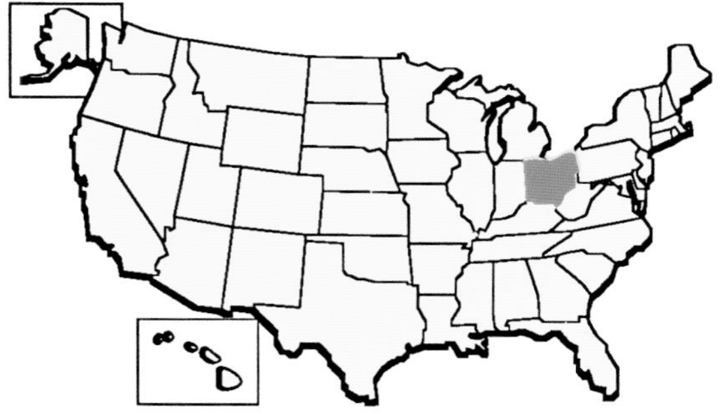

Visited: April 27-29, 1987
Featured in USA TODAY: May 1

"I don't do jokes about Cleveland."

Bob Hope
Comedian
Grew up in Cleveland, Ohio

Ohio

More to life than fun; fun is serious here, too

In Cincinnati (pop. 385,457) more than 400 — some used to cushy corporate dining rooms, others usually carrying metal lunch boxes — came to a "brown bag" lunch town meeting this week to talk about their work.

In Mansfield (pop. 53,927), workers led by Local 8576 President **Linda Parrella** voted last week to take a 13 percent pay cut to keep the Tappan Range plant in town.

Ohioans believe there's more to life than just fun. They take their work very seriously. They also take their fun seriously.

Take Cleveland (pop. 546,543). You've heard the jokes. When it came time to pick a national Rock and Roll Hall of Fame, it was no joke.

More than 110,000 Cleveland rockers voted. **Elvis Presley**'s hometown of Memphis, Tenn., was a distant second. Next year, the hall will open here.

KID LEO: 'We're really rocking.'

Says WMMS radio deejay **Kid Leo**, "Cleveland is sick of the knocking. We're really rocking."

Full-time funnymen and women work seriously at perpetuating Ohio's humorists' reputation.

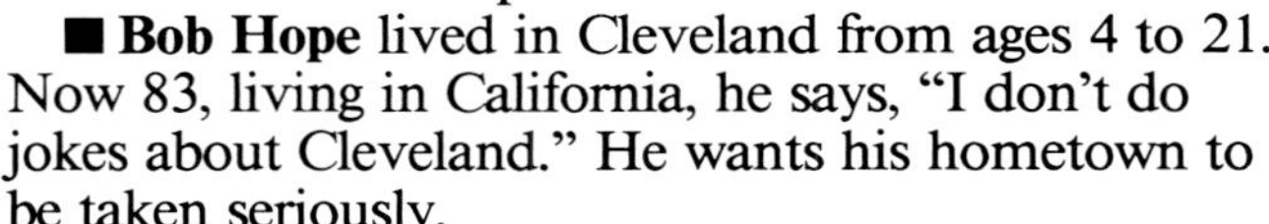

■ **Bob Hope** lived in Cleveland from ages 4 to 21. Now 83, living in California, he says, "I don't do jokes about Cleveland." He wants his hometown to be taken seriously.

■ **Erma Bombeck**, 60, developed her non-stop wit during 44 years in Dayton. Now living in Arizona, she says Ohio has produced more humorists than any other state. Her favorites? The Wright brothers. Yes, they started designing the first airplane here in the 1890s. But listen to Bombeck:

"The Wright brothers said, 'Climb aboard. Here's an oxygen mask. A flotation cushion. A barf bag. Now have a swell time.' Greatest humor Ohio has produced."

Sports is not just fun here. Very serious. Frenzied fans of Reds and Bengals in the south. All Indians and Browns in the north. In the middle, around Columbus, fans are split. Feelings are so fervent, politicians are afraid to choose sides.

"If we get a Cincinnati-Cleveland World Series, we'll widen Highway 71 (249 miles) and make everybody happy," says Gov. **Richard Celeste**, at least semi-seriously.

Back to the really serious. Ohio's unemployment rate is 7.5 percent. Four years ago it was 14.2 percent. State, local, private efforts paid off.

The Cincinnati Human Relations Commission helps the underprivileged find jobs or start businesses. **Robert Harris**, 40, comes in daily in a wheelchair.

"Every day I go to work I help someone else go to work," Harris says both happily and seriously.

Like many middle states, Ohio has lured Japanese corporations here — 24 of them, including Honda, Nissan, Mitsubishi. "Banzai Buckeyes," they're called affectionately by many Ohioans. The current chill between Washington and Tokyo is not felt here.

Joan Pearson Kelly's "Culture Club" in Bellefontaine (pop. 11,888) offers Ohio hospitality to the Orientals. Honda employs 180 Japanese and 4,350 Ohioans in the Marysville-Bellefontaine area.

'CULTURE CLUB': Kelly with Hirobe and Noguchi in Bellefontaine.

Mrs. Kelly, 59, and other local women teach younger Japanese housewives about shopping, sports, speaking English.

Toshiko Noguchi, 39, and **Atsuko Hirobe**, 32, are two beneficiaries. "I love the basketball games. I clap and eat popcorn," says Mrs. Hirobe.

The culture exchange works both ways. Says Mrs. Kelly:

"We eat their raw fish. I like it. They teach us about Japanese holidays like Girls' Day and Boys' Day. Their work ethic rubs off. They've made more Ohioans willing to work all day Saturday or late at night."

That's Plain Talk from Ohio.

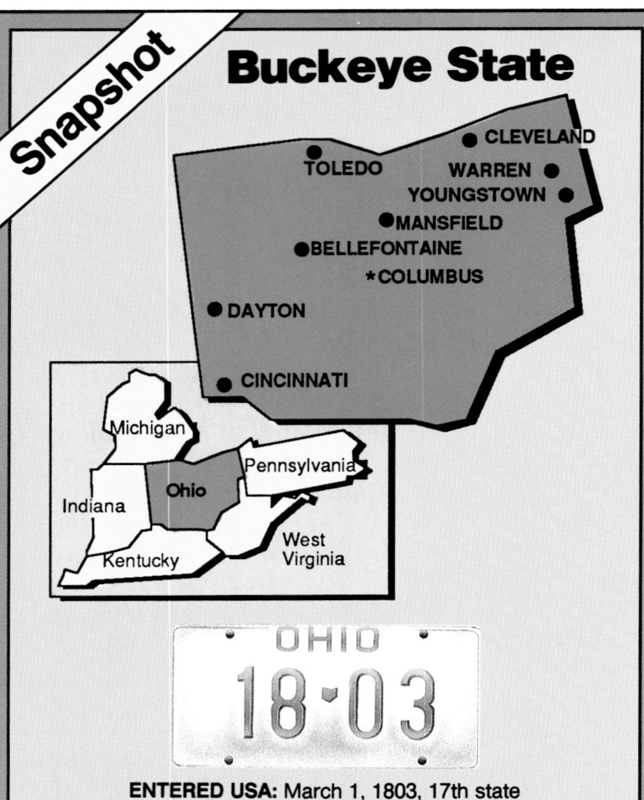

ENTERED USA: March 1, 1803, 17th state

MOTTO: With God, all things are possible
POPULATION: 10,752,000; rank, 7th
LARGEST CITY: Columbus, pop. 566,114
CAPITAL: Columbus
LAND: 41,004 square miles; rank, 35th
POPULATION DENSITY: 262.2 per square mile; rank, 9th
RACIAL MIX: 88.9% white; 10.0% black; 0.4% Asian and Pacific islanders. Hispanic heritage: 1.1%.

Uniquely Ohio

YOU SAY TOMATO: The first edible version of the tomato was developed by Alexander Livingston of Reynoldsburg in 1870.

'H' WORDS: The first 4-H Club was started by A.B. Graham in Springfield in 1902. The 4 H's: head, heart, hands, health.

CANNONBALL: Baldwin-Wallace College in Berea had its English Department windows shattered on July 4, 1979, by the firing of real cannons for the Cincinnati Symphony's "War of 1812 Overture" recording.

CAMPUS COEDS: Founded in 1833, the first co-educational college in the USA was Oberlin College.

PLAY BALL: The Cincinnati Reds were the world's first professional baseball team. Originally called the Redlegs, the team was organized in 1866. Another baseball first: Night baseball was first played May 24, 1935, at Cincinnati's Crosley Field.

Johnny Rongyos, 5 (with mother, Linda)
Kindergarten student
Wickliffe

"I like when the Indians hit a home run. I'm going to be an Indian and I'm going to try to hit a home run."

Mary E. Williams, 65
Tour director for senior citizens group
Blanchester

"I work with the group to keep myself active. You have to keep moving. You can't sit in a rocking chair and think about the aches and pains. You have to keep your hands busy and exercise your mind. I enjoy helping others and I feel that they are helping me in return. I feel that I am getting more out of it than I put in it most times."

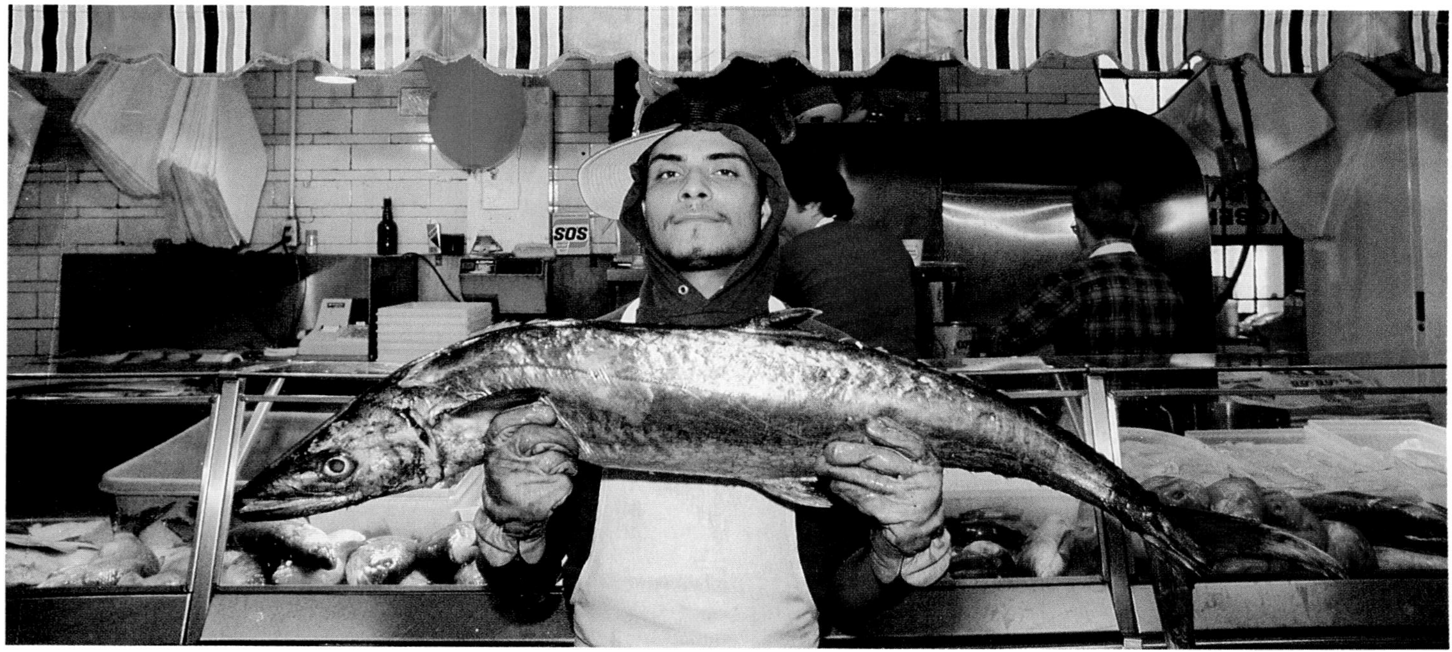

Jose Tirado, 21,
Seafood vendor
Cleveland

"My work gives me the chance to meet a lot of different people. I get to see a lot of different kinds of fish that I have never seen before. A lot of people ask if we get the fish from Lake Erie. I learned a lot of English because I didn't know that much when I came five years ago."

Voices
of Ohio

Maureen Hurst, 35
Bank officer
Niles

"I like a smaller community, but I have access to the bigger cities if I want. The people here are friendly. When the tornado hit (in May 1986), we all banded together as one team. We put our efforts together in one night to assist the victims. The tornado brought the merging of the whole city."

Mike Arcuri, 62
Stadium usher
Cleveland

"Fans from other stadiums like the fact that Cleveland's stadium is spacious and gives you a panoramic view of the game. People can catch foul balls here. I'm proud to be part of this park. I'm proud of being part of this city. Regardless of what people say, 'mistake on the lake,' and all that, I'm proud to be from Cleveland."

Bob Antoine, 36
Construction worker
Columbus

"When you tell someone you're from Ohio, they always mention Ohio State football and the Buckeyes. We have a lot more to offer than just a football team. We're growing. I hear that Columbus is the only city north of the Mason-Dixon line and east of the Mississippi that is growing. The general mood here is positive. We're very comfortable."

Chris Jarman, 32
Program director
Conference of Christians and Jews
Cincinnati

"The people in this community are really starting to reach out to each other. There are growing concerns, particularly minorities and women, and they are forces to be reckoned with. We're going to have to deal with them. We're teaching our young people to have better human relations, understanding and accepting of differences."

Bob Hope was born Leslie Townes Hope in 1903 in England. At age 4, his family moved to Cleveland, where he lived until going on the road as an entertainer at 21. Hope has lived in California for the past 50 years.

No joke, Cleveland's gorgeous in summer

USA TODAY: What are some of your boyhood memories of Cleveland?

HOPE: We were Episcopalian when we left London, and my dad had come over a year before to build the Euclid Avenue Presbyterian Church. When we arrived we looked at that church and loved it so much we became Presbyterians.

USA TODAY: Were you a sports fan?

HOPE: Some of my best memories are of going to watch the Indians play at League Park. One of my greatest memories was when Bob Feller was knocked out of the box and Satchel Paige walked in and took charge. It was dramatic.

USA TODAY: How often do you go back?

HOPE: Two or three times a year. I've got a lot of relatives there — nieces and things. Most of my six brothers settled in Cleveland. The last one — Fred — died two years ago.

USA TODAY: How has it changed?

HOPE: They've built up all the new theaters — the Palace, the State — it's a great theater town. In the last 10 years, they spruced up downtown.

USA TODAY: Why is Cleveland such a favorite target for put-downs?

HOPE: That started on *Laugh-In*. They started doing jokes about Cleveland, made you believe it was a dull city. It could have been anywhere.

USA TODAY: What's Cleveland really like?

HOPE: Cleveland is like Buffalo, Toledo or any town on the lakes. It's cold in the wintertime but gorgeous in the summertime. You get up on the heights — there's nothing nicer anywhere in the world.

USA TODAY: How do you stay healthy?

HOPE: I don't smoke. I don't drink. I walk and play golf. And I watch my diet. When you feel good, it's great; when you get a lot of laughs, it's better.

USA TODAY: You've been married to Dolores for 53 years — long by any standards, let alone Hollywood's. What's your secret?

HOPE: I'm too busy to do anything else. Dolores is busy with her things, and it's a matter of mutual love of activities, I guess.

Topic: OHIO

Our competition is abroad, not next door

USA TODAY: You've just completed one term in office. How do you feel about it?

CELESTE: I feel good about Ohio right now.

USA TODAY: Why?

CELESTE: This week, I spoke before the National Center for Manufacturing Sciences. It's going to try to put this country's machine tool industry and basic manufacturing processes back on the cutting edge. I feel that they will choose to be in Ohio.

USA TODAY: Do you think word of changes in Ohio is getting out?

CELESTE: I was just in Dallas to get an award for the state called the Keeping America Working Award, from the American Association of Community and Junior Colleges. It recognized what our two-year institutions are doing to bring education and economic development together.

USA TODAY: For instance?

CELESTE: In the past, we've been competing with the people next door and the people down the street. Now we need to find ways to cooperate with those folks so that we can compete with the people from Singapore, Brazil, Japan and Taiwan. It doesn't make a lot of sense for Ohio and Indiana to be burning up resources competing with each other.

USA TODAY: How do people feel about foreign investments you've brought to Ohio?

CELESTE: I don't think you'd get a unanimous vote in favor, but you would on the basic instinct toward hospitality. People want to make new visitors welcome, particularly when they invest in their community and bring jobs.

USA TODAY: You've called Lake Erie the state's single most important asset. What is the state of the lake?

CELESTE: There's been an enormous improvement in the quality of water in the lake. Unfortunately, there's also been an enormous rise in the level of the lake, which has caused problems for shoreline communities. But the first and foremost concern has to be with water quality.

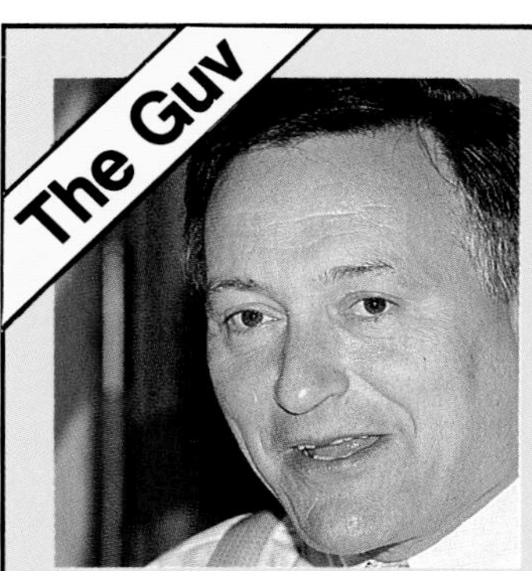

Richard F. Celeste, 49, a Democrat, was first elected in 1982 and re-elected in 1986.

USA TODAY: How are you protecting that?

CELESTE: The Great Lakes Governors Conference is looking at a system for aggressive monitoring to protect water quality. We've done a lot of investment, over a decade now, of upgrading sewer treatment facilities along the lake communities, which has made a major difference.

USA TODAY: What is the state doing to help communities that are hurting economically?

CELESTE: No economic development strategy should focus on big plants. Real growth comes first from existing business. We invest a tremendous amount of job-training money in small plants to help retrain their employees in new technologies.

USA TODAY: What's happening to industrial workers who've lost their jobs?

CELESTE: Part of the transition is that many of the 45- and 50-year-old workers who come out of those old plants have a very difficult time going into another job. There's been a very successful entrepreneurial training program in the Youngstown-Warren area, for former steelworkers. With their maturity and insight, many of them can become entrepreneurs in their own right.

Oklahoma

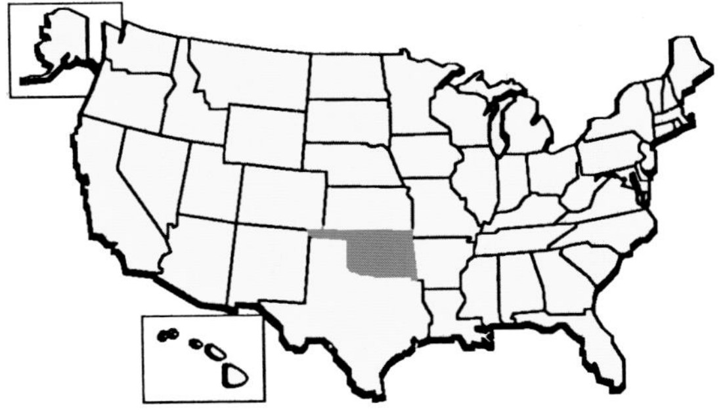

Visited: July 28-29, 1987
Featured in USA TODAY: July 31

"Inherently, cattle people are hopeful and honest. A wink of the eye or a handshake is a cattleman's word. This is one of the few businesses where when you say 'the check is in the mail,' it really is."

Harley Custer
Cattle farmer
Edmond, Okla.

Oklahoma

Sooners: Land grabbers in football, real life

It was 1889. The USA bought 3 million acres of land in Oklahoma territory from the Creek and Seminole Indian tribes. Announced that 1.9 million acres would be open for homesteaders April 22.

Some couldn't wait. Moved in sooner to stake their claims.

When the pistol sounded at noon on April 22, more than 50,000 pioneers poured across the borders. Plenty of land available. But the legal settlers found that folks they dubbed "Sooners" had already grabbed some of the choicest. Nickname stuck and was adopted by the state.

COACH SWITZER: 'They know (Sooners) everywhere.'

Sooners have been land grabbers ever since. The modern-day snatchers are the University of Oklahoma football Sooners. Have taken enough turf away from the opposition to win six national collegiate championships.

Leading the charge for those Sooners on the OU campus at Norman (pop. 78,100) is **Barry Switzer**, 49. One of the USA's winningest coaches. Record at Oklahoma in 14 years: 137 wins. 25 losses. 4 ties. Pct.: 83.7.

"We're a tremendous asset to the state. When you go anywhere and say you're from Oklahoma, people think of the OU Sooners. I just came back from Austria, Switzerland, Italy — they know who we are everywhere," says Switzer.

Football is very big in Oklahoma. But there are other Okie biggies:

- No. 3 in gas production in the USA. No. 5 in oil. No. 5 in beef.
- No. 1 in what the Bureau of Indian Affairs calls resident Indians. 191,981. Arizona is second. New Mexico third.

Oklahoma has 36 Indian tribes. Largest: Cherokees, with 76,000 members.

Their leader is a lady named Mankiller. **Chief Wilma P. Mankiller**, 41. Elected this month. Runs her empire from a farm near Stilwell (pop. 2,369), east of Muskogee, near the Arkansas border.

She likes the Mankiller family name. Is married to **Charlie Soap** but uses Mankiller personally and professionally.

"Sometimes when I try to make hotel reservations, they think I'm pulling their leg," says the articulate and ambitious boss lady.

"I think it's possible for an Indian woman to be elected president. But that's quite a ways down the road. Right now, the tribe is where I'm at. I'm a Cherokee patriot. My position toward the state is that we have certain rights and we intend to protect them. We're going to enter the 21st century on our own terms."

CHIEF MANKILLER: Leads 76,000 Cherokees.

While Oklahoma Indian tribes do have their own political structures, they are also in the mainstream. Have members in the state's House and Senate.

Gov. **Henry L. Bellmon**, 65, talks of Indian relations matter of factly. "Indians in Oklahoma do fairly well. Remember, our most famous citizen, Will Rogers, was a Cherokee."

Bellmon came out of political retirement last year to reclaim the governorship. Said he ran again because Oklahoma "needed a workhorse, not a showhorse." Has his work cut out for him:

- Unemployment: 7.6 percent. The USA average is 6.1.
- Bankruptcies: 13,132 in 1986. Up 56 percent from a year earlier.

But most Okies think the worst is behind them. Typically, those who work the land have the highest hopes. They trust the future, as they trust each other.

CUSTER: 'Wink or handshake is cattleman's word.'

Harley Custer, 77, is a lifelong cattle farmer. Now buys and sells cattle at the Oklahoma City Stockyards. Lives in nearby Edmond (pop. 47,600). Says Custer:

"Inherently, cattle people are hopeful and honest. A wink of the eye or a handshake is a cattleman's word. This is one of the few businesses where when you say 'the check is in the mail,' it really is."

That's Plain Talk from Oklahoma.

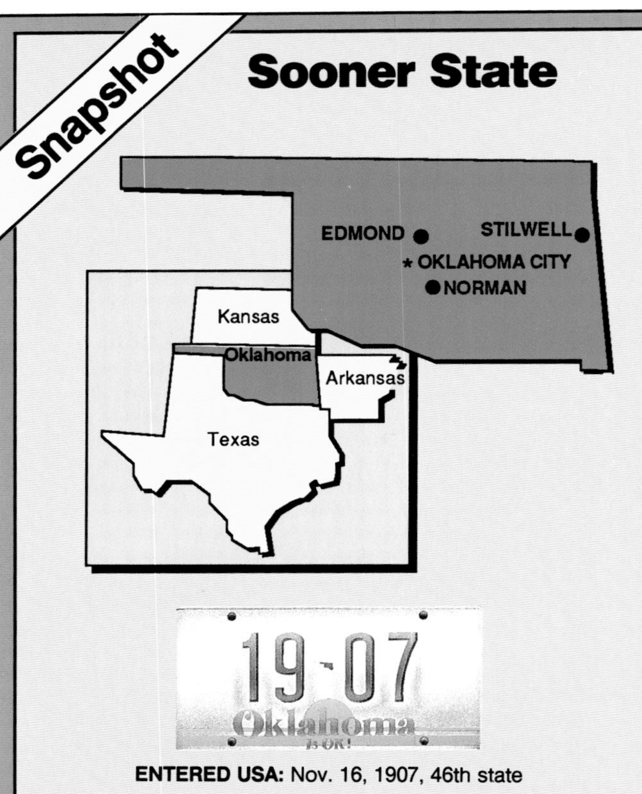

ENTERED USA: Nov. 16, 1907, 46th state

MOTTO: Labor conquers all things
POPULATION: 3,305,000; rank, 26th
LARGEST CITY: Oklahoma City, pop. 443,172
CAPITAL: Oklahoma City
LAND: 68,655 square miles; rank, 19th
POPULATION DENSITY: 48.1 per square mile; rank, 34th
RACIAL MIX: 85.9% white; 6.8% black; 5.6% American Indian; 0.6% Asian and Pacific islanders. Hispanic heritage: 1.9%.

Uniquely Okla.

MARKING TIME: The world's first parking meter was invented by a trio of Oklahoma entrepreneurs and installed in Oklahoma City in 1935.

INDIAN HERITAGE: Among Oklahoma's 36 Indian tribes are descendants of the original 67 tribes inhabiting Indian Territory. The Territory tried unsuccessfully in 1905 to become a separate state called Sequoyah.

BLACK GOLD: More than 500,000 oil and gas wells have been drilled in the state, an average of 7 wells per square mile.

O—K—L—A—H—O—M—A: The state song is "Oklahoma," from the Rodgers and Hammerstein musical that opened in 1943.

HOMETOWN BOY: Cowboy philosopher and humorist Will Rogers was born in Oologah, now home to the Will Rogers State Park. Also named in his honor: Will Rogers Turnpike, Will Rogers World Airport.

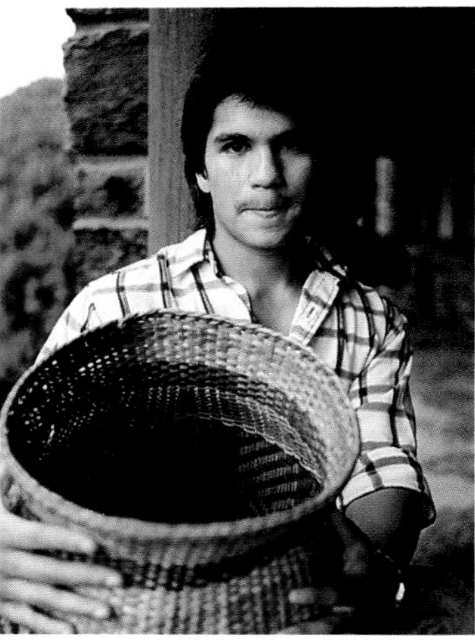

Roger Barr, 17
Student
Tahlequah

"The thing I'm most proud of is that I'm Indian. It's a system so different from anything else. It used to be that no one could own the land. Our nation is real unselfish. Nowadays, people have to pay for land, but we're still unselfish. My father taught me that. A man is as good as his word, he always says."

Carolyn Smith, 24
Medical research technician
Oral Roberts University
Tulsa

"This is the only Christian medical school in the nation and I wanted to be trained with the Christian perspective, not a more secular perspective. I went on a missions trip to Spain with people from here last year and it was incredible the way the healing team made a place for me."

J.R. Hamby, 41
Oil well developer
Muskogee

"People have a romantic idea of the oil business. They think all you have to do is drill a hole in the ground and get the money out. There's nothing romantic about it. You've got to keep your eye on the bottom line. The people that aren't in the oil business anymore forgot that."

Voices
of Oklahoma

Alfred Ginkel, 65
College president
Muskogee

"Native Americans are part of the nature of Oklahoma. They are integrated throughout the community. They are contributing to leadership in churches, businesses, government, art and other cultural endeavors. For example, the Cherokee nation has various industries. Cherokee Nation Industry Inc. is an electronics company; Cherokee Gardens are nursery wholesale and retail garden centers throughout Northeast Oklahoma. It is that type of economic development the Native Americans are doing."

Mike Sanditen, 33
Investments businessman
Tulsa

"Attitudes are getting better. When oil was $12 a barrel, people had poor attitudes. They were going broke. The thing that has helped us along is that people are more optimistic. The price of oil is going up and people are starting to spend more money. Things go in a boom, bust cycle here in Oklahoma. We have a boom about every 10-15 years."

Mary Pepping, 37
Psychologist
Oklahoma City

"When I came here from the West Coast, my friends said, 'Oklahoma . . . oh my God,' and we got out the map. They thought it was rural and backward. It's quiet, but it has a very high-caliber group. I was struck by the fact that so many cities have Indian names. It was amazing to see an 80-year-old man with long hair and young children in costume. Their ethnic pride is neat."

Dalton Young, 18
Student
Norman

"I've always wanted to play football for Oklahoma. The Sooners were the first team I ever heard of. I wasn't blessed with any athletic talent, so it's been an uphill struggle. I've been lifting weights since I was 10. I'm willing to help the team any way I can, even if that means being a tackling dummy."

Jonanna Scrapper, 28
Counselor
Muskogee

"I can't imagine Oklahoma being without Native Americans. Our culture and history is important. It shows where we've been and how far we've come. Each tribe has a lot to offer. For example, each tribe has its own form of government. Native Americans are coming out of a mold that they have been cast in and are contributing to the state in leadership and economics. Native Americans are sensitive and honest people. If you take that out of Oklahoma, it would be missed."

Notable

Reba McEntire, 33, a country singer-songwriter, grew up in Chockie, Okla. Her home now is a ranch in Stringtown, Okla. McEntire is the Country Music Association's top female vocalist.

We'd sing in the car on the way to rodeos

USA TODAY: What was it like growing up in Oklahoma?

McENTIRE: I was born in McAlester, lived 21 years in Chockie and then moved to Stringtown, where I've lived since 1980. My daddy — his name is Clark — was a rancher and a rodeo cowboy. He was world champion in steer roping in '57, '58 and '61. His father, John, was world champion in 1934. There were only 18 people in Chockie, and it was by a real busy highway.

USA TODAY: Were you a rodeo competitor, too?

McENTIRE: Mama would take us kids rodeoing. I competed in barrel racing for 10 years off and on, sharing it with my interest in basketball and music.

USA TODAY: When did you begin singing?

McENTIRE: Mama sang, and when we were off rodeoing, that's how we passed the time, singing in the car. And then every school program — Christmas or Thanksgiving or Valentine's Day — I was right there to volunteer.

USA TODAY: Do you remember your first song?

McENTIRE: In second grade, I sang *He* at the high school commencement. Speaker of the House Carl Albert was there and said, "One of these days, this little girl will be as famous as her daddy."

USA TODAY: How do you describe Oklahoma?

McENTIRE: Very pretty. We have a range of mountains that runs all the way across. People think it's all flat, but Eastern Oklahoma has creeks and streams and some pretty good-sized hills. The people here are friendly and hardworking. Oklahoma will always be my home.

USA TODAY: Your accent plays a major role in your song phrasing. Has anyone ever tried to make you change it?

McENTIRE: Oh, they hinted, but I never wanted to change it. When you start hinting to a redhead, it's like beating your head up against the wall.

USA TODAY: Your voice is so powerful that special recording devices (limiters) must be used. Where did it come from?

McENTIRE: I got the pitch and range from Mama and the loudness from Daddy from his calling cattle.

Topic: OKLAHOMA

Our pioneer heritage is a source of pride

USA TODAY: What is the biggest rallying point for Oklahomans? Oklahoma University's football team, the Sooners?

BELLMON: Not for me. I'm an Oklahoma State University fan.

USA TODAY: How do you handle that?

BELLMON: It's not difficult. I taught at Oklahoma University for a while. We are very, very proud of our football teams.

USA TODAY: What else inspires pride in Oklahomans?

BELLMON: We're very proud of the stage play, *Oklahoma*. We use it as our state song. What we're most proud of is our pioneer heritage.

USA TODAY: At one time, Oklahoma was to be exclusively Indian territory, and it still has one of the largest Indian populations. How are Indians in Oklahoma faring?

BELLMON: Some Cherokees and a few of the Plains Indians still live exclusively in Indian communities and have not found ways of fitting into the total society. On balance, our Indians are better off than the Indians who live on reservations. They're well accepted in our state.

USA TODAY: Humorist Will Rogers was a Cherokee, also. Was he representative of Oklahomans' attitude toward the government?

BELLMON: I think he was very representative. Oklahomans tend to be a little laid back, and I think they have generally a pretty good sense of humor.

USA TODAY: Have agriculture and oil, the state's two biggest industries, improved also?

BELLMON: Oil prices that fell as low as $10 are now up over $20. Cattle prices and production — our biggest farm commodity — are at or near historic highs. We've had a dramatic turnaround in the last six months.

USA TODAY: What caused the turnaround?

BELLMON: The problems OPEC has been having in the Persian Gulf have caused world oil prices to stabilize and get stronger.

The Guv

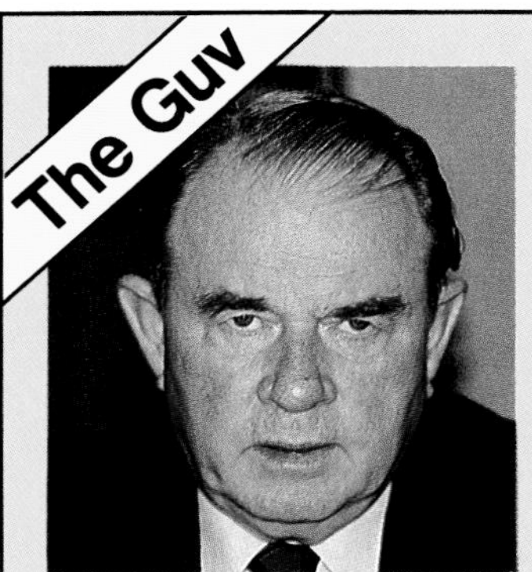

Henry Bellmon, 65, a Republican, was first elected governor in 1962. He served in the U.S. Senate 1969-81 and was re-elected governor in 1986.

USA TODAY: What's the long-range outlook for Oklahoma oil?

BELLMON: Natural gas is really more in our future than crude oil. We probably will not find any more large oil fields, but we have enormous natural gas potential from the deeper horizons, those down around 20,000 feet, even beyond.

USA TODAY: How does the future look for gas?

BELLMON: Gas prices are so low that you can't afford to drill to those depths to find gas, so right now, the gas business is not good. But unlike crude oil, we produce most of the natural gas we use in our country. Our petroleum future is heavily tied to natural gas. We're probably within two years of a major gas shortage again, and then prices will obviously be better, and we'll see another expansion of drilling and development.

USA TODAY: How do Oklahomans relax and have fun?

BELLMON: When you're in Muskogee, you'll be in a fine recreational area, built mostly around water sports: fishing, skiing, swimming. In addition, we have some of the best quail hunting in the world in Oklahoma. We also have at least a few good recreational parks, one in Oklahoma City and one near Tulsa.

Oregon

Visited: July 6-7, 1987
Featured in USA TODAY: July 10

"Whether it's a logger bringing down trees or a radical environmentalist who has chained himself to a tree, you can't question their reverence. They all know the forest is a treasure beyond measure."

John Blackwell
Executive director
World Forestry Center
Portland, Ore.

Oregon

Joggers, loggers, pols: Fast track and laid-back

Their former governor, the late **Tom McCall**, "invited" us all across the USA: "Come visit . . . but don't stay!"

Their most talked-about runner, **Mary Decker Slaney**, fell on the Olympic track . . . and publicly blamed the barefoot lady behind her, sparking an argument aired around the world.

MARY DECKER SLANEY: Olympic outcry.

The mayor of their largest city, Portland (pop. 365,861), is an avowed agnostic and tavern operator. The bearded and mustachioed **J.E. "Bud" Clark**, 55, was called a "born-again pagan" by then-Mayor **Frank Ivancie**. Clark won.

Outspoken mavericks. Oregon has had plenty. U.S. senators. Governors. Mayors. Police chiefs. Sports stars.

Yet, the state is inhabited mostly by laid-back loggers, joggers, farmers, fishermen, businesspeople, students. Why the contradictions in character?

Mayor Clark says simply: "It's because of the mind-set of the people. We think for ourselves."

Those people number just 2,698,000. Small, with very small growth. Sandwiched between Washington to the north (pop. 4,463,000) and bursting California to the south (pop. 26,981,000). Oregon has added only 66,000 people in the last six years. During the same period, California added 3.3 million.

Most Oregonians want to keep their state the way it is. **Jess DeCair**, 67, former county assessor in Salem, state capital (pop. 91,422), expounds the fierce independence of the status-quoers.

"We have no defense industry, no military bases. We have no influx of federal funds and we're proud of that. We take care of our own."

Oregonians' paychecks come from two major industries:

■ Forestry and related products. A $3.4 billion a year business. All the big industry names are involved. Boise Cascade. Crown Zellerbach. Weyerhaeuser.

■ Agriculture and food processing. $2.8 billion annually. Beef and wheat. Corn and beans.

Oregonians are tree people. Those who cut them down and those who want to preserve them. The lumber industry and environmentalists have had their confrontations.

The World Forestry Center, in Portland's Washington Park, tries to bridge differences between the two groups.

Says **John Blackwell**, 43, the center's executive director: "Whether it's a logger bringing down trees or a radical environmentalist who has chained himself to a tree, you can't question their reverence. They all know the forest is a treasure beyond measure."

The many serious runners and many more earnest joggers may best exemplify Oregon's life style. Laid-back about their careers. Undisturbed about Oregon's lack of real growth. Wrapped up in their workouts.

Eugene (pop. 105,100), home of the University of Oregon, is the running capital of the USA. Decker Slaney is based there. So is **Alberto Salazar,** 28, three-time winner of the New York City marathon. Holder of the USA record — 2:08:52 for the 26.2 miles.

Salazar is co-owner of a restaurant. But his heart is on the track and the jogging paths.

Thousands in Eugene and around say running gives them a "wealth of health" and happiness.

Two are **Sandra Huffstutter**, 38, a public relations executive, and her husband **Allen**, 39, a mortgage banker. "We're a two-career family with two teen-age sons and a big house to care for. The only time we really see each other and talk to each other is when we run together," says Sandra. They do that nearly every day at lunchtime.

HUFFSTUTTERS: They run for health, happiness.

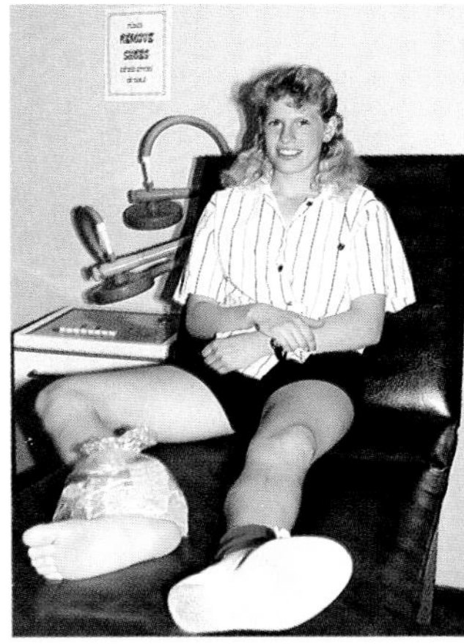

ROBIN: Despite sprain, running is heaven.

Even those who suffer injuries don't lose their enthusiasm. **Robin Raudsep**, 17, from Rainier (pop. 1,655). Is in Eugene for a summer running camp. Sprained her ankle. But she's raring to run again. Says Robin: "I get up at 5 a.m. and run about 5 miles. I expect to be doing the same thing 60 years from now. Running is heaven."

That's Plain Talk from Oregon.

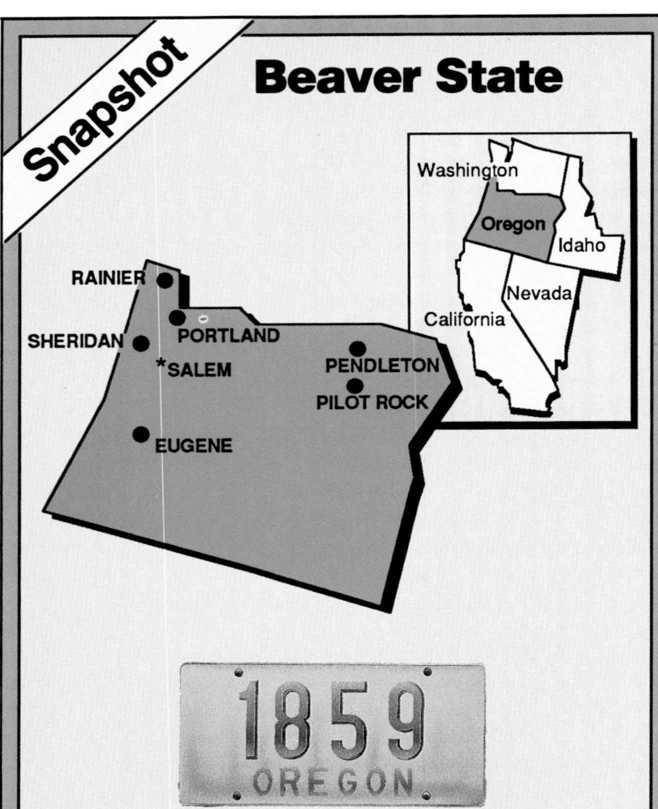

1859
OREGON

ENTERED USA: Feb. 14, 1859, 33rd state

MOTTO: The union
POPULATION: 2,698,000; rank, 30th
LARGEST CITY: Portland, pop. 365,861
CAPITAL: Salem, pop. 91,422
LAND: 96,184 square miles; rank, 10th
POPULATION DENSITY: 28.1 per square mile; rank, 40th
RACIAL MIX: 94.6% white; 1.4% black; 1.3% Asian and Pacific islanders. Hispanic heritage: 2.5%.

Uniquely Ore.

WESTWARD HO: The Oregon Trail was the longest of the great overland routes used in the westward expansion of the USA. The 2,000-mile journey from Independence, Mo., to Oregon's Willamette Valley took six months by covered wagon.

DO-SI-DO: In 1977, the Legislature declared the square dance the state dance.

NATION'S NICKELODEON: Oregon is the source of all USA-produced nickel.

BEACH PARTY: The 1967 Beach Bill guaranteed public access to all 362 miles of Oregon's coastline. It is the longest unrestricted coastline in the continental USA.

FEMALE FORCE: Portland was the first major city to allow women on the police force, shortly after the turn of the century, and the first to have a female police chief, in 1985.

TOPS IN 'P' CROPS: Oregon is No. 1 in peppermint, plums, prunes and winter pears.

Daryl Johnson, 38
Curator
International
Rose Test Garden
Portland

"Portland has an ideal climate for roses. When people ask me what my favorite rose is I tell them I have a favorite rose and it is different every year. This climate is conducive to growing plant life, even though we are behind on rainfall this year."

Jean Starkweather, 62
Gift shop owner
Albany

"Working with myrtlewood is like working on a painting. When it comes out smooth with beautiful grain lines, the woodworker says, 'It's my baby.' You cannot find two things alike made in myrtlewood."

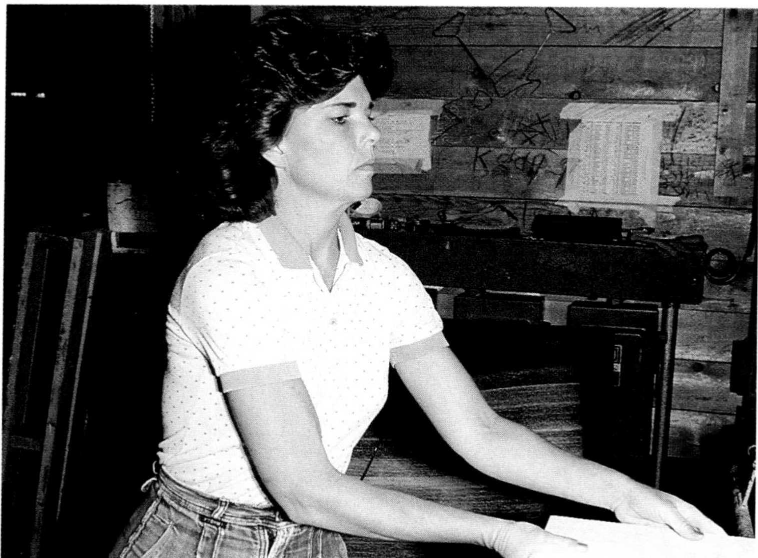

Nancy Bredard, 34
Machine sander
Pilot Rock

"I was frightened when I first started at the factory, but I've kind of settled in. I don't notice the noise anymore. I've got two small boys at home, so it's pretty noisy there, too. I think the women here do as well as the men. We're a little neater at stacking the boards."

Voices
of Oregon

John Hofenbredl, 44
Logger
Grand Ronde

"I think logging is a good occupation for a young fellow. The hills are getting greener from restoration, and it's getting safer. The equipment is getting safer."

Ray Agee, 63
Log marker
Sheridan

"The wood smell is the smell of Oregon. You can smell fresh-cut wood almost anywhere you go. When I come home from work, I've got tree sap all over me. It's on my glasses and in my hair. I mark every log that comes into the cold docks. It's usually 200 loads of logs a day. I measure them so they can be sent to the mills and made into plywood. I like being out in the woods where there's peace and quiet. A lot of states wish to heck they had all these trees. I take care of mental work and the loggers take care of physical work."

Doug Gregg, 53
Production chief
Pendleton

"I've been in the furniture business for 33 years. Most of the furniture in my house was made by companies I work for. But I can still walk through a forest and enjoy nature rather than just see dollars and cents. At home, for a hobby, I make furniture for myself. I just like wood."

Joan Rhinhart, 51
Farmer, homemaker
Pilot Rock

"It's pretty all the time here in Eastern Oregon. From the top of the hill you can look out and see all the different shades of tan grain. It's like a patchwork quilt. Farming is a way of life. You don't plan on a 40-hour week. We go from dawn to dusk. We work until the grain elevator closes at 8. The day ends when you get back from the elevator. We don't do this to get paid. We own it. There's a sense of accomplishment when you're harvesting."

Tom Ellwood, 48
Stained glass artisan
Portland

"When I lived on the East Coast, I felt like the land was deteriorating right under my feet. On the West Coast, the industrialization was wiping out the countryside. I call Portland the least offensive city I've ever lived in. We're more careful on how industry uses land; very environmentally conscious. It's clean because people take care of it. We're slow in growth, but that's just fine with me."

Carl "Doc" Severinsen Jr., 60, was born in Arlington, Ore. (pop. 425). He joined NBC as a staff musician in 1949. Since 1967, he has been musical director of The Tonight Show *band and now lives in Los Angeles.*

Isolation, beauty are state high notes

USA TODAY: What do you think of Oregon?

SEVERINSEN: I'm hard put to find anything remotely comparable to Oregon for sheer beauty. We have everything there: deserts just like the Sahara, the most incredible mountains outside of the Alps, valleys so lush, green and beautiful. The seashore in Oregon is second to none — just miles of clean, pretty beaches, and hardly anybody on them.

USA TODAY: How do you describe Oregonians?

SEVERINSEN: They're different — especially the ones from Eastern Oregon. They're very clannish. If you meet someone from Eastern Oregon, and you're 3,000 miles away from home — as I have been — it's like everybody is a relative. Oregonians — because it is a rather remote place — feel a bond.

USA TODAY: Do you still feel a bond to the people of Oregon?

SEVERINSEN: When I go back now to my hometown, everybody's like family. It's very close. And the people in Oregon take great pride in their state. People don't mess it up.

USA TODAY: Did you ever experience culture shock, coming from a small town?

SEVERINSEN: I'll tell you how much of a shock it was. The first time I joined a band filled with easterners, for about a week I didn't know what the hell they were talking about. I couldn't understand them, and they couldn't understand me. We had a language barrier.

USA TODAY: Still have relatives in Oregon?

SEVERINSEN: My mother lives in Portland; she will be 90 next month, and she's going strong. I also have one half-sister, who lives in Junction City.

USA TODAY: Do you get back often?

SEVERINSEN: A few times a year. Once a year, they have a big river music festival there, with bands from all around. I usually make it back for that.

USA TODAY: Ever tempted to move back?

SEVERINSEN: I wouldn't want to live there full time, but I wouldn't mind having a little ranch back there. There are big, rolling hills like you can't possibly imagine. In other parts of the world they would be called mountains.

Topic: OREGON

People have real love for this piece of land

USA TODAY: What do you think the image of Oregon and its residents should be to those outside the state?

GOLDSCHMIDT: This is a state where people are imbued with a tremendous feeling about the land they've inherited. People come here hauling their possessions behind them down the Columbia Gorge, and it impacts them the same way it has everybody since Lewis and Clark. You can't avoid it. People have a rather intense caring about the real estate here.

Neil Goldschmidt, 47, a Democrat, has been governor since January. He was Jimmy Carter's transportation secretary.

USA TODAY: How do they show their love for the land?

GOLDSCHMIDT: We have a statewide land use plan. Oswald West, who was governor way back, declared the beaches public highways and thereby protected them from anybody building on them.

USA TODAY: How can you tell the difference between a native and someone who's come here from somewhere else?

GOLDSCHMIDT: Oh, you can't. You know, it's a little bit like converts to Judaism, or Catholicism, or whatever religion they choose. The converts are much tougher than the natives. This is not a place that's easy for a transient to wander into. If you decide to come here, it's because you heard about it and you want to be here, or you've been here and you want to come back.

USA TODAY: The eastern part of the state and the western part of the state are very different. What challenge does that present?

GOLDSCHMIDT: Today, we have 40 percent of the state's population and 50 percent of the state's economy in three counties around Portland. Twenty percent of the income growth has been in one county for the past five years.

USA TODAY: And the rest of the state?

GOLDSCHMIDT: Central Oregon is almost its own state in the sense that its climate is so different, and its economy is so different. But it's also got assets that none of the rest of us have, the most important of which is that 300 days a year, you can be out and enjoy the weather. The problem there has been transportation. The three counties in the area have done such an incredible job of getting themselves together. They now have PSA Airlines flying into Redmond Airport twice a day from San Francisco.

USA TODAY: How has modernization affected the timber industry?

GOLDSCHMIDT: Changes have hammered the timber industry — very substantial increases in productivity. When I grew up in Eugene, in 1950, when I was 10, there was a mill that had over 1,000 employees. Today, there's a mill in Eugene that has about 160 employees turning out double the board footage. We have to do it to be competitive.

USA TODAY: Can you tell us the story of how Portland got its name?

GOLDSCHMIDT: The intellect here, you know, is very deep. We are a people of deep and abiding creativity, and we give long and deep thought to all our decisions, and that was one of those decisions where they couldn't decide whether to name it Boston or Portland, because some of the guys who lived there were from Boston, and some were from Portland, Maine, and they flipped a coin. Very creative.

Pennsylvania

Visited: April 29-May 1, 1987
Featured in USA TODAY: May 4

"The Constitution verbalizes everything the USA stands for. It's all written down there, and it started here in Philadelphia."

Carla Draluck
Student
Philadelphia, Pa.

Pennsylvania

Patriotism on display every day, every way

"Certain inalienable rights . . . life, liberty and the pursuit of happiness." — Declaration of Independence, 1776.

"We, the people . . . do ordain and establish this Constitution." — the Preamble, 1787.

This is where it all began, for all of us. They all gathered here. **Ben Franklin**. **Thomas Jefferson**. **George Washington**.

This year, we will gather here. Millions of us. In Philadelphia, the City of Brotherly Love. To celebrate the 200th anniversary of our Constitution.

The curtain went up last Friday on this heartwarming drama. It was May Day, Law Day — and especially — Magna Carta Day.

Patriotism was on parade. Anthems were sung. Bagpipers marched. People clapped . . . and cried. They lined up to stroke the crack in the Liberty Bell. (Yes, you're allowed to touch it.)

Standing in the doorway of historic Independence Hall were:

■ Britain's **Princess Alexandra**, 50, first cousin to **Queen Elizabeth II**.

■ U.S. Attorney General **Edwin Meese III**, 55.

■ American Bar Association President **Eugene Thomas**, 56.

■ **H. Ross Perot**, 56, superpatriot and superbillionaire.

PEROT: Presents Magna Carta.

Perot came to loan to Philadelphia his $1.5 million copy of the 13th century Magna Carta.

The princess reminded that "many of the concepts of your Constitution stem directly from our Magna Carta."

Members of local British-American societies cheered.

Meese participated in the ceremony for 43 new citizens, from the Soviet Union to El Salvador.

BURGER: Heads commission.

"You have paid us a tremendous compliment by making your way to our doorstep. . . . Now we repay that compliment. . . . We are adopting you as citizens of our nation," Meese said.

ABA president Thomas told them: "Our highest office is that of citizen."

It will all climax here on Sept. 17, 1987. Constitution Day. The USA's highest citizens will be here then. **President Reagan**. Cabinet and Court dignitaries. Retired Chief Justice **Warren Burger**, head of the constitutional bicentennial commission. In spirit or in person, you and I. Why?

James Michener, 80, Pennsylvania's Pulitzer Prize-winning novelist, says it's a wonderfully warm "Peasant Patriotism." He's caught in it, too.

Michener, who has written verbosely about Hawaii, Texas, Alaska, says he'll have a "short, dramatic, intense novel" out this fall.

Title: *The Constitution*, of course.

Most Pennsylvanians will get in on the act. In Harrisburg, the state capital, Gov. **Robert Casey**, 55, is inviting the governors of the original states to join him May 24 and share their views on the celebration of the Constitution.

Joining Pennsylvania in the Colonial 13: Delaware, New Jersey, Georgia, Connecticut, Massachusetts, Maryland, South Carolina, New Hampshire, Virginia, New York, North Carolina and Rhode Island.

"Our challenge is to bring the Constitution to life for our people . . . to show how meaningful it is today," Casey says.

This summerlong show includes showmanship as well as patriotism.

Ralph Archbold, 45, and his wife, **Sue**, 32, are show people. But patriotic, too.

Sue portrays flag maker **Betsy Ross**, 13-star flag in hand. "Of course, I can sew," Sue assures.

Ralph roams Independence Square in Ben Franklin regalia. His birthday and Ben's coincide (Jan. 17).

Says Ralph: "I'm not just an actor with a wig. Ben was the unifier, the peacemaker during the constitutional convention. He needs to be here now. I bring Ben to life."

That's Plain Talk from Pennsylvania.

'BETSY' AND 'BEN': Archbolds' family act helps bring Philadelphia's history alive.

Snapshot

Keystone State

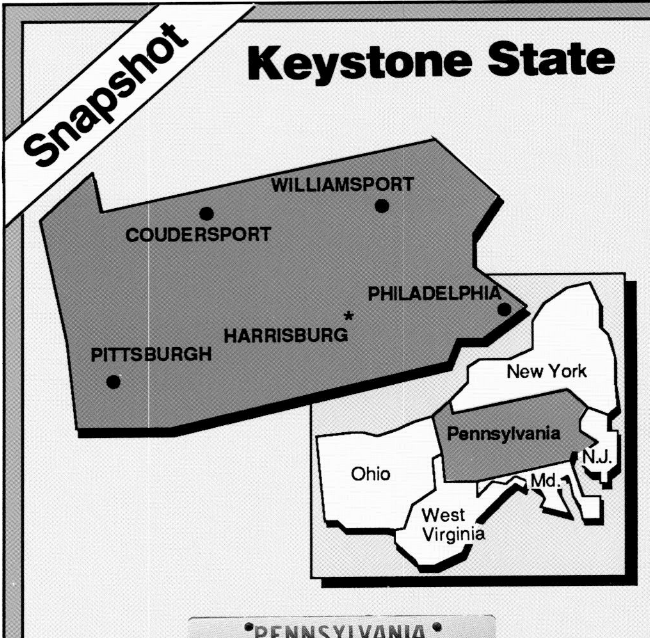

PENNSYLVANIA 17 87 KEYSTONE STATE

ENTERED USA: Dec. 12, 1787, 2nd state

MOTTO: Virtue, liberty, and independence
POPULATION: 11,889,000; rank, 4th
LARGEST CITY: Philadelphia, pop. 1,646,713
CAPITAL: Harrisburg, pop. 52,200
LAND: 44,888 square miles; rank, 32nd
POPULATION DENSITY: 264.9 per square mile; rank, 8th
RACIAL MIX: 89.8% white; 8.8% black; 0.5% Asian and Pacific islanders. Hispanic heritage: 1.3%.

Uniquely Pa.

ZOO KEEPER: Philadelphia was the first USA city to have a zoo. It opened in 1874.

CHANGE OF SEASONS: At the Ice Mine in Coudersport, nature causes icicles up to 3 feet thick to form during summer.

FORE SCORE: The oldest golf course in continuous use in the USA is in Foxburg. The original clubhouse is now the American Golf Hall of Fame.

FOUNDING FATHER: Pennsylvania means "Penn's Woods," but it wasn't named after founder William Penn. It was named for his father, Admiral Sir William Penn.

FUTURE ALL-STARS: Little League Baseball started in 1939 in Williamsport, home of the Little League World Series.

BATTLE WEARY: More Revolutionary War battles were fought within a 50-mile radius of Philadelphia than in all of New England.

Voices
of Pennsylvania

Phyllis Polk, 53
Public relations coordinator
Philadelphia

"It's been a very fulfilling year working on the constitutional bicentennial celebration. I've been involved with it since it was born, in November 1983. To participate in the communicating of the full meaning of this bicentennial and the full meaning of the Constitution, what it means to all of us, this city and state and country, to watch and see how it's grown and see the response from people from all walks of life has been very gratifying."

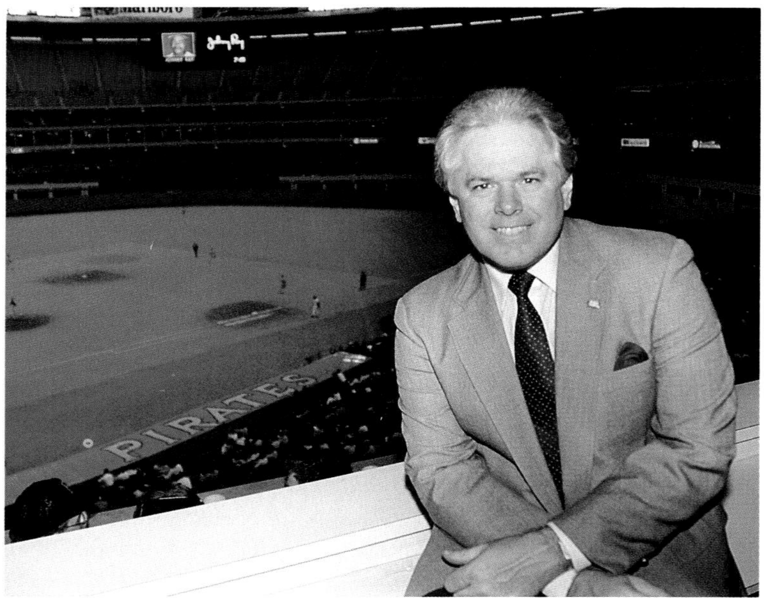

Nelson Briles, 43
Former Pirates pitcher
Pittsburgh

"People here have strong commitments to the family. They have long-lasting friendships. The Pirates benefited from that. The citizens and the corporations banded together to keep the ballclub in the city. There's a deep loyalty to the black and gold."

Jessica White, 10
Student
Wernersville

"We learned about the Liberty Bell in our social studies book. I like the history because it's neat to learn about all the different stuff that happened in Philadelphia. I like Independence Hall the best. I like looking at the room where they signed the Declaration of Independence."

Carla Draluck, 20
Student
Philadelphia

"The Constitution verbalizes everything the USA stands for. It's all written down there, and it started here in Philadelphia. What the Constitution stands for has become such a part of everybody's life that it's really easy to forget how unique it is in the world today. The Constitution stands for individualism. It shows that it's not only OK to be an individual, it's good to be one."

Marian Zeiset, 18
Cashier/farmer
Goodville

"I've been driving a horse and buggy since I was eight or nine. I was out driving a tractor around this morning — a diesel, on steel wheels. Our Mennonite church doesn't allow rubber wheels. I quit school when I was 15. Our church only goes to 8th grade. We studied writing, math, spelling — not science."

Bill Hertrich Jr., 38
Food service trainer
Cheswick

"Pittsburgh is the friendliest city I've ever been in. You can break down on the expressway and people will help you. Everybody's basically alike — 98 percent of the people here have somebody in their family who's been in steel. So people unite here and it makes a strong city. If you moved here, it would take two days and you'd have a friend."

Johnny Kitt, 36
Geriatric nurse
Harrisburg

"I don't think Harrisburg is as depressed as the media make it sound. In Harrisburg we've got the minor league baseball and two football teams. I don't see any need for young people to move out of here. It's all right here, if they apply themselves."

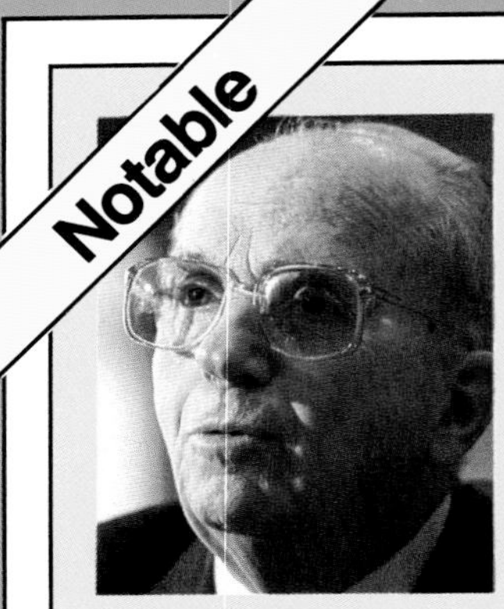

James Michener, 80, who grew up in Doylestown, Pa., has written 40 books, including Tales of the South Pacific, Hawaii, Centennial, Poland, *and* Texas. *He just completed a book about Alaska.*

It's a first-class state and it's my home

USA TODAY: You've written about some wonderful places — the South Pacific, Hawaii, Texas. Yet you've always called Pennsylvania home.

MICHENER: I've never left home. This is my home state. I would never live overseas.

USA TODAY: What is it about Pennsylvania that holds on to you?

MICHENER: When I was a boy, Pennsylvania was the third largest state in the nation and maybe the third in importance — New York, Illinois and Pennsylvania. I have lived to see it drop way down to fifth or sixth. So I have seen a kind of political and geographical decline, but still there has been a wonderful retention of quality. Pennsylvania's a first-class state.

USA TODAY: What's special about Doylestown, where you grew up?

MICHENER: It's in Bucks County, which is one of the few counties in America which is known by its own name — it has its own importance. It was the home of a great many writers and artists, and it had its own little Renaissance. Doylestown itself was a town of about 3,000. I delivered papers at 4 in the morning, and I knew every house on every street in Doylestown.

USA TODAY: What impact did it have on your becoming a writer?

MICHENER: Doylestown had a fine little library, the Melinda Cox, which started about the time that I was born. The first two people to enlist for cards at that library, I was told some years ago, were Margaret Mead and me.

USA TODAY: What were the other students like?

MICHENER: In my class in high school, about half of the students had German as their language at home. So it was a Germanic-English mix of very nice quality. It was a very religious area.

USA TODAY: Since you have written so much about other places, when can we expect a book about Pennsylvania?

MICHENER: I don't rule that out. I have a real goodie all outlined. But when I'll get to write it, I don't know.

Topic: PENNSYLVANIA

We're going to start accenting the positive

USA TODAY: You're finishing your first 100 days in office. Are things better or worse than you expected?

CASEY: One of the things I've been stressing is what Pennsylvania has to offer. Historically, Pennsylvanians have had an inferiority complex.

USA TODAY: Why?

CASEY: We have been losing manufacturing of steel and coal. And frankly, in a lot of national articles about Pennsylvania, there are these labels that are really tyrannical, the "Rust Belt," for example.

USA TODAY: What are you going to do about it?

CASEY: We've got to start emphasizing the positive. It's high time the people made up their minds they're not going to take a back seat to any other state.

USA TODAY: What are the positives?

CASEY: We've got the best work force in the world. Hard-working people, family-oriented, the salt of the Earth. A lot of people left, but many stayed behind. The people of this state in World War II out-produced the world. The steel mills may be gone, but the people are still here. The values are here.

USA TODAY: Can you offset the manufacturing loss?

CASEY: In recent years, it has been somewhat offset by gains in hi-tech and the service economy. But you cannot sustain the economy with hi-tech and service jobs alone. You've got to have that undergirding of manufacturing support. We do have a strong secondary market here in high-specialty steel products.

USA TODAY: What changes could attract businesses?

CASEY: One thing that's very important, and it doesn't cost five cents, is the personal commitment of the governor.

USA TODAY: In what way?

CASEY: How many times have you heard the story of the chief executive officer who goes to South Carolina, has breakfast with the governor, and the governor takes out his personal card, writes his home phone number, hands it to the fellow, and says, "If I can be of any help, please call me." I've heard these kinds of stories about former Tennessee Governor Lamar Alexander.

***Robert P. Casey**, 55, a Democrat, won election as governor in 1986 on his fourth try. He is a former state senator and auditor general.*

USA TODAY: Did that help Tennessee get the Saturn auto plant?

CASEY: Saturn came about in significant measure because Alexander was a better salesman.

USA TODAY: There will be a lot of celebrations in your state because of the bicentennial of the Constitution.

CASEY: The Statue of Liberty observance was an easier kind of thing. Our challenge is to bring the Constitution to life for our people . . . to show how meaningful it is today.

USA TODAY: Do Pennsylvanians want the speed limit raised to 65?

CASEY: Some do, but I don't. We're going to stick with 55.

USA TODAY: Why?

CASEY: Because it saves lives, and it saves gasoline, in that order. We're not New Mexico. We have icy roads in the wintertime.

USA TODAY: Do you mind if we do 65 going home?

CASEY: At your peril! I think we're going to stick with 55.

Rhode Island

Visited: May 11-12, 1987
Featured in USA TODAY: May 15

"A Rhode Island swamp Yankee is an independent, industrious, backwoods, strong-willed, stubborn, tight-lipped person scratching and scrounging to make a living in today's society."

Liz Peterson
Public librarian
South Kingstown, R.I.

Rhode Island

Smallest state, but big on spunk, self-reliance

The Independent Man. His statue tops the dome of the state Capitol. The symbol bespeaks the spirit of the smallest state in the USA.

Rhode Island. At its longest point, 48 miles. At its widest, 37. All told, 1,055 square miles.

You could fit 46 Rhode Islands into Iowa. 91 into Nevada. 220 into Texas. 485 into Alaska.

But don't mistake size for soul. They're not just independent, but indestructible. Cautious, yet cocksure. Fixed in their ways and do-it-yourselfers.

"That independence goes back to our founding fathers," says restaurant owner **William Nelle**, 42, in Wakefield (pop. 3,300).

"Rhode Island is for rebels," adds lawyer **Paul Singer**, 44, in tiny Carolina (pop. 501).

That old-line rebelliousness rubs off on some newcomers.

MR. INDEPENDENT: State's symbol.

Latest and most noted — **Amy Carter**. Once a shy pre-teen in the White House with parents **Jimmy** and **Rosalynn Carter**. Now a highly publicized protester on the campus of Brown University, atop College Hill in Providence (pop. 154,148).

AMY: Once shy, now a Rhode Island rebel.

Tried in a Massachusetts district court on disorderly conduct charges stemming from a protest against CIA recruiting. Found not guilty. Amy says she might spend the rest of her life protesting. "I can't sit around and preach to other people if I'm not going to be one of them."

Outsider Amy's unfettered feelings fit well here. Republican Gov. **Edward DiPrete** loves the "fiercely independent" ticket-splitters who re-elected him last year. At the same time, they voted in a heavily Democratic state Legislature.

From the capital of Providence, you can journey to any of the not-very-far corners of the state and find:

- A diversity of lifestyles and ideas.
- But a unity of self-esteem and self-reliance.

Rhode Island calls itself the Ocean State. It has 384 miles of Atlantic Coast line to back up the motto.

From Narragansett Bay to Newport (pop. 29,259), fishing and boating are big. Digging the sea banks for the oversize clams you eat in New England clam chowder are sons and daughters of immigrants who did the same thing. They call themselves Quahaugers.

Newport is most famous as the longtime home of the America's Cup races. **Dennis Conner**, who brought the cup back from Australia to San Diego this year, was wined and dined in Newport last week. They made him an honorary commodore of the exclusive Commodore's Club.

But most doubt the cup races will be back here. **Jock West**, 43, director of Morris International Incorporated's Newport facilities located on America's Cup Avenue, says, "Conner is not going to let tradition get in the way of making a lot of money." West thinks San Diego and Hawaii will far outbid Newport for the 1990 races.

The tiny villages that dot the smallest state may be the best measure of its spirit and soul.

Take the mill village of Carolina. Nestled in the hillsides of the south, 10 miles from the ocean. Most of its 501 residents were born near here, have lived here most of their lives, or have come back. Hope to stay here. Expect to die here.

The youngest Carolinian is **Stephen Collins Cellar**, 9 weeks old this Sunday. The seventh generation member of his family to live here. Grandson of **John C. Quinn**, USA TODAY editor and one of the biggest landowners in Carolina.

One of Carolina's oldest is retired mill-weaver **John Grimes**, 79. "I'm a swamp Yankee, goddamit," he says with pride.

GRIMES: 'I'm a swamp Yankee.'

Swamp Yankee? **Liz Peterson**, 27, public librarian in nearby South Kingstown (pop. 23,000), defines the term:

"A Rhode Island swamp Yankee is an independent, industrious, backwoods, strong-willed, stubborn, tight-lipped person scratching and scrounging to make a living in today's society."

That's Plain Talk from Rhode Island.

Snapshot: Ocean State

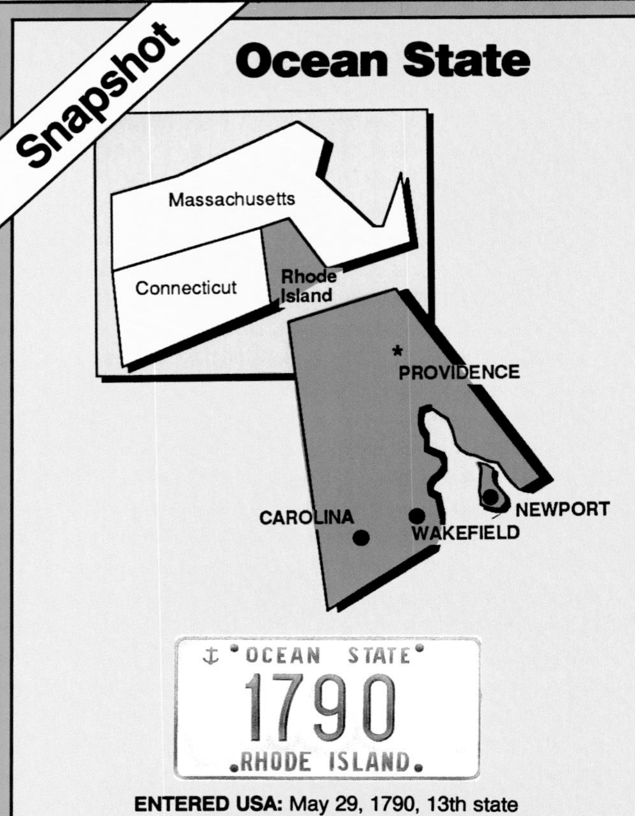

ENTERED USA: May 29, 1790, 13th state

MOTTO: Hope
POPULATION: 975,000; rank, 42nd
LARGEST CITY: Providence, pop. 154,148
CAPITAL: Providence
LAND: 1,055 square miles; rank, 50th
POPULATION DENSITY: 924.2 per square mile; rank, 2nd
RACIAL MIX: 94.7% white; 2.9% black; 0.6% Asian and Pacific islanders. Hispanic heritage: 2.1%.

Uniquely R.I.

GREEK TO HIM: Italian navigator Giovanni da Verazzano, who visited in 1524, is said to have likened the state to the Greek Island of Rhodes.

BREWMASTER: Newport's White Horse Tavern has been serving ale since 1673.

WIDE SPAN: The widest bridge in the world is Providence's Crawford Street Bridge. At 1,147 feet, it spans part of Narragansett Bay.

DIGGING DEEP: The Limerock quarry has been in operation since 1643.

FORWARD MARCH: The Newport Artillery Company, chartered in 1741, is the USA's oldest active military organization.

YANKEE DOODLE DANDY: Providence-born composer George M. Cohan was actually born on the third of July, not the fourth as he liked to claim in song.

Voices
of Rhode Island

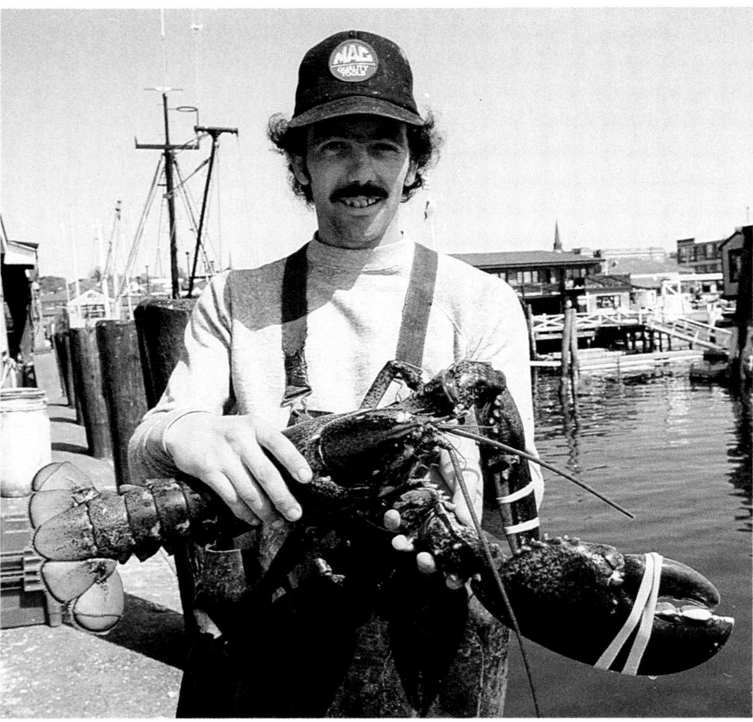

Frank Frenette, 27
Fisherman/dock worker
Newport

"I'm a lobster-trician. It's like an electrician, but we work with lobsters. It's hard work, but it's good for you. If you don't like to work hard, you ain't gonna make it. It gets really cold, but it keeps you awake. You can get all dirty and don't have to worry about staying clean. You can make good money fishing. I made $600 in one six-hour night sea clamming."

Candy McKenna, 40
Store manager
Middletown

"I moved away, but I came right back home. Like most people from this part of the country, I love my roots. I have access to the rest of the world, but I live on an island."

Michael Hall, 34
Boat captain
Carolina

"I've been doing this for about 16 years, but I used to filet fish and work on my uncle's lobster boat. Can you think of another job where you never have to see another stop sign, look at another clock or get caught in a traffic jam? It's a completely different life with no restrictions, no boundaries. You work for yourself, and then do what society makes you do when you come ashore."

Betty Dean, 40
Hotel manager
North Kingstown

"Everything here is small. The stores are small, the shops are small. It's mind-boggling if you're used to going to large supermarkets and then having these small ones. It's not really fair to compare it to other states. It's like comparing apples and oranges. This is just a scaled down version of everything else. I'm from Houston, and there it takes two days of driving before you leave the state. Here, you drive 25 minutes in any direction and you're out."

Col. William Long Jr., 68
Director, International Tennis Hall of Fame
Newport

"This whole city is a living museum. This is an intoxicating place to live. Newport has many layers: the old wealth, new wealth, and the young, creative people. Living here in the winter is like taking a beautiful lady to a ball. Everybody dances with her, but you have to take her home."

Grace Trofa, 40
Photographer
Cranston

"No one is ever happy with the place where they were born except Rhode Islanders. Many of my friends have moved away in search of hi-tech jobs. But then, they move right back. Many of those who find work elsewhere continue to live in Rhode Island and commute to their jobs."

Scott Johnson, 34
Student
Saunderstown

"This state is so small that everybody always knows what's going on. If something happens at the opposite end of the state, we know about it here. Because of that, you feel a part of everything."

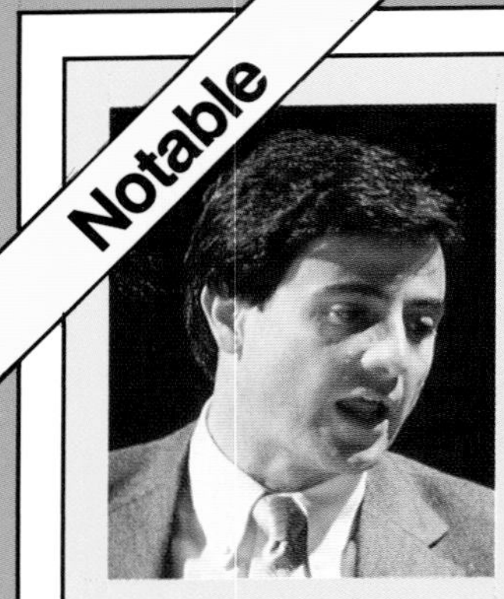

In two seasons as basketball coach at Providence College, ***Rick Pitino****, 34, turned an 11-20 team in 1985 into a 25-9 team that reached the Final Four of the 1987 NCAA Tournament.*

Friars are still first love in Providence

USA TODAY: You've been courted by several pro basketball teams, including the New York Knicks. Why did you decide to stay in Providence?

PITINO: I've traveled about 48 out of the 50 states for recruiting and other matters, and this is one of the more comfortable states to live in for family atmosphere. It really is a great place to raise a family. You're never more than 20 minutes from the ocean, you have great restaurants, you're an hour from Boston, two and a half from New York — access to everything is tremendous.

USA TODAY: What attracted you to Providence?

PITINO: It goes back to when I was a player in 1973 at the University of Massachusetts. We had an outstanding team. There were only 24 teams, and making the NCAA and the NIT was very big. Every year for a four-year period, it came down to beating one team for an NCAA berth, and that was Providence College.

USA TODAY: What did Rhode Island derive from your team's trip to the NCAA finals?

PITINO: It's built up a tremendous pride and interest. Wherever you go, you see signs in downtown, "Thank you, Friars," and rather than talking about the Patriots or the Red Sox, they're once again talking about the Friars, which is their first love.

USA TODAY: The Big East is probably the most successful basketball conference in the country. Yet the teams aren't caught in the web of cheating and dishonesty that seems to run through college athletics these days. Why?

PITINO: Putting academics first is the major common denominator — it's true of most of the schools in the Big East. In a five-year period in 21 sports, both male and female, we've had 100 percent graduation. That's probably the No. 1 statistic in the USA today. You can't do any better than that.

USA TODAY: You're a well-known figure in Rhode Island. Does that go with the territory?

PITINO: Obviously, the head coach of Providence has always been looked on in a different light because of the entertainment quality we have here, but just after the Final Four, it has picked up tremendously. That's something I believe in, and I get a big thrill from helping charity causes.

Topic: RHODE ISLAND

We're a small state, but we're on a roll

USA TODAY: How do the people of Rhode Island feel about their state?

DiPRETE: For years, Rhode Island has gone around with an inferiority complex. But I think the state is on a roll now.

USA TODAY: In what way?

DiPRETE: We had our 350th anniversary of the founding of Rhode Island in 1986. Estimated attendance was around 240,000 — roughly 25 percent of the state's population. We had a poll taken and, in 1984, one out of three people felt the state was headed in the right direction. That figure is now up to 70 percent.

USA TODAY: Any other indications of this new mood?

DiPRETE: Construction is booming — a 45 percent increase in contracts in 1985 over the prior year, and 1986 figures will be higher than that. Another indirect indication that people feel good about the state — sales tax collections that show people are not only making money, they're willing to spend it. To our surprise, sales tax revenues have continued to climb.

USA TODAY: How important has the sea been to the state?

DiPRETE: The sea is very important. Commercial fishing is prosperous in the state. The sea is also very important from a recreational point of view. Tourism now has become a major industry; it was not five years ago. The America's Cup has a lot to do with it. The America's Cup is traditionally in Newport.

USA TODAY: What are the chances of bringing back the cup races?

DiPRETE: If the powers that be reject San Diego, our chances are better than 50-50. There are three prime sites: San Diego, and then a close tie between Newport and Hawaii. It's the next leading contender. All seven members of the site committee come from San Diego. Now, that's a hurdle we have to get by.

Edward DiPrete*, 52, a Republican, has been governor since 1984.*

USA TODAY: How have Rhode Island officials dealt with hunger and homelessness?

DiPRETE: We have our share of the homeless and people who need help. I have tackled the problem head on, and I'm sure there are people who will say we should do more. We established line-item appropriations in the budget for the homeless and hungry. I now recommend an additional $10 million allocation.

USA TODAY: Does Rhode Island deserve its image of being a base for organized crime in New England?

DiPRETE: I don't think so. A lot of that was probably exaggerated. As a small state, anything that happened made its way into the statewide media. Whatever may have been true in the '70s and early '80s is not true today.

USA TODAY: Rhode Island elects a governor every two years. Isn't it difficult to get anything accomplished in a two-year term, when you're constantly campaigning?

DiPRETE: I don't think it makes it impossible to get things accomplished. As a matter of fact, in 1985 the media said it was probably the most productive session of the General Assembly in its history.

USA TODAY: What do you do for relaxation?

DiPRETE: I've got a Winnebago motor home. I usually drive down by the ocean. I go frequently, even if it's only for a few hours.

South Carolina

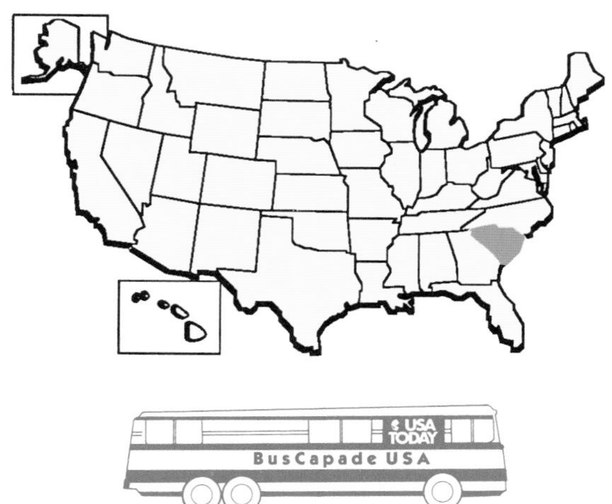

Visited: Aug. 24-26, 1987
Featured in USA TODAY: Aug. 28

"I've always felt that if it goes out with my name on it, it should be the best."

Georgia Smith
Cloth inspector
Laurens, S.C.

South Carolina

Old South, new outlook: Gracious & aggressive

This is deep South country.

First state to secede from the Union, Dec. 20, 1860. The Confederate flag still flies — along with the Stars and Stripes — atop the state Capitol in Columbia (pop. 98,634).

Antebellum ambiance and elegance still reign in Charleston (pop. 67,000). Perhaps the most gracious and refined city in the USA, as it was in Civil War days.

But the future is catching up with the past here:

■ Industrial development has lured big money from West Germany, France, Great Britain. Companies with some foreign ownership have invested more than $3 billion in the last six years, created 21,000 new jobs.

■ The textile industry is on the rebound, led by a strong "Made in the USA" campaign. Employs about 150,000 — almost 10 percent of the state's work force.

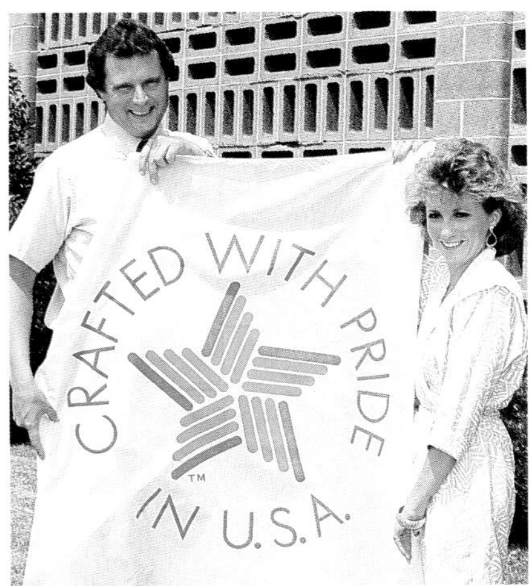

PHILLIPS and GARRETT: Proud and patriotic people.

The area around Greenville (pop. 58,300) is the textile center. Heavy promotion campaign has enlisted such popular personalities as **Bob Hope**, **Barbara Mandrell**, **Don Johnson**.

Receptionist **Phyllis Garrett**, 24, at the Woodside Mills plant in Fountain Inn (pop. 4,226), displays the pride. Plant manager **Bob Phillips**, 36, explains it: "If we don't buy our own products, we're cutting our own throats. We're also patriotic and we're trying to get the rest of the country to feel the same way."

Aggressive business recruitment means manufacturing in chemicals, tires, automobile parts will join textiles as the way of the future. But the agrarian past has a place here.

Tobacco, soybeans, peaches are the three top crops. Farm income is low, holds down the state average:

■ Income per person in 1986 averaged $11,096.

■ The USA average was $14,461.

Many of South Carolina's wealthy have homes or hideaways on its 187 miles of Atlantic coastline. From Myrtle Beach (pop. 26,700) on the north to Hilton Head (pop. 17,622) on the south. Hilton Head also has become a haven for retirees and a golfer's paradise.

Whether well-off or poor, on the farms or in the cities or on the coast, South Carolinians are churchgoers. Heavily Protestant — Southern Baptists, United Methodists and Presbyterians, in that order.

The University of South Carolina in Columbia is promoting a year of "religious awareness." Has brought in the archbishop of Canterbury, leading Jewish rabbis, the head of the Greek Orthodox Church.

The climax comes Sept. 11 when **Pope John Paul II** will fill 72,400-seat William-Brice Stadium. Even though fewer than 2 percent of residents are members of the Catholic Church, the state is united in pride over the visit.

In recent months, much of South Carolina's — and the USA's — awareness of and attention to spiritual life has been focused on PTL's **Jim Bakker** and wife, **Tammy**.

Critics of the PTL say it stands for "Pass The Loot," not "Praise The Lord," as Bakker originally labeled it. The PTL's Heritage USA, at Fort Mill (pop. 4,162), has sharply divided detractors and defenders.

Gov. **Carroll Campbell Jr.**, 47, first-term Republican, is outspoken on the issue: "I think it's caused people to examine things and to understand you don't buy heaven."

But he hastens to add: "South Carolina has much more to offer than Jimmy Bakker or **Donna Rice** or **Rita Jenrette**. Those things just grab the headlines. I don't think they hurt our image particularly."

HARDISTER: A dedicated defender of PTL and Heritage USA complex.

The PTL, Heritage USA and the Bakkers have their staunch supporters. Among them are club executive **Don Hardister Jr.**, 36, and **Millie Freeman**, 51, sales clerk. She still does a brisk sale of Tammy Faye cosmetics.

Says Millie: "We try to stay beautiful for the Lord. He wants his people to have the best. Tammy believes that and so do I. I don't think the Lord wants you to look haggard."

That's Plain Talk from South Carolina.

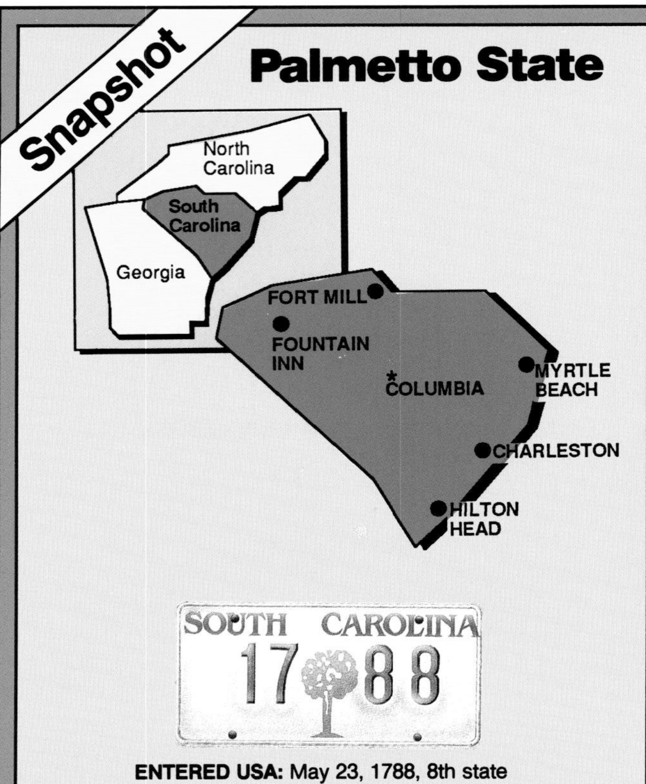

ENTERED USA: May 23, 1788, 8th state

MOTTO: While I breathe, I hope
POPULATION: 3,378,000; rank, 24th
LARGEST CITY: Columbia, pop. 98,634
CAPITAL: Columbia
LAND: 30,203 square miles; rank, 40th
POPULATION DENSITY: 111.8 per square mile; rank, 20th
RACIAL MIX: 68.8% white; 30.4% black; 0.4% Asian and Pacific islanders. Hispanic heritage: 1.1%.

Uniquely S.C.

SERVING TIME: People go to jail voluntarily at Pickens. The 1890s jail is built like a small castle and now houses county history and art museums.

ALL ABOARD: The first USA steam locomotive used for passenger service, "The Best Friend," was built for the South Carolina Railroad in 1830. It was the first train to carry U.S. Mail.

CENTER STAGE: Charleston's Dock Street Theatre, built in 1736, was the USA's first building devoted solely to theatrical productions. First play: "The Recruiting Officer."

READ ON: In 1698, South Carolina offered the first free library in the USA, in what is now Charleston.

SCARY TALES: Georgetown County is known as the "Ghost Capital of the South," with more than 30 ghostly legends, including the Pawleys Island specter, "The Gray Man."

Jody Taylor, 35
Peach farmer
Lexington

"I love to see the peach trees blossom in the orchard. It's somewhat in my blood. My father grew peaches before me. We eat them every way you can eat them. I love them in daiquiris, ice cream, pies."

John Farrell, 25
Assistant golf pro
Hilton Head Island

"Hilton Head is a golfer's paradise. There are 21 championship golf courses on one island. For a golf professional, this is the ideal place to be."

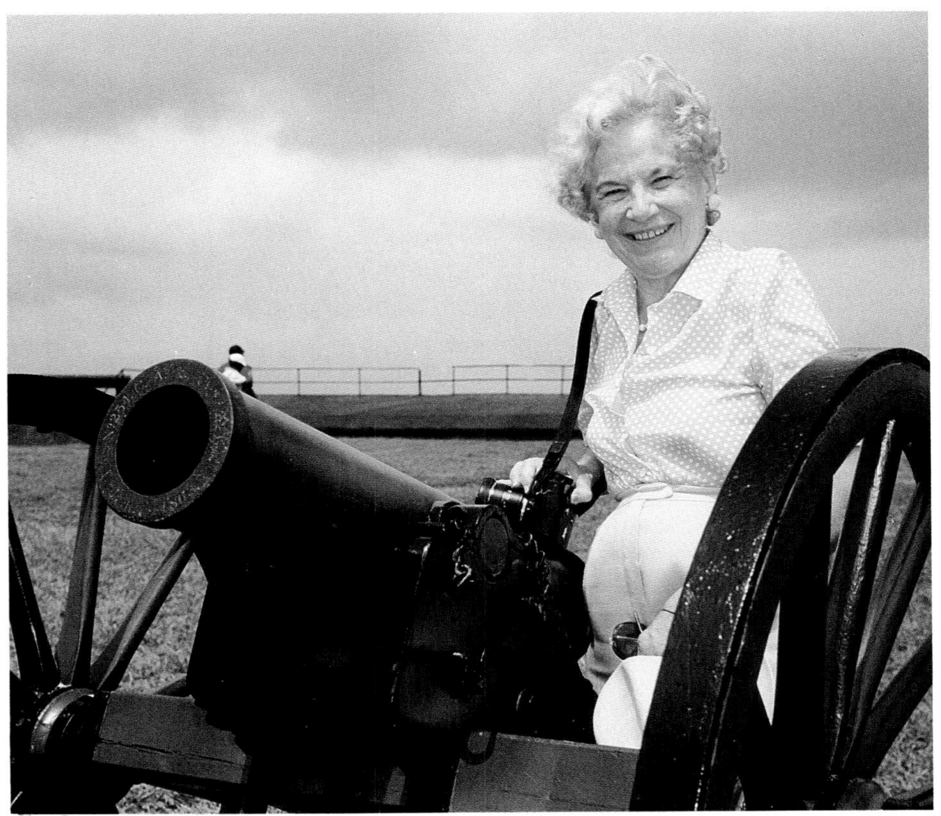

Voices
of South Carolina

Jean Pearce, 63
Retired
Charleston

"I'm a great admirer of the past, but I think we should learn from it. I think what our forefathers accomplished was inspirational — their trials and tribulations. I've been here 41 years, but I'm not a real Charlestonian. You have to be born here, and your daddy has to be born here, and your granddaddy."

Jerman Disasa, 38
University administrator
Columbia

"In Columbia, people are trying to step into the future, yet respect the past. The university is coming out of its Deep South concept to a real international reputation. We're working toward the future, targeting the year 2000. Students are learning hi-tech studies, getting a more diversified education."

Georgia Smith, 55
Cloth inspector
Laurens

"Our material winds up as surgical bandages, casket linings. We usually don't get complaints from those customers. I've always felt that if it goes out with my name on it, it should be the best. Most textile mill workers check for 'Made in the USA' labels on everything. I even have a car made in this country."

Bob Cohen, 35
Assistant manager
of cable company
Lexington

"The work ethic here is unbelievable. One day, I showed up at work and sitting on my desk was a petition signed by every employee. It said, 'We request not to receive the annual pay increase until business improves.' I couldn't believe it. It's nice to come to a community that's concerned with your success."

Ulla McPherson, 28
Homemaker
Charleston

"I came to Charleston from Sweden 10 years ago. I married into a family that was involved in the Civil War, as most people were. They were all officers on the right side. People here still talk about the Civil War. They don't talk about it in hatred, but as a vital part of their history."

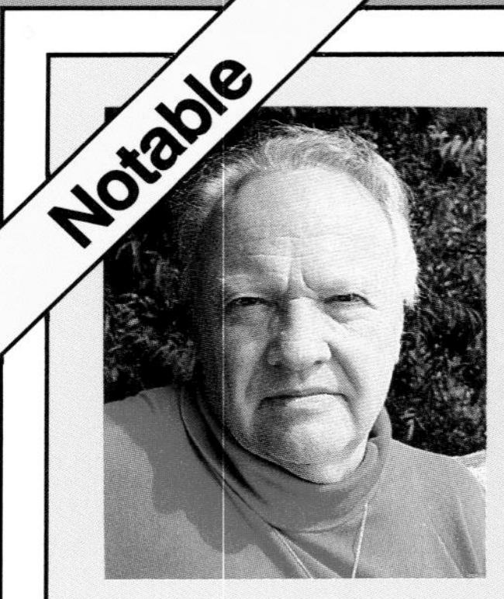

James Dickey, 64, is a novelist, poet, and screenwriter. Dickey grew up in Atlanta, Ga., and moved to Columbia, S.C., to teach at the University of South Carolina. His best-known work is Deliverance, *later made into a movie.*

Southerners know all of their cousins

USA TODAY: Why did you move to South Carolina?

DICKEY: I had been at the Library of Congress in Washington for two years as poetry consultant, and a friend asked me to come down here and give the university a look. I liked what I saw. I'm a Southerner, and I hadn't lived in the South for a while.

USA TODAY: What was your first impression of South Carolina?

DICKEY: The heat — it's very hot here, and humid. And the luxurious vegetation. The soil here will grow anything. There were lots of flowers and birds.

USA TODAY: How would you characterize the people?

DICKEY: They have a combination of old aristocracy here and a lot of people who are agrarian. South Carolina is not a very wealthy state; per capita income is kind of low here. We're trying to do something about that.

USA TODAY: How do you see Columbia?

DICKEY: Columbia's about halfway between the ocean and the mountains. I have a second home at Pawleys Island, right on the Atlantic Ocean. It has the best beach I ever saw.

USA TODAY: Do you also go to the mountains?

DICKEY: We have eight mountain counties here, and I love Appalachia and Appalachian people.

USA TODAY: What about Appalachia's poverty?

DICKEY: There's plenty of that, but they've got their pride, they've got their music, they've got their folkways. It's unique.

USA TODAY: What are the South's charms?

DICKEY: The traditionalism, the sense of past. I particularly like the cooking. Fried chicken is a very great contribution to world culture.

USA TODAY: Are family ties strong here?

DICKEY: When I went into the service in 1942, I was shocked to be in a platoon with a lot of Northern boys who didn't even know who their first cousins were. I sure know who mine are — all the way down to the third cousins. I don't have to *like* 'em all, but they're all blood kin, and that's the difference.

Topic: SOUTH CAROLINA

Our climate, workers attract foreign firms

USA TODAY: We've never seen so much "Buy USA" sentiment in a state. Why is that?

CAMPBELL: The textile industry mounted a major campaign to encourage people to buy USA, to recognize that their jobs are affected by their neighbors' purchasing habits.

USA TODAY: Is there a conflict between "Buy USA" and the search for foreign firms?

CAMPBELL: They make it in the USA. Many companies we consider to be USA companies are part of international conglomerates. Companies like Electrolux AB of Sweden that own subsidiaries operating as American companies like White Consolidated Industries Inc. — we've been very successful in recruiting them.

USA TODAY: How is the economy in Columbia, the state capital, doing?

CAMPBELL: Columbia has had a recession-proof economy. It's an economy based on government and the university. We have Fort Jackson here and the University of South Carolina. Columbia is growing — becoming a true capital city.

USA TODAY: Who are your competitors in recruiting?

CAMPBELL: It's regional. All of the foreign people coming into the USA — Japanese, Koreans, Germans, British — look at the United States objectively. They say, where do we need to go in the marketplace to be competitive? If you use that as the single criterion for location, they all look to the Southeast first.

USA TODAY: What do they see as the advantages?

CAMPBELL: We don't have major labor problems; we don't have a harsh environment where you lose work days to the weather. We've got a lot of water. We attracted the Michelin Corp. Germany has just announced expansions of its two facilities here.

USA TODAY: Although Georgia is known as the Peach State, South Carolina grows more peaches.

Carroll Campbell Jr., 47, a Republican, was elected governor last year. Campbell is a former U.S. representative and state legislator.

CAMPBELL: We have a very strong peach and apple market. For the first time in several years, we've got a decent crop. We had a disastrous drought last year. We are diversifying our agricultural base.

USA TODAY: Segregated private clubs have been in the news here. What should the state's role be in this issue?

CAMPBELL: First, I found out that the state was subsidizing employee use of clubs, and I stopped that. To support segregated clubs with taxpayers' funds is absolutely wrong. However, where there's no government involved, people have a right to associate any way they want to.

USA TODAY: The Confederate flag still flies atop the Capitol. Is that controversial?

CAMPBELL: It's not a major issue. It flies by resolution of the General Assembly. Unfortunately, it polarizes along racial lines, but it's not something that comes up very often.

USA TODAY: What has the Jim and Tammy Bakker episode done for religion in the Carolinas?

CAMPBELL: It's done a lot to hurt the TV ministers. But it's probably restored support for mainstream beliefs. Rev. Billy Graham's popularity actually increased. He's a great leader.

South Dakota

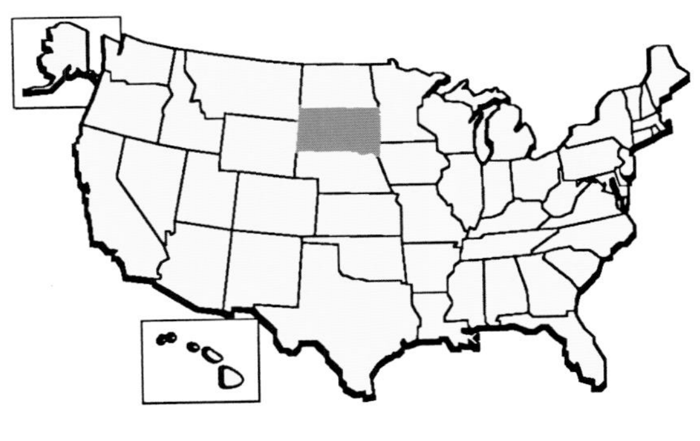

Visited: June 17-20, 1987
Featured in USA TODAY: June 22

"We took a one-room drugstore and built it into the largest drugstore in the world, bringing in $5.2 million a year. But we still serve a 5-cent cup of coffee."

Bill Hustead
President, Wall Drug
Wall, S.D.

South Dakota

Open letter to Mom: You CAN go home

*USA TODAY Founder **Al Neuharth** was in his native South Dakota last week, 28th state on the BusCapade. His father, **Daniel**, died there after a farm accident in 1926, when Al was two. His mother, **Christina**, died in 1979 at age 86.*

* * *

Dear Mom,

Your ears must have been burning this weekend. Dad's too.

I went back to Eureka. Saw hundreds of aunts and uncles and cousins and friends. You know how they love to jabber. They tattled about some things you never told me.

1915 WEDDING: They danced all night.

Said you and Dad drank and danced nearly all night at your wedding in 1915. Sounded pretty wild. To think he was only 20 and you just 22.

You're probably surprised I was back in Eureka. First time in 34 years. You and I used to argue about my going back with you. Wish I had. But I told you **Thomas Wolfe** said *You Can't Go Home Again.* I remember you spit out that you didn't know who Thomas Wolfe was and you didn't care what he said. You were right. He was wrong. So was I.

Eureka had its Centennial celebration. 100 years old with 1,349 people. 63 years ago when I was born there it had 1,228. Everybody relived the old frontier days:

■ A lot of the men grew beards. Brother **Walter** had one of the wildest-looking ones. Came back from California.

■ Most of the ladies wore long, old-fashioned gowns. **Aunt Hulda** had one of the fanciest ones. She and **Julius** still live on that 2,000-acre farm east of town.

I made the talk at the big reunion at the high school gym. Over 1,100 people were packed in. Reminded me of when I won the 5th grade speaking contest in 1934. You always said I hammed it up too much when I spoke. But they gave me a standing ovation.

I told them about my secret 4th grade crush on **Adelaide Bjertness**. She was in the audience and stood up and waved. Everybody cheered. She's still cute. Of course, she's married.

We went out to the house where we lived. **Rudy Hager** lives there now. Keeps it nice and neat. But he painted it pink. You wouldn't like that. You always said a house should be white and clean looking.

At night, **Uncle Richard** had a party at his house for all the Neuharths. About 150, ages one to 83.

Uncle **Art**'s 75. He has to have an oxygen tank with him to help him breathe. But it doesn't bother him too much. He just sat in his chair and everyone shot the breeze with him.

The twins, **Uncle Elmer** and **Aunt Lillian**, are 68. Elmer runs the Eureka municipal liquor store. Knows how much and what everybody in town drinks. He'd make a good gossip columnist for the newspaper.

Your grandchildren **Dan** and **Jan** were with me. She's quit practicing law and is a farmer now, like Dad was. Except hers is a trendy horse farm called Paper Chase in Middleburg, Va. Dan is in school — again — in San Francisco. He has a bachelors, a masters in journalism and is working on a graduate degree in psychology. Guess he wants to figure out what makes the world work. You did that with a 3rd grade education.

We went to Alpena to yours and Dad's graves. Brought some flowers and picked off a few weeds. It's so peaceful on that prairie cemetery. No wonder they named it "Rest Haven."

We came to South Dakota on the USA TODAY BusCapade. You remember that little paper *SoDak Sports* I started in 1952. USA TODAY is like that. Only bigger. Nearly 5 million people read it every day.

It's less than 5 years old and already made money last month. So, we won't have to auction off the typewriters and furniture the way we did when *SoDak Sports* went broke in 1954.

I know USA TODAY isn't available yet where you are. But we are very expansion-minded. So, like you always said: "You never know what's coming next."

Hope you don't mind my sharing this letter with all those people. It won't hurt them to know the two strongest memories I came away with after going back home:

■ Life should be fun. In Eureka or anywhere. You knew that. So you always kidded a lot and made the best of everything, even in the Depression days.

■ Life is finite. You knew that too. So you prepared yourself and us for your death when you were 75. That made your last 11 years peaceful and even more pleasurable.

Thanks for teaching me those things. Say hi to Dad. Love you both. See you one of these years.

Allen

Coyote State

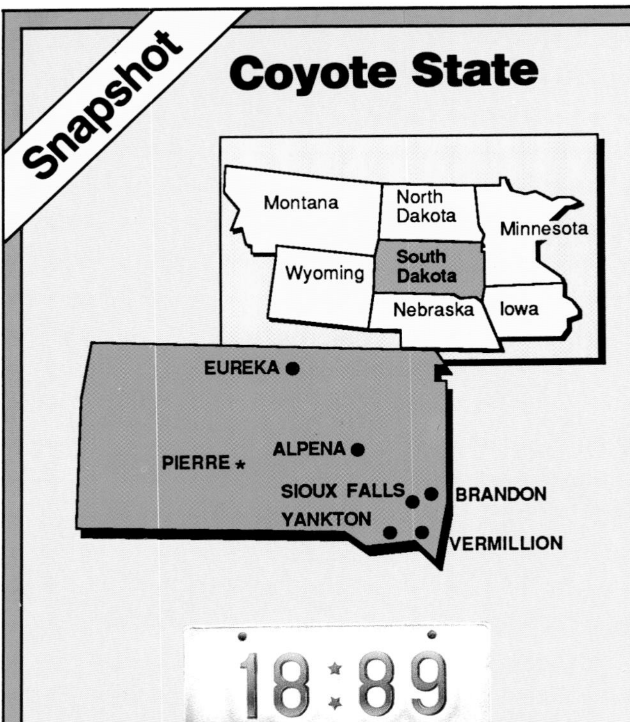

18 89
SOUTH DAKOTA

ENTERED USA: Nov. 2, 1889, 40th state

MOTTO: Under God the people rule
POPULATION: 708,000; rank, 45th
LARGEST CITY: Sioux Falls, pop. 87,611
CAPITAL: Pierre, pop. 12,900
LAND: 75,952 square miles; rank, 16th
POPULATION DENSITY: 9.3 per square mile; rank, 46th
RACIAL MIX: 92.6% white; 6.5% American Indian; 0.3% black; 0.3% Asian and Pacific islanders. Hispanic heritage: 0.6%.

Uniquely S.D.

HEAT WAVE: The world's greatest variance in temperature occurred in Spearfish in 1943 when it went from 4 degrees below zero to 45 above — in two minutes.

GUARANTEED RESERVATIONS: South Dakota has the most "treatied" — federally recognized — Indian reservations in the USA: nine.

GOLDEN OPPORTUNITY: Homestake Gold Mine in Lead is the largest gold mine in the Western Hemisphere. It has processed more than $1 billion worth since 1876. It still leads the USA in production.

IN THE MIDDLE: The geographic center of the USA is 17 miles west of Castle Rock. It moved 6 miles in 1959 when Hawaii became the 50th state.

LITTLE HOUSE ON THE PRAIRIE: Six of Laura Ingalls Wilder's popular children's books were based on her years in DeSmet, S.D.

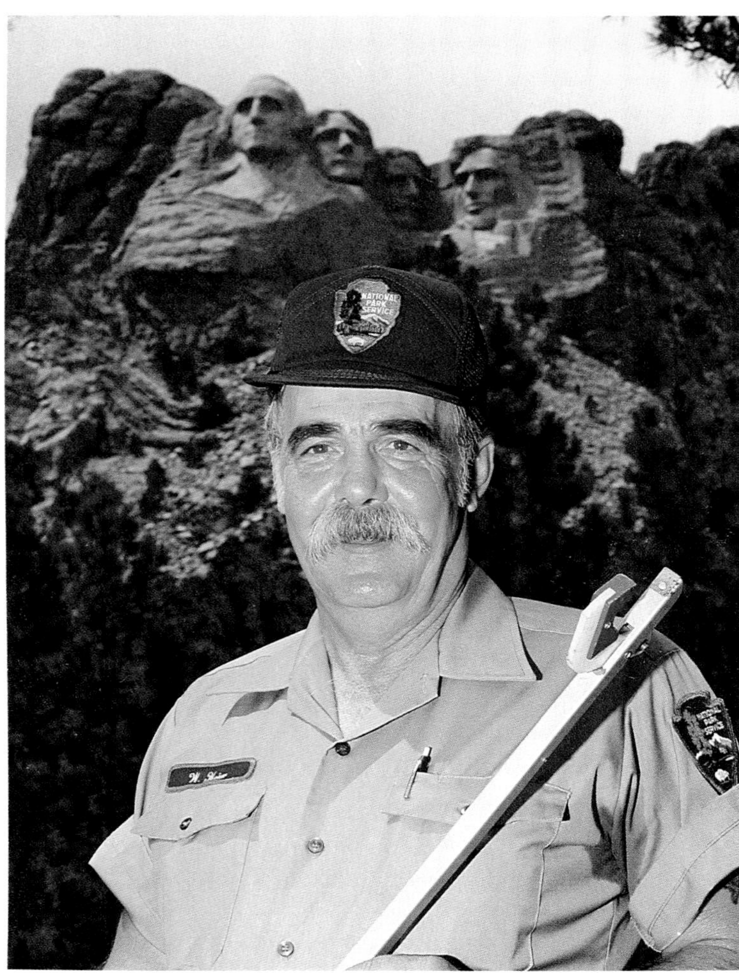

Wayne Heiar, 53
Maintenance worker
Keystone

"It's a spectacular sight. I never get tired of seeing it. I don't just see four presidents' faces, I see what they did for the country: Washington, freedom; Jefferson, the Constitution; Lincoln, slavery freedom; and Roosevelt, go forward."

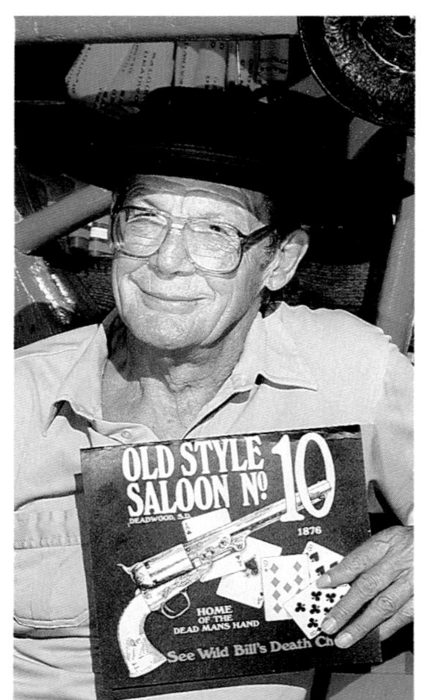

Lew Keehn, 70
Saloon owner
Deadwood

"People come here because of Wild Bill and Calamity Jane. That history in this place is known from all over the world. Wild Bill consumed his share of booze and it's said that every morning, he'd slip on pants and shoes and scoot into this saloon. Calamity Jane was tough, but with a big heart."

Voices
of South Dakota

Ruth Ziolkowski, 61
Chairman, Crazy Horse
Memorial Foundation
Custer

"Chief Henry Standing Bear wrote to my husband, Korczack, asking him to build a monument so the white man would know the red man had heroes, too. We're carrying out his dream."

Burton Ode, 64
Farmer
Brandon

"The first thing the pioneers did when they got here was to build a house. Next they built a church and a school. I think that those priorities have carried through all these years. Home, church and school are still the most important things. They're basic. That's what it's all about."

Kathy Murphy, 20
Student
Yankton

"Farming is really important to a lot of people here. Some of my relatives had to declare bankruptcy. They thought they could make it work, but they went under. They ended up moving in with some other relatives. People are really giving."

Claricie Collins, 60
Alumni director
University
Of South Dakota
Vermillion

"Too often, we sell our resources short in South Dakota. I think people apologize for being from South Dakota at times. They apologize when their kids go to college in South Dakota, when they could have gone to a more prestigious school in the East or West. But I doubt very much if they'd get an education any better."

Bill Hustead, 59
President, Wall Drug
Wall

"We took a one-room drug store and built it into the largest drug store in the world, bringing in $5.2 million a year. But we still serve a 5-cent cup of coffee. We wanted to be known as more than 'that little store with all the crazy signs.' "

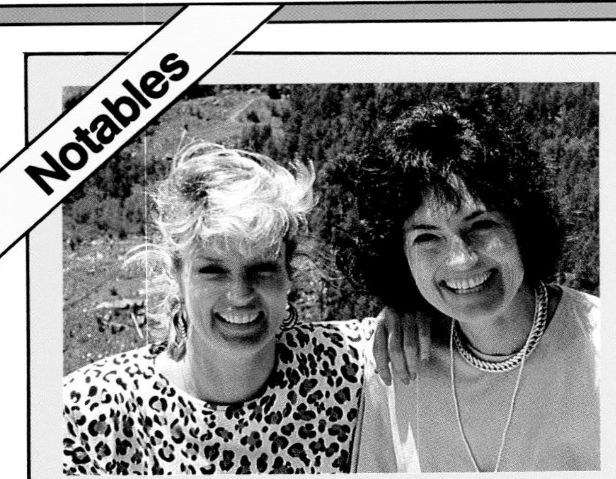

Mary Hart (left), 35, and Meredith Brokaw, 46, after traveling up Crazy Horse Mountain on the USA TODAY BusCapade. Both are former English teachers and Miss South Dakotas. Hart is Entertainment Tonight *hostess, and Brokaw, married to* NBC Nightly News *anchor Tom Brokaw, owns four Penny Whistle Toy boutiques in the New York area.*

Here, it's easy to feel relaxed and down home

USA TODAY: When you come back to South Dakota are you treated as celebrities?

BROKAW: South Dakota prevents me from feeling like a celebrity. It's too easy to feel really relaxed and down home and one of the people here. There's a real sense of being yourself and yet not being too different from everybody else around you.

HART: Especially in our family you could never get too big of a head because you'd get cut right down to size. I don't know whether that's indigenous of the area, but there's something about being real that's important.

USA TODAY: You've been on a whirlwind tour of the Black Hills. Do memories sweep back?

HART: A lot. I was 2 years old when we lived here, and I remember some of our first family vacations were coming up to the Black Hills and seeing the Badlands and remembering at a very early age being awestruck by Mount Rushmore. Loving the buffalo, tasting my first buffalo burger, then moving to Europe and trying to explain to Scandinavians that no, indeed, the cowboys and the Indians were not still shooting at one another in the streets.

USA TODAY: What kind of reaction do you get when you tell people you are from South Dakota?

BROKAW: This has probably happened to you, Mary, but it constantly amazes me. I live in New York City, which supposedly contains the most sophisticated people in the world, yet time after time I'm asked, "Where are you from? I can tell you don't have a New York accent." I say South Dakota, to which they reply, "Gosh, I've never met anyone from South Dakota!"

HART: All the time! It's like E.T., the extraterrestrial. It's alien to them. It's like saying you're from Mars. I wear green ears on weekends.

Topic: SOUTH DAKOTA

We'll take some risks to make progress

USA TODAY: What would you like South Dakota's image to be?

MICKELSON: We're working very hard on image and self-perception. My goal is to diversify our economy. We're the most agricultural state in the nation. In the last several years, when the agricultural economy has been hurting, it has provided some real challenges.

USA TODAY: Is that a continuation of former Gov. William Janklow's work?

MICKELSON: In many ways, he kicked the state in the pants to ensure we were flexible in legislation, which resulted in Citibank, and in putting South Dakota on the map, by being a very strong advocate for rural America. My approach also recognizes that we need additional tools.

USA TODAY: Such as?

MICKELSON: I am a big believer in developing higher education. We get less research and development money in this state than the U.S. territories do. I was happy that the Legislature agreed that we needed to put money in that.

USA TODAY: Does diversification mean the family farm is a thing of the past?

MICKELSON: No, but the definition of the family farm is changing. You can't buy a $70,000 tractor anymore and, with today's prices, make it pay off by farming a quarter section of land. So the size of the farms is increasing, but it's never going to be a thing of the past. I'm very aggressively seeking some markets for our agricultural producers in terms of processing and different ways of producing. We're going to do some things differently. We have always been afraid to take some risks in this state, and I'm going to take some risks in the hope that we will be able to make some progress.

USA TODAY: In the years since Wounded Knee, have relations improved between the Indians and the state?

MICKELSON: There has been an improvement. I have a new

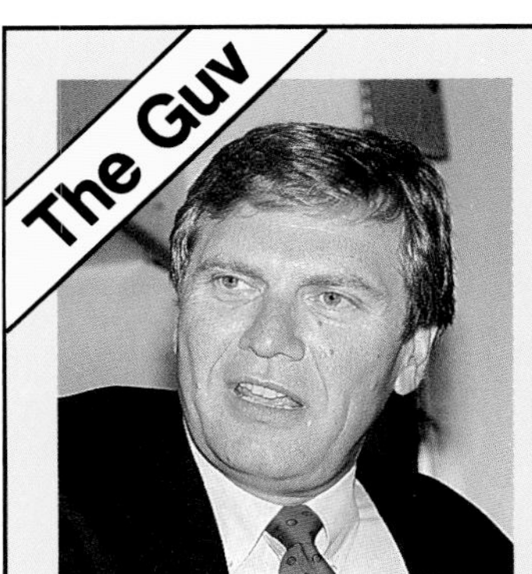

George Mickelson, 46, a Republican, was elected governor of South Dakota last year. His father, George T. Mickelson, was the 18th governor of South Dakota from 1947-1951.

division of economic development, which is directed solely toward the Indian reservation employment. They don't even have retail establishments, let alone manufacturing or something which holds some potential. So we're starting from absolutely square one.

USA TODAY: Your father was governor 40 years ago. Are you doing anything differently as a father and a governor?

MICKELSON: I'm doing some things differently. My dad's parents homesteaded in Walworth County in 1884. They were married when they were 16, had 10 kids, worked themselves to death, and one day laid down and died. Work was his whole life. As a result of growing up while he was attorney general and governor, I made a conscious decision that I was going to do the Boy Scouts and fish and hunt with my kids.

USA TODAY: How do you manage with such a busy schedule?

MICKELSON: I schedule 10 days in a row in every month that, no matter how many hours there are in a day, I know I'm going to be home for supper. I want to take Sundays off, and I've stuck close to that schedule. I've got a 15-year-old son who very much likes me. I want him to continue liking me.

Tennessee

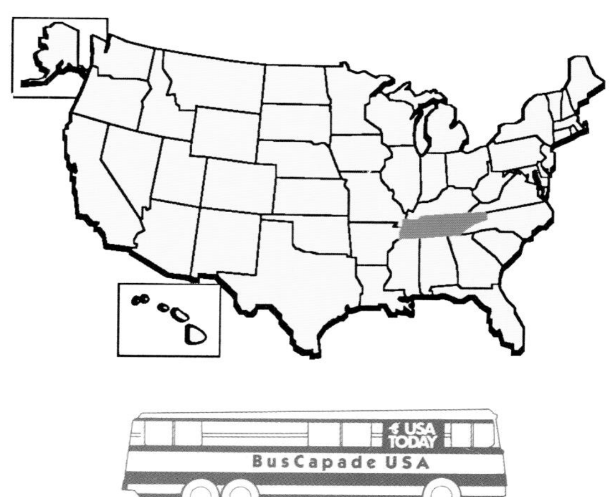

Visited: April 7-9, 1987
Featured in USA TODAY: April 10

"Tennessee is like a new car — you want to show it off."

Joan Hughes
Receptionist
Spring Hill, Tenn.

Tennessee

Teachers and kids; politics and the prez

A state that has given the USA more than its share of presidents — three of 39 — is eager to offer up another.

The state in which New York multi-millionaire **Cornelius Vanderbilt** chose to fund a prestigious private university in 1873 is debating in 1987 how to upgrade sub-par public education for its young.

Education and politics are the two most talked about topics in Tennessee. There are others of intense interest, like:

WILLIAMS: Country music entertainer of the year.

■ Music. The entire state sang when **Hank Williams Jr.** was named entertainer of the year by the Academy of Country Music in an NBC telecast Monday night.

Williams grew up in Nashville (pop. 462,450). He rebelled against the Nashville establishment that idolized his father, grew long hair and developed his own rowdy and raucous style of music. But he told the academy audience, "I'm as gentle as a lamb and just as sweet as sugar." The leader of the establishment, Gov. **Ned McWherter**, responded: "He's my favorite country music performer."

■ Jobs and industry. In Spring Hill (pop. 989), south of Nashville, blasts and bulldozers are clearing more than 2,200 acres for a new General Motors Saturn auto plant.

Some folks hate to see the farmland flattened. But most agree with **Wilson Herbert**, 62, owner of Herbert's Bar-B-Q in nearby Franklin (pop. 12,407). "This is our time to grow," he says.

■ Tourism. In Memphis (pop. 648,399), Graceland still draws 500,000 **Elvis Presley** fans annually, 10 years after his death. In Jackson (pop. 49,131), folk-hero worshipers still look to the house where legendary railroader **Casey Jones** lived. In East Tennessee, just 30 miles from Knoxville in Pigeon Forge, **Dolly Parton**'s Dollywood soon will be a big tourist bus-stopper.

Back to the two top topics:

■ Political interest, always hot here, boiled over this week. U.S. Sen. **Al Gore Jr.**, 39, said he would announce by this weekend whether to seek the 1988 Democratic presidential nomination. "Al Gore for President" buttons burst forth immediately.

Tennesseans adore Gore. In fact, they love most of their politicians. Party lines are hazy. You are a Tennessean first, a Republican or Democrat second.

The Volunteer State gave us presidents **Andrew Jackson**, **James Polk** and **Andrew Johnson**. It is eager for another — of either party.

"I think the odds are only 36-1 that the 1988 presidential election will be an all-Tennessee match. Al Gore for the Democrats and **Howard Baker** (Reagan's White House chief of staff) for the Republicans," says perennial political prognosticator **John Jay Hooker**.

GORE: Democratic prospect.

BAKER: GOP prospect.

Hooker himself ran twice unsuccessfully for governor.

He helped start Minnie Pearl Chicken. Now, he's huckstering a "Hooker's Hamburgers" stand on wheels.

■ A $68 million "Master Teacher Program" based on merit was adopted in 1984. Former Gov. **Lamar Alexander** was the architect. But public school teacher salaries still are near the bottom, nationally.

Now, the politically powerful Tennessee Education Association wants a 25 percent boost in minimum starting salaries — from $14,700 to $18,500. Gov. McWherter is sympathetic, but says "Be patient." Maybe next year. TEA President **Velma Lois Jones**, 56, is impatient. "They've been taking bites out of the teacher's apple and all that's left is the core," Jones says. She and hundreds of others sported "apple core" buttons during Tuesday's Teacher Unity Day at the state Capitol.

JONES: President of Tennessee Education Association.

Students are helping the teachers' campaign. Says **Mandy Schackelford**, 15, an 8th-grader at Bolivar Junior High: "Teachers should get paid more. I know. My mom's a teacher." Mandy says the low salaries are why she doesn't want to be a teacher. "I want to be a model. They definitely get paid more."

That's Plain Talk from Tennessee.

Snapshot

Volunteer State

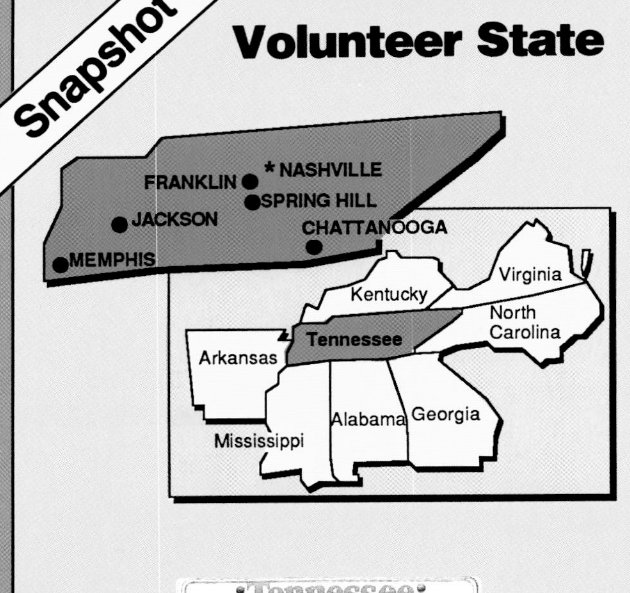

Tennessee
1796
Volunteer State

ENTERED USA: June 1, 1796, 16th state

MOTTO: Tennessee — America at its best!
POPULATION: 4,803,000; rank, 16th
LARGEST CITY: Memphis, pop. 648,399
CAPITAL: Nashville, pop. 462,450
LAND: 41,155 square miles; rank, 34th
POPULATION DENSITY: 116.7 per square mile; rank, 18th
RACIAL MIX: 83.5% white; 15.8% black; 0.3% Asian and Pacific islanders. Hispanic heritage: 0.7%.

Uniquely Tenn.

FRONTIER FOLKLORE: Davy Crockett was not "born on a mountaintop in Tennessee" as the song says. He was born on the banks of Limestone Creek near Greenville.

LIQUOR LICENSE: In 1866, the Jack Daniel Distillery at Lynchburg became the USA's first registered distillery. It's located in a county where liquor can't be bought or sold.

COKE IS IT: Coca-Cola was first bottled in 1899 at a plant on Patten Parkway in Chattanooga. Two Chattanooga businessmen purchased the bottling rights to the fountain drink for $1.

SCENIC VIEW: Lookout Mountain at Chattanooga is the only place in the USA where seven states can be seen from one spot — Alabama, Georgia, Kentucky, North Carolina, South Carolina, Tennessee and Virginia.

LION'S ROAR: The original MGM lion was a resident of the Memphis Zoo.

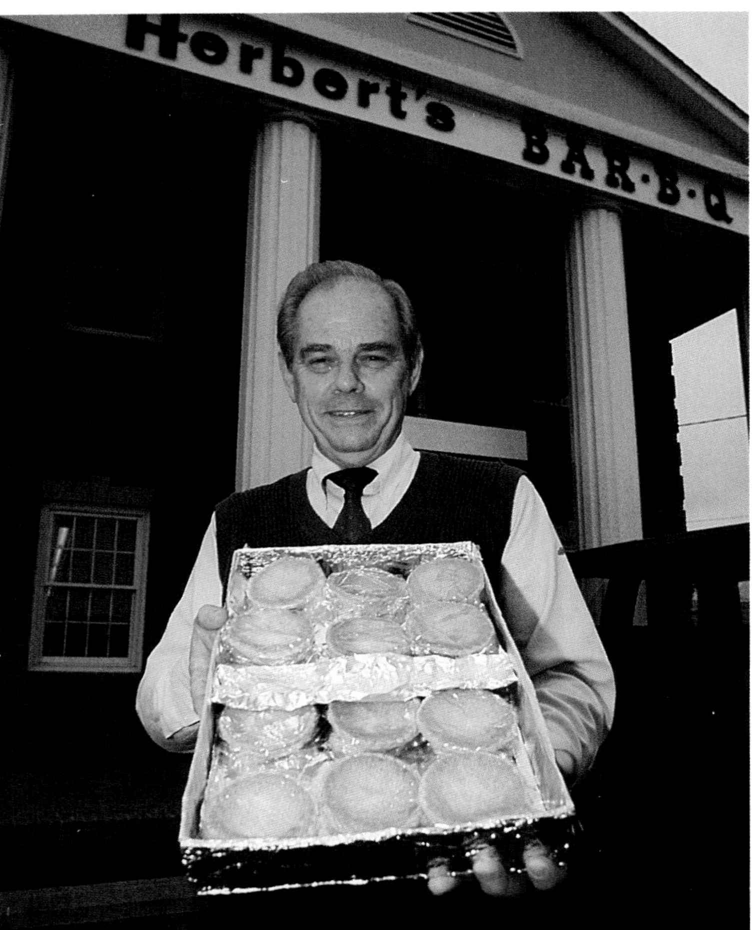

Wilson Herbert, 62
Owner, barbecue restaurant
Franklin

"Franklin is an historical town. We have an old country square that has an old country Southern charm that brings people in here. Years later, they come back and live here. It's the magnet that brings them back. This entire area in the Nashville region is growing. It's a lot different. Before you could let your kids ride bicycles out on the street. Now you just don't see much of that anymore. Some things are better and some things you don't want to change."

Dianne Frances Bradley, 33
Construction worker
Spring Hill

"Tennessee has great fishing. I love to fish down on the Tennessee River. I catch bass and catfish. I use Tennessee crickets for bait. Not many women get to do construction work. It's a challenge. It takes guts. You have to put up with the men and the weather."

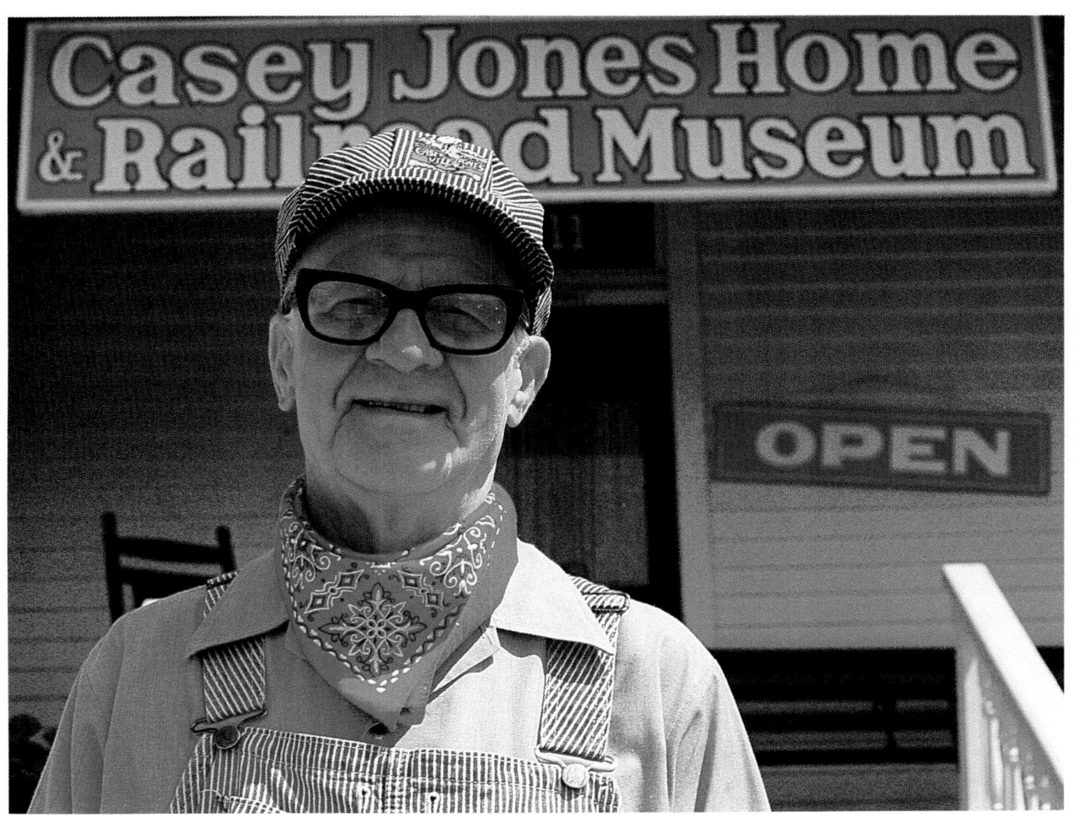

Voices
of Tennessee

James C. Barlow, 77
Assistant museum director
Jackson

"I like the good people. They're friendly; everybody enjoys life. We've got the Smokey Mountains. The children like the mountains and we like the flat country of West Tennessee. I wouldn't want to live anyplace else."

Tom Walton, 36
Waiter
Nashville

"If you can't find it in Nashville, you shouldn't be looking for it."

Joan Hughes, 27
Receptionist
Spring Hill

"I get to meet a lot of different people. My job as a receptionist may be the only link between our company and the public. I try to make them feel comfortable. There's so much I like in Tennessee that I don't think about it 'cause it's home. Tennessee is like a new car — you want to show it off."

Marion Cross, 35
Teacher
Bolivar

"You need good teachers in order to have good classrooms. No classroom is better than its teachers. I won't change jobs because of the money. I'll just do what I can within the system to change it."

Hedge Burt, 19
Valet parker
Nashville

"Why does everybody stereotype Nashville? I mean, not everybody is a hillbilly who is a country music fan. I've never seen the Country Music Hall of Fame and neither have any of my friends. Tennessee's economy is really growing. They say we'll be the next Atlanta with all the new corporations moving in."

Tammy Wynette, 44, lives in Nashville. She signed her first record contract in 1966. She is the "First Lady of Country Music," with a string of hits including D-I-V-O-R-C-E *and* Stand By Your Man *(also the title of her autobiography).*

Tennessee people are very down to earth

USA TODAY: You've lived in Tennessee 21 years, and you've toured everywhere. What sets Tennessee apart?

WYNETTE: I was born in Mississippi and raised in Alabama. And Tennessee to me is an awful lot like where I came from. The trees, the land, everything is so much like what I was used to where I was born. And it's where the music is that is my life. I feel very lucky to do what I've wanted to do all my life.

USA TODAY: How would you describe Tennesseans?

WYNETTE: Very down-to-earth people. Very humble people. They're the salt of the earth.

USA TODAY: Is it easier for a woman in the music business now than when you started?

WYNETTE: I think it's harder. There were so few of us in the beginning, we didn't have the competition that the country artists have now. I wouldn't want to start now. The traveling situation is much easier — I traveled in a car with three kids for years, eating peanut butter and jelly sandwiches on the side of the road.

USA TODAY: When you listen to music purely for pleasure, whose albums do you listen to?

WYNETTE: Well, I love Merle Haggard. I love George Jones. I think Reba McEntire's wonderful. But I also like Gladys Knight and the Pips! I like Ray Charles, I love Lou Rawls. Other than country music, rhythm and blues would be my favorite.

USA TODAY: You're recording a new album. How many have you made now?

WYNETTE: I'm real excited about it. This would be 50 or 51. And with the albums that I've had released in foreign countries, I've got about 100 out.

USA TODAY: You've had a lot of health problems recently.

WYNETTE: I went to the Betty Ford Center because I had been dependent on pain pills for four years, because of an operation I had. While there, I had to have surgery all over again.

USA TODAY: How are you doing now?

WYNETTE: I'm starting back to work. Most of the pain's gone. I feel wonderful, so I'm not pushing it.

Topic: TENNESSEE

Progress in education has been tremendous

USA TODAY: What has the new Saturn plant meant to Tennessee's economy?

McWHERTER: It's important to us. We're very proud that a corporation like General Motors would pick Tennessee. Spring Hill's an excellent location. Nissan is a very important ingredient of our economy. They're working about 3,300 people.

USA TODAY: Tennessee has a lot of industry that other people want, but there is also some — such as the proposed nuclear waste storage depot, known as the monitored retrievable storage facility or MRS — which many people don't want.

McWHERTER: That's true, including the governor.

USA TODAY: What, if anything, can be done to enforce your opposition to it?

McWHERTER: I've notified the federal government that we would veto MRS coming to Tennessee. The majority of the legislature feels the same way.

USA TODAY: Why are you opposed to an MRS?

McWHERTER: Some of us just can't understand why we need a temporary site in Tennessee, without a permanent site designated out West. Temporary becomes permanent in many cases. I've just opposed Tennessee becoming a nuclear storage site, a dumping ground.

USA TODAY: Tennessee became known four years ago as a leader in education reform. This past week, William Bennett, the secretary of education, said education reform is under attack. Is that happening here?

McWHERTER: No. We continue to improve education. Lamar Alexander, the former governor of Tennessee, pioneered some changes. For example, we pioneered a merit pay concept, including the career ladder. We established summer schools for our gifted students. We have a tremendously high dropout rate, so we're going to incorporate the dropout rate and the adult illiteracy programs into our education reform. We'll make a recommendation on that at the next general assembly.

Ned McWherter, 56, a Democrat, was inaugurated in January.

USA TODAY: How about the college level?

McWHERTER: We're perceived as making tremendous progress in higher education. We created centers of excellence, and the legislature complemented that with what we call "chairs of excellence." We funded 73 chairs of excellence to go to our different campuses; they're on a matching basis with the private sector, and the private sector has matched 35 of those thus far.

USA TODAY: In light of Tennessee's long history of debate over religion and the schools, should values and morals based on the Bible be taught in the classrooms?

McWHERTER: Both should be taught. That's my personal belief.

USA TODAY: Do you like country music?

McWHERTER: Yes.

USA TODAY: Is there a country song that typifies your personal style?

McWHERTER: *Just Walk On By, Wait On the Corner*. I really am a country music fan. I come from a rural background. I started listening to the Grand Ole Opry on one of those old Philco radios. So I was raised in a community where maybe there'd be one of those radios, and everybody'd gather on Saturday night, and go to their neighbor's house, and listen to the Grand Ole Opry.

Texas

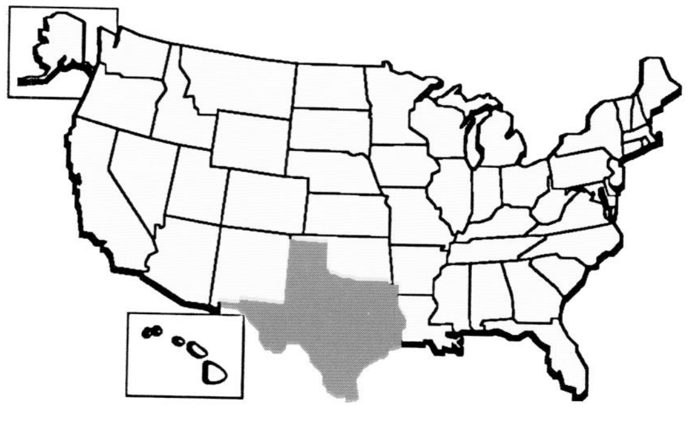

Visited: April 14-17, 1987
Featured in USA TODAY: April 20

"Texans look for tomorrow to be better. Then we try and make it so."

Lady Bird Johnson
Johnson City, Texas

Texas

They brag on the best; worst can't whip 'em

Traditionally, Texans have touted themselves as the best and the biggest. In everything.

But the Lone Star State is not so alone anymore. Many a worker is out of work. Many a millionaire has run out of money. The worst got worse here than elsewhere in 1986:

■ Unemployment over 10 percent, highest of the USA's most-populous states.

■ 32,568 bankruptcy filings, most in the USA.

Says **Lady Bird Johnson**, 74, still the belle of them all here: "Chapter 11 (bankruptcy) has become a way of life." But she adds quickly, "Texans look for tomorrow to be better. Then we try and make it so."

Gov. **Bill Clements** says the "tick up" has started. Statistics bear him out. Unemployment is down from 10 to 8 percent. Oil prices are up from $10.77 to more than $18 a barrel.

The "tick up" is reflected in an upbeat mood. Texans are thinking big again. Here's what some of them told us as our BusCapade rolled across 1,170 miles of Texas highways and byways last week.

■ Austin (pop. 397,001). State capital. Home of 48,000 University of Texas students and the fabled Longhorn football team.

Says UT freshman **Melissa Lotz**, 19: "Even if everybody was broke and dying of the plague, they'd still be proud Texans. I've been saying, 'Hook 'em, Horns' since I was five."

■ Houston (pop. 1,705,697). The biggest city. At nearby San Jacinto Junior College, construction worker-turned-student **Ralph Jolly**, 44, says culture is much more consequential to Texans than are cowboys. His heroes are philosophers.

"Socrates and Aristotle wouldn't fit in Texas, but Plato would. He aspired to ideals, the biggest and best. That's Texas," says Ralph.

■ Tyler (pop. 70,508). "Rose Capital of the World." "The Yellow Rose of Texas" is grown here. So are 400 other varieties — 12 million roses a year. But that's not good enough for **James Ervin**, 27, gardener at the city's 22-acre rose garden.

"We're experimenting and trying to find a black rose. That's an elusive color to breed." But Ervin leaves no doubt that if a black rose is developed it will happen in Texas.

■ Dallas (pop. 974,234). Home of Neiman-Marcus. Says saleswoman **Bea Mazzola**, 35: "Everyone in the country knows what Neiman-Marcus is (22 stores across the USA). But the important thing is it's a Texas store. It started here. We made it famous."

Adds salesclerk **Ezzard Owens**, 23: "Still lots of rich people here. Look outside — Jaguars, Mercedes. **Tony Dorsett** (Dallas Cowboys) and **Mark Aguirre** (Dallas Mavericks) shopped here last week."

■ El Paso (pop. 463,809). Fronts on the Rio Grande. Across the river: Juarez, Mexico. Illegal aliens overrun the area. Population over 60 percent nonwhite. **Roy Glasgow**, 31, a native of Panama, says he's a 100 percent Texan now. He shines shoes at Cielo Vista shopping mall. $3 a shine.

GLASGOW: 'You can do anything you want in Texas,' the Panamanian-turned-Texan says.

"Texas is much more than cowboy hats and cowboy boots. You can do anything you want in Texas," Roy says. His dream: to study real estate and own a real estate company. "We have enough land to even build new cities if the country wants them."

■ Guthrie (pop. 250). Real cowboy country. **Buster McLaury**, 29, is one of 12 cowboys who work the 208,000-acre 6666 Ranch 100 miles north of Abilene, near the Oklahoma border. His three horses are Spider, Jigger and Pedro. He herds and brands cattle, harvests hay, fixes fences, often sleeps by campfire.

Says Buster: "I'd like for one of those weekend honky-tonk Oklahoma cowboys to ride fence with me just one time. He wouldn't last until noontime."

That's Plain Talk from Texas.

SCRATCHED FROM SPACE: The 363-foot-long Saturn V was to have been used on the Apollo XVII moon mission, but was scratched for budgetary reasons. It's now an attraction for the 1.2 million people who visit the Johnson Space Center in Houston each year.

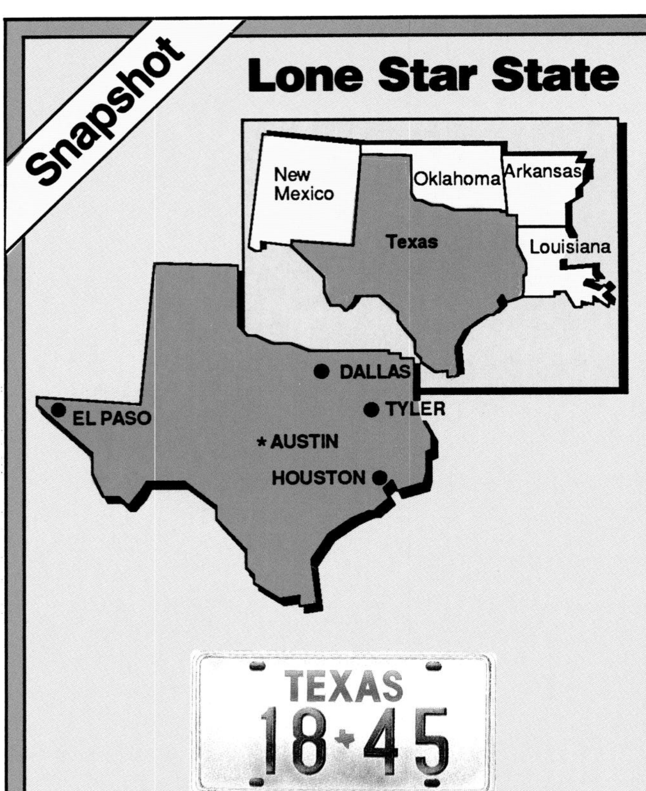

ENTERED USA: Dec. 29, 1845, 28th state

MOTTO: Friendship
POPULATION: 16,682,000; rank, 3rd
LARGEST CITY: Houston, pop. 1,705,697
CAPITAL: Austin, pop. 397,001
LAND: 262,017 square miles; rank, 2nd
POPULATION DENSITY: 63.7 per square mile; rank, 29th
RACIAL MIX: 78.7% white; 12.0% black; 0.8% Asian and Pacific islanders. Hispanic heritage: 21.0%.

Uniquely Texas

PIPELINES: Texas has 202,623 miles of oil and gas pipelines — more than the states of Alaska, California, Hawaii, Oregon, Pennsylvania and Washington combined.

FAVORITE FARE: Texas-style chili is the official state dish.

CAPITOL CAPITAL: The state Capitol in Austin is the only one in the USA that wasn't built with taxpayers' money. Some 3 million acres of land in the Panhandle were traded to the Capitol Freehold Land and Investment Co. in exchange for building the Capitol, completed in 1888.

LATE NEWS: The last battle of the Civil War was fought at Palmito Ranch May 13, 1865, more than a month after Lee's surrender at Appomattox. The Confederates won.

COOL AT LAST: The world's first public air-conditioned building was the First Presbyterian Church at Orange, completed in 1912.

Voices
of Texas

Charlie Dunn, 89
Retired bootmaker
Smithville

"Texas is one of the best places to make boots. There is more of a demand for them in Texas, although we get orders from all over. Texans want boots and they want them to be fitted properly. Most of the people I make boots for have wanted them all their lives. . . . The summers are hot here. It's the kind of heat that can condition you to take the heat in hell."

Janice Pettit, 46
Homemaker
Spring

"Texans are nationalistic. You've heard of the myth: the United States of Texas. Well, they believe it! I've never seen or heard such pride, and they're so loud about it."

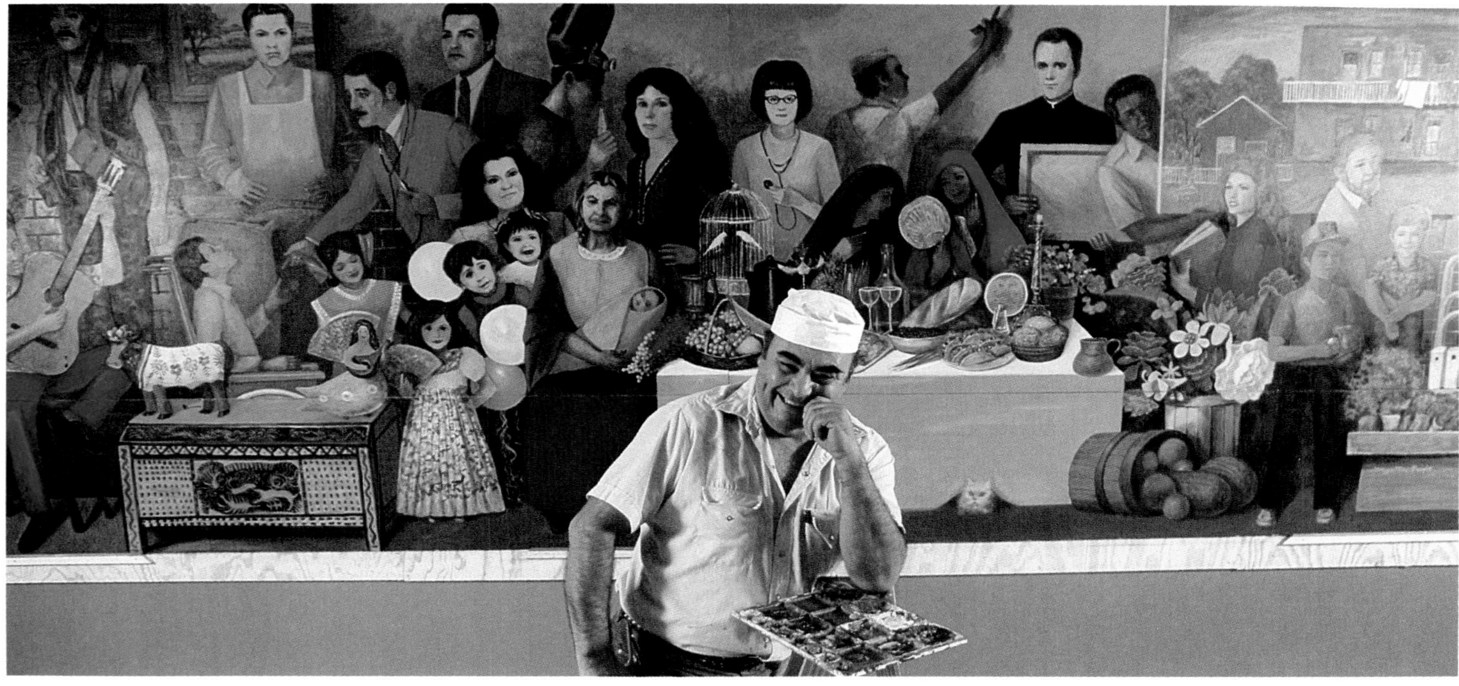

Manuel Acosta, 66
Artist
El Paso

"I painted the La Fe Clinic mural with real people. I wanted neighborhood people to see real people who have done well and achieved. I put in my grandmother, my nephew who served in Vietnam, several lawyers, mothers, all Mexican Americans. All someone here."

Maria Teresa Aranda
Secretary
El Paso

"This is my land. We were here even before the Mayflower. My husband's family dates back to 1850 when the county seat was in San Elizario. History is so vivid here. It's all in our laps."

James Henry, 32
Truck parts retailer
Pasadena

"People's image of Texas comes from cowboy movies, but it doesn't do any harm. We're as down home as anybody. I know nuclear engineers that are as cowboy as I am. There's cowboy in everybody. I define cowboy as honest, hard-working."

Merv Jordan, 45
Mechanic
San Antonio

"In the last couple of years, Houston got just about devastated, but it seems to be starting to grow again slowly. This is the best place I've ever been — you don't have to shovel snow. I left Oregon 2 1/2 years ago. I'm a better Texan than the Texans who were born here because I WANTED to come down here — they were just born here."

Joe Birdwell, 63
Park ranger
Chamizal
National Memorial
El Paso

"We're the closest park to an international bridge. We see it everyday here, the culture, the people, all friendly. Working here just enables me to do the things I've been doing since I was a kid. As a projectionist, I show and see our different cultures."

Lady Bird Johnson, 74, widow of President Lyndon Johnson, lives in Johnson City. She has donated land and money for the National Wildflower Research Center in Austin, Texas.

We try to make tomorrow better

USA TODAY: Texans seem to be optimistic about the future. Is that part of their character?

JOHNSON: Sam Rayburn used to say, "It's a great big 18-year-old boy, just eating and growing." We do feel the work ethic is alive and kicking here. Texans look for tomorrow to be better. Then we try and make it so.

USA TODAY: You're working these days with the National Wildflower Research Center. What are the center's goals?

JOHNSON: To encourage the use of native wildflowers, trees and shrubs in the landscaping patterns of the country. That was four years and four months ago. In those years, I guess what we have done is to increase awareness of the possible disappearance of this heritage.

USA TODAY: Do you find this work as personally satisfying as other work you've done?

JOHNSON: Oh, yes. Because if I had to remember what days I've enjoyed in the last months, I'd have to single out the unstructured days where I just lit out in the morning and did what I wanted to. Last Saturday, we drove down to Eagle Lake, through a lovely little town. We saw the most beautiful church on a hill, with three white crosses in front of it and an expanse of bluebonnets leading up to it. I thought, those people have a sense of beauty and love of the land, and that's pretty close to religion.

USA TODAY: When you go back to Washington, D.C., what holds your interest there?

JOHNSON: Well, certainly I left a piece of my heart there after living there 30 years. You're not married to the place; you just have a very loving relationship with it. At least that was the way it was with me.

USA TODAY: Does the public have an accurate sense of who President Johnson was?

JOHNSON: I do not know whether enough time has passed. I also know that people forget you quickly. Sometime ago, I made a little talk at a college. The president was a dear friend, and he said, "Now Lady Bird, remember, these young folks were three years old when you were in the White House!" Today you would have to say they weren't born. Time passes.

Topic: TEXAS

Our economy is up and so is our morale

USA TODAY: You're in your second term as governor. Are the serious economic problems behind you?

CLEMENTS: Most people who are well-informed across the state acknowledge that our economic upturn has begun.

USA TODAY: What made it happen sooner than expected?

CLEMENTS: I'm not sure. It has to do with spirit and focus. The election was a factor because we now have leadership that came out of the business community.

USA TODAY: What were the first signs that the economy was improving?

CLEMENTS: When the price of oil started turning around, that was the first signal. Our unemployment rate started to fall. Over the last few months, it's fallen off 2 percent. That builds morale and confidence, and people start perking up.

USA TODAY: The prison system is a major headache in Texas. Is private ownership of prisons a solution?

CLEMENTS: It's an option, but it is not a solution. In the past, we built conventional prisons. But we have changed our direction 180 degrees.

USA TODAY: Why such a dramatic change?

CLEMENTS: This is largely due to federal court intervention. We need more facilities for minimum-risk inmates. We put them in urban areas where they can work in the daytime and come back to minimum security at night. At the same time, they pay restitution to their victims.

USA TODAY: Hasn't this been tried in other states?

CLEMENTS: Not in the degree that we're getting ready to try it. Between now and Sept. 1, we will put under contract four 500-bed facilities in the metropolitan areas, where this theory will be put into practice for low-risk, non-violent inmates.

USA TODAY: What impact will the new immigration law have on Texas?

William P. Clements Jr., 70, a Republican, is serving his second term.

CLEMENTS: I don't think the rest of the country understands the sheer numbers of illegal aliens we have in Texas and California. That law represents some real problems to us in Texas. Amnesty is going to affect services of all kinds. It will affect the political scene, our economy.

USA TODAY: Southern Methodist University has been rocked by the football scandal. Will SMU be as strong as ever in a few years?

CLEMENTS: I don't think it will return as strong as ever, but I have consistently refused to get into the controversy. Too much has already been said about it.

USA TODAY: Why do Texans have a reputation for having the biggest egos in the union?

CLEMENTS: I find most Texans rather self-deprecating, and more humble about their surroundings and accomplishments.

USA TODAY: But Texans have a lot of pride in their state.

CLEMENTS: Texans do have an enormous pride in their state. It's deserved. We are different.

USA TODAY: You have deep roots in Texas?

CLEMENTS: My grandchildren are the seventh generation born in Texas. I started out with absolutely nothing, and Texas has been good to me. I'm proud to be a Texan.

Utah

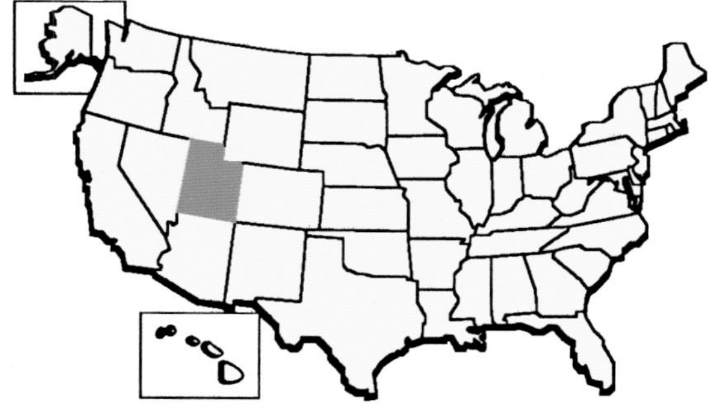

Visited: July 15-17, 1987
Featured in USA TODAY: July 20

"I feel safe here. There's this security of having the mountains surround you. Nothing can get to you."

Susannah Erickson
Teacher/singer
Provo, Utah

Utah

Tidy Mormon piety; church IS the state

Brigham Young led his troop of 148 Mormon pioneers into Salt Lake City 140 years ago this Friday. July 24, 1847.

Now, there are 1,252,000 Mormons in Utah. 75 percent of the state's population. Another 1.1 million in nearby California, Idaho, Arizona. 6.1 million worldwide. Missionaries across the USA and around the world bring in 200,000 converts a year.

Now, as then, The Church of Jesus Christ of Latter-day Saints, as the Mormons call it, stands for:

- Godliness
- Familyness
- Cleanliness.

For most across the USA, the voice of the Mormons is the Tabernacle Choir. Heard every Sunday on nationwide radio since 1929.

Jerald Ottley, 53, directs the 325 singers. "We're the best-known choir in the world. Our listeners are looking for something uplifting. Music can be an antidote for a lot of the problems of society, as well as a vehicle for worship."

Active Mormons worship willfully. No smoking. No alcohol. No caffeine. No premarital sex. While some of the young rebel, the church dictates most of Utah's lifestyle. Socially. Politically. Economically.

CHOIR DIRECTOR OTTLEY: Music can be an antidote.

■ Business: The Mormon Church is by far Utah's biggest business. Estimated annual income: $2 billion. Assets: $8 billion. Church officials do not give out actual figures.

■ Politics: The governor is a Mormon. So are 90 percent of the members of the state Legislature. Conservatives. Republicans. Mormons are missing from the registered list of lobbyists at the state capital. No need. The church IS the state. It lobbies from within.

■ Society. The family is the center of everything. Plural marriages were an original Mormon practice. Officially ended in 1890, a condition for Utah to become a state.

But, early marriages, lots of children are still the style. Women are encouraged to stay home, have children. Results:

■ Utah is No. 1 in percent of population under 17. National average is 26.4. Utah's is 37.4. Infinite infants.

Much is made of Mormon motherhood. **Julie Pacini**, 32, Salt Lake City (pop. 164,844) calls herself a full-time mother. Had a day's outing at Great Salt Lake last week with her six children, ages 20 months to 9 years. Brought along a young niece.

PACINI: Full-time mother says children are everything.

"The church encourages us to have large families. But I have a large family by choice. As far as I'm concerned, children are the whole joy of life," says the young and youthful looking Mormon mega-mother.

The young look as clean and neat as the older. When thousands camp out on the streets of Salt Lake City for this week's 140th anniversary celebration, you can be sure they'll leave the place the way they found it. Squeaky clean. Streets look as though they've been scrubbed with a toothbrush every day. Probably the cleanest city in the USA.

Elsewhere across Utah:

■ Provo (pop. 78,000). Home of Brigham Young University. A sports power. Won the national collegiate football crown in 1984. Noted BYU alum include Chicago Bears QB **Jim McMahon**; 1985 Miss America **Sharlene Wells**; recording stars **Marie** and **Donny Osmond.** McMahon's popularity has dropped here since he criticized BYU's conformist lifestyle.

■ Park City (pop. 2,823). Home of U.S. ski team. **Robert Redford**'s film festival. Mrs. Fields' chocolate-chip cookies. Former model **Debbie Fields** has developed an $80 million-a-year business. 420 stores across the USA. Why Park City? "We fell in love with the community, the environment, the people," says the cookie queen.

■ Cedar City (pop. 10,972). Tourist mecca tucked away in southern Utah. Noted for its Shakespearean Festival. Started last week. Lasts through Labor Day. 26th year. Draws performers, spectators nationwide.

James Carroll, 34, is on stage. A 2nd-year Yale drama student. Hometown Washington, D.C. Says Carroll:

"Being a little East Coast colored fellow, I had my reservations. I didn't know what to expect in Mormon country. But everybody is so honest here. I leave my apartment unlocked at night. I leave my bicycle unchained at night and it's still there in the morning. That's awfully refreshing."

That's Plain Talk from Utah.

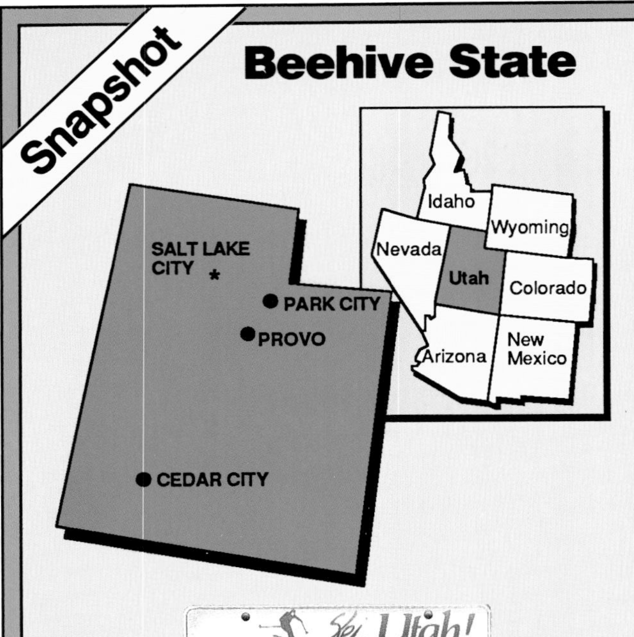

Ski Utah!
1896
GREATEST SNOW ON EARTH

ENTERED USA: Jan. 4, 1896, 45th state

MOTTO: Industry
POPULATION: 1,665,000; rank, 35th
LARGEST CITY: Salt Lake City, pop. 164,844
CAPITAL: Salt Lake City
LAND: 82,073 square miles; rank, 12th
POPULATION DENSITY: 20.3 per square mile; rank, 42nd
RACIAL MIX: 94.6% white; 1.3% American Indian; 1.0% Asian and Pacific islanders; 0.6% black. Hispanic heritage: 4.1%.

Uniquely Utah

SALT LAKE STATS: Only the Dead Sea has a higher salt content than the Great Salt Lake. Percentages of salt have been as high as 27 percent, 8 times saltier than the oceans.

OVER THE RAINBOW: Rainbow Bridge, on the shore of Lake Powell, is the world's largest natural bridge at 290 feet high and 270 feet wide. It is a sacred place for Navajo Indians.

VALLEY VISION: July 24 is Pioneer Day. On that date in 1847, Mormon leader Brigham Young first looked upon Salt Lake Valley and said, "This is the right place."

GOLDEN SPIKE: East met West with the joining of the rails at Promontory Summit in Northern Utah May 10, 1869. It made North America the first continent with a coast-to-coast rail line.

STOP 'N' GO: Lester Farnsworth Wire of Salt Lake City invented the traffic signal in 1912.

Inalee Herbert, 42
Tour guide/hostess
Salt Lake City

"One of the values of our church is the belief that we should not take things into our body that are harmful to us. We believed this long before the surgeon general issued his warning. We've known this all along, and now the rest of the world is hopping to it."

Fred Adams, 56
Drama teacher
Cedar City

"Utahans have an inordinate love of the arts. It goes clear back to Brigham Young and the first wagonload of people who produced The Merchant of Venice the first week they set up! In Utah, we've got a major ballet company, the symphony orchestra and our Shakespeare Festival."

Voices
of Utah

Gail Haury Peart, 43
Forest ranger
Panguitch

"We call it Utah Color Country. The rock formation is red because of the iron in the soil from the volcano. The rain runs down the side of the limestone and dyes it red. What's amazing is that Utah's national forests are a well-kept secret in the states. But walk into any pub in Germany or France and mention Utah, and they'll whip out post cards!"

David Mayfield, 44
Genealogical library director
Salt Lake City

"Genealogy has to do with our commitment to families. We believe that families can continue beyond the grave into eternity, that those who have gone before can be sealed to their families. Genealogy goes beyond names of the deceased. It's a means of tying us together as one family. You don't have to go back very many generations until we all come together."

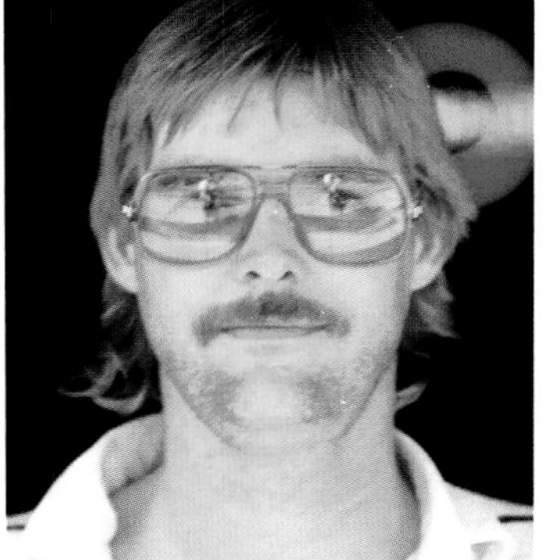

Dennis Godfrey, 32
Bartender
Ogden

"Mormons constitute 75 percent of the people who go to bars here. It correlates to the population. We call Mormons who don't follow the church exactly Jack Mormons. There are a few of them."

Jim Silver, 39
President, Saltair Resort
Salt Lake City

"Everyone in Utah has an opinion about the lake. You either love it or hate it. I love it. My family has been on the lake for six generations. The lake is kind of in my blood, but I know it can be mean. We have a saying for everything that goes wrong around here. We blame it on the lake effect."

Susannah Erickson, 36
Teacher/singer
Provo

"I feel safe here. There's this security of having the mountains surround you. Nothing can get to you. Utahans feel about their mountains the way other states feel about their water. People take their families there for hikes and skiing so there's good memories in the mountains."

Marie Osmond, 27, started her show business career 20 years ago with the family singing act, The Osmonds. During the mid-70s, she and her brother Donny hosted a TV show and recorded numerous albums together.

For 'Valley Girl' it's a great getaway

USA TODAY: You were born in Ogden, Utah, and grew up near Los Angeles, but your family moved back to Utah. Why did you go back?

OSMOND: I was in Utah until I was about 3 years old. And then we moved to Los Angeles because my brothers were working in the studios a lot. I'm a Valley Girl. We had a house in the San Fernando Valley. We always maintained Utah as a residence because we always loved Utah.

USA TODAY: What's the big attraction?

OSMOND: Once you've been to Utah, there's just something there that really gets a hold on you. It is so beautiful. It will take your breath away. At sunset it really looks like a post card.

USA TODAY: What distinguishes Utah from other states?

OSMOND: There is more scenic beauty in Utah than any state. There are four beautiful seasons. There are a lot of beautiful places to drive through and literally take your breath away.

USA TODAY: Do you take advantage of the lakes and the parks, go camping and things like that?

OSMOND: Absolutely. Just a little while ago, we drove down to Zion and saw the Great White Throne. We drive down to St. George. They have some beautiful places back there. And they have some of the best skiing in the world. The U.S. ski team trains in Utah. They have Park City and Snowbird and Alta, Deer Valley. We live a few minutes from Sundance.

USA TODAY: How tall are the mountains?

OSMOND: Right in our back yard, the mountains are about 12,000 feet. It's just a beautiful place.

USA TODAY: Utah is certainly not the hub of show business or the music industry. Do you ever feel like you might be out of it?

OSMOND: Well, Jaclyn Smith has a place here. Willie Nelson. Robert Redford. I know so many friends who have property here just to get away. John Schneider has a place here because he loves to take his Jeep up, and he loves to fish. When you're a hunter, it's a paradise. I don't hunt, but I know a lot of people who enjoy the sport. A lot of our friends have places here and just like to get away. Really, that's what Utah is for our family.

Topic: UTAH

The state is changing from isolated society

USA TODAY: Governor, you're a Mormon; 90 percent of the state's legislators are Mormon. Is there less separation of church and state in Utah?

BANGERTER: No, I don't think so. That's always a topic of discussion, with this being the headquarters of the Mormon Church. Obviously, you tend to reflect your upbringing and the culture in which you reside. Certainly, the church doesn't come in and say, "You will do this," or "You won't do that."

USA TODAY: Is it tough for a non-Mormon to move to Utah and become accepted?

BANGERTER: I feel we tend to make our own breaks. I've been a very active Mormon all my life, and my business partner of 20 years is not a Mormon. Some of my very best friends happen to not be members of the Mormon Church.

USA TODAY: One of your major concerns as governor is overcrowded schools. How do you handle that issue?

BANGERTER: As I tell people, I've taken the pledge — I'm not having any more children. But I already have six. While the school-age population in the nation has been going down, ours has been going up.

USA TODAY: Will that continue?

BANGERTER: We estimate that public school enrollment will peak in 1993, and then for the next decade, we will have an absolute numerical decline. Our birthrate has dropped, but is still above the national average. That gives us a challenge that we've always had.

USA TODAY: Drinking and gambling are frowned on in Utah. Would the state change to attract more tourists, or will it remain fairly conservative?

BANGERTER: Every place in the world is going to change. And we're going to change in Utah. We are no longer an isolated society. It used to be that the Mormon Church said, "All people who join the church, come to Utah." Now they say, "Stay where you're at." That trend will continue. A Mormon population will be diversified more and more as years go on. And that will have an impact on the state. There's no question about it.

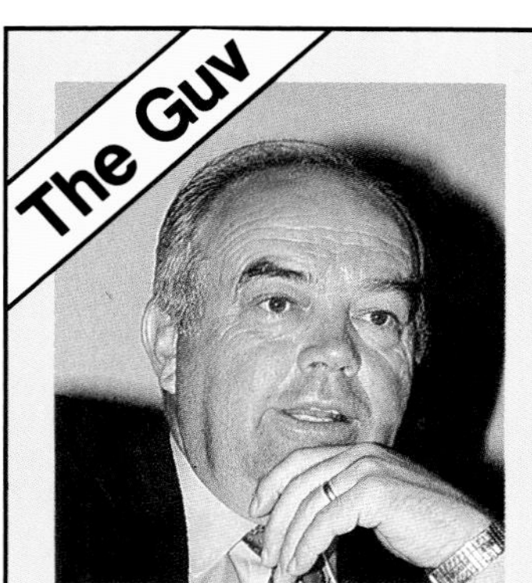

Norman Bangerter, 54, a Republican, was elected governor in 1984. He previously had held several leadership posts in the Utah Legislature.

USA TODAY: Speaking of change, you've had some difficult decisions: the largest tax increase in recent history —

BANGERTER: You can play that one down, if you'd like!

USA TODAY: — was passed by the Legislature last year. Will you run for re-election, and what do you think of polls that show that there isn't anybody you could beat?

BANGERTER: I don't worry about that. That's today. The polls are taken on Election Day. Are they unhappy because of the tax increase? Is my opponent going to be for lower taxes? No. Whether he'll articulate that will remain to be seen. I don't think that's the issue. You've got to have the issues.

USA TODAY: So you like your job?

BANGERTER: You bet. It's exciting and challenging, but it's a difficult time to be a governor.

USA TODAY: You went to Brigham Young and the University of Utah. How do you divide your sports loyalties?

BANGERTER: I wear a red sweater under a blue blazer.

Vermont

Visited: May 19-20, 1987
Featured in USA TODAY: May 26

"I could have made a much better living somewhere else, but I've always been careful not to confuse my living and my life. In Vermont, we draw that distinction."

Eric Bye
Insurance representative
Saxtons River, Vt.

Vermont

Town meets shape fate of land of syrup, cider

They say town meetings were invented here. They still shape the fate of this tiny state. Pop. 541,000. No. 48 in the USA.

They keep Vermonters close to their leaders and to their land. "My first town meeting blew my mind. You really get involved. People speak their minds," says **Bob Falta**, 45, gym owner in Middlebury (pop. 7,574).

Look at what that process has produced:

■ A liberal lady governor.

Democrat **Madeleine Kunin**, 53. One of only three female guvs in the USA. Swiss-born. A bit shy, genteel, queenly. But, also plucky and persevering. Lost her first gubernatorial election, after serving in the Legislature. Squeezed through with 50.026 percent of the vote next time.

■ A Socialist mayor of Vermont's largest city.

Bernard Sanders, 45. Only Socialist city boss in the USA.

Brooklyn-born. Won his first term in 1981 by 10 votes in Burlington (pop. 37,817). Elected to a fourth term last March with 56 percent of the vote. Feisty. Appeals to non-traditional voters. Targets the poor, homeless, elderly.

SANDERS: Burlington mayor is a Socialist.

The mayor attended a Burlington town meeting of some 250 vocal Vermonters last Tuesday. He didn't speak out, but his followers and foes did.

Ed Moore, 55, unemployed, complained: "I am a veteran. I'm not an alcoholic. I'm not a derelict. I'm just a person who happens to be homeless. A lot of us are on the way down."

Joseph Bello, 32, hotel manager, countered: "Eight years ago I was a security guard making $2.90 an hour. I manage this place now. You can go wherever you want to go."

The Vermont political pattern is explained by **Kerrick Johnson**, 25, a legislative aide in the state capital of Montpelier (pop. 8,241).

"When people in New York or Boston make enough money to move to the country, the conservatives go to New Hampshire and the liberals come to Vermont."

Despite the liberal or non-traditional political picture, many stick to tradition. Especially the love of their land.

"Vermont is the way America used to be" read bumper stickers from Brattleboro in the south (pop. 8,596) to Barre in the middle (pop. 9,824) to Barton in the north (pop. 1,062).

Keeping Vermont the way it used to be means preserving the summer green, the fall foliage, the white winter on the ski slopes.

The threat to that is acid rain. Sulfur particles spewed from coal-fired utilities in the Midwest and Canada worry Vermonters. Environmental issues heat up town meetings.

"We can see the progression of damage from the softwood trees, which are first to go, then to the hardwoods. Maple trees are hardwoods," worries **Francine Chittenden**, 35, of Waterbury Center (pop. 500).

Maple trees and maple syrup mean a lot to Vermonters. Financially and sentimentally.

Suzy Chaffee, 40, Olympics ski star from Rutland (pop. 18,436), now lives in Marina del Rey, Calif. She reminisced about maple syrup making when she came home for the premiere of her movie *Fire and Ice* recently.

"Our family had about 30 acres. We had fun collecting syrup. Maple syrup is the greatest thing you can put in coffee for sweetener. It's better than honey. It's better for little babies," says Chaffee.

CHITTENDEN: She squeezes apples, gets thousands of gallons of cider.

Apple cider hasn't quite the high visibility of Vermont maple syrup. But it's a big business.

The Cold Hollow Cider Mill has been run by Francine Chittenden and her husband, **Eric**, 44, for 13 years.

They squeeze 2,000 to 3,000 gallons of cider a year. Mostly from McIntosh apples. In Northern Vermont, apple cider is as all-American as apple pie.

Whether they are natives or "flatlanders," as newcomers are called, most Vermonters share a rugged individualism. Dead set against anyone pushing them around.

Says **Gene Benjamin**, 44, a roofer in Putney (pop. 1,100), "I don't give a damn if I'm first in line or last in line, as long as I get there."

That's Plain Talk from Vermont.

Snapshot

Green Mountain State

Vermont
New Hampshire
New York
Massachusetts
BURLINGTON
MONTPELIER *
BARRE
MIDDLEBURY
RUTLAND
BRATTLEBORO
GUILFORD

GREEN MOUNTAINS
1791
VERMONT

ENTERED USA: March 4, 1791, 14th state

MOTTO: Vermont, Freedom, and Unity
POPULATION: 541,000; rank, 48th
LARGEST CITY: Burlington, pop. 37,817
CAPITAL: Montpelier, pop. 8,241
LAND: 9,273 square miles; rank, 43rd
POPULATION DENSITY: 58.3 per square mile; rank, 30th
RACIAL MIX: 99.1% white; 0.3% Asian and Pacific islanders; 0.2% black. Hispanic heritage: 0.6%.

Uniquely Vt.

WELCOME MAT: The first interstate highway welcome center in the USA opened in 1966 on Interstate 91 in Guilford.

FIRST CLASS: In 1845, the USA's first postage stamps were issued in Brattleboro.

SEA MONSTER: Lake Champlain, at Burlington, is reportedly the home of a sea monster named Champ.

THIS WON'T HURT: Laughing gas (nitrous oxide) was invented by Gardner Colton of Georgia, Vt. Horace Wells of White River Junction in 1844 became the first person to use laughing gas as a dental anesthetic.

GOVERNMENT PAYOFF: The first beneficiary of monthly Social Security payments was Ida M. Fuller of Ludlow. She received check No. 00-000-001 for $22.54, Jan. 31, 1940.

FAR FROM SHORE: Vermont is the only New England state that has no coastline on the Atlantic Ocean.

Voices
of Vermont

Milo Marshall, 53
Chainsaw carver
Waterbury Center

"I got started a few years ago when a fellow from Arizona came by. He was a traveling chainsaw carver. He set up on my piece of property here and I learned from him."

Don Ostler, 34
General manager
of cider mill
Morrisville

"Apples are not our biggest agricultural product, but they're very important. Cider is becoming more and more popular as people are turning to natural drinks instead of the sodas. Apple cider is Vermont's natural juice. I've lived in Vermont 17 years."

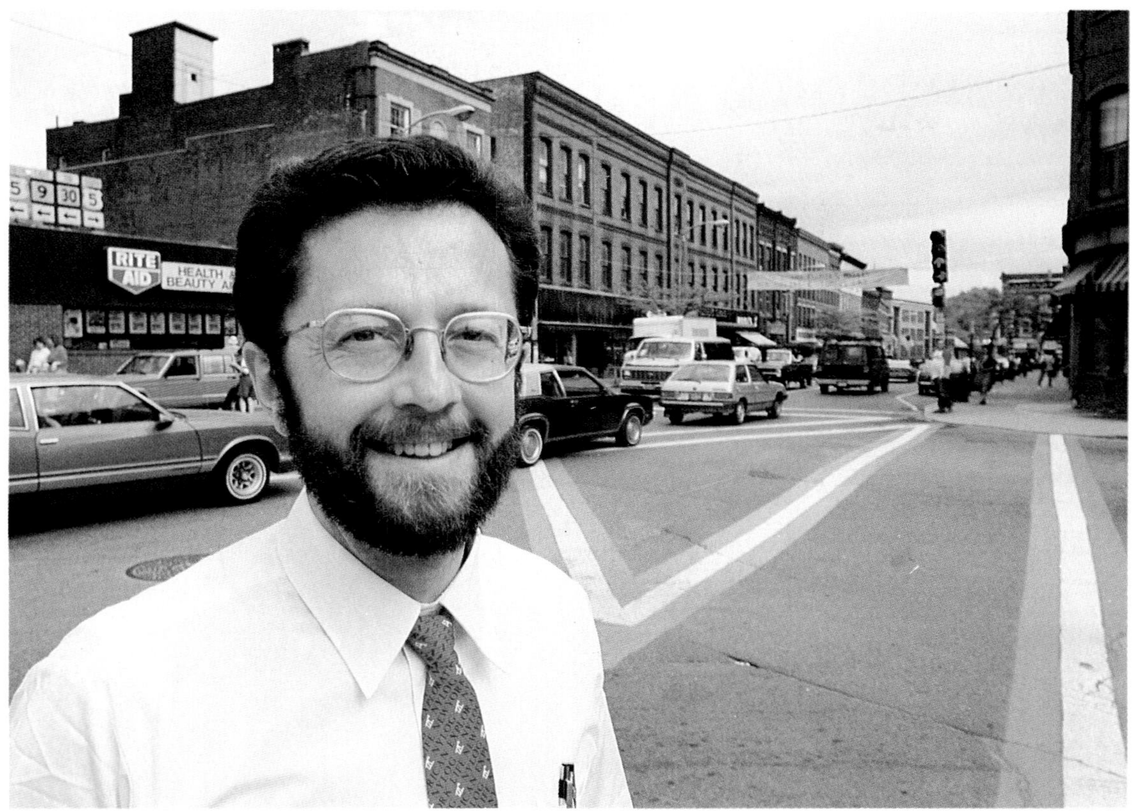

Eric Bye, 39
Insurance representative
Saxtons River

"I could have made a much better living somewhere else, but I've always been careful not to confuse my living and my life. In Vermont, we draw that distinction. I could strap on my skis in my back yard and ski to the Canadian border. There's a stream in my yard where I can see blue herons. That's worth more than $10,000 a year. It's priceless."

Gene Benjamin, 44
Roofer
Putney

"People come to Vermont from the city, and bring the city with them. To fit in up here, you have to get into the laid-back rural atmosphere. I don't give a damn if I'm first in line or last in line, as long as I get there."

B.J. McClellan, 13
Student
Bennington

"Town meeting gives people a chance to express their thoughts and ideas about what should be done. My parents bring home the topics and discuss it with us. I can express my opinions and they can bring it to the next town meeting."

Emma Marshall, 53
Store owner
Waterbury Center

"We've got one of the best skiing resorts, Stowe, just three miles away. But it's very expensive. I think it's the well-to-doers that go rather than the regular Vermonters. More and more, they're getting into cross-country skiing. That way, you don't have to go to a mountain. Most Vermonters are just average people. We'll leave the skiing to the tourists."

Carol McFeeters, 40
Insurance agent
St. Albans

"I love being able to walk down the street and see people I know. I really like a small town. You know your kids' friends and that's really beneficial. I think the fact that I know who they are makes for a better understanding. You always hear about the generation gap — I don't want that to happen."

Notable

***Suzy Chaffee**, 40, who was born in Rutland, Vt., and was a member of the 1968 USA Olympic ski team, became known as "Suzy Chapstick" after appearing in commercials for a lip balm.*

Change is minimal, mystique remains

USA TODAY: In Rutland, where you grew up, was skiing a tradition?

CHAFFEE: My role model is Andrea Mead Lawrence, the first American skier to ever win two gold medals, in 1952 in the Olympics. I just brought my movie *Fire and Ice* back for a premiere in Rutland. It was a homecoming and celebration of all the greatness of the skiers of Rutland. It's really part of the culture of our hometown and our state.

USA TODAY: You're from a family of skiers.

CHAFFEE: My brother Rick was captain of two Olympic teams. And my brother Ken was captain of the Harvard ski team. My mother was an alternate on the Olympic team, and my father was one of the first pioneers of skiing.

USA TODAY: Where did you learn to ski?

CHAFFEE: I learned at Pico Peak, which is nine miles from our house. Andrea Mead Lawrence's family started Pico. We used to ski to music. That's where I learned the beginnings of free-style skiing, which I was one of the inventors of.

USA TODAY: How much has Vermont changed since you were growing up there?

CHAFFEE: Very minimally. It's a slow growth, which means it hasn't overbuilt itself and lost its charm. It still has a mystique.

USA TODAY: How would you compare Vermont to other ski states, like Colorado?

CHAFFEE: Colorado usually has better snow, but every once in a while, Vermont can outdo it. Vermont is close to major population centers, such as New York and Boston.

USA TODAY: Many people remember you for the "Suzy Chapstick" commercials. How do you feel about that?

CHAFFEE: I got the commercial when I was working with President Ford getting the first bill through Congress to protect the rights of athletes. The advertising guy said, "You can have any commercial you want." I said I'd like to get one with a fitness message because fitness was very uncommon in commercials. So he had the Chapstick commercial. And he said, "It came to me in the middle of the night. You should be 'Suzy Chapstick.' "

Topic: VERMONT

Tempered by tradition, but not out of date

USA TODAY: How does the nation perceive Vermont?

KUNIN: Vermont is seen as a green space, a place of beauty and escape, where values are more genuine and old-fashioned.

USA TODAY: In what ways?

KUNIN: There are more traditional values and work ethic and respect for individuality, but it is also a very modern place with high technology and good jobs and culture. People know more about the nostalgia part of Vermont than they do about the contemporary Vermont. We're not caught in a time warp, but we still are different. And we're happy that we are.

USA TODAY: Kentucky Gov. Martha Layne Collins said that some women's groups had expressed disappointment because she didn't push their issues hard enough. Have you had a similar problem?

KUNIN: That's not been my experience. I've been supported by women's groups, but I have not had a set of issues that have exclusively been women's issues. I've incorporated women's issues among my issues.

USA TODAY: Educational funding was a very important item on your agenda this year. Will it be on your agenda again next year?

KUNIN: One specific project I asked the business people to consider getting involved in was redistricting. We have more school districts per capita than any state in the union. This leads to great inefficiencies as well as to different tax burdens.

USA TODAY: Acid rain is a big issue here. What would you like to see the federal government doing about it?

KUNIN: Supporting Vermont's U.S. Sen. Robert T. Stafford, basically, in his initiatives and really having some limitations with teeth on emissions. The knowledge is there. The call for delays in terms of further study just doesn't hold water anymore. We need someone in the White House, frankly, who will lead the charge in the Congress.

The Guv

***Madeleine M. Kunin**, 53, a Democrat, was born in Zurich, Switzerland. The first woman governor of Vermont, she was elected in 1984 and re-elected in 1986.*

USA TODAY: A recent news story said that the state's only black lawyer is moving to Wisconsin after trying unsuccessfully for six years to get a job in a private firm here.

KUNIN: I don't feel Vermont is prejudiced. We don't have a lot of experience with a black population, which may lead to some sense of unfamiliarity, but I wouldn't describe us as biased.

USA TODAY: Why aren't more women running for state houses and Congress?

KUNIN: It is harder for anybody to get into politics. It's a fairly rough and tumble, highly competitive world. We're beginning to build support structures, and traditional political men's groups are becoming more inviting to women. There are also some internal barriers that women have to overcome.

USA TODAY: What is your proudest achievement?

KUNIN: I have raised the consciousness about the importance of education. It is an important value for the future of this state, that people are willing to commit themselves to, not only at the state level, but also at the local level. When some people come up to me and say, "I'm glad you're doing that," that is reassuring. Environmental issues are very important to me, as well.

Virginia

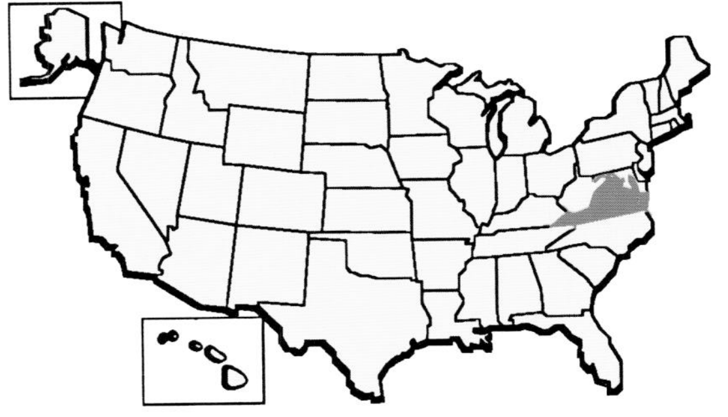

Visited: Aug. 18-19, 1987
Featured in USA TODAY: Aug. 21

"Sometimes when I walk out my back door I feel like I'm walking into a history book."

Vickie Francis
Shoe saleswoman
Lynchburg, Va.

Virginia

Love history, horses, presidents, precedents

"Virginia is for Lovers," the slogan goes. Virginians have a lot to love.

The past whispers patriotically and romantically at the state's nearly 6 million residents and 29 million annual visitors.

■ The first permanent English settlement in North America. Jamestown, 1607. Nearby Williamsburg (pop. 10,900), now displays much of the earliest colonial memorabilia in one of the USA's largest outdoor museums.

WASHINGTON

JEFFERSON

MADISON

. . . Virginia: 'Mother of Presidents' . . .

■ Virginia gave us four of our first five presidents. Eight in all. More than any other state. Ohio second with seven. Presidents **Washington**, **Jefferson**, **Madison**, **Monroe**, **Harrison**, **Tyler**, **Taylor**, **Wilson** born in the state called the "Mother of Presidents."

■ Capital of the Confederacy. Richmond, now the state capital (pop. 216,700) was the "other White House" in 1861-65. Virginia Gen. **Robert E. Lee** led the South's forces. More Civil War battles fought in Virginia than in any other state.

"Sometimes when I walk out my back door I feel like I'm walking into a history book," says **Vickie Francis**, 19, shoe saleswoman in Lynchburg (pop. 66,500).

Proud as they are of their history, Virginians optimistically are looking ahead:

Gov. **Gerald Lee Baliles**, 47, 1st-term Democrat, talks of being on the cutting edge of change, of setting precedents:

"Everyone has a very healthy respect for our history and our early leaders. But Virginia is a hot property right now. Transportation and education are our building blocks. Our neighbors used to be North Carolina and Maryland. Now they are Brussels and Peking and Brazil."

World trade has been a major thrust for the Guv and his predecessor, **Charles (Chuck) Robb**, who left in 1986.

Results:

■ The port of Hampton Roads, in the Newport News-Norfolk area, (pop. 1,261,200) is the largest export port in the USA. 42 million short tons of freight annually. Baltimore is second with 11 million. New York third with five million.

■ Virginia's airports are the power passages of the USA and the world. Dulles and National. Congress recently authorized a regional airport authority that is expected to spend $799 million to $800 million for modernization and expansion.

Many across the USA confuse those airports as being in Washington, D.C. Two other high-visibility facilities on Virginia soil but with a D.C. identification: the Pentagon, Arlington National Cemetery.

The Virginia suburbs around Washington are home to the rich and famous. Business giants, present and former Cabinet members, senators, congressmen, diplomats.

"On any trip to the store you meet people from around the world. There are 46 different languages spoken in the Fairfax public schools," says **Emily Solomon**, 47, in the commercial department of the United Virginia Bank in Arlington (pop. 155,400).

Distinctly Virginia is the northern horse country. Middleburg, Leesburg, Upperville, Warrenton. All just an hour or so west of the White House. Historic small towns surrounded by fancy farms owned by the **Mellons**, **Firestones**, **du Ponts**, other big money names. Smaller hideaways owned by such as **Jackie Onassis**, U.S. Sen. **John Warner** (his ex-wife **Liz Taylor** lived there, too), TV weatherman **Willard Scott**.

Many, like Washington Redskins owner **Jack Kent Cooke**, 74, and his new bride, **Suzanne Martin**, 31, ride on the privacy of their estates. Many more who are hooked on horses take their pleasure publicly at professional training, riding and boarding farms. One such is the trendy two-year-old Paper Chase Farms, near Middleburg (pop. 619). Run by daughter **Jan Neuharth** and her Swiss-born husband **Joseph Keusch**.

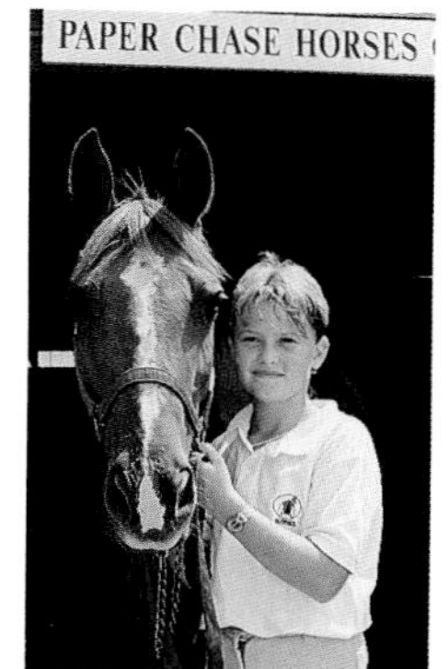

LENAH and APPOLLO: Olympic dreams.

Paper Chase is a haven for international horse lovers from the pre-teens on. One regular is **Lenah Ueltzen**, 9, from nearby Aldie (pop. 125). Her family owns horses and farms in England and Spain as well as the USA. Her mother, **Helen**, is author of *The Racing Breed.* Lenah, with her horse Apollo, has her sights set on stardom:

"I've been riding ever since I was three. Being on the back of a horse is such fun. It may sound like a silly dream, but I want to go to the Olympics and make it there."

Dreams. Memories. That's Plain Talk from Virginia.

Snapshot

The Old Dominion

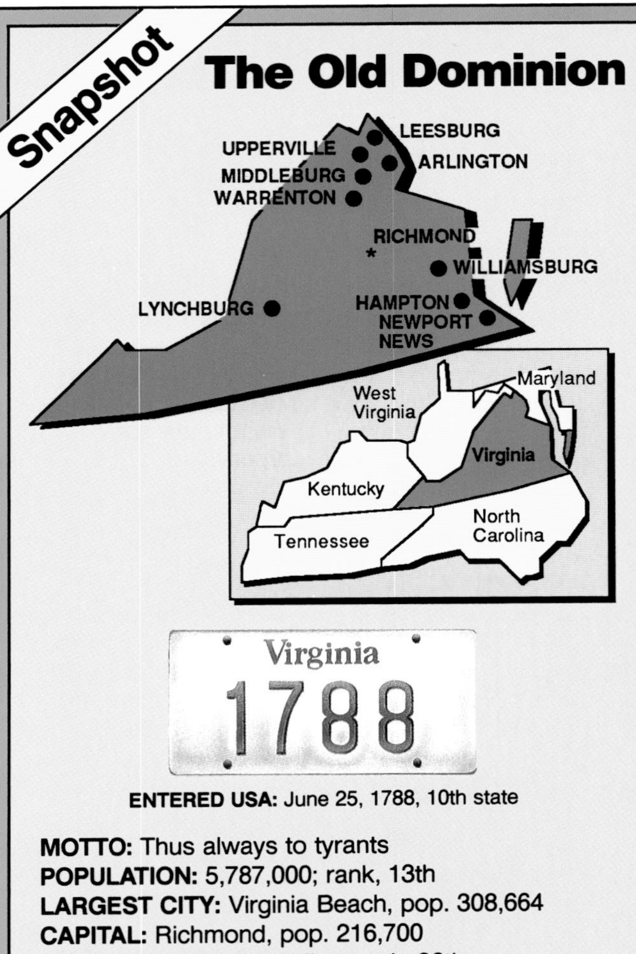

ENTERED USA: June 25, 1788, 10th state

MOTTO: Thus always to tyrants
POPULATION: 5,787,000; rank, 13th
LARGEST CITY: Virginia Beach, pop. 308,664
CAPITAL: Richmond, pop. 216,700
LAND: 39,703 square miles; rank, 36th
POPULATION DENSITY: 145.8 per square mile; rank, 16th
RACIAL MIX: 79.1% white; 18.9% black; 1.2% Asian and Pacific islanders. Hispanic heritage: 1.5%.

Uniquely Va.

ORGAN DONOR: The world's only "stalacpipe" organ is in Luray Caverns. The organ's pipes are stalactites (they hang down) that have been tuned to particular notes. Leland Sprinkle of Springfield conceived the idea while touring the caverns in 1954.

CONFEDERATE CAPITAL: Monument Avenue in Richmond is lined with monuments to the Confederacy, Gens. Robert E. Lee, Stonewall Jackson, J.E.B. Stuart and Confederate President Jefferson Davis.

WHITE FLAGS: The surrenders ending both the American Revolution (Yorktown) and the Civil War (Appomattox) occurred in Virginia.

FRATERNITY ROW: The first college fraternity was Phi Beta Kappa, founded in 1776 at William and Mary College in Williamsburg.

PASSIONATE PLEA: Patrick Henry delivered his plea for "liberty or death" in St. John's Church at Richmond March 23, 1775.

Voices
of Virginia

Cpl. Gregory Frey, 19
Honor guard
Arlington National Cemetery

"Each of the headstones is a person, some of them famous, some of them not. That doesn't matter. When I stand out there and look at the tomb, it's not just a piece of marble. It's a shrine. I think about what it means, and about how proud I am to be there."

Emma Tramposch, 7 (with Aaron Flach, 10)
Student
Williamsburg

"In some ways it would be fun to live back then, to help your mom cook and stuff. But they had to wear hot clothes. They're pretty, but they're hot."

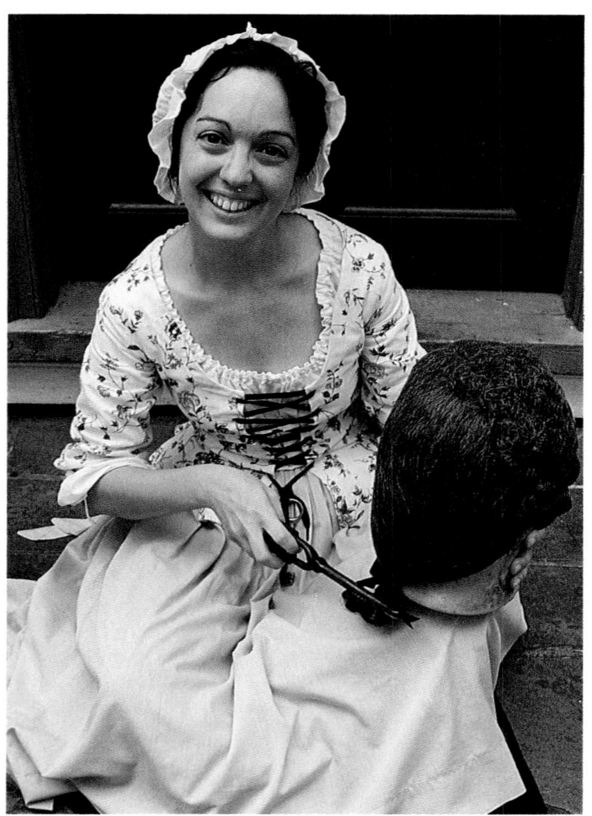

Janea Whitacre, 27
Wigmaker
Williamsburg

"I have a degree in art history and after studying that, I wanted to come here and get a job. I visited here at 9 years old and thought it would be wonderful to come here and dress up. Wigmaking was so very important as a trade in the 18th century. Wigs were an obvious status symbol, just like clothing was. You couldn't move a plantation, so wigs, clothes and horses were their way of saying, 'I'm wealthy.'"

Elizabeth Dowling Taylor, 36
Visitor services supervisor
Monticello

"I think the beauty of Virginia and the glorious history go hand in hand. It's an attractive place to pick up your American heritage. You're getting in touch with your roots here. We're very proud of our heritage in Virginia."

Terry Wood, 41
University administrator
Charlottesville

"The influence of Thomas Jefferson is amazing. You get the feeling he's behind a tree somewhere. It's invigorating and stimulating. He's certainly on the minds of students and faculty. It's interesting that he's always referred to as 'Mr. Jefferson.' He's toasted quite often at university functions."

Lisa Dixon, 18
Student/cashier
Lynchburg

"We were one of the first colonies. I appreciate that — what it cost us, what it bought. The Civil War, which was fought on a lot of Virginia ground, symbolized freedom and our people's rights. I look at how it changed my ancestors' lives and caused a change in mine. It makes me proud to be from here."

David Bundy, 31
Museum director of development
Richmond

"Richmond is unique. It was the capital of another nation. The Confederacy was incredibly important for us to understand. The South back during the Confederacy was a special time. People believed in honor and personal conviction. Southern women then were genteel and elegant. But when the war broke out, they were forced to be working women; women in charge of their own destiny."

Robin Drucker, 21
Student
Virginia Beach

"At school I couldn't wait to get home to the beach. After studying for exams, I can come to the beach and I don't have to be serious. The summer tourist business opens up a lot of jobs. A normal summer is going to the beach in the day and working as a waitress at night. I usually try to save money to buy books and groceries during school."

Willard Scott, 53, is the weatherman on NBC's Today *show. Scott was born in Alexandria, Va., and owns a farm in Virginia. An American University graduate, with a philosophy and religion degree, he is the author of* Joy of Living.

Blessed with love of family, friends

USA TODAY: Your autobiography is called *Joy of Living.* Were you happy growing up in Virginia?

SCOTT: When the colonists originally settled this Western world, they had everything from Chile and the South Pole all the way up to Nova Scotia to settle, but they chose Virginia. Even the Pilgrims were originally headed for Virginia. I say that to emphasize I have a warm feeling about my hometown.

USA TODAY: What is there about Alexandria, your hometown, that produces such warm feelings?

SCOTT: Alexandria had a population of 35,000 when I was born. It was a sleepy little town in Northern Virginia when I was born. Virginia has managed to combine the graciousness, the charm and the cavalier spirit of the good part of the Old South with the modern times.

USA TODAY: What influenced you to choose a career in broadcasting?

SCOTT: When I was 8 years old, my mother left me at a theater to watch a movie. The movie got out early. I wandered up to the radio station in the building. Right then, I knew that's what I wanted to do for a living. I have never had a desire to do anything else.

USA TODAY: You own a farm in Upperville. What is it like?

SCOTT: It's a small, 20-acre farm. My grandfather had a dairy farm up in Maryland, which I've always loved and admired. Like most people who ever came from a farm background, it's in the blood.

USA TODAY: What kind of community is Upperville?

SCOTT: It is a little kingdom of its own. The people are simply lovely. It's only a block long. But there's an Exxon station and a little grocery store. So it really is, literally, a village.

USA TODAY: Off camera, you seem as upbeat and effervescent as you are on the air. Were you always like this?

SCOTT: I've been blessed with a wonderful family, a great job, and all the money I could ever ask for. But in my heart is love. That's just the way I grew up. From people in my hometown to members of my own family, who shared with me a lot of love.

Topic: VIRGINIA

We revere history; we also want to make it

USA TODAY: Virginia is rich in history, having sent more presidents to the White House than any other state. What effect has that had on the state's self image?

BALILES: In Virginia, tradition is very important. Two hundred years ago, Virginians led the nation. We were the writers, the fighters and the thinkers. They were willing to face change, and to grapple with it, and we must do the same. As much as we like to read history, we ought to be more concerned about making it.

USA TODAY: Do Virginians feel slighted by Massachusetts' claim that it originated the celebration of Thanksgiving?

BALILES: We had it first. To set the record straight, the Thanksgiving celebrated in 1619 in Virginia did predate the observance in Massachusetts. There's enough room in our history books for Plymouth Rock and Virginia's Thanksgiving — as long as it notes Virginia was first.

USA TODAY: What should the rest of the USA know about Virginia?

BALILES: Virginia is first in per capita income in the Southeast, 10th in the country, and climbing. One of our great resources is geography. Virginia's location, midway on the Atlantic Seaboard, provides us with great access to the American market, within a day's drive of 60 percent of the nation's population.

USA TODAY: What shape is the economy in?

BALILES: When you consider that Dulles International Airport is not only the fastest growing air facility in the country, but increasingly is the international gateway for travelers, and that the port of Hampton Roads is the fastest growing seaport, you recognize that we have the ingredients for a very successful economy. Unemployment is half the national average. The challenge is how to sustain that kind of prosperity in the future.

USA TODAY: How is your "no-read, no-release" program to promote literacy among prisoners working?

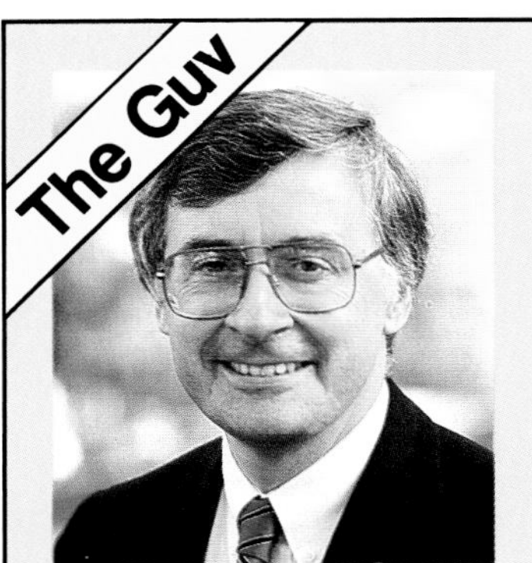

Gerald Baliles, 47, a Democrat, was elected last year. Baliles also has served as state attorney general and as a state legislator.

BALILES: The program was implemented almost a year ago. It seems to be meeting with increasing success. Two-thirds of our prisoners — and I suspect the numbers are pretty much the same nationally — do not have high school diplomas. About a third are functionally illiterate — can't read at a sixth-grade level.

USA TODAY: Is the program expensive?

BALILES: Many of our prisoners are repeats and are likely to continue that pattern unless we can break that cycle. Education is cheaper in economic terms. In terms of social costs, I don't think we really have a choice.

USA TODAY: What did the 1985 election of your ticket, which included a black lieutenant governor and a female attorney general, say about the voters of this state?

BALILES: We won handsomely because we brought to the campaign credibility, a record of accomplishment, and a commitment to the future. We were successful in raising money, and telling people this ticket reflected a modern Virginia.

USA TODAY: Is the country ready for a mix like that in the top political offices?

BALILES: I hope so. It would say a lot about us as a country.

Washington

Visited: June 30-July 2, 1987
Featured in USA TODAY: July 6

"If you put economics and environment side by side, environment's going to win."

Washington Gov. Booth Gardner

Washington

Jet, apple capitals keep Evergreen State green

If "an apple a day keeps the doctor away," Washingtonians help us avoid lots of doctor calls. 5 billion apples were harvested here last year and consumed across the USA.

Around the USA, New York and Los Angeles have the jet-setter reputation. But here in Seattle (pop. 488,474), Boeing builds more jets than anyone else anywhere in the world.

Jet building is the key to Western Washington's economy. Apples feed the cash registers east of the Cascade mountain range. Facts and feelings:

■ No. 1 apple producer in the USA. Provides us with 48 percent of our fresh apples. Plus juice and applesauce. A $700 million a year business. About 80,000 people involved.

■ No. 1 jet manufacturer in the world. Boeing had sales last year of $16.3 billion. 84,074 Washingtonians work there. They'll turn out 313 big commercial jets this year. The "smaller" 737 sells for about $17 million. The huge 747, for about $126 million.

Washington's jet builders and apple growers have profuse pride in their No. 1 position.

"If it ain't Boeing, I ain't going," says **Ed Satterlee**, 40, a mechanic on the Seattle assembly line. "Pilots say Boeing is their favorite. Washington's got a better grade of workers. We're not irritable. It's not too hot, never too cold. So everyone's relaxed. We take great pride in our jets."

SATTERLEE: Boeing pride flying high.

Pride at Boeing now is greatest over the building of the new Air Force One and its backup for the next president of the USA. Scheduled for delivery in May 1989. Cost for the two: $250 million.

The new Air Force One will have 4,000 square feet of floor space — double the size of the average USA family home. A range of 6,000 miles. Farther than a non-stop from Washington to Moscow.

Apple growers are as proud as jet builders. **Gary Dahlstrom**, 52, works "Woodring Acres" near Cashmere (pop. 2,240), off the beaten path north of Yakima (pop. 181,700), west of Spokane (pop. 175,600).

"We're the apple capital. We grow them, pick them, eat them, drink them. We make applesauce, apple pie, apple strudel, baked apples, fried apples. I drink three quarts of apple cider a day. Ever since my wife's been drinking it, she hasn't had a cold," says Dahlstrom.

Of course, there's more to Washington than jets and apples.

■ Shipping. Seattle's port is No. 5 in the USA. 90 percent of its trade is with Asia. Only Alaska and Hawaii have a better position on the Pacific Rim. The Port of Seattle has a bright future.

DAHLSTROM: Cider chases apple grower's colds.

■ Beer and hops. Olympia and Rainier beer are brewed and exported. And this is the home of hops, the vine used to flavor beer.

Washington is the No. 1 hop producer in the USA. Supplies 70 percent of the hops for brewers everywhere.

When you add up all of Washington's economic factors, the beauty of the environment still overwhelms you.

Gov. **Booth Gardner**, 50, first-term Democrat, explains it: "If you put economics and environment side by side, environment's going to win."

Across the USA, Washington's environment got special attention when Mount St. Helens erupted on May 18, 1980. Threw boulders the size of dump trucks in the air. Hurled huge trees 35 miles. Turned daylight into darkness. Three days later, the ash cloud crossed the USA and eventually circled the globe.

John Fraenzi, 41, a forestry technician in Woodland (pop. 2,340) at Mount St. Helens' base, recalls the eruption and what's happened since:

"It was a moonscape out there — a real wasteland. But we've planted 9½ million trees in the ash. Today, it looks fantastic. Life is returning and we're speeding up the process."

The beauty of the land — from the waters of Puget Sound to snow-capped Mount Rainier — is what hooks most people in the Evergreen State.

Many who have to choose between career concerns and their love affair with Mother Nature opt for the latter. **Thom Beamish**, 52, a financial analyst in Bellingham (pop. 46,000), sums it up:

"It's almost magical. This kind of scenery gets you outside yourself a little and gives you a sense of proportion. You begin to value something other than scurrying around."

That's Plain Talk from Washington.

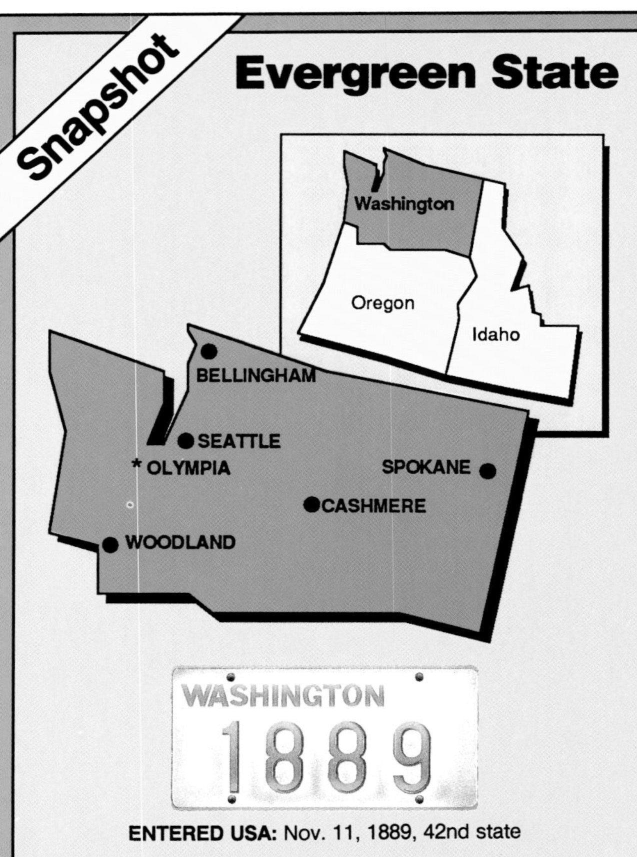

ENTERED USA: Nov. 11, 1889, 42nd state

MOTTO: By and by
POPULATION: 4,463,000; rank, 19th
LARGEST CITY: Seattle, pop. 488,474
CAPITAL: Olympia, pop. 27,447
LAND: 66,511 square miles; rank, 20th
POPULATION DENSITY: 67.1 per square mile; rank, 28th
RACIAL MIX: 91.4% white; 2.6% black; 2.5% Asian and Pacific islanders. Hispanic heritage: 2.9%.

Uniquely Wash.

ISLAND HOPPING: Washington is home to 32 island groups, including the San Juan's 172 islands. Whidbey is the longest at 50 miles.

GRAPES GALORE: No point in the state is more than an hour's drive from a winery. Washington has more than 65 wineries and 11,000 acres of grapevines.

BELLY BUSTER: The English translation of the Indian word Yakima is Big Belly.

NORTH OF THE BORDER: More than 15,000 vehicles pass through the Bellingham-Vancouver border crossing each day. The state has 13 border crossings with Canada.

MOUNTAIN MOVER: The eruption of Mount St. Helens, on May 18, 1980, had a force 500 times greater than the atomic bomb dropped on Hiroshima. Enough timber was blown down to build 500,000 homes, and the mountain itself lost 1,300 feet, dropping in height from 9,677 to 8,377.

Voices
of Washington

Mike Osborn, 28
Seafood barker
Seattle

"What I like best about being on the water is watching the sunrises and sunsets. There's nothing like Washington sunrises and sunsets. The sun rises over the Cascades and sets over the Olympic Mountains. All you have to do is come here once, and you're hooked."

Paul Decou, 37
Brewmaster
Olympia

"There are only a handful of brewmasters in the whole country. I think there's a mystique surrounding us because beer has been promoted so much. Washington is No. 1 in the country for growing hops. But it's the water here that makes a difference. It's not too hard, not too soft, and has all the right minerals."

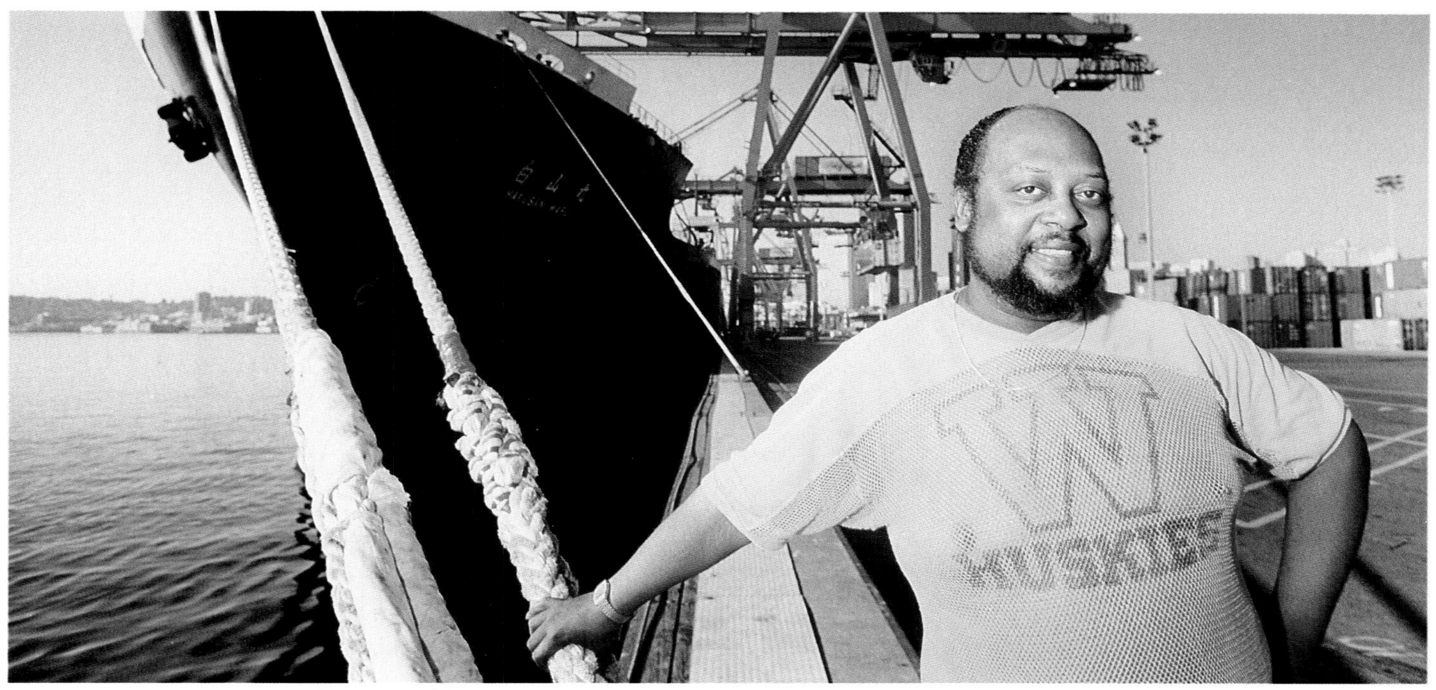

Gerald Tanner, 43
Longshoreman
Seattle

"The job used to be done by rough, tough hairy-chested bar-brawling guys. Now you've got your college-educated guys out here. And women, too. Things are changing. We've got to use our minds more than our backs."

Brett Renfroe, 19
Machinist
Opportunity

"The name fits. There are lots of opportunities in this country. You've just got to get a goal and go for it. I've got a job, and I'm thankful for it. But I'm not satisfied. You can't just sit and watch the world go by. I'm starting out from nothing and I'm going to give 100 percent. I'm going back to school so that I can get ahead."

Stephanie Rowe, 18
Student
Olympia

"Olympia is famous for its water. It has the best. I don't drink water anywhere else because it tastes funny. Whenever I say I'm from Washington, everyone always thinks of Washington, D.C. My friend went away to college and she was constantly saying, 'I'm from Washington . . . the state.' Then when they do think of the Northwest, they think of all the beauty and Mount St. Helens. Even here we were given these masks to wear in case the ashes got too thick in the air."

Jean Brownlee, 35
Laundry worker
Spokane

"I was born and raised in apple country, in a town with 850 people. My mother makes the best home-made bread and apple pie in the world. But everybody here says that. There's a lot of competition between the mothers and the grandmothers around here."

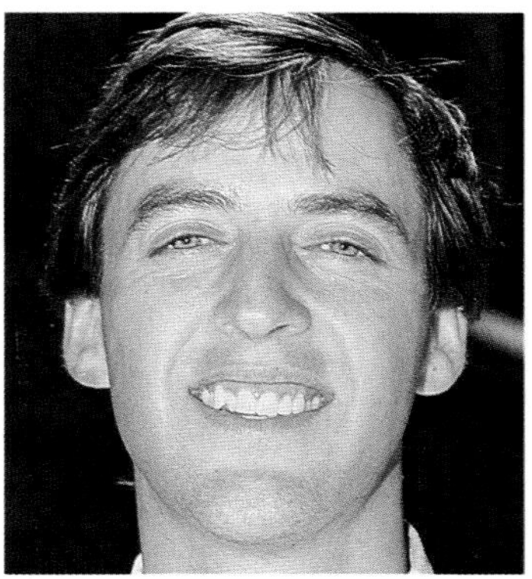

Matthew Crane, 30
Law clerk
Tacoma

"To most, we're one big national forest. We're the evergreen state. I think Washington would like to be known as environmentally progressive. We do protect our parks and wilderness and we're trying to protect the Puget Sound against further pollution. It rains so much that they say there is a Seattle Rain Festival that lasts from October through April. You can buy hats that have umbrellas built in."

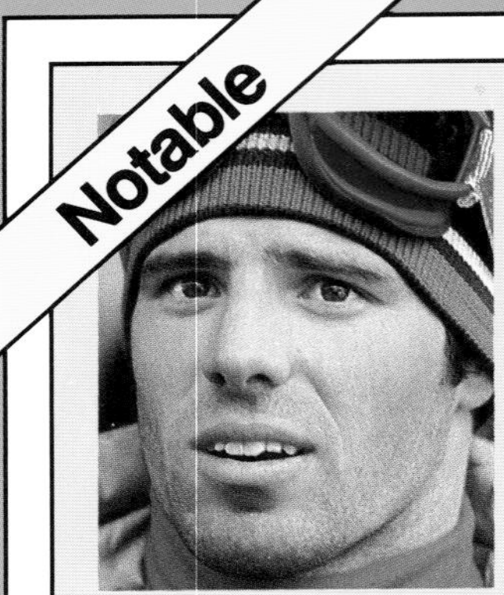

Phil Mahre, 30, still lives in his hometown of Yakima, Wash. He won medals in the 1980 and 1984 Olympics and was World Cup champion 1981 to 1983. He and twin brother, Steve, retired from competitive skiing in 1984.

Skiing a family affair for former Olympian

USA TODAY: You've traveled around the world. How do you compare Washington to some of the more exotic places you've been?

MAHRE: Washington basically has everything that anybody else has. I think we actually have a little more variety than a lot of states. Over near the West Coast, it's a little bit greener, a little lusher, and maybe a little bit damper. You come to the east side of the mountains, and the area is a lot drier.

USA TODAY: Do you think of yourself as a Washington state person or a Westerner?

MAHRE: Westerner. Even to travel to the East Coast is like traveling to Europe for me. The culture from the East Coast to the West Coast is dramatically different. I kind of view the East Coast as Europe. It was just like a foreign country to me.

USA TODAY: How do you rate the skiing that's available in the Northwest?

MAHRE: It's funny; a lot of people ask me, "Where is your favorite place to ski?" I'd just as soon go back home and ski White Pass as anywhere in the world, I think, mainly because I grew up there. And it's a small area. It has everything a big area offers, just on a smaller scale.

USA TODAY: After you skied all those years as a racer and skiing was almost your profession, how do you react now when someone says, "Let's go spend the day skiing for the fun of it"?

MAHRE: When I first retired, I almost wanted to take a whole year and not ski at all. Just get away from the sport. There are times when I do think if I ski 10 days a year on my personal time, that would be enough. I have two youngsters, a little boy who's 3 and a little girl who's 4, and they both ski now. It takes on a little bit different meaning. When they get excited about it, it becomes a family event or sport.

USA TODAY: What do you and your brother, Steve, have planned now?

MAHRE: We continue to be involved in the ski industry. We do a lot of promotional work as well as product development with different companies. We started our own clothing line. We're both pursuing car racing. So that's kind of from one competitive field to another.

Topic: WASHINGTON

It's two states — and both are beautiful

USA TODAY: Washington has a rainy reputation. But people seem to love it anyway. Why?

GARDNER: You're within an hour of some of the best skiing in the United States. You're within an hour of some of the best sailing. We have a tremendous cultural base. While we're constantly trying to improve our schools, they are considered excellent.

USA TODAY: Is it really that wet here?

GARDNER: Yeah, it rains. But it rains differently than you're used to. It could be raining out there with some measurable rainfall, and you could walk through it in the clothes you're in half the year. Most of us wear light- to medium-weight suits. It's essentially a mild climate most of the year.

USA TODAY: What do you think distinguishes Washington from other states?

GARDNER: We're doing a lot more movie production in this state because you can virtually film as though you're in any other state. We've got mountains, mesas, desert, water, canals, and small, old communities to give you a New England flavor. In a lot of respects, we have two states here, and they're both beautiful: The West, which is made up of mountains, the Sound, numerous lakes, and tremendous beauty, and Eastern Washington, which is a desert state, but highly irrigated. So we have a tremendous range of agricultural products — next to California, probably the greatest diversity.

USA TODAY: Washington is the closest of the contiguous states to the Far East. How much are you involved in Pacific Rim trade?

GARDNER: Tonnage out of our ports has increased significantly, and we're very competitive with other West Coast ports. We don't have the population base here, probably never will. I'm not sure that we want to be a major market. But in terms of being a financial center, being an end point for shipment to the Far East or for imports from the Far East, Washington is tremendously well located. We have the highest income per capita on trade of any state.

***Booth Gardner**, 50, a Democrat, has been governor since January 1985. He's a former state senator, county executive and businessman.*

USA TODAY: Mount St. Helens caused great damage when it erupted in 1980. What's the status of that area now?

GARDNER: Everything is basically back to normal.

USA TODAY: The state is legendary for its apples, but aren't some Washington residents now looking into seaweed farming?

GARDNER: We have environmental concerns, but if we can work our way through those, I'm very confident of aquaculture. We'll grow seaweed, and salmon, and shellfish.

USA TODAY: You're a soccer booster and coach. What other spectator sports interest you?

GARDNER: None. I go to my obligatory football game between the University of Washington and Washington State.

USA TODAY: If the Mariners brought the World Series out here, wouldn't you go to that?

GARDNER: Sure. Although I have a cardinal rule: I will not be announced, or throw out a ball, or do anything official.

USA TODAY: Why?

GARDNER: My first name is Booth. And I've been unable to distinguish between "Booth" and "Boo."

West Virginia

Visited: Aug. 12-13, 1987
Featured in USA TODAY: Aug. 17

"Fiddlin' runs in families. My two brothers play. My mother and father play. My aunts and uncles play. We call it blue-eyed soul. The music comes in through your ears, goes down through your soul and comes out your feet."

Mack Samples
Dean of records
Glenville State College
Linn, W.Va.

West Virginia

Loyalties: To the USA, families, farms, fiddles

Many across the USA have talked about seceding from the state they're in and forming their own. West Virginia did.

Part of Virginia as one of the original 13 states. But, when Virginia joined the Confederate forces in 1861, folks in the west broke away and fought on the Union's side.

President Lincoln decreed West Virginia the 35th state in 1863. Their independence created the state's motto: "Mountaineers are always free."

Free and fiercely loyal. To their country. Church. Family. Farms. Fiddles.

John Denver put it to words and music:

"Country roads, take me home,
to the place I belong . . ."

Mountaineers jump to their feet and hoot and holler when it's played. That's often. Fiddlin' and singin' is still a big part of life in the Mountain State.

SAMPLES: Loves to fiddle 'blue-eyed soul' music.

Mack Samples, 48, of Linn (pop. 100), is dean of records at Glenville State College. But he'd rather talk about his 30-acre farm and his fiddle than his job.

"Fiddlin' runs in families. My two brothers play. My mother and father play. My aunts and uncles play. We call it blue-eyed soul. The music comes in through your ears, goes down through your soul and comes out your feet."

Samples exemplifies the vast majority of West Virginians who wouldn't want to live anywhere else and/or those who left and came back.

"Like a lot of people, I went away, but I came back home. I was working on my Ph.D. and was on my way up. One day I asked myself, 'What the hell am I doing?' and I came back home where I belong. I won't get rich or get famous but all the things I like to do are right here."

"Right here" for most Mountaineers is on the farm or in small towns or cities. Sixty-one percent of the 1.9 million residents are classified as "rural." Only two cities have more than 50,000 population. Charleston, the capital (pop. 63,968), and Huntington (pop. 63,684).

Despite their pride in their land, folks here resent the backwoods "barefoot and pregnant" stereotype that persists with some comedians and some writers. Some facts back the Mountaineers. West Virginia has:

■ Lowest birthrate in the USA. 12.6 per 1,000 people. Average for all 50 states is 15.5.

■ High Scholastic Aptitude Test (SAT) scores. Math average: W.Va. 502, USA 475. Verbal: W.Va. 462, USA 431.

■ Lowest crime rate in the USA. 2,316.7 per 100,000 population. USA average is 5,207. West Virginia has been No. 50 in state crime rate since 1973. Last year, Wheeling also had the lowest crime record of any USA city.

West Virginia's national image traditionally has been linked to coal mining. Actually, it ranks No. 3 in coal production, behind Kentucky and Wyoming.

About 25,000 miners dug 130.7 million tons of coal in 1986. Most of those still working the mines stay with it because it's a family tradition.

Dave Gearde, 48, Route 1 in Rivesville (pop. 1,327), has been working the mines for 19 years. "My father was a coal miner. It's a job like any other. But the hazardous conditions limit what you can think about at work. It doesn't pay to daydream when you're down there."

GEARDE: No place for daydreams in coal mine shafts.

As traditions go in the Mountain State, the family church may be the strongest of all.

"When you think of church in West Virginia, think of family. People go to the church where their grandpa went. I've lived all over West Virginia. There are churches on every corner. The harshness of life makes religion a serious thing," says the Rev. **Charles R. Echols**, 44, minister of the United Methodist Church in Huntington.

Adds the Rev. **Edwin S. Harper**, pastor of the Apostolic Church in Huntington:

"The church here is the basis for the family structure. It's the anchor during our boom-bust cycles. It's the moderating influence. The hardest thing to find here is someone who admits to being a sinner."

That's Plain Talk from West Virginia.

Snapshot

Mountain State

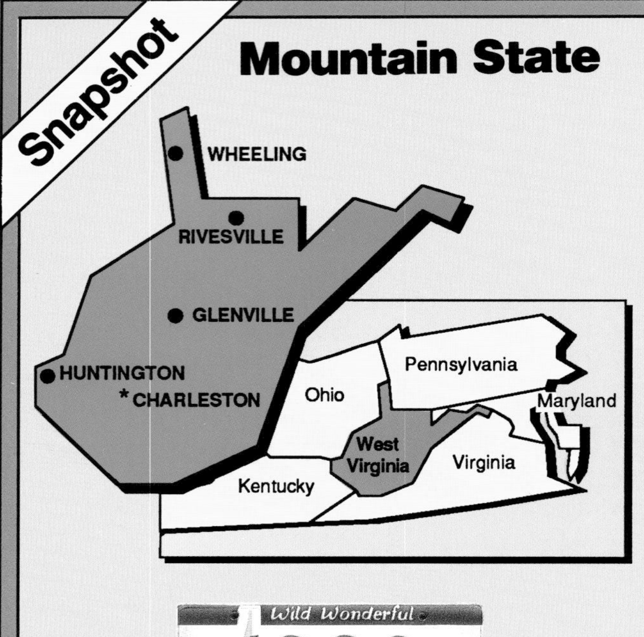

Wild Wonderful
1863
WEST VIRGINIA

ENTERED USA: June 20, 1863, 35th state

MOTTO: Mountaineers are always free
POPULATION: 1,919,000; rank, 34th
LARGEST CITY: Charleston, pop. 63,968
CAPITAL: Charleston
LAND: 24,119 square miles; rank, 41st
POPULATION DENSITY: 79.6 per square mile; rank, 26th
RACIAL MIX: 96.2% white; 3.3% black; 0.3% Asian and Pacific islanders. Hispanic heritage: 0.7%.

Uniquely W.Va.

TAX INCLUDED: West Virginia was the first state to have a sales tax. It took effect July 1, 1921.

BILLBOARD BIRTH: Outdoor advertising originated in Wheeling about 1908 when the Block Brothers Tobacco Co. painted bridges and barns with the slogan, "Treat Yourself to the Best; Chew Mail Pouch."

HOUSE OF COAL: White Sulphur Springs is home to Coal House, the only residence in the world built entirely of coal. Mr. and Mrs. David T. Myles have lived there since June 1, 1961.

BLOCK PARTY: The 1500 block of Virginia Street in downtown Charleston is the USA's longest block — four-tenths of a mile.

RAPID TRANSIT: River runners call the first rapid on Cheat River below Albright "Decision." Reason: Once you enter Cheat Canyon, there's no turning back.

Jerry Cornell, 44
Coal stacker operator
Huntington

"I feel pretty lucky to have a job in coal. It's not the cleanest job, but it's a job and it's steady. You have to take the bad with the good. West Virginia would be nowhere without coal. We supply the coal that makes energy for the power plants. I guess that makes me partly responsible for lighting up the world. A little part of the world anyway."

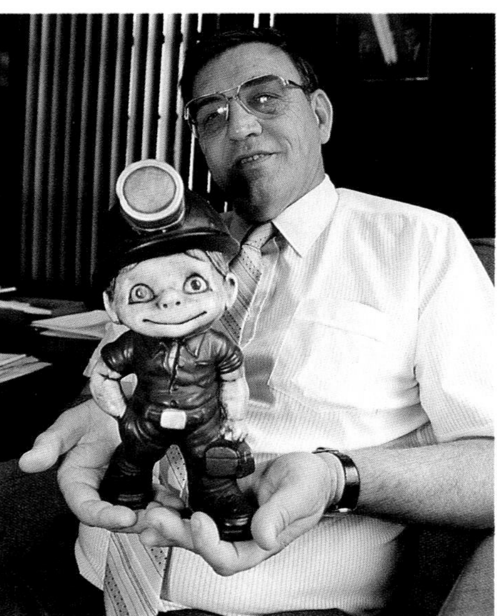

Eugene Claypole, 49
President, Local 31
United Mine Workers
Fairmont

"There's a strong camaraderie among coal miners. You have to depend on each other. When something goes wrong, you may have to depend on guys 10 miles away. Most miners have fathers who were miners and brothers and uncles who were miners. It's a family tradition."

Voices
of West Virginia

Darrell Meadows, 44
Glassblower
Culloden

"I like working glass. It's satisfying. You take a blob of glass out of the furnace and you get to pulling and yanking and twisting and you form it into something. Hopefully you have some idea of what you're doing."

Linda Hazelwood, 38
Factory worker
Lindside

"There's not a lot of hustle and bustle here. You can sit on the front porch in peace. You're not distracted by pollution or traffic. Everybody is family where I live, even if they're not kin. People trust people. Everybody knows everybody else, their parents and grandparents. They want the respect and admiration of their community and they don't mind earning it."

Ruth Prickett, 55
Receptionist
Monumental

"When our children started growing, we decided we didn't want them exposed to the problems of the big-city environment, so we moved back and built a house on land that had been in my husband's family for almost 200 years. Now I can't see myself living any place else. The people here all feel like family."

Harold Brookman, 59
Salesman
Princeton

"We're West Virginia mountaineers; always free. Out here in the mountains, you have to learn to trust others. You never know when you might need them. You know the saying, 'Only the strong survive.' Well, that's us. We're more Southern than Yankee, but we have our share of Yankee ingenuity."

Sharon Gresham, 29
Personnel specialist
South Charleston

"People here are more into home, church and family. They aren't very materialistic. You don't see people wearing designer clothes. Moving here has given me more of an appreciation for people. A lot of folks here are church-going. The first question most people I meet ask is what church I belong to."

***Chuck Yeager**, 64, who was born in Myra, W.Va., has set nearly 40 aviation records. Yeager, a retired Air Force brigadier general, in 1947 became the first to break the sound barrier. He wrote* Yeager: An Autobiography.

We took advantage of every opportunity

USA TODAY: You grew up in Hamlin, W.Va. What was life like when you were a kid?

YEAGER: We were very well-disciplined kids, meaning we had chores to do. We had to milk cows, work in the garden, hoe, and plow and cut wood. You didn't argue and you kept it clean, and you were Boy Scouts. And you learned to honor your country.

USA TODAY: In your book, you described the time you bailed out, grabbed the top of a pine tree, and let it bend over to the ground. Did you learn to do that in West Virginia?

YEAGER: As kids, we used to climb a tree up to about 30 or 40 feet and bend the top of the tree over to the next tree and get on it, climb up it, and bend it over. We could travel for miles in the woods and never touch the ground.

USA TODAY: How else did your upbringing help you as a pilot?

YEAGER: You learned to take advantage of everything you had presented to you. We went to school like all kids do, from 8 to 4, but then we'd go to a garage at night to learn to weld, and repair machinery.

USA TODAY: Is that sort of education unique to West Virginia?

YEAGER: I would say West Virginia is like all rural areas where you can't just go buy anything because, No. 1, you didn't have the money, and secondly, it might not even be available. Dad taught me what machinery meant, and how to respect it. That helped me to survive in combat and research flying.

USA TODAY: Do you get a big thrill now working with the astronauts?

YEAGER: I get a charge out of new technology.

USA TODAY: How do you want the nation to remember you?

YEAGER: You don't have much control over what people think of you. Primarily, I think they all admire my dedication to my job and to the country. Also, don't forget that you have to be at the right place at the right time to accomplish something.

USA TODAY: Isn't it more than that?

YEAGER: Primarily, you've got to know your equipment. And there's a lot of luck involved, too.

Topic: WEST VIRGINIA

Our quality of life is low-key, low-crime

USA TODAY: What have been the major changes in West Virginia since you were first elected governor in 1968?

MOORE: If I had talked with you 12 years ago, Massachusetts Gov. Mike Dukakis would have had the highest unemployment in the country, and West Virginia would have had the next to the lowest. In 12 years, we've seen an absolute reversal. I came back to the governorship in West Virginia in 1985 after the state had led the nation in unemployment for six years. So, our positions in that time frame have changed dramatically.

USA TODAY: Why?

MOORE: The demand for energy, the transition in the U.S. economy, has not been kind to West Virginia. The Rust Belt syndrome had a tremendous impact upon us, because we were a heavy manufacturing state.

USA TODAY: So it was a combination of factors?

MOORE: Bad economic days were compounded because we were furnishing the energy in the country to the manufacturing base, the steel complex, and so on down the line. So we got hit on both ends of the spectrum. We saw a great deterioration in the manufacturing industries and then in the energy base of our state, which still represents more than 50 percent of the total economy of West Virginia.

USA TODAY: Coal production is down?

MOORE: Oddly enough, we've produced more coal in the last year than we've done at any time. But it's been at a lower price per ton because of world market conditions. That gives us a much smaller base to tax.

USA TODAY: Are you making progress in reversing the overall economic downturn?

MOORE: We've made some progress, but we've got to diversify the economic base of the state to match what's happening in the country. For example, West Virginia trails the country in sharing in the distribution of defense-spending dollars, where you get something like $200 million out of that total monstrous defense budget.

***Arch Moore Jr.**, 64, a Republican, is West Virginia's first three-term governor. He also served six terms in the U.S. House of Representatives.*

USA TODAY: What has changed for the better?

MOORE: We have a modern highway system. We maintain a high structure of cultural activities in the cities. Our budget has increased from $700 million to $1.6 billion so it was a significant escalation. But in order to generate those funds, we had the highest personal income tax rate. We've now given that crown back to New York.

USA TODAY: What's West Virginia's best-kept secret?

MOORE: A lot of people do not realize we're a state. When you say you're from West Virginia and somebody says, "Well, I have a cousin who lives in Richmond," that's great, but Richmond is the capital of another state.

USA TODAY: How would you describe the quality of life in West Virginia?

MOORE: We have the lowest crime rate of any in the country. Our system of state parks is the finest on the Eastern Seaboard. We've got more fresh water than any other state east of the Mississippi. There is a quality of life here that is perhaps a little lower key, less pressure. We're a state that's tremendously proud of the talent of our people.

Wisconsin

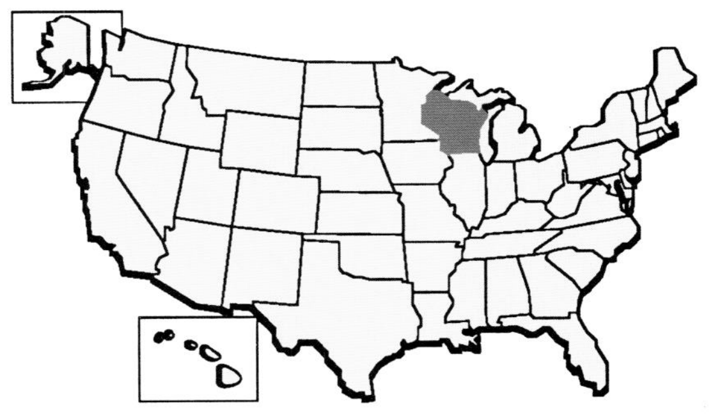

Visited: March 23-24, 1987
Featured in USA TODAY: March 27

"Government here is really by the people . . ."

Mary Ann Opelt
Retired
Madison, Wis.

Wisconsin

Social tinkering out; beer, bowling still in

"The beer that made Milwaukee famous" — Schlitz — isn't brewed there anymore. Stroh's now makes Schlitz in six other states.

The politics of progressive populism — fathered by **"Battling Bob" La Follette** — is gone.

But across the bountiful Badger State, settled by hardy Germans, Irish, Scandinavians and Swiss, the people in 1987 still enjoy most of the old pleasures and some new politics.

The ABCs of life in Wisconsin:

- **A**ctivism, right and left.
- **B**eer, bratwurst and bowling.
- **C**ows, cheese and crackers.

People here always have had their say and taken turns getting their way. Conservatives. Liberals. Populists. Even Socialists. Now the conservatives are in command.

Republican Gov. **Tommy Thompson**, 45, a former butcher boy and farmer, later a lawyer and legislator, from Elroy (pop. 1,540), upset Democratic Gov. **Anthony Earl** last November.

Thompson makes it clear social tinkering is out. "We were spending ourselves out of business. Now we're going to budget to stay in business," says Thompson.

He has ordered all government to reduce spending to 95 percent of last year's level. That's generally being accepted, even at the University of Wisconsin at Madison, the 1960s hotbed of rebellion against anything establishment.

SHAW: Activism not dead on University of Wisconsin campus.

Ken Shaw, president of the 150,000-student, 26-campus university system, says student activism is not dead, it's just different.

Twenty years ago, it was protests against Vietnam and racism. "Now activism includes a conservative campus newspaper and extensive ROTC participation," says Shaw.

Off campuses and outside government houses, most Wisconsinites are conciliatory and content, if not always comfortable. Fun is foremost with most.

BEER STOP: 'Milwaukee has the best of everything — beer, sausage, cheese,' says bartender Douglas Haese, 38.

Beer drinking is big, although Gov. Thompson says alcoholism is no more a problem here than elsewhere. That may be because many bars serve complimentary cheese and crackers or popcorn with their beer. Bars are social centers.

Wisconsin now leads the USA in the number of bars per person, according to the most recent U.S. Census data. Across the USA, there is one bar for every 2,273 of us. In the most recent national census, five Wisconsin cities were on top of the list with three times the average:

1. Eau Claire. . . . 1 for every 629
2. La Crosse . . . . 1 for every 676
3. Kenosha . . . . . 1 for every 693
4. Green Bay . . . 1 for every 703
5. Milwaukee . . . 1 for every 843

"I'm the one who brings up the level of consumption of beer," boasts **Paul Soffa**, 21, student at Milwaukee Area Technical College in Milwaukee.

"I like the quality of life here. I can cross the street and get 28 kinds of cheese," says **George Tautch**, 64, a retired banker in Westport.

At Marquette University, freshman **Patrick Burgess**, 21:

"Milwaukee has five distinct aromas. Four are awful — from a tannery, yeast factory, rendering plant, brewery. But one is great — when the wind blows off the lake you can actually taste the chocolate from the Ambrosia chocolate plant."

That's Plain Talk from Wisconsin.

Snapshot

Badger State

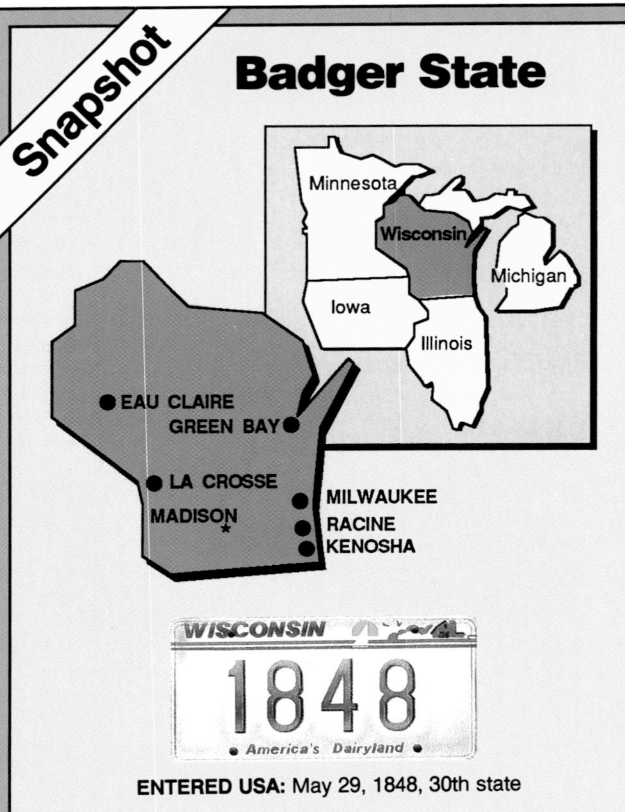

ENTERED USA: May 29, 1848, 30th state

MOTTO: Forward
POPULATION: 4,785,000; rank, 17th
LARGEST CITY: Milwaukee, pop. 620,811
CAPITAL: Madison, pop. 170,745
LAND: 54,426 square miles; rank, 25th
POPULATION DENSITY: 88 per square mile; rank, 24th
RACIAL MIX: 94.4% white; 3.9% black; 0.4% Asian and Pacific islanders. Hispanic heritage: 1.3%.

Uniquely Wis.

GONE FISHIN': In Wisconsin, a leading fishing state, there are 2,444 trout streams. End to end, they would stretch 9,235 miles.

MALT SHOP: The first malted milk was made in Racine in 1883.

LUCK O' THE IRISH: The first St. Patrick's Day parade in the USA was held in 1843 in Milwaukee. It was sponsored by a temperance society.

SCHOOL DAYS: Former Israeli prime minister Golda Meir attended public schools in Milwaukee.

MARCHING BEAT: "On Wisconsin," written by Carl Bech in 1909, became the official state song in 1959. Ex-Beatle Paul McCartney owns the rights to the song.

NAME GAME: The city of La Crosse was named by the French for a game that Indians played with long-handled rackets that resembled bishop's crosses.

Voices

of Wisconsin

Dan Eggert, 39
Computer technician
Appleton

"I was born and raised in the Fox River Valley. I like the outdoors, recreation, fishing, camping and canoeing in Wisconsin. They have a great state park system here in Wisconsin. There are many, and they are quite unique in themselves as far as the environment goes. The last couple of years we've tried to visit some of the ones we haven't been to. We've visited about a dozen so far."

Brian Jooss, 12
Student
Green Bay

"I like Wisconsin because it's a bigger state, with more things to do than other states. It's also a dairy state, so you get products like milk and ice cream."

Nick Smith, 45
Insurance firm executive
Wausau

"Wausau offers a unique blend of rural and urban living. Residents are concerned with the quality of life in the area and actively support cultural activities that are uncommon for a city the size of Wausau. The local spirit is one of pride and optimism with a concern for progress."

Mary Ann Opelt, 69
Retired
Madison

"Wisconsin people are hardworking, very practical. There's a work ethic here, and we are very civic-minded. People came here for freedom, and the government here is really by the people, for the people. We're responsible for making the state what it is."

Kevin Hermening, 27
Advertising salesman
Wausau

"When I was in Iran, I missed the outdoors in Wisconsin. I missed the skiing. I didn't even realize what I missed the most until I had been back for almost a year and the leaves began to change color. It was so beautiful, I began to cry." (Hermening was held hostage in Iran from Nov. 4, 1979, to Jan. 20, 1981.)

Steve Maertzweiler, 37
Production supervisor for brewery
Milwaukee

"I think the people here are real down to earth. There's a lot of ethnic diversity. I'm a sports fan and I enjoy watching the different teams here compete. And I like to party. There's so much good food here in Milwaukee, and good beer to go with it is needed. I like making beer in the city that made it famous."

Sheila Butzine, 20
Student
Fond du Lac

"I like the changes of the seasons. There's always variety. You can get outside and do things like go swimming; just being outdoors. The wilderness, hilly areas and farmlands are interesting to see. We sometimes go to Wisconsin Dells in the central part of the state. I like to visit some of the different natural, wilderness areas. We live right by the Mississippi River."

Ray Nitschke, 50, was a linebacker for the Green Bay Packers during their glory days under Vince Lombardi. The Packers retired Nitschke's No. 66, and he was enshrined in the Pro Football Hall of Fame.

Fans work harder after the team wins

USA TODAY: How do you explain the strong emotional attachment Green Bay has always had for the Packers?

NITSCHKE: It's really a unique, marvelous thing. When I came into Green Bay in 1958, from Chicago and the Bears, I didn't really know what the Packers were all about. Then I found out that the community really cares about their team. They were concerned about your welfare, and how you behaved.

USA TODAY: Do you notice a difference in the mood in the town after a Packers victory?

NITSCHKE: Yes. The people in all the factories and in the paper mills work a little better than they do when they don't win. You know when the Packers win and you know when they lose.

USA TODAY: Three Packers have been involved in sexual-assault cases. What impact has that had?

NITSCHKE: It takes away from the image of the Packers, and it's sad. The community is forgiving. I think they will continue to support the team.

USA TODAY: Do the Packers play dirty?

NITSCHKE: I think a few players play dirty, and other teams have players who do.

USA TODAY: How would a great coach like Vince Lombardi have handled that situation?

NITSCHKE: Lombardi would have been very disturbed, naturally. Guys do make mistakes. I know he would have been tough on them, though.

USA TODAY: What was Lombardi like?

NITSCHKE: He could have been successful in any effort that he chose. He was a very bright man, a Christian. He had this tremendous intensity.

USA TODAY: Why do you live in Green Bay?

NITSCHKE: It's the way of life. I have many friends, and I feel a part of the community. In Wisconsin I've been treated with open arms.

USA TODAY: When you look back at your career, what great moments stand out?

NITSCHKE: Just being a Packer player. And playing as long as I did play. I played 15 years. To represent Green Bay all over the country on the football field was a wonderful experience.

Topic: WISCONSIN

Our state has become world bio-tech capital

USA TODAY: You're on your third month at your new job. How do you like it?

THOMPSON: I enjoy it. It's been a tremendous experience, and I think that I have probably had more monumental issues thrown at me for a new administration than any other governor.

USA TODAY: Such as?

THOMPSON: The attempt to put together a loan package to allow American Motors to stay in business here; the contest between all the other communities that have General Motors plants — to build GM's new truck line, which Janesville won — and then we had several major labor strikes, plus putting together a government, and a budget, and having the legislature in session and solving the prison issue.

USA TODAY: To many people, Wisconsin means dairyland and beer drinking. Is that an accurate image?

THOMPSON: It's a misconception. The University of Wisconsin is the No. 1 public university receiving research grants. In the last several years, we have become the bio-tech capital of the world; we have over 100 small bio-tech companies that have started up. It isn't just the beer drinking any more — it's bio-tech, it's manufacturing, it's tourism, it's agriculture, it's a very diversified economy.

USA TODAY: Many of your farms are in financial trouble. Have you considered a moratorium on foreclosures?

THOMPSON: That is counterproductive. All you do there is hurt the individual farmer who's doing well and going in to get a loan from the bank. If you put a moratorium on foreclosures, the bank is not going to loan money on agricultural pursuits; therefore, you hurt the people you're trying to help. It's the wrong approach.

USA TODAY: When this crisis ends, how many farmers will you have lost?

THOMPSON: We're down to about 40,000 dairy farmers right now. In 1970, we had 95,000.

***Tommy Thompson**, 45, a Republican, was elected last fall. A lawyer, Thompson was elected to the Wisconsin Assembly in 1966 and elected Republican floor leader in 1981.*

USA TODAY: What would you say is Wisconsin's worst problem right now?

THOMPSON: Our biggest problem is that we have not been competitive. We have not sold ourselves as a state. We have been unable to increase our exports, and we need to do that.

USA TODAY: What is the message you want to get out?

THOMPSON: Wisconsin's a beautiful state. We've got a diversified economy, a great educational system, and a lot of things to offer economic development. We've got the greatest group of people in the world and a quality of life second to none.

USA TODAY: Care to make a prediction on either the Milwaukee Brewers or the Green Bay Packers this year?

THOMPSON: The Brewers are going to have at least a .500 season. We've got a brand-new coach by the name of Tom Trebelhorn, and we have some very talented young people. The Bucks, our basketball team, have been hurting, but they'll be back fairly strong in conference play next year. The Packers? They've got some internal problems. But as Vince Lombardi in 1966 was able to make the unsung and the unknown a world-championship team, I am sure the Pack will be back.

Wyoming

Visited: June 9-11, 1987
Featured in USA TODAY: June 15

"Drugstore cowboys overdo everything. Bola tie, hat, boots, vest, the works. Mainly you can tell from their attitude. Real cowboys are quiet. Withdrawn. And they always have chew in their mouth."

Gordon Prickett
Assistant manager
Western Ranchman Outfitters
Cheyenne, Wyo.

Wyoming

Western, but not wild; women work a legacy

It has a Wild West image. Only half true. Wyoming. Pop. 507,000. No. 50 in the USA. The whole state has roughly the same number of people as Atlanta. Or Cleveland. Denver. Seattle.

Yet in size it ranks ninth. 365 miles across. 275 north to south. In those 97,914 square miles:

- 1,325,000 cattle.
- 819,000 sheep.
- 92,000 horses, 44,000 classified as "Wild."

No wonder the Wild West image. It IS very Western. But not really wild. The horses and hoopla hype the image. Locals feed it. Tourists love it.

Gov. **Michael J. Sullivan**, 47, added to it when he said in his campaign: "We in Wyoming need to get a little wild and crazy, because we have something special."

FIRST LADY: Digs own way.

The first-term Democrat explained what he meant as he met with BusCateers on the patio of the ranch-style governor's mansion in Cheyenne, state capital (pop. 47,283). Working at home while recovering from back surgery, the Guv wore faded blue jeans, heavily scuffed brown cowboy boots.

"I just meant we should trumpet our wares a little." When he made the remark, the Guv and his wife had just returned from New York's traffic jams. Said he wanted to put up a billboard next to the Lincoln Tunnel reading:

"If you lived in Wyoming, you could be fishing now."

Fishing, hunting, riding, rodeoing, gardening is what Wyoming people do to take advantage of their great outdoors.

Right outside the governor's mansion. First Lady **Jane M. Sullivan**, in tan jeans and flowered gardener's gloves, was digging flower ditches. "The guys were having a tough time getting started. I have a pretty good idea of where I want everything to go."

Wyoming women have gone where they want to go for a long time:

- First state to elect a woman governor. **Nellie Tayloe Ross**. 1924.
- First to give women the right to vote and hold office — while still a territory. 1869.

Modern-day Wyoming women take advantage of that legacy. They work at whatever pleases them. Teachers and secretaries, sure. But also ranch hands. Construction bosses.

Lauri Hepper, 29, is foreman of a railroad gang in Gillette (pop. 14,545). She and her crew dig ditches, haul away rotten ties, lay new track. "When I first started, one guy said I should get a waitress job. But I'm stubborn." She stayed, got promoted. Now she supervises nine burly guys.

LAURI: Happy bossing railroad gang.

Wyoming guys do their thing too. In the coal fields. In oil or gas production. On horseback. Coal, oil and gas has been a roller coaster way of making a living. Horsing is steady.

Wyoming cowboys are legend. Drugstore cowboys and the real thing. How do you tell the difference?

Gordon Prickett, 46, assistant manager of Western Ranchman Outfitters in Cheyenne, tells you:

"Drugstore cowboys overdo everything. Bola tie, hat, boots, vest, the works. Mainly you can tell from their attitude. Real cowboys are quiet. Withdrawn. And they always have chew in their mouth."

GORDON: 'Cowboys are quiet.'

The real cowboys have a busy season coming up. Rodeo time is big time in Wyoming. Frontier Days in Cheyenne July 17-26 will draw 1,000 cowboy and cowgirl contestants, 300,000 spectators. They call it the "Western Mardi Gras."

To many in the USA, Wyoming is Yellowstone Park. First national park and the largest in the lower 48 states. 2.3 million visitors a year.

Old Faithful erupts, faithfully, about every 71.2 minutes. Breathtaking. Says **Roger Anderson**, 56, a machinist from Bremerton, Wash., on vacation with his wife, **Kay**, 52:

"You wonder what the first mountain men thought when they saw this. This couldn't just happen. It has to be God's work."

That's Plain Talk from Wyoming.

Snapshot

Equality State

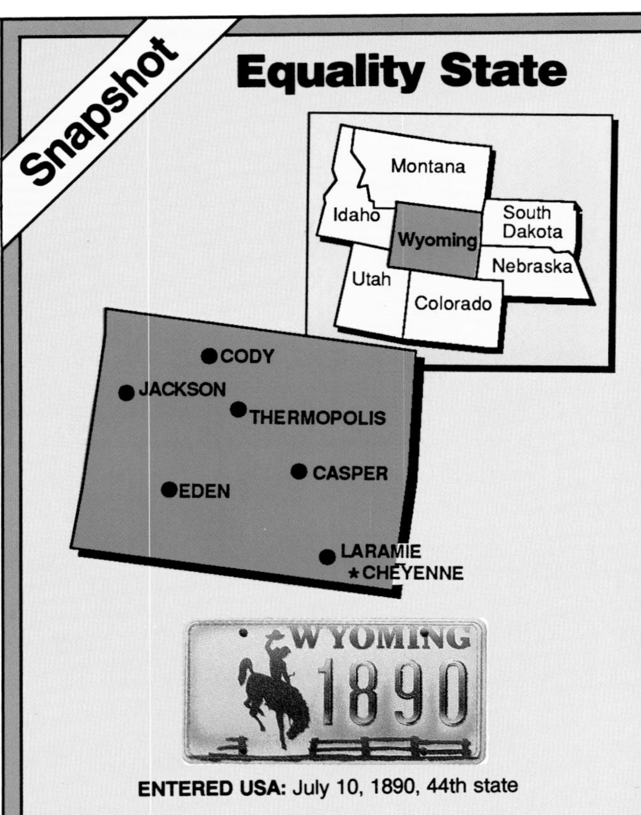

ENTERED USA: July 10, 1890, 44th state

MOTTO: Equal rights
POPULATION: 507,000; rank, 50th
LARGEST CITY: Casper, pop. 50,935
CAPITAL: Cheyenne, pop. 47,283
LAND: 97,914 square miles; rank, 9th
POPULATION DENSITY: 5.2 per square mile; rank, 49th
RACIAL MIX: 95.1% white; 1.5% American Indian; 0.7% black; 0.4% Asian and Pacific islanders. Hispanic heritage: 5.2%.

Uniquely Wyo.

SPACE ENCOUNTER: The spaceship in the movie "Close Encounters of the Third Kind" landed at Devils Tower National Monument in the Black Hills of Northeastern Wyoming.

NAMESAKES: A city, frontier port, mountain range, river and county are named for French fur trapper Jacques LaRamie.

BRIGHT IDEA: Thomas Edison was fishing on Battle Lake in 1878 when he came up with the idea for the incandescent electric lamp, a local tale says.

DOWNHILL RACERS: Jackson Hole Ski Area has the greatest vertical rise among all USA ski mountains — 4,135 feet.

HOLES IN THE WALL: Mountainmen and fur trappers described Wyoming valleys totally surrounded by mountains as "holes," as in Jackson Hole. A Wyoming box canyon was a hideout for Butch Cassidy and his outlaws — the Hole in the Wall gang.

Voices
of Wyoming

Mona Divine, 32
Park ranger
Yellowstone National Park

"I have a great deal of respect for the wildlife. Yellowstone is the animals' home. We have to remember that we're guests."

Cari Lammey, 20
Student
Cheyenne

"When you're a Wyoming woman, you're not looked at like, 'you can't do this or that.' I was raised around the rodeo way of life. I know I'm tougher than your average city girl. I could do just as good as any boy, even better."

Mike Tobin, 26
Oil field worker
Casper

"It's good money working in the oil field. I take pride in my work. There's lots of danger out here. You've got to keep a level head and use common sense. That's the way people are in Wyoming."

Ron Levene, 45
Realtor/founder
of Gunslingers Assn.
Cheyenne

"I figure I was born a hundred years too late. I always wanted to be a gunslinger. Lots of people come and say, 'Where are the cowboys and Indians?' They're surprised to see we have paved streets. Well, you can't run around dressed like this, shooting off guns, even in Cheyenne. It sounds corny, but this is still where the deer and the antelope play."

Katy Jane Irvine, 56
Homemaker
Thermopolis

"Thermopolis means hot city in Greek. We've got the second largest mineral hot springs in the world. The largest is in Germany. I swim in the water twice a day and I drink the water. People from the East would ask should they pack a gun. They can if they want to, but we don't go out in the street and shoot each other."

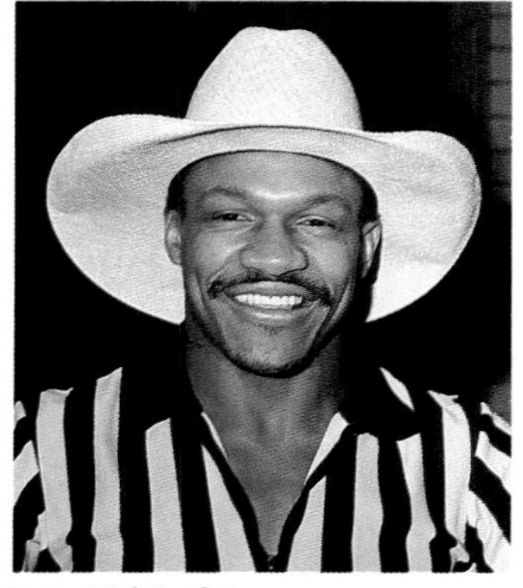

Bob Hill, 31
Bouncer
Cheyenne

"This is where a man is a man. Regardless of his color, it's the Grizzly Adams mentality. Nobody messes with you here. I guess it goes back to the old days of trappers and mountainmen. And out here, they're not prejudiced. Traditionally, black guys aren't into cowboys and westerns. I've learned to like it."

Mary Ann Grubb, 36
Homemaker/
horse trainer
Eden

"Open spaces are what we have the most of in Wyoming. Almost everywhere you look there's a park. We're proud of our state and our park. People all over the world know about Old Faithful. People save up for months to come here, and it's right in our back yard."

Jim Stone, 51
Boot store owner
Jackson

"The real working cowboy won't buy the fancy boots. He'll buy the best pair he can afford and keep getting them repaired. He'll take a boot as far as it will go. The real working cowboy is a different breed."

***Curt Gowdy**, 68, grew up in Cheyenne, and now lives near Boston. One of the USA's best-known sportscasters, he called every All-Star Game and World Series for NBC from 1966-75. He's won four Emmys.*

Fishing's great here; so are the people

USA TODAY: What was life like growing up in Cheyenne?

GOWDY: Fantastic. I had the greatest boyhood a boy could ever have. Wyoming is a big, vast place loaded with great fishing streams and wilderness. And lovely, open, honest people. And the outdoors. I had a big back yard and the whole state to claim.

USA TODAY: You're an avid fisherman. Is the fishing good in Wyoming?

GOWDY: Wyoming and Montana are the two best trout-fishing states in America. And it's still good.

USA TODAY: Any favorite fishing spots?

GOWDY: My dad and I would go fishing around Laramie where I went to college. There was the Little Laramie River there and the Big Laramie. We'd fish the Trout River a lot. If we saw one car, my father would leave — he thought it was overcrowded.

USA TODAY: Do you get to Wyoming often?

GOWDY: Quite often. I own two radio stations in Laramie, and I go back and tend to business there. My mother lives in Cheyenne. She's 89 now.

USA TODAY: You're also on the board of directors at the Buffalo Bill Historical Society. What does the society do?

GOWDY: It's a great Western museum. When James Michener wrote *Centennial*, he visited all the Western museums, and he said this was the best.

USA TODAY: What kinds of things does the museum feature?

GOWDY: We have four arms there. We have the Whitney Gallery of Western Art. We have the Buffalo Bill wing. We have the Indian Plains wing. And we have the Winchester wing, which is all the gun collections that they had going back 2,000 years, back to the Chinese crossbow. Every year, 200,000 or 300,000 people go through it.

USA TODAY: Wyoming's also named a state park after you.

GOWDY: They passed this through the Legislature in recognition of all the promotion and plugs I'd done on behalf of the state. It's between Cheyenne and Laramie. They couldn't do anything nicer for a fellow than do that.

Topic: WYOMING

Independence thrives in wide-open spaces

USA TODAY: You've said a lot of people outside Wyoming still think it's cowboy-and-Indian country. Do people here also embrace the Wild West image?

SULLIVAN: We're proud of it. It is a part of our heritage and our tradition. I think that heritage, that tradition, makes not only the quality of life but the people, and the way we treat people, different as well. At least, we like to think that we make people feel welcome.

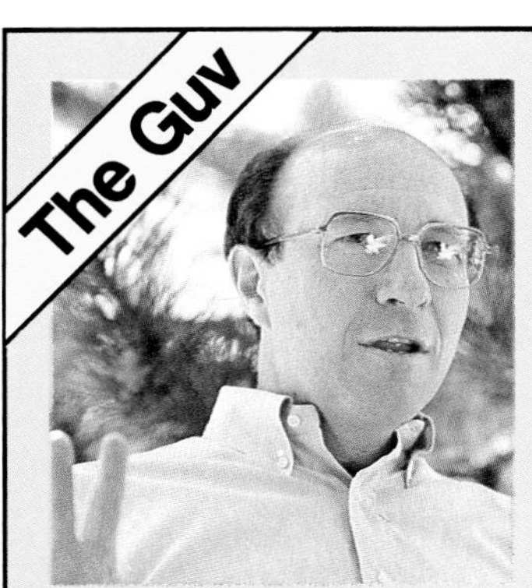

***Michael Sullivan**, 47, a Democrat, was elected governor in 1986. He was a medical malpractice attorney before his election.*

USA TODAY: What are the biggest surprises for visitors?

SULLIVAN: The wide-open spaces and the blue skies. They just can't believe how blue the sky is.

USA TODAY: Montana calls itself "Big Sky country." Your sky's just as big, isn't it?

SULLIVAN: I can't imagine that you can get many places with a bigger sky or a more beautiful one. One of the most beautiful parts about this end of the state is that every evening, the huge thunderheads develop. If you go from Casper to Laramie, there's the Shirley Basin area. You talk about open spaces, this time of year it's absolutely beautiful.

USA TODAY: How would you rate Wyoming with neighboring states, such as South Dakota, Montana, Colorado?

SULLIVAN: What distinguishes Wyoming from any state is the sparse population and the wide-open spaces. Now, all of the states that you've mentioned have wide spaces, but they're not quite as sparsely populated as we are. That gives us an independence and a sensitivity to people that may not exist in many of the other states.

USA TODAY: There's pressure for more development in the state. How do you balance development against environmental concerns?

SULLIVAN: We've been engaged in that process for many years. Particularly during the boom of the late '70s and '80s, those were serious problems, and continue to be. Now there's a concern that we might move toward development and forget the environmental resources. That struggle will continue. It should continue, notwithstanding the need for economic development. The environment and our quality of life, and the nature of Wyoming, are our major long-term resources.

USA TODAY: Your state has always had a boom-bust economy. Can you escape that cycle?

SULLIVAN: We're looking for ways. Any state that's as dependent upon natural resources and energy as we have been is going to go through a boom-bust cycle that we've seen nationwide in the energy business.

USA TODAY: How can you guard against the ups and downs?

SULLIVAN: Our efforts are to try to diversify, to attract other industries, to increase and encourage the tourist industry. That is such an important part. We're hit with a double whammy, as are many of the Midwestern and Central states, because we have both the energy crisis and the agricultural problem.

USA TODAY: How do you feel about the MX missiles, which are based at Warren Air Force Base in Southeastern Wyoming?

SULLIVAN: It's one of those issues that I'm still watching. I am concerned about the continuing defense escalation.

The White House

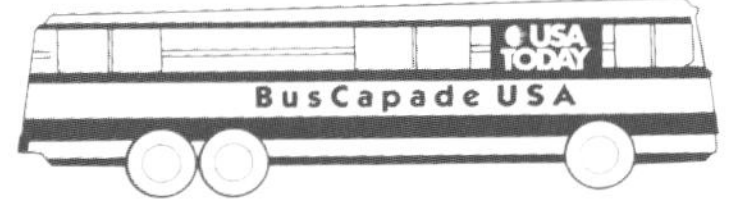

Visited: Sept. 10, 1987
Featured in USA TODAY: Sept. 11

The White House

Being governor is best training for presidency

USA TODAY: During our travels across the USA, the BusCapade team interviewed all 50 governors. You've been the governor of California, and now you're the president. Which is the tougher of the two jobs, and which one is more fun?

REAGAN: I found a certain excitement and pleasure in both of them, but being governor was the best training school for this job. Earlier in our time, that was normally the source of presidents. It is the nearest thing to this job; the only addition that you have here is the national security part of the job, which is supposed to be the most important, according to the Constitution. But governors are the chief executives in their states, and we have to remember that. Our government was created to be a federation of sovereign states.

USA TODAY: Is being governor better training than being in the U.S. Senate?

REAGAN: Yes — with all due respect to the senators.

USA TODAY: We also visited former Kansas Gov. Alf Landon at his Topeka home, just as you recently did for his 100th birthday. Do you also want to live to be 100 and do you think you will?

REAGAN: Considering the alternative, I'm in no hurry to go. Yes, I was quite impressed. I didn't remind him of the fact that when he ran for president, I was on the other side. I was a Democrat.

USA TODAY: The press pointed that out.

REAGAN: They did. But I was amazed at how sharp he is, how up on everything he is. Physically, he has a little problem walking and has to have assistance, but he also bore out something that I have believed in for much of my life, and that is the old cavalry slogan, "Nothing is so good for the inside of a man as the outside of a horse." Up until past 90, he was still riding every day.

USA TODAY: On the BusCapade trip, we were struck not only by the diversity of the USA, but also by its common bonds. What is it that makes this truly one nation?

REAGAN: Let me explain that with something that is not original with me. It's a concept that was written to me once in a letter. You can go to another country to live. You can go to France. But you can't become a Frenchman. You can go to Japan, and you can't become Japanese. But people from every corner of the world can come to America and become Americans.

USA TODAY: And that's something we share.

REAGAN: That is one of the great things that

***Ronald Reagan**, 76, a Republican, is the 40th president of the USA. He was interviewed on the last stop of the BusCapade tour at the White House by USA TODAY founder **Allen H. Neuharth** and reporters **Ken Paulson, Dan Greaney, Paula Burton** and **Johanna Neuman**.*

we're representative of — and the only thing we have in common — that someplace back in the ancestry of each one of us were people who had the courage and the love of freedom to uproot themselves from country and friends and come here, not even knowing the language to begin with, to become a part of this. They did so because they saw here something that met that inner demand.

USA TODAY: You were born and raised in small towns in Illinois, and several of your predecessors grew up in small communities. Is there something in small-town values that makes for a better president?

REAGAN: I don't know whether it makes for a better president, but I have to tell you that one of my regrets with my own children was that they had to be raised in a city. There is something about a small town — the very fact that you know everybody by name. I was born in a town of 850 people — Tampico. But then we moved to Dixon, where I really did my growing up and going through grade school and

OVAL OFFICE CHAT: President Ronald Reagan meets with Allen H. Neuharth.

high school. And that was about 10,000.

USA TODAY: What kind of town was Dixon?

REAGAN: As a boy, I had a dog that was the love of my life. He was named Bobby Jiggs, and Bobby Jiggs ran away. He was lost. And I was broken-hearted. Then I looked out a window, and here came a squad car down the middle of the street. And leaning out the window was the policeman who wasn't driving, and in front of them, coming down the middle of the street, was Bobby Jiggs.

USA TODAY: The squad car was herding Bobby Jiggs home?

REAGAN: Every time Bobby Jiggs tried to sashay, they were behind him, and the policeman was yelling. Even knew his name. They ran him right into our yard. They'd found him clear over on the other side of town. And they knew where he belonged. And it wasn't just us. We were small fry. You had to say, "My golly, they probably know everybody's dog in town!"

USA TODAY: Vice President Bush has portrayed himself as the candidate with experience. Can you give us an example or two where he has been a pivotal player in policy decisions?

REAGAN: I can't answer in that context. I don't know that there has ever been a vice president who has been more completely involved in all that goes on than this vice president. When I was governor, I made up my mind that the lieutenant governor should be like the executive vice president of a corporation. He should not be just sitting over on the sidelines waiting for something to happen to the governor.

USA TODAY: And you took the same approach with Vice President Bush?

REAGAN: I had the same resolution when I came here about the vice president. You don't leave that kind of ability out in another room while you're discussing all the decisions to be made. And so, he hasn't just been feeling my pulse, sitting by. He has been actively engaged. He's been all over the world in our behalf as an emissary. And, not just at funerals. With actual missions.

USA TODAY: How have you felt about facts concerning your health being portrayed so graphically in the media?

REAGAN: Sometimes the sketches on the air bothered me. I recognize that you give up a certain amount of privacy when you take this job. But I did get a little weary of reading all the diagnoses and prognoses that were being made during that time, and particularly more recently, when I found that I was supposed to be shuffling and hesitant and aged beyond my years. That was absolutely bothersome.

USA TODAY: Were you embarrassed?

REAGAN: I tried not to be. The biggest wound that I have suffered in all of that, though, just simply has to do with the most recent incident (of skin cancer). For seven years, beginning in my teens, I was a lifeguard. And most of my life, I have never been without the marks of a bathing suit because of tanning. During my motion picture days, it gave me extra sleep because I was one of the few who didn't have to wear makeup. I had a year-round tan. And now, as a result of this, I can't do that anymore. I'm a missionary for telling you all: "Don't lie on the beach and get tanned."

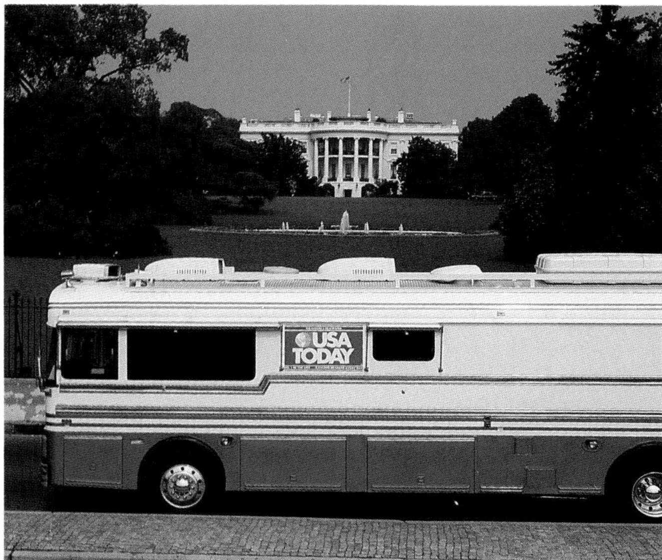

THE BUS STOPS HERE: BusCapade USA ends its nationwide tour at the White House.

USA TODAY: You've indicated that after you leave office, you will campaign for various candidates and causes. What might some of those include?

REAGAN: I would like to remove the amendment to the Constitution that limits the president to two terms, once I'm not in this job. I think it's an invasion of the democratic rights of the people to tell the people that they can't vote for whoever they want to vote for and for as long as they want to. A Congress has people who have been there for 30 or 40 years telling the American people they can't have a president they might want for more than two terms. I'd like to see that changed.

USA TODAY: The pope, who's visiting the USA, leads 630 million Roman Catholics and holds his position for life. As president, you lead 250 million people and can hold office for no more than eight years. Which is the better job?

REAGAN: It's hard for me to conceive of someone ever being in that position of having such a choice. The pope's calling is certainly to a higher level than even this one is, although I call upon his superior, I think, maybe as often as he does for help. I don't know of any president who's ever failed to do that. Lincoln said that he had been driven to his knees many times because there was no place else to go. And he also said that he couldn't meet the responsibilities of this position for 15 minutes if he did not feel that he could call upon someone who was stronger and wiser than all others.

Next stop

JetCapade to tour world

BusCapade will be followed by a worldwide "JetCapade" in 1988.

USA TODAY Founder Allen H. Neuharth and a small news team are planning a seven-month assignment that will take them to about 30 of the major countries in the world.

JetCapade reports will run weekly in USA TODAY's domestic and international editions from March through September. USA TODAY circulates in more than 50 countries from printing plants in Switzerland and Singapore.

BusCateers

The people behind the scenes and up front

Though Allen H. Neuharth's BusCapade team was made up of a small core of reporters and photographers who made the entire tour of the USA, many others helped in coverage of individual states.

There also were many who joined the tour to promote USA TODAY and assist with its nationwide circulation.

Others joined in to help produce this book.

Here is a list of those who helped:

Editorial:

Steve Anderson, Caesar Andrews, Joe Armstrong, Sam Atwood, Molly Badgett, Phyllis Bailey, Ashley Barnes, Theresa Barry, Jeff Beauchamp, Victoria Benning, Cathleen Black, Hal Bodley, Lark Borden, Ramon Bracamontes, Lou Brancaccio, Peter Bronson, Dean Brown, Robin Brown, Maxwilliam Brown, J. Taylor Buckley, Paula Burton.

Lisa Carlson, Melinda Carlson, Susan Catron, Don Collins, Monica Collins, Kathy Cook, James Cox, Byron Crawford, Diane Culbertson, Richard Curtis, Emilie Davis, Brian Donlon, Ernest Dumas.

Jerry Easterling, Gaynelle Evans, Mimi Feller, Joanna Firestone, Elizabeth Flansburg, Doug Fowler, Henry M. Freeman, Mary Freeman, Phil Fuhrer.

Bob Gabordi, Sheila Gibbons, Dale D. Glasgow,

BusCapade regulars

LOU BRANCACCIO
. . . editor

PAULA BURTON
. . . reporter

LISA DIXON
. . . promotions

JOEL DRIVER
. . . bus driver

GAYNELLE EVANS
. . . reporter

DAN GREANEY
. . . reporter

SCOTT MACLAY
. . . photographer

ALLEN NEUHARTH
. . . chairman

KEN PAULSON
. . . chief of staff

JUANIE PHINNEY
. . . secretary

PHIL PRUITT
. . . editor

BARBARA REYNOLDS
. . . reporter

BOB ROLLER
. . . photographer

DAVID SILK
. . . circulation

KATHLEEN SMITH BARRY
. . . photographer

Dan Greaney, Tom Green, Lance Gurwell, Susan Hall, Theresa Harrah, Rebecca Hood-Adams, Phil Hudgins, J. Ford Huffman, Warren Isensee, Lee Ivory, Pam Janis, Linda Lord Jenkins, Jeanette Jordan, Joe Junod.

David Karvelas, Gregory Katz, Dennis Kelly, Randy Kirk, Danica Kirka, Joe Lewandowski, Rod Little, Sandy Lunner, Elizabeth Martin, Rudy Martzke, Mike Mathis, Mark Mayfield, Charles McCauley, Paul McMasters, Doug McMillen, Leslie Miller, Everett Mitchell, Nancy Monaghan, Martha Moore.

Allen H. Neuharth, Dan Neuharth, Johanna Neuman, Mike Oakland, Dick Patrick, Ken Paulson, Mark Pearson, Rick Pearson, Lynne Perri, David Peyton, Fred Pfeiffer, Pam Platt, Gene Policinski, Peter Prichard, Phil Pruitt, John C. Quinn, Jim Rasmussen, Barbara Reynolds, Kevin Riordan, Hal Ritter, Matt Roush, Tim Ryan.

Valerie Salembier, Ray Sarracino, Cathy Sarault, Laralyn Sasaki, John Seigenthaler, Rachel Shuster, Dolph Simons Jr., John Simpson, Dan Sperling, Susan Spielman, Warren Springer, Julie Stacey, David Patrick Stearns, Judy McConnell Steele, Jim Stevenson, Paul Stigers, Andrea Stone, Jo-ann Swanson.

John Taylor, Jerry Thompson, Maura Thurman, Tom Topousis, Joe Urschel, Hilary Waldman, Sam Ward, Larry Weisman, Susan Weiss, Chris Wells, George White, Joe White, Steve Wieberg, Vanessa Williams, Bob Woessner, Nancy Woodhull, John Yaukey, Dave Zimmerman.

Photography:

Mark Angeles, Charlie Archambault, Toby Armstrong, Associated Press, Bill Baptist, John Barr /Gamma Liaison, H. Darr Beiser, Bettmann Archives, John Biever, Porter Binks, Eileen Blass, Sydney Brink, Vandy Brisbon, Jim Britt, Brian Broom, Rob Brown, Jim Callaway, Rebecca Company, George Ceolla, Cindy Charles/Gamma Liaison, Ann Clifford, Ron Cortes, Margaret Croft, Dean Curtis.

Robert Deutsch, Tim Dillon, Terry Farmer, Frank Folwell, Garvin/Ron Gallela Ltd., Gary Gaynor, Sandee Gerbers, Monique Gray, Steve Haines, Tom Hardin, Acey Harper, Nancy Hart, Itsuo Inouye, Jason Johnson, Brent Jones, Michael Keating, Joe Kennedy, Barbara Kinney, Steve Koger, Bob Linder, Dan Loftin, Scott Maclay, Maine State Development Office, Jason Martin, Jim Mayfield, Rick McKay, Jack Mitchell, Eric Munch, Brent Nicastro, Rob Orcutt, Don Parsons, Mary Pember, Alan Petersime, Patrick Pfister, Bill Powers, Steve Purcell.

Eli Reichman, Barb Ries, Bob Riha Jr., Scott Robinson, Bob Roller, Tom Roster, Rhode Island Department of Economic Development, Anthony Savignano, Leslie Smith, Kathleen Smith Barry, Craig Stafford, Tom Stanford, Rich Stefaniak, Don Stevenson, Tom Strickland, Rob Swanson, Clarence Tabb Jr., Jeff Thompson, Charles V. Tines, David Tulis, University of South Dakota photo service, Kevin Vandivier, Luis Villalobos, Jason Wachter, Alan Warren, Paul Whyte, Kevin Winter/DMI.

Administration:

Claudia Baldwin, Randy Chorney, Joan Dunphy, Christie Golden, Beth Goodrich, Suzette Karelis, Carolynne Miller, Trini Peltier, Juanie Phinney, Andrea Redding, Ellen Schnur, John Simonds, Nancy Wiltzius.

Circulation:

Helmut Adler, Bob Alcorn, Carol Alka, Larry Aronson, Gene Asmussen, Brenda Baich, Paul Barbetta, Frank Bardonaro, Diane Barrett, Rick Beaty, Tom Beckette, Ric Bender, Vic Benintende, Clyde Benton, David Berks, Kevin Berry, Tom Bibs, Charley Boles, Gary Borsuk, Jim Bost, Gary Boyd, Carol Breitinger, Darrell Brotherton, Joice Buckley, Doris Burgess, Mike Butler.

Dennis Calvey, Angela Carmen, Jim Carter, Mike Caswell, Tony Catatao, Lee Caylor, Valeria Cheatham, Fran Cianciola, Paul Cimino, Kate Cleary, Bob Cochran, Kevin Cooper, Pat Corella, Dan Creacy, Dan Cruey, Mickey Cruey, Barry Cullen.

David Daniels, Bob DeMatteis, Rick DeMichele, Tom Dillinger, Debbie Dixon, Sharon Doerr, Jim Donivan, Mike Donohue, Pete Donohue, Jean Downs, Donna Dworkin, Ed Egan, Dave Enderle, Willie Etundi, Darcy Falk, Ron Farmer, Dave Fiedelman, Mickey Finn, Russ Ford, Dennis Francis, Carla Freeman.

Norbert Gallian, Jeff Garant, Dennis Gardner, Rick Gebensleben, Guy Gilmore, Arthur Gonick, Linda Greenwood, Leslie Hall, Bob Hamlin, Chris Hansen, Novella Harden, Bob Hart, Dick Hartnett, Mike Harvey, Phil Haun, Carl Helbig, Jim Henderson, Kathy Henderson, Bob Herring, Kevin Hickey, Chuck Hilgedick, Bryan Holland, George Hooper, Jeff Howard, Jim Hull, Ed Humphrey, Mike Huot.

Felicia Ingwers, Ron Jackson, Newel Jensen, Chris Jensen, John Jewell, Bob Johnson, Jeff Johnson, Bill Jones, Ken Kain, Ellen Kaminski, Jerry Kane, Leo Kelly, Tom Kelly, Chris Kennedy, Karen Kietzer, Ken Knapp, Ellis Knowles, Paula Kristiek, Chris Lacy, Dave Lack, Jerry Lee, Paul London.

Don Madigan, Barb Madine, Mike Malie, Don Malone, Bob Marciale, Kevin McCarthy, Charlie McClaren, Mary McClory, John McGee, Mike McKillip, John Micksich, Suzie Miles, Wayne Milzarek, Gail Mitchell, Robert Mitchell, Dennis Mosby, Liz Moscatelli, Jeff Myers, Kelly Myles.

Eileen Navish, Reggie Nester, Dwight Newton, Tom Norton, Dennis Ohira, Ruth Parise, Mary Patterson, Susan Payler, Jim Pinnex, Ted Popis, Tom Raia, Linda Ramsey, Rich Randles, Kelly Rounds, Susan Rovegno, Gary Ruffin, John Rutland.

Ben Sahr, Jeff Scharfeld, Cindy Schneider, Paul Seehusen, Jerry Shapiro, Jill Shirley, Ron Siemering, Craig Siemssen, David Silk, William Simmons, Eric Smith, Beth Watson Sousa, Dave Spiess, Gary Steele, Fritz Stellrecht, Jim Stephens, Richard Stone.

Dave Thomas, Dick Timm, Dean Tortora, Neil

Truax, John Truitt, Tracey Ulmer, Jonny Valente, Jeff Webber, Beth Wells, Joe Werlinich, Bill Windsor, Ed Wood, Chuck Wooten.

Promotion:

Paul Czachowski, Lisa Dixon.

Production:

Allison Ames, Hrayr Avakian, Bill Bogert, Dianna Carroll, Danitria Carruth, Robin Cohen, Gary Coppola, Wanda Dandy, Dai Chang Dee, Jay Embree, Neil Ferris, Guido Gomez, Mike Grinder, Gary Gunnerson, Bruce Hawkins, Shonna Jones, Brian Kuendel, Dang Limanpai, Thong Luong, Cherie Millar, JoAn Moore, Dale Parkhurst, Danny Pei, Gina Porretta, Paula Prettyman, Bob Smith, Jim Smith, Etchie Yap.

Purchasing:

Lori Chafin, Mike Ciarimboli, Fran Jolles.

Telecommunications:

Joe Bellacosa, Walt Halfpap.

Bus driver:

Joel Driver.

About the author

When Allen H. Neuharth was 11 years old and living in Alpena, S.D., he got a job delivering *The Minneapolis Tribune* — and never looked back. Journalism was it for him. He had found his life's work.

In 1952, at age 28, Neuharth launched his first newspaper — a statewide South Dakota weekly called *SoDak Sports.* It went bankrupt two years later. Neuharth spent the next 10 years rising through the ranks of the Knight newspapers in Miami and Detroit. He joined the Gannett Co. in 1963. That started another rapid rise. He became president in 1970, chief executive officer in 1973, chairman in 1979.

Along the way, Neuharth launched *Today* in Brevard County, Fla., in 1966 and, on Sept. 15, 1982, USA TODAY, now the nation's most-read newspaper.

Gannett publishes 90 daily newspapers, 39 non-daily newspapers and *USA WEEKEND,* a newspaper magazine. It also operates eight television stations, 16 radio stations and owns the largest outdoor advertising company in North America.

Gannett also has marketing, television news and program production, research satellite information systems and a national group of commercial printing facilities. Gannett has operations in 40 states, the District of Columbia, Guam, the Virgin Islands, Canada, Great Britain, Hong Kong, Singapore and Switzerland.